GREATER THAN A MOTHER'S LOVE

THE SPIRITUALITY OF
FRANCIS AND CLARE OF ASSISI

GREATER THAN A MOTHER'S LOVE

THE SPIRITUALITY OF
FRANCIS AND CLARE OF ASSISI

By

GILBERTO CAVAZOS-GONZÁLEZ, OFM

FOREWORD BY
INGRID J. PETERSON, OSF

UNIVERSITY OF SCRANTON PRESS
SCRANTON AND LONDON

Library of Congress Cataloging-in-Publication Data

Cavazos-González, Gilberto, 1957-
  Greater than a mother's love : the spirituality of Francis and Clare of Assisi / by Gilberto Cavazos-González ; foreword by Ingrid J. Peterson.
    p. cm.
  Includes bibliographical references (p.   ) and index.
  ISBN 978-1-58966-213-1 (pbk.)
  1. Francis, of Assisi, Saint, 1182-1226--Family. 2. Clare, of Assisi, Saint, 1194-1253--Family. 3. Christian saints--Family relationships--Italy--Assisi. 4. Family--Religious aspects--Catholic Church. 5. Spirituality--Catholic Church. I. Title.
  BX4700.F6C38 2010
  271'.3022--dc22

                                                    2010011615

Distribution:
University of Scranton Press
Chicago Distribution Center
11030 S. Langley
Chicago, IL 60628

PRINTED IN THE UNITED STATES OF AMERICA

Con amor y gratitud a Dios,
deseo dedicar esta obra
a mis padres
Gilberto Cavazos DeLeon
y
María Emma González de Cavazos
y a mis hermanos
Sergio, José Luis, y Gustavo.
Los quiero mucho.

CONTENTS

FOREWORD

In today's culture, the topic of relationship—whether of a personal nature or in a broader scope—is timely. *Greater Than a Mother's Love: The Spirituality of Francis and Clare of Assisi* is a thorough investigation of kinship in the lives of Francis and Clare of Assisi and their consequent use of familial language in their spiritual writings. In this work, Friar Gilberto Cavazos-González, OFM, studies how the family experiences of both Francis and Clare influenced the way they understood and expressed their relationship to God. This is the first extensive study of the lives of Francis and Clare primarily focusing on the theme of kinship in its historical context within the dynamics of their families.

The introduction to this book presents brief biographies of Francis and Clare in the context of the High Middle Ages. Then the author describes what he calls a socio-spiritual methodology, an application of the social sciences to the study of theology and religion. Such a method sharpens the perspective on each figure and underscores the common language of their spirituality. Cavazos-González contends that, in order to analyze the letters, rules, testaments, and prayers of Francis and Clare, it is necessary to begin with the anthropological, social, and spiritual preconceptions which influenced writers and readers of the Middle Ages. He explains how theirs is a movement from human experience to the experience of God.

The first chapter, "European Family of the High Middle Ages," traces the place of the family in the context of medieval social and religious culture. It provides a necessary groundwork for understanding the role of the family, one that is very different from the current popular experience of family. The chapter treats marriage in its Christian context, conjugal love, and the roles of the husband, wife, and children within the family. A section on unconventional families treats virginity and male and female sanctity.

The material in chapters two (about Francis) and three (about Clare) is presented in parallel forms, beginning with what is known of the parents of Francis and Clare, the significant players in their upbringing, and their struggles to break with the expectations of their families in response to the inner call of the Gospel. Chapter two, "Francis: Son of a Merchant Family," traces the saint's family background. It recounts Francis's birth and early youth, the role of his mother, Lady Pica, and his father, Pietro di Bernadone, and his conversion as presented by his early biographers: Thomas of Celano, Julian of Speyer, Henry of Avranches, Bonaventure, and the *Anonymous of Perugia*. Breaking with the ways of the merchant class, Francis's conversion became public before the bishop of Assisi when he denounced his father and his family's values, demonstrating through a ritual of stripping that his father no longer had a claim on him. Francis's struggle with his father echoes the stories of the Christian martyrs whose faith brought them into conflict with their culture.

In a parallel manner, chapter three, "Clare's Noble Family," presents Clare's early experiences and her break from an aristocratic family. Clare's mother and father, Ortulana and Favarone, belonged to a higher social class than that of Francis, so Clare had to sever her identity with them in order to follow the way of the Gospel. She refused to marry, causing her family a potential loss of property, power, and prestige, and she eventually split up her family by attracting and convincing many of her kinswomen to follow and join her at San Damiano. Cavazos-González shows that, where Francis *broke with* his, Clare *broke up* her family.

Having dealt with family relationships in the lives of Francis and Clare, the author, in the next two chapters, demonstrates how their writings adapt their domestic experiences to describe their relationships to the family of God. These chapters support the thesis of *Greater Than a Mother's Love*, for they reveal how the spirituality of Francis and Clare flows from their human relational experiences.

Chapter four, "Kinship in the Opuscula of Francis," traces imagery from the Scriptures. References to the relationship of the three persons of God also occur repeatedly in Francis's writings. As a child of the celestial Father, Francis understood himself as brother and mother to everyone, and he enjoined them all to love one another. In the First and Second redactions of the Letter to the Faithful, Francis describes the faithful as God's children. He joins the role of brother to that of mother and sister and spouse to develop his spirituality of mystical union, accomplished as the Holy Spirit unites the faithful soul to God. In *Greater Than a Mother's Love*, Fray Gilberto combs Francis's writings to demonstrate his countless invitations to the faithful to experience for themselves a relationship of kinship with Jesus involving the tenderness of a spouse, the strength of a brother, and the fecundity of a mother.

Francis left behind more writings than Clare, yet her spirituality contains all the kinship themes that permeate Francis's prayer and thought. In chapter five, "Kinship in Clare's Opuscula," the author mines the writings of Clare as they employ human understandings to convey divine realities. Her works, too, are filled with images expressing the union of the soul and God through relational images of father, mother, sister, brother, spouse, and handmaid. As had Francis, Clare drew kinship images from the Scriptures and from her experience in an extended noble family. Reaching beyond the scriptural images used by Francis, Clare also draws popular metaphors from the spirituality of her time, using the concept of speculum, the mirror, to illustrate her likeness to God.

The conclusion of the book reviews and expands upon how both Francis and Clare ultimately belong to the household of God in which the tensions of their human experience of family shape the ways in which they understand their place within God's family. The inclusive reaches of the language used by both Francis and Clare draw Cavazos-González to his final sentence and the meaning of his title, the description of a love that is "greater than a mother's love," for it is experienced as both maternal and fraternal.

The research supporting this work is at once impressive in its clarity and organization and impeccable in its detail. The bibliography attests to the extensive primary sources Cavazos-González investigated. It presents an exhaustive list of primary sources, translations, commentaries, and studies, including the most prominent recent authorities. He includes the standard Latin primary sources in their Italian editions which are used for Franciscan scholarship. In addition, six appendices refine and expand upon the bibliography. In itself, such a compilation of primary and secondary source material is a truly valuable resource.

With new translations and editions of the primary sources for the study of Francis and Clare of Assisi readily accessible in the English-speaking world, a spate of scholarly interpretation as well as popular writing has attempted to relate the message and example of Francis and Clare to contemporary life. Many aspects of their lives, writings, and related early biographical materials have been addressed in books, articles, and translations of European scholars; these have been published for the English-speaking world. No one, however, has addressed the topic of kinship relationships in the lives and writings of Francis and Clare with the clarity, background, and depth of Cavazos-González's *Greater Than a Mother's Love*.

The insight into Francis's family, the treatment of Clare's family, and the exploration of how both applied their relational experiences to their spirituality—all are original and fresh. This book is at once easy and profound. Because the organization is so clear and the book so well-written, a reader can move easily through its pages. But at the same time, absorbing and appropriating all of its content is the work of a lifetime. This book can be read for meditation or used as a text for courses in medieval social or religious history, theology, spirituality, or Franciscan studies. It can be appreciated by readers either new to or well versed in the Franciscan universe.

The contemporary world appears insatiable in its pursuit of the message of Francis and Clare. Both of them are known and admired, yet they remain curiously elusive. *Greater Than a Mother's Love* brings the reader into the spirit of Francis and Clare and, with them, closer to the heart of God.

Ingrid J. Peterson, OSF

ACKNOWLEDGMENTS

Greater than a mother's love—the phrase captures the imagination. For those of us who have had good and loving parents, the phrase immediately raises the question: "What can be greater than a mother's love?" Francis and Clare of Assisi both insist that the love of brothers and sisters in the Spirit has to be just that. This surprising twist, found in both the Rule of St. Francis and the Rule of St. Clare, captured my imagination almost fifteen years ago and has led to this book. Francis and Clare both invite their brothers and sisters to love each other with maternal and fraternal affection. This does not mean that they want us to love each other as contemporary western mothers do their children or as brothers and sisters do their siblings. They want us to go beyond a mother's natural and socialized love, thus the title for my book: *Greater Than a Mother's Love.*

This book began as my doctoral dissertation for the Pontificium Athenaeum "Antonianum" in Rome in 2000. In considering a topic for my thesis, I began by wanting to write about the divine maternity of believers— which is to say, about how Christians "give birth to Jesus" in imitation of Mary. Both Francis and Clare indicate that the imitation of Mary is important to Christian life. As I continued to read their writings, however, I began to wonder about all the family imagery they used. At that time, I also had the opportunity to speak with Franciscan scholars Marco Bartoli; Optatus van Asseldonk, OFM Cap.; and Thadée Matura, OFM. With their encouragement and insight, I came to realize that I had to consider the importance of the maternal–fraternal language in the writings of Francis and Clare. I began to study and write about what lay behind the language that Clare and Francis used to express their experience of God and community.

In 2000, I successfully defended my dissertation and began to share my insights on the maternal–fraternal tension of Franciscan life with different Franciscan groups and with my students at the Catholic Theological Union. During the last nine years, different people have invited me to consider publishing my work. With the help of Carmen Nanko-Fernández, Jean-Pierre Ruiz, and Orlando Espín I was able to get my dissertation to medieval historian Chris Bellito who enjoyed my work and encouraged me not to give up on it. So with the help of Ulrike Guthrie I edited and updated my dissertation for publication. I am greatful to Carmen, Jean-Pierre, Orlando, Chris, and Ulrike for their help and support.

I had problems finding the right publisher until I met Jeff Gainey, director of the University of Scranton Press. I am grateful for his support in the process of getting this book to print. Our meeting was a chance encounter that I thank God for. At the same time I met Jeff, Ingrid Peterson, OSF, read my work and encouraged me to get it published. I am thankful for her encouraging me and agreeing to write the foreword to this book. God has a way of making things happen in due time.

Muchisimas Gracias.

The adventure of writing this book has taken me to various places around the globe where I spent time with any number of brothers and sisters in the Franciscan family as well as the greater Christian community. Consequently, I am grateful to many people.

I would like to begin by thanking my family of origin. Antes de nada, deseo agradecer a mis padres Gilberto y Emma por el don de la vida y en especial el don de la fe y del amor. Agradezco también a mis hermanos Sergio, José Luis, y Gustavo por enseñarme lo que es ser un hermano. Agradezco asimismo a mis cuñadas Norma Linda, Herminia Guadalupe e Yvonne. Además les doy las gracias a mis sobrino/as Larissa Irazemma, Sergio, Eliana Linda, José Luis, Gilberto, y Emma Lilia.

As regards the Franciscan Family, I would like to thank the professors and community of the Antonianum for their advice and fraternal support. I met so many friars in Rome to whom I am grateful that time and space do not allow me to mention by name. But I do want to give a special *grazie mille* to Alex Arias, Stefano Cecchin, Jorge Horta, Lorenzo Ago, Jimmy Zammit, Alessandro Caspoli, Giampaolo Cavalli, and Stephano Cavalli.

I want to thank my friends in Rome, Luigi Miranda, Fernando Harris, Federico Fiorucci, Margarita Gatta, Tarcisio Gotay, Gerald Cadieres,

Paola Martorelli, and the Gruppo Redenzione. While I was in Rome, they were my sanity and perseverance. *A voi cari amici, sarò sempre grato.*

I am very grateful to my brothers in the Franciscan Province of the Most Sacred Heart. I want to thank, in a special way, Arturo Ocampo, Kurt Hartrich, Robert Karris, Robert Hutmacher, Ray Shuhert, Arthur Anderson, and William Burton. I am particularly grateful to David Rodriguez, Phil Hogan, Gil Ostdiek, and Charles Payne, who make up my local community, Holy Spirit Friary.

In conclusion, I want to thank my friends in Chicago and the Midwest for their encouragement and support as I worked on the revisions and publication of this book: Gary Riebe-Estrella, José Alexander Gaitan Montez, Jaime Bascuñan, Denise and JoKay Joseph, Carmen Guzman, María de Jesús Lemus, Amanda Quantz, Vanessa White, Mary Frohlich, Mark Schramm, Avis Wright, Ed Foley, and Dawn Nothwehr.

Deo Gratias
Fray Gilberto

Introduction

Francis and Clare of Assisi never met my mother or yours, and of course we never met theirs either. Nevertheless, both of these saints encourage us as brothers and sisters in Christ to love each other with a love that is greater than a mother's love. But what does that mean? I have been blessed with a very loving mother and a loving father, and consequently I am not sure how I would love anyone more than my parents love me. Yet, called by these two medieval saints to do precisely that, I'm pushed to wonder what they mean. To discover that, I necessarily have to find out what I can about their relationships with *their* parents that in some way prompted them to urge us to love even more than a mother does.

In 1980, three other Franciscan novices and I were sent to a two-week "Mary-Martha experience." We were told that we would take turns being mothers to each other as described in Francis's "Rule for the Hermitages" (RegEr), in which he states that the mothers should care for and protect the sons (those attempting contemplation) from the distraction of others. Essentially this means that while two friars (Mary/sons) spent the time in prayer at Jesus' feet, so to speak, the other two (Martha/mothers) spent the time cooking, cleaning, and making sure that the "sons" were free from distractions and well cared for. Those who were "Mary" during the first week got to be "Martha" during the second. At first, this type of language seemed quite strange, but as I grew in my understanding of Francis and (eventually) Clare, I became accustomed to the maternal–fraternal nature of Franciscan life.

Later, however, I began to question my comfort with this Franciscan maternal–fraternal language. Perhaps I'd made too many assumptions about what they meant, assumptions based on my experiences of my mother's love for me. So I began to wonder what lay behind this challenging language that our saints, Francis and Clare, used to express their experience of God and community.

I decided to consider the entire spectrum of kinship language in their writings. So I read their vitae (lives) and opuscula (works)[1] from the perspective of the social construct of the family of their time and place. We can of course read and learn a great deal about Francis's and Clare's parents without ever actually meeting them. And in an effort to do what we can to come closer to knowing them, we can research the medieval European family. Presumably, this can help us understand the spirituality that Francis and Clare expressed using kinship terms such as *father, mother, brother, sister,* and *spouse.*

When my formation directors emphasized our being mothers as well as brothers to each other in our attempt to love each other in community life, they insisted that this was what Francis and Clare wanted. Yet, these medieval saints never intended us to love each other as contemporary western mothers love their children, nor for that matter did they simply want us to imitate the love of medieval Italian mothers. Francis and Clare wanted us to go beyond a mother's natural and socialized love.

All Christians, not just those who call themselves Franciscans, are called to a love that is much more than maternal, which is to say a love that is greater than a mother's love.[2] The concept of brothers (or sisters) loving and caring for each other as mothers do their children can be found in all three of Francis's Rules—"Non-Bulled Rule" (RnB), "Bulled Rule" (RB), and "Rule for Hermitages" (RegEr), as well as in Clare's "Form of Life" (RCl). Francis and Clare do not limit the maternal role to loving each other in community; both highlight the idea of Christians actually mothering Christ. This curious notion is found in Francis's Letter to the Faithful (1EpFid)—as well as in Clare's Letters to Saint Agnes (1EpAgn–4EpAgn), and because of its very curiosity, it stirs up the minds and hearts of the Christian faithful to ask how such language can be lived today. When contemporary Christians seek to interpret these mothering images, however, they tend to do so with the contemporary mother or the Virgin Mary in mind— and that, as we shall see, is quite insufficient.

OUR SAINTS IN BRIEF

My earliest recollection of Francis came with the popular hymn, "The Prayer of St. Francis" (Make Me a Channel of Your Peace). Many people know Francis of Assisi only through this song (based on a prayer which he never wrote), or because they have seen his statue decorating a bird-bath in a garden. He is usually associated with the peace movement, ecology, and animals because of his love of humanity and nature. But there is so much more to Francis.

I first read the life of St. Francis at the recommendation of my spiritual director. I had never heard of the man, but I was captivated by what I read. And so, without ever having met a Franciscan, I decided to become one. When I told my family about my decision, I was surprised to discover that my parents and other members of the family had heard of the Franciscans and knew a bit about Francis and Clare. Mexican Catholicism was planted and nurtured by Franciscan missionaries and the image and stories of Francis are all around us.

It seems that many people have a vague familiarity with Francis and Clare of Assisi, thanks to the mission and influence of the Franciscans over the centuries. In the last century, many books have been written and movies produced about these two saints, helping to popularize them. We are used to images of Francis talking to animals and birds and are becoming familiar with images of Clare holding up the Eucharist to frighten off the Saracen army. But again, there is more to these two saints than just their miracles.

FRANCIS OF ASSISI

There are many good biographies and hagiographies written about Francis, so I will not go into his whole life. Briefly, the Francis most of us know is the converted playboy. His own conversion was from that of a spoiled rich young man who went off to war to gain fame and fortune. All he got was a year in prison, followed by a year of sickness and depression that caused him to reevaluate his life. At the end of it all, he kissed a leper, the thing that had repulsed him most in this world. His conversion led him to volunteer in the leprosarium and rebuild ruined and abandoned churches at the command of a voice he heard coming from a crucifix. All of this was too much for his parents to handle, and it led to a break with them, a break that probably lasted the rest of his life.

In place of his former family, God gave him followers, men and women, single and married, who were attracted by the change they saw in him and the work that he did. Although he was rejected and ridiculed at first, in time many noblemen and women, theologians, priests, and peasants joined him in living the Gospel in chastity, obedience, and without anything of their own.

Francis was a simple man who completely trusted God, so he turned to the Gospel to learn what to do with his followers. In the process, he was inspired to send his brothers out, two by two, to preach the good news and greet people with peace.

In time, he was persuaded for the good of his brotherhood to ask the Pope for approval of his Order. His community was recognized in 1209, and by 1223 his Order of Friars Minor had a "Bulled [approved] Rule." In 1211, with the conversion of St. Clare and the women who later joined her in the Monastery of San Damiano, his brotherhood included sisters. Eventually, he formed a "third order" for married men and women who wanted to live a simple life at home in service of the poor.

Francis was known to be a gifted preacher who was said to be able to get even birds to listen to his words. He is also said to have tamed a ferocious wolf in the town of Gubbio. His preaching ministry took him to the Crusaders' camp in the Middle East. Disgusted with what he saw in the Christian encampment, he made his way to the Muslim sultan, hoping to be martyred for the faith or to convert the Muslim leader to Christ. He gained only the respect of the sultan and free passage in the Holy Land.

Eventually, he made his way back to Europe where he found his brotherhood in disarray. With the permission of the Pope, the many theologians and doctors of the law who entered his Order were busy building schools for the training of preachers. Try as he might, he was never able to call the community back to his original ideals of a simple life.

In 1224, distressed by what he saw and no longer able to lead his community, he went to Mount La Verna for prayer and solitude. It was during this time that Francis received the stigmata of Jesus on his own body.

In his early forties, wearied from his ministry, asceticism, and the stigmata, Francis was taken back to the Porziuncola where he had first lived with his brothers, and where Clare had joined the Franciscan family. There he died on the night of October 3, 1226. Two years later, he was canonized a saint.

CLARE OF ASSISI

For centuries, Saint Clare's memory was overshadowed by that of Saint Francis; she was all but ignored. Not even Franciscan sisters gave her much attention. That has changed in the recent past thanks to several insightful biographies that have been written about her. As I did with Francis, here I offer only a brief glimpse of this powerful woman.

Clare outlived Francis by twenty-seven years and was twelve years his junior. She was born circa 1193 and, unlike Francis, was part of the *maiores*,[3] the noble class, and spent most of her youth being prepared for a suitable marriage and to run a noble household. The witnesses for the process of her canonization tell us that she belonged to one of the finest families in Assisi. There were seven knights in her household, including her father, Favarone. Her mother, Hortulana, was a pious woman who spent much time on pilgrimages and caring for the poor.

We can quickly discard all the romantic notions of Francis and Clare having been in love with each other prior to their conversions for, in fact, societal norms would have kept them from ever having met. She was a *maiore*, engaged to marry a suitable man of her family's choosing. He, on the other hand, was a *minore*—belonging not to the lower class per se, but to the new and growing merchant class.

Clare eventually came to hear of Francis only after his conversion. He had heard of her holiness, and they began to have secret meetings in which he instructed her in the ways of poverty and minority.[4] On Palm Sunday, in 1211, she ran away from home. Her being received into the Franciscan family sent her noble family into frenzy. Led by her Uncle Monaldo, the head of her household, the family's knights went to the monastery, where she was working as a servant, to drag her home.

What happened next is legendary. She revealed her tonsured head and held onto the altar cloth like a common criminal seeking asylum. Frustrated, the family left her to her new life—only to repeat the scene a week later when one of Clare's sisters fled the family to be with her.

Clare, her sister Agnes, and a few of their friends eventually ended up in the Monastery of San Damiano, which Francis had rebuilt a few years earlier. There they underwent many hardships, and Clare proved her holiness by performing many miracles. On several occasions, when she found that there was nothing for the community to eat but a small loaf of bread, Clare blessed it and managed to feed sixty sisters—and still have some left over. When sick people from the area came to her for prayers and left liberated from their illnesses, she became known as a healer. Twice she was able to liberate the town of Assisi and her own sisters from Saracen attacks by praying before the Blessed Sacrament that she had placed at the entrance to the monastery.

As time went on, Clare and her sisters founded many other monasteries[5] in Italy and other countries. Various popes and cardinals tried to impose first the Benedictine Rule and then their own Rules on the Damianites (the Poor Ladies, or the Poor Sisters, as they were originally called).[6] Clare nonetheless insisted on being Franciscan and following the Franciscan way of life. She finally wrote her own Rule, the first Rule ever written for women by a woman. It was approved on August 9, 1253 only two days before her death.

Despite her having challenged and stood up to popes, bishops, and cardinals, precisely such men were present for her burial and insisted on promoting her cause for canonization. Only protocol kept them from canonizing her at her own funeral. Like Francis, she was added to the canon of saints only two years after her death.

SOCIO-SPIRITUAL METHOD

Every theologian is a product of personal background and life experience.[7] For Latin@[8] theologians, important influences on our theology include our culture, our social location, and our life and faith experiences. For this reason, *cotidianidad* (quotidianness/dailiness)[9] is critical to our approach to spirituality. *Lo cotidiano* (quotidian/daily), the everyday routine of life with all its ups and downs, is where God is found. As such, it is the locus for spirituality as ontological reality and existential experience. *Lo cotidiano* is where spirituality is "traditioned"[10] by the family in both its religious and cultural contexts.

My own *cotidiano* as a Latino leads me to have a close connection to *mi familia*. Consequently, I am intrigued by the family imagery found in these saints' opuscula (their writings). These two medieval saints infused their spirituality with their own *cotidiano*, choosing to explain their concept of the Christian spiritual life with the ordinary roles of motherhood, sibling relationships, and paternity.

In considering the use of family terminology in Francis's and Clare's opuscula, I have to admit that I am a nonparticipant[11] of their *cotidiano*. So, I have turned to history, sociology, and other human sciences in order to enter as best I can into their understanding of family and kinship.

I refer to this interdisciplinary approach[12] as a socio-spiritual method. This method is based on the understanding of the Christian message as one that seeks to penetrate all aspects of the socio-spiritual[13] life of the human race with God's reign. Without denying the faith and theology implicit in the study of Christian spirituality, my method relies on cultural studies and other human sciences. Spirituality is a social and anthropological reality, but for Christians it is above all the work of the Holy Spirit in the social and cultural *cotidiano* of the believer. Therefore, I like to think of my method as a social, faith-filled, and spiritual look at *la cotidianidad divina*, the place where God dwells and acts.

The socio-spiritual method that I employ seeks to use *la cotidianidad divina* in which (to quote Carmen Nanko-Fernández) I privilege "*lo cotidiano* in theologizing *latinamente*."[14] It is based heavily but not exclusively on the method explained and used by Adriana Destro and Mauro Pesce, in *Antropologia delle origini cristiane*.[15]

Today's spiritualogians (theologians who research, teach, and write about spirituality) seek to appropriate Christian spiritual classics—letters, poems, rules, testaments, prayers, and vitae—produced by spiritual writers who wrote for the readers of their day, readers who shared their social, cultural, political, economic, and religious milieu and who's *cotidiano* would have enabled them to understand the material.

The work of Destro and Pesce inspires me to read our two saints' vitae and opuscula within the social construct of the Italian family of their time and place. So, I engage the Franciscan sources with a socio-spiritual method of study that arises out of the fact that the message of any historical text, even a spiritual one, is socially, culturally, and religiously determined by its *cotidiano*. This supposes that both the writer and the "intended readers" are immersed in a common religious, cultural, and social process, which forms their "social imagination." Social imagination (*immaginazione sociale*) refers to what a person believes his/her society is or should be.

In the case of Francis's and Clare's opuscula, where maternal language is tied to fraternal love, I need to consider that the medieval Italian mother is not the Mexican-American mother I grew up with. The *cotidiano* I share with *mi madrecita* will not be enough to understand the strange way in which these two saints saw the role of mother. I must discover what their social imagination has to say about the maternal role in the *cotidiano* of the family of thirteenth-century Assisi. This, in turn, will help me discover how they wanted their readers to respond to their message.

Spiritual texts, like Francis's and Clare's opuscula and vitae, were not written simply to impart information but to provoke action and modification in the life of the reader. The writing and reading of the text takes place within a concrete operative process. Moreover, like all texts, they may continue to be read after the intended audience no longer exists. Spiritual in nature, they provoke religious transformation in new generations of readers who no longer share in the operative religious, cultural, and social process of the writers. These new audiences can read the texts for information and/or for transformation. In any case, it will be better if they understand something of the writer's context and social imagination.

LITERARIZATION

Spiritual classics (religious texts, sacred imagery, and devotional practices) are conditioned by time, culture space, and the personal experience of the writer, artist, or practitioner. The authors of such spiritual classics produce a synthesis of their cultural system and its dynamics and condense them into concrete forms by means of selection and translation. Destro and Pesce refer to this process as "literarization"—which should not be confused with "literaturization."

Literaturization is the process by which a writer produces literature. *Literarization*, on the other hand, is the process by which an author takes material from his/her *cotidiano* and research and assimilates it into his/her knowledge. As previously noted, the process of assimilation creates a social imagination which is made up of categories-classifications and social, spatial-temporal realities (institutions, rites, practices, precepts, relationships, and so on). An author can then take from this social-cultural imagination some personal knowledge and redact it within a unifying form. Clare and

Francis did this in their letters and rules. This is the literarization of the socio-cultural imagination.

The text, which is the outcome of this process, contains several cultural levels that can be considered. First is the implicit cultural presupposition or what the author and the intended audience participate in as common knowledge and experience because of a shared *cotidiano*. Then there are the expressed and specific cultural factors of the group that the author and intended audience are a part of—and which are specifically dealt with in the classic. The third and final level to be considered is the differentiation whereby authors express the principal explicit intention of their work, which helps the audience see things that, until then, their natural inclinations and social imagination had not allowed them to see.

In my work with these saints' opuscula, their implicit cultural presupposition is that the reader understands the medieval Italian family, so they feel no need to explain what they mean by the terms *mother, brother,* or *sister.* In writing about the maternal–fraternal tension of community life, the specific cultural factors that they deal with are the roles of mother and siblings as found in their thirteenth-century Italian *cotidiano*.

I realize that there are those who question the validity of applying social sciences to spiritual classics. Truly, this method has its limitations. Medieval spiritual writers are often not writing for specifically social or cultural reasons. Their focus is on life in the Spirit and its religious movements. Yet the Spirit dwells and acts in the *cotidiano* of the authors and their audiences. This *cotidiano* is often no longer available to the spiritualogian of a later era who must accept his/her status as a non-participant, all the while researching the *sitz im leben,* social-location, and especially the *cotidiano* of the spiritual authors and their original audiences.

Secondly, relying too much on the social and cultural factors of the author and audience could cause some to miss the movement of the Spirit and the influence of the Gospel on the authors, their intended audience, and successive audiences. To keep from falling into these traps, one must truly believe that God's Spirit can build on and enlighten human nature, that *lo cotidiano* can indeed be *divino*—which is to say, infused with God's continual presence.

We should not be afraid to apply the social sciences to the academic discipline of spirituality. Nor should we forget or negate the movement of the Spirit and the influence of the Gospel on these authors and audiences.

Believing that God's Spirit builds on and enlightens human nature, I give special attention here to the possible influence that the medieval family might have had on the writings of these two saints. To that end, I focus my attention on the use of kinship imagery and terminology in the writings by and about Francis and Clare.

The words *family, spouse, father,* and *mother* were part of Francis and Clare's social imagination and were usually used without explanation, due to the implicit cultural presupposition of the text. When they did explain the kinship terminology in their writing, it was to highlight specific cultural factors and spiritual imaginings that they wanted to share with the reader. They did so because they wanted to transform these words into a way of expressing the explicit spiritual intention of their work. With this in mind, I will endeavor to give a brief overview of the Middle Ages as a time of reforms and changes that affected not only religious life but family life as well.

CHRISTIANITAS AND THE HIGH MIDDLE AGES

Latin@ Catholicism was born at the end of the Middle Ages,[16] and as such it shares the medieval sacramental mindset that sees God at work in the *cotidiano.* A common ground of Christian belief and Gospel values unites all contemporary Catholics to the medieval communion of saints. Yet, we will forever remain the nonparticipants of their lived experience, a reality that we will never really know or completely understand. As a spiritualogian, I have to peruse history and read the spiritual classics in order to attempt to find the anthropological, cultural, social, religious, and spiritual preconceptions that influenced both the writers and readers of that past age.

Francis and Clare lived and wrote in a specific historical moment; for this reason, we need to consider the European family of the High Middle Ages. Ideally, we would consider families in Assisi, but unfortunately the *cotidianidad* of family life was not important enough to be discussed with much detail in historians' analyses of that period. Nonetheless, it was influenced by the regulations and tensions of that time.

The High Middle Ages was a period in which Church and State, culture and religion were united into what is called *Christianitas*. Christianity had become the official state religion of Europe in 381. Yet, the Christianizing of Europe was a superficial one; it took much of the Early Middle Ages to penetrate the consciousness of society. By the time of Francis and Clare, Europe was strongly under the influence of Christianity. Thus, *Christianitas* occurred because European society as a whole proclaimed itself as doctrinally and socially Christian.

During this time, ecclesiastical authorities found themselves having to care for both the spiritual and the temporal well-being of the flock. This blending of social and spiritual care eventually led to increasing tension between Church and State in the Late Middle Ages and Renaissance. This tension was beginning to be felt in the time of Francis and Clare, as can be seen in the war between Popes Innocent III (1160–1216), Gregory IX (1170–1241), and Innocent IV (1190–1254) and the Emperor Frederick II (1194–1250).

For *Christianitas*, the High Middle Ages was a time of great change. The feudal system was breaking down. With the death of the Holy Roman Emperor Charlemagne (†814), Western Europe was subdivided into three kingdoms—France, Germany, and Italy—with a hierarchical system of kings, nobles, and knights who lorded it over serfs and freemen. This feudal society was based on land ownership and agriculture rather than commerce, on military force rather than civil rights and morality. The feudal system was even felt in the Church, where landed monasteries ruled many a countryside. Consequently, Christianity was seen as a part of the feudal system of power with lord bishops who ruled on behalf of emperors, kings, and other nobles. Society was divided into three orders of men based on their function in society: those who pray, those who fight, and those who work the land.[17] Women were divided into their own tri-functional scheme based on their body, gender, and relationship to family: maid, wife, and widow.

The Early Middle Ages offered no guarantee of equality, and in time the people of the High Middle Ages sought political participation and liberty, which gave rise to the communes. The freemen who had worked for many of the lords were now becoming prosperous merchants and artisans in towns and cities. Even serfs were breaking free from their Teutonic overlords and flocking into urban centers in hope of a better life. The search for liberty and freedom, the growth of urban centers, and the development of a middle class that sprang up between nobility and serfs especially characterized the High Middle Ages.

The period from the twelfth to the thirteenth century was especially traumatic for urban centers like that of Assisi, where old values were questioned through the sword and the slow rise of the individual. As individuals became more self-determined, they chose not to be ruled by their roles in *Christianitas*. Rather, they desired to have the freedom to choose how they would live their lives. This newfound self-identity demanded a breaking away from lords and nobles, and in many cases, this included a break with one's kin.

In the High Middle Ages, Christianity began to penetrate deeply into the soul of the faithful, which helped the Church gain ground both in a peace movement for the war-torn Europe and in the popularizing of the early Crusades. The penetration of Christianity also helped in separating the Church, somewhat—as it searched for greater liberty and autonomy— from the power of noble families. This deeper penetration of the faith helps to explain the rise in reform movements among already established monastic orders, the penitential movements, and the heretical sects that came to life in that time period. These movements, calling for a new look at the Gospel by following the example of the poor and crucified Jesus, were especially popular among the laity of the time.

Both men and women were attracted in droves to the reform movements of the twelfth century. Monastic reform movements like those of the Cistercians welcomed these converts by reforming already existing, single-sex monasteries, or opening new ones. In the early twelfth century, some monasteries, like those of St. Gilbert of Sempringham, opened their doors to both men and women in what came to be known as double monasteries that were run by either an abbot or an abbess. The Premonstratensians worked for reform as itinerant preachers who attracted both men and women to new experiences of apostolic life.

Penitential austerity was a given in the spirituality of the Middle Ages. As the Church developed its penitential nature, Christians came to understand themselves not as a community of saints, but rather as a society of sinners in need of God's mercy. With the gradual move to child baptism in the early medieval period, conversion became a lifelong process in the life of the already baptized rather than a requirement for baptism. Some Christians found themselves in serious states of sin and in need of penance, which was imposed on them by bishops and priests. Penance might involve a year or two of fasting and abstinence. Long pilgrimages to Rome, Santiago de Compostela, or the Holy Sepulcher in Jerusalem were oftentimes the penance imposed on people stained by mortal sin. Thus, groups and movements of obligatory and even voluntary penitents sprang up throughout much of Western Europe. These men and women aspired to do penance not only for their own sinfulness but also in reparation for the sins of others. Such was the world in which Francis, Clare, and their families lived.

A QUESTION OF STUDIES

There are very few studies of the families of Francis and Clare. Certainly, both Fortinis (Arnaldo and Gemma) did an excellent job of perusing the archives of both the commune and the diocese of Assisi in order to piece together what was happening in Assisi before, during, and just after Francis's and Clare's lifetimes. Arnaldo Fortini's *Nova vita di San Francesco*[18] was published in five books and devotes a good portion to the families of both saints. Without going into the emotional attachments that there might have been in those families, Fortini limits himself to genealogical research and to describing the family holdings of the di Bernardone and the Offreduccio families.

Gemma Fortini continued her father's study and, in 1982, published new information about Clare's family tree.[19] This material is an attempt to trace Clare back to the noblest of European families and does nothing to describe her home life or the members of her family. It would seem that historians are much more interested in tracing Francis's and Clare's family trees than in discovering how the members of those families interacted with them or how family ties and relations affected their personalities and futures.

Despite the lack of the human element in these works of the Fortinis, contemporary biographers owe them much for the historical research they have given the field of Franciscanism. Francis's and Clare's biographers have attempted to add some life to historical data in writing the lives of these saints. However, many of them are so caught up in these saints' sanctity that they give little if any attention to their lives before conversion, usually focusing in on the break with the family.

Just over a hundred years ago, in 1894, P. Sabatier wrote his famous *Vie de S. François d'Assise*. His work sparked a whole series of debates now known as the "Franciscan Question" which has come to be "the thorniest question of medieval hagiography."[20] His book also ignited a renewed interest in the life of Francis of Assisi and eventually in the life of Clare of Assisi. Sabatier was not content to simply report Francis's holiness. He desired to set Francis in the context of his day, so he included a brief chapter on Francis's home life. Interestingly enough, Sabatier's description of Francis's youth is completely centered on his father with hardly a nod to his mother's influence. He describes how Pietro was caught up in the family business and in his travels. These travels would have been recounted to the child Francis until the time at which he would have joined his father's business trips. As far as Sabatier is concerned, Francis was his father's son and Pietro unknowingly prepared Francis for religious life.[21]

In the 1920s, the Franciscan Ciro Ortoladi da Pesaro wrote a (now, almost forgotten) book on Francis's mother, Pica. Although he attempted to do a serious historical work addressing the Luccan origin of Francis's family and criticizing the notion that Pica was from France, he fell into the trap of romanticizing the mother–son relationship. He tried to explain the horrendous picture of family life found in Celano's *First Life of St. Francis* (1Cel; *First Celano*) as an exaggeration meant to make Francis fit into the literary model of conversion, with Pietro di Bernardone as the villain in his son's life and conversion.[22]

Omar Englebert dedicated the first chapter of his life of Francis to describing Francis's world and, in this context, Francis's parents. But aside from brief descriptions of each parent and the mention of Francis's brother, the biographer focused his attention on Francis's break with the family.[23]

In 1980, Raoul Manselli published his own biography of Francis. In a chapter entitled "The Merchant," Manselli bemoans the fact that little can be said with certainty about Francis's parents and home life. He spends most of his description of Francis's father and mother on their roles in the story of his conversion. In his telling of it, Francis's mother ultimately lets her son go, and his father pushes him out of the family.[24]

Another medieval historian, Franco Cardini, admits that, given the lack of testimony, seeking to describe Francis's family and family life is historically risky. He admits that the Pietro found in the source literature is a bit of a caricature of what many medieval fathers were like. He points out that all that can be said about Pica was that she was a good mother, at least according to the source accounts.[25]

Medieval historian Jacques Le Goff also wrote a short biography of St. Francis that is worth noting because he recognizes that Francis built his order on the ideal of the family. Unfortunately, he spends only a few lines on Francis's actual family and does not really explain the medieval concept of family and family roles.[26]

Among the recent biographers of St. Francis, Adrian House does a decent, albeit brief, job of looking at Francis's family life. This he does in the context of Francis's education, pleasure-loving youth, and work, three things that marked the family life of most merchant sons in the Middle Ages. He gives primacy of importance to Pietro, without completely ignoring Pica.[27]

Clare's life has also attracted biographers, especially in the later part of the twentieth century. Anton Rotzetter, Ingrid Peterson, María Victoria Triviño, and Marco Bartoli are foremost among them.[28] These authors do a wonderful job of situating Clare in the context of her time.

Although Bartoli and Rotzetter do a good job of describing Clare's life at home, Triviño, and Peterson do even better. All of these authors' attempts at describing Clare's home life rely heavily on historical research done on the noble household of that period. Peterson, however, adds to her life of Clare the work done by feminist historians and theologians. As a result, her Clare is much more situated in the feminine context of her time, and the feminine realities of pregnancy and child rearing are looked at in depth. Without singling out the feminine movement of that era, Triviño seeks to place Clare in the total context of her time. She depicts Clare of Assisi—in turning her back on her family—as repudiating the aspirations of the nobility of that period.

A few authors have attempted to do psychological studies of these saints' personalities. Inevitably, these authors have had to refer to the influences of Francis's and Clare's families. The Franciscan Roberto Zavalloni has written two books, one exploring Francis's personality, and the other, Clare's. In both of these books, he applies the science of psychology to show that both Francis and Clare had mature personalities. He considers the influences of their time and the effects of their conversions on the development of their personalities. He fails to seriously consider, however, the affects that growing up in their respective households had on them. Rather, he limits his discussion to how the family affected each one of them and to the importance of the mothers in their lives.[29]

Another Franciscan scholar who has applied the science of psychology to Francis is Jean-Marc Charron. He attributes to Francis a move from narcissism to true Christian identity. This seems to take the path of moving away from serving the father figure (and Pietro's dreams for his son's future) to the service of Christ, expressed in maternal imagery. He does a good job of placing Francis in what could be called a medieval search for the mother and the feminine. Because of this, Charron shows a preference for Francis's mother over his father, a preference that I do not think Francis shared.[30]

For the last century, scholars have attempted various approaches to understanding the lives, writings, and spirituality of these two saints. I have mentioned here just a few works that have given some attention to the beginning of their lives. I have discovered that, for the most part, their families of origin are either ignored or blended into what we know of the family structures of their day. Scholars in reality can do little more than situate Francis's and Clare's families in their period. The sources for studying them offer little information about the *cotidianidad* (day-to-day reality) lived in the houses of these saints. Attempts have been made by certain authors to reconstruct conversations in Francis's household, but, though well informed, these are always nothing more than the inventions of vivid imaginations.[31]

With the exception of Charron, none of the authors mentioned have attempted to express how Francis's and Clare's family experiences might have influenced any of their writings. Others, such as Thaddée Matura,[32] Optatus van Asseldonk,[33] Norbert Nguyên-Van-Khanh,[34] and Carlo Paolazzi,[35] have referred to the influence of his kinfolk (especially his mother) in Francis's writing and spirituality.

Of those who have written on Clare's writings—Chiara Giovanna Cremaschi, Chiara Agnese Acquadro,[36] Marco Bartoli,[37] and René Charles

Dhont[38]—none has indicated any possible correlation between her use of kinship terminology and the medieval family. In her formidable biography of St. Clare, Peterson sets Clare in the context of the women of her period with a few allusions to women's roles in the family.[39] She, however, was writing about Clare's life, not about her opuscula.

All in all, those who have written on the opuscula of Clare and Francis might have made some reference to the influence of one or the other family member on them, but they fail to consider the influence of the medieval family system and roles of Western Europe. Rather than negate the work done by these specialists, I aim to fill in the lacuna left by them—namely, to place Francis's and Clare's use of kinship terminology and symbolism in the context of the medieval family in order to gain insight into their spirituality.

SOURCES OF INFORMATION ON THE SAINTS' FAMILIES AND HOME LIFE

Of course, the primary and most direct sources for family imagery in the spirituality of Francis and Clare of Assisi are their opuscula. It is in their writings that we are privileged to find their thought and their experience in a literary form. But in order to better understand our two saints, we must consider their vitae (see Appendix D). Although they are indirect sources, vitae are the primary material we have to research the lives of Francis and Clare. Because they are not strict biographies, however, we cannot be sure what in these is based on actual lived experience and what is hagiography. The Franciscan sources, especially as regards Francis, have an added limitation in so far as Francis's vitae increasingly became a polemical tool in the struggle between the "Spirituals" and the friars of the "Community."

Without going into the entire debate concerning the Franciscan question about the dating and interdependence of these vitae,[40] I have chosen them because most Franciscan scholars will agree to their having come from the first Franciscan century. Although they are not all equal in importance, I have decided to use all of them for my work. They are the vitae closest to the time of Francis and Clare and thus reflect cultural presuppositions and factors that these saints of Assisi might have also shared regarding the medieval family.

Keeping in mind that not all of these vitae are of equal significance in their overall content and use by Franciscan scholars, I will nonetheless consider them in a thematic way. Consequently, Francis's and Clare's lives before their conversions will be divided into the various events and persons found in the vitae. These will give us the themes to be dealt with. And because they are varied in their treatment of these events and persons, I will consider what each has to say about these events and persons, keeping in mind that some are official sources while others are not. Even though we have met neither Francis's nor Clare's parents, we can get glimpses of them thanks to hagiography and contemporary historical research into the medieval family.

I will go on to consider their families in the context of the European family of the High Middle Ages. Then, with all of this in mind, I will plunge into the saints' opuscula in order to consider how the social and anthropological reality called kinship influenced or helped define their spirituality. I will end by looking at some similarities and differences and sharing my conclusions about the way Francis and Clare used kinship language to speak of God the Father and their relationships to the Lord Jesus, the Holy Spirit, and Mary. I will pay special attention to the maternal–fraternal tension of the way of life they created, and I will try to answer these questions: What does it mean to be mother to our brothers and sisters?—and even more important—What does it mean to love them with a love that is greater than a mother's love?

CHAPTER I:

EUROPEAN FAMILY OF THE HIGH MIDDLE AGES

In doing a study on family imagery in the spirituality of Francis and Clare of Assisi, we need to establish the socio-anthropological concept of family that was lived by them and their biographers, for they did not write in a vacuum, but were people of their time period, with a social and cultural experience of kinship and family that was presupposed in their readers. When they use the words *mother, father, brother, sister, son, daughter, maid servant, lady,* and *spouse* (*mater, pater, frater, soror, filius, filia, ancilla, domina, sponsus,* and *sponsa*), they are using them as implicit cultural presuppositions and as specific cultural factors of their and their reader's *cotidianidad*.

We cannot enter the minds of Francis and Clare, so we will never truly know what their personal perception of the family was, but we can attempt to reconstruct the general perception of their time. All social constructs of any period are a blend of traditions and practices inherited from the past. For the Italians of the thirteenth century, this meant the pre-Christian family construct of Roman, Jewish, and Germanic societies. But what did these look like, and what did the medieval family of Umbria inherit from them in terms of family construct and familial roles?

For the most part, when historians have delved into the Middle Ages they have paid little if any attention to the medieval family. The European Middle Ages have been studied as a period of historical conflicts and power struggles, of philosophical and scholastic education, of Crusades and witch hunts, of nobles (*maiores*) and serfs (*minores*), and of Chivalry and courtly love. Yet in all of this the family has been largely ignored except as it served the importance of lineage for the great figures of nobility. Those families that have been studied have been examined for their lines of ancestry and not for *lo cotidiano*—the daily lived experience of what it meant to be a husband or a wife, or of how children were raised. It is only recently that gender studies have caused an interest in the family constructs of the European Middle Ages. These contemporary studies have tried to shed light on the roles of different family members—those of parents and children, husbands and wives.

Any family portrait of that time period will necessarily be painted by modern scholars with a dispassionate, analytical approach that cannot take into account the lived experience of medieval family members. Historians, sociologists, and anthropologists studying the medieval family have no choice but to turn to the sources of that period. These are social and ecclesiastical law codes, cartularies, and tax records which relate data about the family as viewed within *Christianitas* for the purpose of controlling and placing the family at the service of the common good. They also include theological and secular writings, paintings, murals, frescoes, sculptures, poetry, song, and prose that, with the exception of bawdy drinking songs, tend to portray their subject in an idealized fashion while critiquing (or ignoring) anything that falls short of the ideal. Finally, the sources used by those studying the family of the Middle Ages must necessarily include tombstones, hagiographies, and autobiographies that give a hint of the emotions involved in family life without truly explaining them. Together, all of these sources point out bonds based on friendship and on blood; they refer to hostilities, indifferences, and reconciliation; they paint an ideal and hint at how the real family did or did not live up to it.

No element in social history is more prevalent than the family, kinship group, or clan. These groupings usually went beyond the limitations of domesticity or the nuclear group of parents and children living under the same roof. They have always been the environments where human beings learn to eat, walk, and speak, and acquire their sense of identity and modes of behavior. Every culture, past and present, has included the institution of the family as an economic, political, and social unit needed for the survival of society. The family has provided solidity, stability, and protection by joining with other families in order to form a society.

Yet, the way in which cultures have lived and defined family has changed over the centuries. In some cultures and times, the family has been understood in a much reduced fashion as parents and children living under one roof, with all other relations being recognized as relatives or kin, but not part of the "nuclear" family. In others, the family has been understood to include biological and legal relatives whether or not they live under the same roof.

In the Early and High Middle Ages, the European family was undergoing a slow and gradual transformation. It was moving from the ancient patriarchal system (in which a family or household gathered under a paterfamilias) to a structure that tied family units of genitors and their offspring to others of common blood lines. As noble families desperately strove to maintain their status, they found themselves threatened by a rising merchant class. This class was made up of those who had freed themselves from lords—from being part of their noble households. Yet, despite their freedom, they sought to gain noble status and emulate noble families.

Some of Francis's vitae give testimony to this. Just before his conversion, Francis dreams that his family house is transformed into a palace full of trophies and coats of arms that he is told belong to him and his followers (household). Like all merchants, he and his father sought to emulate the *maiores*. This emulation included a desire to turn their small merchant family into a powerful household like that of Clare's family in Assisi. But, I am getting ahead of myself. Let's turn now to the roots of the Christian family of Medieval Europe.

PRE-CHRISTIAN FAMILY

The cement of human society is found in the give and take of relationships. It is in this type of relationship that the anthropologist, Marvin Harris, drawing on Darwinism and socio-biological factors, claims the concepts of marriage and family find their origins in pre-classical times as a means of propagating the human species. A type of give-and-take relationship took place between a man and a woman and was extended to the woman's children by the man.[1] Eventually, in many societies, this give-and-take relationship became monogamous, and in most cases, led to patriarchal family structures like those proposed by the Hebrew Scriptures and Roman law.

JEWISH PATRIARCHY

According to the anthropologist, Dieter Lenzen, the figure of the father developed in ancient Asia Minor in the period from 2385 to 1728 BCE (before the Common Era). It was during this time that the cause and effect between sexual intercourse and pregnancy was discovered.[2] The cultures of Asia Minor and especially that of Egypt developed a tri-functional role for the father who was to generate, sustain, and educate his children.

The concept of patriarchy, however, was born in Israel.[3] In ancient Judaism, the concept of father took on new and particular connotations, which greatly affected the concept of patriarchy in medieval Christianity. These connotations were primarily two: (1) God's election of a people with the call of Abraham and, eventually, in the Exodus experience, and (2) the people becoming a kingdom in which David takes the place of the people, thus becoming the chosen son of God (cf. 2 Sam 7:14; Ps 2:7). In these two moments, God acts as the one who adopts the child and thus sanctifies him through official recognition. Thus, adoption moved paternity from being solely a biological function to having an important social and affective role. After all, almost anyone can biologically generate a child, but only a good man can take responsibility for the education and welfare of that child and others. The God of Israel, although a patriarchal God, blends the social and educational role of the father figure with affective maternal imagery—without, however, being proclaimed as mother. In this blend of paternal and maternal imagery, the mercy, wisdom, and soul strength attributed to fathers are referred to as feminine in the Hebrew Scriptures.[4]

The word *patriarch* is Greek in origin and comes from the Septuagint and other biblical manuscripts. In the Greek Scriptures, *patriarch* was used to refer not only to heads of households, but also to the chiefs of the tribes of Israel or men who governed companies of at least one hundred men. *Patriarch* in the Hebrew Scriptures was also an honorary title given to the twelve sons of Jacob and specifically to Abraham, Isaac, and Jacob who were the origins of the people of Israel. Although he is never called patriarch in the Hebrew Scriptures, in the Christian Scriptures, the title *patriarch* refers exclusively to David, Abraham, and the twelve sons of Jacob. These patriarchs however were no longer seen as direct ancestors but as spiritual figures in the new people of Israel, the Church.

In Israel, God's paternity becomes the role model for human fathers who need to pity their children as well as correct them (cf. Prov 3:12; 5:11;

Job 5:17). The educative role given to fathers is an extension of God's paternity. In the Hebrew Scriptures, the role of the father is that of paternally and affectionately sustaining the "needy" child by raising and educating her/him with freely given love. Because of the father's commitment to the well-being of the child, the child owes the father respect and honor. Thus the father's role was not primarily generative. Rather, he was the head of the family whom all others served and obeyed in their various domestic and familial roles.

Patrilocality was the primary form of the Hebrew family in Ancient Israel. In this form, the entire family—even married sons along with their wives and children—gathered around the person of the father; all were expected to live with the father. The father was the lord of his house and had the power of life and death over the members of his family.[5] He had the role of judge and was expected to maintain the family, to teach them the Torah, to form them in labor, to correct his children, and to arrange their marriages. The father, however, was warned in the scriptures not to ruin his children by loving them more than he should (I Sam 2:12–36). Correction seems to be the key to raising and educating children worthy of God (Prov 13:24; 29:15, 21; Sir 22:3–6; Ws 11:9). It is important to note that, even with the supreme power of the father of the family, the Hebrew Scriptures presuppose equality between father and mother.[6] But this equality is only as regards the shared responsibility of raising a child. The child in question is to honor both parents equally. This equality of father and mother, however, does not translate into an equality of husband and wife.

Medieval noble households learned much from Jewish patriarchy. Just like the Jewish patriarch, the Christian head of the family sought to gather a family of offspring and servants into a common household. Women were sought for their male offspring and brought into the household for its continuation. Female offspring were given over to powerful families to establish ties that were mutually beneficial to both families. Yet in all of this, we note that the noble head of the family was more like the Roman paterfamilias than a Jewish patriarch.

THE ROMAN FAMILY

For centuries, Western cultures have used derivatives of the Latin word *familia* to speak of the conjugal unit. Yet, neither classical Greek nor Latin had a term which corresponds to the contemporary English word *family* or the *familia* of Romance languages, because the conjugal unit did not exist in isolation as it does in many of today's societies.[7] In the classical period, the Greek word for family was *genea* which meant blood descent, while the Romans used *familia*, which described the property and dependents of the head of a household.[8] Both of these definitions excluded the *dominus*—head of the household or paterfamilias—from the definition of family, thus establishing a crucial distinction between the ruler and the ruled, the father and his dependents. According to juridical texts of ancient Rome, the father's role went beyond the generative function to a punitive one that gave him the power of life and death over the familia. In accordance with Roman law, all the misbehavior of his dependents would also fall upon him.[9] Having the paterfamilias included in the familia would compromise this role as administrator, judge, and lord of the household. As *pater*, he was expected to fulfill a protective role, while as dominus he was expected to have punitive responsibilities. Yet he was also to act with *pietas* and not *atrocitas* when exercising his role.[10]

The father's dependents were subject to his authority either by nature (offspring) or by law (wife, adopted children, and servants). All of these were considered part of the family; obviously some were related by blood, while others were given over to the manus (jurisdiction) of the head of the family through either marriage or commerce. The role of the paterfamilias was a political and social reality whose function it was to provide a defense system in union with other families of the same society. The functions held by the family gave great importance and authority to the person of the paterfamilias resulting in a family structure that was definitely patriarchal. However, even in this patriarchy, there was room for a type of matriarchy in which the male of a weaker family would move in with his wife's family and enter the service of the stronger clan.[11]

In Roman history, the creation and continuation of a family came to depend largely on the institution of marriage, an institution that could only be entered into by Roman citizens. The unions of noncitizens or a citizen and a noncitizen were considered legalized concubinage.[12] Marriage and concubinage, besides being a combination of sexual relations and parenting, became a publicly approved and legal contract defining the relationship of the two spouses as well as that of parents and children. The community in which the spouses lived gave public approval. In ancient Rome, this community was constituted by the families involved, especially the fathers of the bride and the groom.

In primitive Roman law, marriage had the effect of placing the woman in the manus of the paterfamilias, who arranged marriages for his sons. She came to the family on the same footing as the children (*filius familias*). This custom centered marriage not on love but on the good of the family. Love in fact had nothing to do with marriage. A wife was given to her husband so that the two might procreate and thus provide continuity to the clan by giving children to the family. This "handing over" to the jurisdiction of the head of the family was done in one of three different ways: *confarreatio, coemptio,* or *usus. Confarreatio* was a type of ritual sacrifice conducted in the presence of ten witnesses by a priest or the paterfamilias. The sacrifice was usually of a *panis farreus* (a type of bread) signifying the sharing of life. *Coemptio* was the delivery of the woman in a fictitious sale. *Usus* was done through matrimonial cohabitation for a year without the couple having spent more than three continuous nights apart.[13]

In the classical era, these three forms fell into disuse and were replaced by public mutual consent. Consent became so central to marriage that not even consummation was necessary for the validity of a marriage. This consent began to focus more on the groom, however, and not simply on his paterfamilias. The same however could not be said for the bride in question. She was still seen as a vassal of the family, and thus her free consent to marriage was not required. Consent, which included an exchange of promises and gifts between the bride's father and the groom, became "a private act, based solely on the consent of the parties involved (which of course included parents or guardians), and requiring no further external gesture"[14] or sanction from the civil government.

Early Christianity and Family

Any study on marriage and family in the High Middle Ages cannot simply consider the Jewish and Roman influences on those institutions. Despite the Jewish roots of Christianity, it was the pagan family—eventually transformed into the Christian family structure—that greatly influenced the societies and cultures of medieval Europe. Christianity took into itself Roman custom, law, and practices that were not contrary to the spread of the Gospel. These included family structure and the concept of marriage by consent. This concept could be easily adopted into Christianity, as it did not contradict the Gospel. In fact, Modestino, at the close of the classical period of Roman jurisprudence in the early third century, had defined marriage as "the union of husband and woman in a lifelong, divinely and legally communicated consortium."[15] This definition certainly agrees with Jesus' own concept of the insolubility of marriage

The medieval European family was a Christian reality. *Christianitas* did much to ensure that Europe lived by evangelical norms and thus the family could not help but turn to Jesus and the Christian Scriptures. This was especially true as scholars struggled to make sense of marriage and the sanctity of procreation and family in the eleventh and twelfth centuries.

Even though Jesus defended marriage as a lifelong commitment, his relationship with his own family and his references to leaving one's family in order to follow him, show that he was not defending the dignity of the family in doing so. In the first century, family (or rather, kinship) was the primary instrument for giving a person a sense of identity and belonging. It was in the clan that people would establish and act out their function and role in society. Nonetheless, Jesus challenged kinship identity as an essential socio-cultural category without condemning it completely. Jesus and the early Church did much to establish a new style of social identification, that of discipleship. It is through discipleship and not through socio-familial identity that a person comes to know and belong to the Family of Christ. Despite the apparent break with the clan/family, Jesus and his followers polemically use kinship terminology (except for *father*, which is reserved exclusively for God) in order to describe their relationships with each other.[16]

Jesus, who never married, insisted that marriage was a lifelong indissoluble commitment (Mt 19:3–9; Mk 10:6–12). This teaching of Christ was not to be found in either Jewish custom or law. Furthermore, despite Modestino's definition of marriage as a lifelong commitment, it would seem that, for the most part, pagan custom and law allowed for divorce. Thus, Jesus' definition of marriage as an indissoluble union of husband and wife who have left their parents gave Christians food for thought in their consideration of marriage. It required Christian couples to make a lasting commitment to each other despite conditions that caused Jewish and pagan spouses to leave each other.

Despite Jesus' teaching on the divine establishment of marriage, it would seem that he did not respect the familial practices of his day. He insisted on a personal commitment that denied the obligations of family life. He gave mixed messages about the importance of family ties. While he gave back the son to the widowed mother (Lk 7:11–15), he asked his disciple not to love their parents more than Him (Mt 10:37). He proclaimed that he came to divide families and that the members of one's household will be one's enemies (Mt 10:35–36). His own pronouncement on marriage—that a husband leaves his parents in order to cling to his wife and form a new unit—seems to indicate that marriage was not meant for the continuation of a patriarch's household but rather for personal union of the husband and wife. This concept, now ingrained in contemporary Christianity, was a radical concept for the whole of the first Christian millennium and much of the early centuries of the second.

Besides Jesus' pronouncement on the indissolubility of marriage, *Christianitas* had to contend with Pauline teaching on marriage and family life. Marriage as an indissoluble union founded on sacrificial love caused Paul and others to use it as a means of describing the union of Christ and his Church (Eph 5:23–32). Yet this understanding of marriage was not new to Christianity. The Hebrew Scriptures had already used it to refer to God and Israel, with Israel usually referred to as an unfaithful wife and even a prostitute. In the Christian Scriptures, however, the Church is seen more as a waiting bride than an unfaithful wife, the difference being that the Church/bride is being prepared for the heavenly wedding feast in which she will finally, after a long period of preparation and expectation, be welcomed by her Spouse[17] (Rv 19:8; 20:2, 9, 17).

Many in the early Church shared Paul's understanding of marriage to symbolize Christ's union with the Church, extending it to refer also to a bishop's relationship with his see and God's mystical marriage to the soul. This sacramental use of marriage, however, had in mind a "spiritual" marriage, free of carnal knowledge. Although Paul never excluded carnal knowledge from Christian marriage, he had explicitly ranked celibacy as higher than marriage. This led other writers to wonder how marriage could symbolize the relationship between Christ and His Church if not in a celibate marriage.[18] And, although Paul gave sacramental significance to marriage by using it as a symbol of Christ's relationship to the Church (Eph 5:23–32), the Church itself did not consider it a sacrament—and, therefore, something worthy of a follower of Christ—until as late as the thirteenth century.[19] This should come as no surprise given Jesus' ambiguous stance on family relationships and Paul's insistence on the supremacy of the celibate state and description of marriage as a "prophylactic against incontinence."[20]

There seems to have been no specifically Christian wedding ceremony during the first three centuries of the Common Era. Christian couples were wed according to the customs of their society. Most early Christians were not Roman citizens, and, oftentimes, those who were had to marry "beneath them" in order to find a Christian spouse. Officially, they could not be married, so they lived in legal concubinage. It was not until the fourth century, when many Roman citizens became Christians, that Christianity began to develop marriage rituals. These were originally nothing more than a blessing of the marriage that had already taken place. Although some marriage rituals were being developed in different areas of Europe, the Church had no standard nuptial liturgies before the eighth or ninth century. This lack of a common nuptial ritual or liturgy was probably due to the fact that, while some Christians insisted that it was required for all, others totally opposed marriage.[21]

THE ORTHODOX POSITION

The early centuries of Christianity did little to develop Christ's and Paul's teachings on marriage and family. Rather, they did much to defend and a support a way of life that in both Jewish and pagan circles was considered unnatural and counter to the good of the family: virginity or celibacy. This new way of life was promoted for some members of the Church, yet some heretical Christian sects proposed it for all its members. This heretical and total condemnation of marriage is understandable when, even among patristic Christianity, marriage was seen as a lesser state in life and virginity was promoted as the way of perfection. What ultimately distinguished the orthodox position from heretical points of view, however, was that the patristic writers appointed themselves as guardians of marriage and procreation. The orthodox position affirmed the dignity of the married state. The Church promoted a growing awareness that marriage and family life were also a part of God's original plan and not just something that resulted after the fall.

Despite their acceptance of two sexes, marriage, and procreation as part of God's original plan, patristic writers, tainted by Stoicism, had a difficult time accepting conjugal relations as good. Even within marriage, Origen presented sexual relations as an indication of humanity's flawed corporeal state and "original sin was identified as the first sexually transmitted disease."[22] Origen and other patristic writers did not seek to eliminate the conjugal act altogether; rather they sought to discipline and contain it by stressing its procreative function as being the primary ends of marriage. They presupposed that couples would refrain from conjugal relations during certain periods of the liturgical year since prayer and sexual relations are incompatible. They also insisted on sexual abstinence during pregnancy and lactation. Patristic writers expected that couples would eventually move into a chaste relationship that would exclude the conjugal act altogether after having had a certain period of normal sexual activity.

In an attempt to settle a debate between Jerome and Jovian, Augustine was the first Church father to develop an explanation of marriage that was not dependent on the conjugal debt. Jerome was adamant in his denunciation of marriage, while Jovian used the marriage of Mary and Joseph as his defense for claiming that marriage should be considered more noble then virginity. Augustine refuted Jovian's denial of virginity. He tried to correct Jerome's condemnation of marriage; "he did not believe that the elevation of the one (virginity) required the vilification of the other (marriage)."[23] Augustine evolved his position on marriage and procreation from believing that Adam and Eve had spiritual bodies to admitting that they had sexually differentiated corporeal bodies before the fall and would have procreated even if they had never sinned.[24]

Augustine, though, never claims that Adam and Eve had conjugal relations before the fall. It was only after the fall, when marriage had already lost its original beauty, that the conjugal act took place. Yet the dignity of marriage was not totally lost; rather, this dignity is safeguarded by the three goods of matrimony: procreation, fidelity, and indissolubility. It remained humanity's first social bond, but after the fall it took on the role of channeling concupiscence. Augustine espouses the Roman concept of marriage as a free act of consent that does not need to be consummated in order to be valid. "In line with this secular framework, Augustine distinguishes between the end of marriage (which is procreation) and the essence of marriage, which is agreement between spouses."[25] In this way, Mary and Joseph were said to have been truly married even if they never consummated their relationship.

Besides dealing with issues of sexual consummation and procreation, some of the patristic writers tried to establish married life as being spiritually beneficial for both partners. Clement of Alexandria, in Stromata 3, attributed Christ's words of being present where two or three are gathered in His name (Mt 18:20) as being applicable to the Christian family. Yet this emphasis on mutual spiritual help did not seem to be enough to justify marriage in and of itself. Marriage was much too entrenched in a family's need for children to warrant any other focus. Even Clement, who did so much to defend marriage, was at a loss as to how the wife is a helpmate for her husband apart from the conjugal act and the raising of children. Moreover, where Jesus had specifically mentioned that a man leaves his parents to cling to his wife, in fact Christian marriage became in the first few Christian centuries an institution for the good of the groom's family. Thus the groom did not leave father and mother; rather he brought his wife to his father's household.

GERMANIC INFLUENCE ON CHRISTIAN MARRIAGE

Christian marriage in the High Middle Ages was not simply an institution inherited from Jewish patriarchy and Roman practice. Toward the middle of the sixth century, the Italian peninsula was subjected to a series of invasions, especially that of the Lombards of Germanic descent. Eventually the Lombards were Christianized and their own views of marriage and family began to challenge the Roman Christian position. While Roman law had settled on consent as the principal agent in the legal formation of marriage, the Lombards insisted on consummation for the validity of a marriage, and this stance slowly entered into the Church's teaching on marriage as Christianity struggled to define the dignity of marriage and procreation.

The Church had always taken the Roman position that only consent given by the parents of the bride and groom was needed for the validity of a marriage. Consummation was not required and, in many cases, it never occurred, in keeping with the example of Mary and Joseph. This non-consummation definition of marriage helped feed dualistic tendencies within Christian groups. As heretical groups like the Cathars, which had taken up dualistic notions against the flesh, increasingly assailed the Church, the orthodox position on marriage slowly began to require consummation for the validity of a marriage. Especially as an aid for channeling sexual energy, marriage became the Church's tool against those who completely condemned the flesh and its functions.

Another Germanic practice that slowly influenced the Christian concept of marriage was that of personal and not familial consent. This concept was reserved only to the groom by Germanic tribes. Germanic fathers had great authority over the lives of their offspring, although it was not as absolute or permanent as that of Roman fathers. The male offspring became *persone sui iuris* when they came of age. Among other things, this meant that the male offspring—and not the father—sought his own bride. A daughter, however, never gained autonomy; she passed from the authority of her father to that of her husband. Indeed, in Italy, the Lombards did not consider it possible for a woman to commit to a juridical act on her own. Thus, marriage took on a more businesslike approach, treating the woman as a sales item passing from one owner, the father, to another, the husband. In the High Middle Ages, this transaction was done in two phases, neither of which required the consent of the bride in question, only the consent of her father. The two phases were juridical acts and consisted of the *desponsio* (by which a bride is promised to the future husband) and the *traditio* (by which she is actually handed over to the husband). By these two acts, the couple was considered married, but that marriage was not considered completely valid and indissoluble until after consummation.

Eventually, in the late twelfth century, the Church not only approved of the groom's personal consent to marriage but also sought to extend this concept of personal consent to the bride. It was one thing to insist on consummation, but the Church's insistence on the consent of both the bride and groom was more than just a countercultural move; it was an outright attack on the noble family system. In feudal times, the lord or paterfamilias seeking to protect his interests controlled the giving and taking in marriage of his children, vassals, and their children. A person's choice in marriage (or celibacy) affected the present and future service of the lord and his finances. Thus, the idea of personal consent, especially on the part of the bride, was not a welcome one to most noble families. And although the Church slowly promoted it, feudal society did not completely accept it.[26]

THE CHRISTIANIZATION OF MARRIAGE

In the first Christian millennium, the Church did not have its own fully developed theory or ideal of marriage or family but rather had adapted itself (not without criticism) to the structures of the different peoples to which it spread. Nevertheless, a Christian ideal of marriage is discernable from the very beginning. "This Christian ideal emphasized the relation between the spouses rather than the view, characteristic of so many forms of extended family, that saw marriage in terms of the need of the larger social structure."[27]

The ninth century is a decisive period in the long history of the Christianization of matrimony for it was at this time that Europe was brought under Carolingian domination. During this period, governed by the notion of *Christianitas*, it became difficult to distinguish between Church and society. European peoples recognized a king as sacred and the Church as a means of educating people for the needs of society. Carolingian Society sought the Church's aid in regulating the structure of marriage and family life.

The Christian notion of marriage as personal and not proprietary provided a criticism for the varied marriage customs of Europe in the Late Roman Period and the Early Middle Ages. Thanks to *Christianitas* in the High Middle Ages, Christian thought on marriage penetrated Western Europe; society and family structures changed accordingly, but not without resistance.

Family life had always been structured and controlled by society, since it is more than just the coming together of a couple and the raising of offspring. Marriage and family involve the continuation of a society's power, influence, peace, and patrimony. This was especially true in feudal society.

Marriage aided the common good by joining noble families together, which helped to bring peace to society. Therefore, the nobility of the feudal period could not risk secret marriage among its members. In brief, secret marriages and illicit unions produced unwanted heirs that could destroy a family's patrimony and seriously endanger peace. While the Church was espousing the idea of personal consent, *Christianitas* gradually required priests to assist in the public act of the marriage ritual and in the formation of family life.[28]

THE UNCONVENTIONAL FAMILY

Jesus' teaching on celibacy as a valid option for the kingdom of God became a widespread phenomenon in patristic Christianity and in *Christianitas*. Contrary to the Hebrew Scriptures, which promoted a family bound by blood, Christian Scriptures espoused an unconventional family system where the waters of baptism were stronger than bloodlines. Jesus himself had an ambiguous relationship with his own blood kin, preferring to build a new family based on the doing of God's will.

While blood families depended on marriage and procreation for their continuation, patristic Christianity came to the realization that virginity and celibacy perfected Jesus' household. Consequently, as the Roman Empire slowly disintegrated and Europe became Christian, many Christians who wanted to be freed of the ties of blood family turned to virginity instead. This freedom from familial responsibilities was not a simple refusal of the institution of marriage and family but an attempt to live more perfectly the teachings of Christ.

For most of the first Christian millennium, despite the examples of female martyrs, such as Agnes and Lucy, the celibate or virginal lifestyle was more common among men. Many of them chose to live as hermits, while most of them opted for an unconventional family system that centered on a paterfamilias, known as an abbot. These monks rejected their own families of origin and set up an entirely different type of family. Women who chose to do the same were fewer in number and came to be known as nuns gathered in families led by abbesses. With the coming of the penitential movements in the High Middle Ages, nuns slowly came to outnumber monks and friars.

VIRGINITY VERSUS MARRIED LIFE

The rejection of earthly marriage was nothing new in the Middle

Ages. As is well known, patristic authors, following the teachings of Jesus and St. Paul, exalted virginity over matrimony from early on in Christianity. Although marriage and family life came to be defended as compatible with Christian life, virginity was still the preferred state for those seeking evangelical perfection. This prejudice of patristic authors made its way into the writings of medieval authors. Nevertheless, although virginity was the preferred state at the time of Clare, marriage was finally proclaimed a sacrament of the Church during her lifetime.[29]

The writings of many medieval authors manifest misogynous tendencies. Women, as the daughters of Eve, were held suspect because of their sex. As a result, women practiced exaggerated forms of the many penitential practices that were begun by men. These austerities were a way in which women could overcome their own sex. Fasting for long periods would stop the monthly cycle of menstruation, which was a woman's most obvious "weakness." At a time when being a woman meant a life limited to the household and the raising of children, the penitential life, especially the vow of chastity, became an attractive "way out" offered them by the Church. Religious life assisted women in breaking free of social conventions that kept them tied to one or the other family. In overcoming their own sex, women chose a life that went against the traditional family expectations of patriarchal societies. In the tri-functional society of the High Middle Ages, which defined women as virgins, wives, and widows, a woman refuted the status of wife (and mother) that most families desired for them by choosing virginity.[30]

Medieval men saw chastity and asceticism as ways in which women could confront the dark powers that were associated with being a woman. Virginity was suggested to them as a good higher than marriage and as a way of perfection. It was a way of denying womanhood, while holding on to femininity. Because of their femininity, inspired by the many commentaries to the Song of Songs, women turned chastity into a positive force in their spirituality. Their virginity was the virginity of a *sponsa* (bride) that waited for her *sponsus* (bridegroom)[31] to come to her. The virgins of the women's religious movement were women who spurned carnal joys for Christ, clinging to him in their poverty and humility. They were women whose fertility gave birth to many children.[32] Chastity was a way of entering the chambers of the Bridegroom and of being even more fertile than is the "mother of seven sons."

MALE AND FEMALE SANCTITY

One testimony to the influx of women (especially virgins) in the reform movements of the medieval Church is the number of women saints canonized during the High Middle Ages. According to Donald Weinstein and Rudolph Bell in their book *Saints and Society: The Two Worlds of Western Christendom*, women were only ten per cent of the canonized saints of the Church in the tenth century. During the twelfth and thirteenth centuries, the number of women saints grew to 22.6 per cent of the total, but then dropped back down to 14.4 per cent by the seventeenth century.[33]

The vitae of male and female saints show few differences in their pious practices and devotions. In the High Middle Ages, male and female saints were reading the same Scriptures and spiritual writings, listening to the same sermons, and using the same metaphors to express their spirituality. Yet this age can be called the "Era of the Feminization of Sanctity,"[34] for during this period, both male and female saints used terms and "spiritual themes that modern commentators have assumed to be gender-specific (e.g., the vision of nursing the Christ child or of being pregnant with Jesus)"[35] in order to express their relationship with the Divine.

The hagiographies of this age show that, where male saints usually underwent a sudden conversion during late adolescence or in their early twenties, women saints steadily grew in holiness from childhood into their adolescent years. Clare and Francis are both good examples of this. Male saints often underwent a conversion that involved a rejection of wealth, power, and sexuality. On the other hand, women saints demonstrated holiness either by rebelling against family in order to insist heroically on guarding their virginity or by humbly consenting to a prearranged marriage. Male saints were often seen as men of action for the sake of the Gospel while female saints were usually considered models of suffering for Christ.

"The notion of renunciation of the world—i.e., following the naked and suffering Christ by renouncing status, power, personal comfort, and family—was at the heart of medieval Christianity."[36] In this way, both men and women were freed from worldly burdens, concerns, and pleasures, like those of family life, to devote themselves to God and to the things of God. This freedom from worldly and familial ties was also expressed, in symbolic language, as freedom from gender-specific roles and expectations. Through this symbolic language, the religious man and woman seem to be seeking wholeness and holiness by integrating the masculine and the feminine found within each human person. This symbolic language, which broke the traditional family ties, nevertheless used family roles to explain the roles in the unconventional family of religious life.[37]

Anthropologists suggest that gender reversal in symbols and symbolic language is proof of "liminity,"—which is to say, an escape from role and status. It is a powerful social critique, which helps to transcend boundaries and limitations in such a way as to reaffirm normal structures and roles, but with a new understanding.[38] In the language or symbols of role reversal, however, men and women again show themselves to be different. Women subconsciously used role reversal to protest male power and dominance in their lives. Men, on the other hand, referred to themselves as brides, mothers, and children in spiritual literature, and used role reversal to express a renunciation of male power, authority, and/or status.[39] Both, however, revealed their dependence on God in their language and symbols.

The dichotomy of gender-specific roles and expectations seems to be what religious men and women sought to overcome. In telling their brothers and sisters to love each other more than a mother loves her son, and to give birth to Christ, Francis and Clare are encouraging Christians to overcome this dichotomy. They had grown up being told that men are strong and women are weak, that men are rational and women are emotional. In these dichotomies, masculine qualities were logic, thought, decision, organization, and order. On the other hand, female qualities were creativity, intuition, feeling, affectivity, and relationship.

THE SONG OF SONGS

Symbolic gender reversal along with a renewed appreciation for the humanity of Christ slowly worked its way into the spirituality of the High Middle Ages. This helped both male and female saints and mystics develop an affective spirituality of union. Bernard of Clairvaux had recalled the humanity of Christ in the twelfth century by stressing his passion. In the thirteenth century, Francis of Assisi recalled the humanity of Christ by stressing the Incarnation. Early and medieval imagery of the Church had presented Jesus as the Glorified Lord even as he hung triumphantly on the Cross (for example, the Cross of San Damiano, the figure of which spoke to Francis during his conversion). In the mid-thirteenth century, this representation began to change into the image of the Nazarene who died painfully on an instrument of torture. Prayer, for many of the period, and especially for women, became a way of emotionally uniting with this "Suffering Servant" whom they claimed as Spouse and Lord. Clare, herself, was especially fond of praying to the five wounds of Christ and saying Francis's "Office of the Lord's Passion," but she did so before the image of the triumphant Lord upon the Cross of San Damiano.

So the image of Church/bride found in the Christian Scriptures came to be seen as a symbol of the union of the human soul with God. This was especially true in the unconventional family structure of religious life. Monks and nuns in the early part of the second Christian millennium not only turned to the spousal imagery found in the Christian Scriptures, but increasingly to a mystical experience of the love of God through the Song of Songs in the Hebrew Scriptures. When speaking of the soul's union with God, the Song of Songs was undoubtedly the most discussed book of the Hebrew Scriptures in Christianity. This book overflows with depictions of human passion that have been allegorized to explain a soul's passion for God.

"The basic element of the analogy is the loving relationship which, according to the story of the Song of Songs, exists between husband and wife. Their love is reciprocal and so intense that it causes illness, languor, suffering, and even torment (*cruciet*). Love causes souls to melt; . . . . The actions of love are multiple: it speaks to the spouse when he is present, invites him to return when he is absent."[40]

The Song of Songs reflected for both the female and male mystics of the Middle Ages an ultimate source of love imagery to express their love and yearning for God. At this time, such human love-sickness was considered "womanly," yet, in regard to the soul's relationship with God, the spiritual writers and mystics of the period encouraged that love-sickness.[41] The faithful are to be the Bride in the canticle anxiously awaiting her lover/groom so that she might enjoy the rapture of his erotic embrace and the kisses of his mouth. For Christians, this book from the Hebrew Scriptures became an expression of the Church's relationship to Christ. For Bernard of Clairvaux, the lover yearned for is God, and the young woman is the soul in search of mystical union with the Divine. The Song of Songs was influential for virgins who saw chastity as preparation for the heavenly marriage bed.[42] The woman who chose to live in chastity saw herself as "destined for a higher consumption. She scintillated with fertility and power. Into her body, as into the Eucharistic bread on the altar, poured the inspiration of the Holy Spirit and the fullness of the humanity of Christ."[43] Male mystics were also sensitive to this imagery of the Song of Songs; but in women these nuptial themes first articulated by men become more erotic and affective.

THE HOLY FAMILY

No look at the development of marriage and family life in Christianity would be complete without taking the relationship of Jesus, Mary, and Joseph into consideration. For all practical purposes, theirs was definitely an unconventional family. While solemnities and feast days for Jesus and Mary grew in this period, there were no feasts for Joseph or the Holy Family in the Middle Ages. Strangely enough, St. Joseph was never used as a patriarchal figure until after the fifteenth century. New studies show that a matrilineal tradition developed in medieval hagiographic works, which centered on the person of St. Anne, the mother of the Virgin Mary.[44] In this saintly matriarchy, many female saints took on complex and contradictory roles. These took them out of traditional female gender roles; they took on the gender prescriptions of the male roles in medieval culture and society. According to Ashley and Sheingorn, the visual image of St. Anne, not Joachim, is presented in medieval art as the founding parent of Mary's family.[45] Thus, even in the Holy Family, Mary is presented as the principal parent, with Joseph being assigned a minimal and almost insignificant role in the life of Jesus. It was thanks to Mary that Jesus entered the human family. It was this role, centered on the humanity of Jesus, which endeared Mary to the medieval Christian.

Holy women of the Scriptures, such as Hannah, Elizabeth, and the Virgin Mary, stood out as models of a matrilineal tradition that gradually moved the faithful past patriarchal structures and mindsets. They each conceived a child with the blessing of God and had the audacity to usurp the paternal role in the naming of their sons. In their stories, the husband/father is a lesser figure that many times gets lost in the light of the wife/mother's virility. If the husband—consider Joseph as the prime example—is remembered at all, it is for his service to the valiant woman and her offspring.

LOVE AND THE CONJUGAL DEBT

Strangely enough, at the same time that male and female religious were turning to the eroticism of the Song of Songs in order to express their loving union with God and Joseph was being all but left out of the Holy Family, Christian concepts of marriage were beginning to include romance. It was not until the twelfth century that marriage was connected with erotic or romantic fulfillment.[46] Indeed, as far as law, theology, and even popular imagination were concerned, marriage should not be based on sexual attraction. Given the reality of arranged marriages, and the legislation by canonists, it would seem that the institution of marriage was devoid of love, that it was a juridical matter in which two people were expected to cooperate, while true love was to be found elsewhere.

In reality, Canonical literature in the twelfth century gave much space to a form of attachment known as *affectio*, referring to is as "marital affection," "affection for one's wife," or " conjugal affection,"—what a man should feel for his own wife. At least according to law, it is true that in medieval society a man was both to dominate and to esteem his wife at the same time, and, even though parents arranged many marriages, couples were still expected to love and respect each other. Most men may not have married the women they loved, but many came to love the women they married.[47] This affection included a sense of grace, since spousal love was recognized as a gift from God, which the spouses were obliged to care for and cultivate. In the early twelfth century, love was associated with Augustine's three goods of marriage (procreation, fidelity, and indissolubility), especially fidelity. With this development, love came to be seen as necessary in matrimony, and the conjugal act as a normal, but not indispensable, manifestation of that love.[48]

The theological schools of the twelfth century grappled with the question of the need for consummation in Christian marriage.[49] This was a struggle between the old Roman view of "consent only" marriage and the Germanic understanding that consummation was needed to validate any marriage. This struggle was found not only among theologians, but also more importantly among canonists who espoused the need for the consummation of a marriage. Gratian, like most theologians of the period, argued that consent alone made the marriage, citing the example of Joseph and Mary. However, he also admitted that marriage was ratified by coitus. Thus, he distinguished two moments in marriage: initiation through consent and ratification by consummation.[50]

Not all canonists agreed with Gratian's position that marriage is begun by consent and ratified by consummation. The problem of accepting a consummation-based definition of marriage came with the strong belief that Joseph and Mary were truly married although their marriage was never consummated. Huguccio, the canonist who originally saw coitus as being outside natural law seems to come to accept Gratian's definition of marriage. Huguccio safeguards Mary's virginity by insisting that Mary and Joseph were married, because the intention to consummate was present, if God allowed it, which of course God didn't. Huguccio and Gratian both agreed that once a marriage was consummated, however, both parties were obliged to render the conjugal debt from then on, and both parties had equal rights to asking that this debt be paid by the other.[51]

Peter Lombard, on the other hand, insisted that consent given in the "present tense" made a marriage and thus Joseph and Mary's marriage was complete without the need for consummation.[52] In his Sentences (4.31.8.1), Lombard excused coitus from sin if it is done with Augustine's three goods present. However, if any one of these was missing, the act would be rendered sinful and Lombard warned husbands of the evil of excessively desiring one's wife (4.31.5.1–2). Hugh of St. Victor, in a definition of marriage which took up the patristic-consensual vision of the marriage of Mary and Joseph, divided marriage into two sacraments: a contract of love, which involves only consent, and an office for procreation, which requires consummation. Hugh was "careful to stress that if the consent to carnal union is part of the marriage agreement, both parties are obliged to observe this agreement."[53]

Peter Lombard seemed to accept Hugh's consensual definition of the bond of matrimony, which required no consummation, but maintained that there is only one sacrament of marriage. Eventually, with Pope Alexander III,[54] marriage became defined by only two criteria: consent and marital affection. In Alexander's definition, marriage is legitimized by consent, but it is cultivated through marital affection. Innocent III later ratified this position. This was especially liberating to a family's offspring who no longer were required, at least on paper, to accept under coercion an unwanted spouse. This emphasis on an individual's right to give or withhold consent to marriage was seen to undermine the power of families, especially that of the father.[55]

As we consider what we have culled from our research on the medieval family and marriage we underscore that the Christianization of marriage and family owes much to the teachings of both the Hebrew and Christian Scriptures, to Roman law, and to Germanic influence.

Christian and Hebrew Scriptures are at odds as to the importance of marriage and family ties. Thus, while Jewish society saw permanent virginity as opposed to God's will, patristic Christianity opted for virginity as the state of perfection while defending marriage and procreation from dualistic heresies.

Monks and nuns became a popular unconventional religious family system within Christianity. They were busily refusing the "age" along with all of its institutions and concerns. Consequently they were inclined to resist marriage and blood families as something that stains the person, troubles the soul, and hinders contemplation.

As marriage became more acceptable in orthodox Christianity[56] and monastic and eremitic families grew in importance, the Latin Church slowly required its priests to adopt the celibate lifestyle of the religious. The Church recognized the importance of the sexual act for procreation, yet it could not allow a priest who consecrated the flesh and blood of Christ to contaminate himself in such a way. It should be noted, however, that priests, by strict definition, are not religious; thus, priestly celibacy took several centuries to implement.[57]

Although, in the twelfth century, love and making love were recognized as essential to Christian marriage, the penitential manuals of the period encouraged preachers and confessors to teach couples to limit copulation and to regard it simply as a tool for procreation.

The Church tended to spiritualize matrimony,[58] accenting the engagement of souls, the need for consent, and the spiritual exchange, which together make marriage a sacramental expression of the love of Christ and the Church. In this spiritualization process, the Virgin Mary is slowly turned into a symbol of the Church, as the spouse of Christ, and mystical literature takes on nuptial themes. Added to this spiritualization of marriage was a stress on individual choice for either marriage or virginity, much to the chagrin of medieval parents who lost the means of carrying on bloodlines, expanding family trade, and augmenting their wealth.

During the Carolingian period, priests slowly became more and more involved in the marriage ritual itself, going from simple blessings over the couple to rituals at the church door and, eventually, (at the end of the eleventh century) to celebrating the once domestic ritual within the church building itself.[59] In 1215, marriage was finally recognized as one of the seven sacraments of the Church. Some theologians called it the oldest Order, founded not by holy men like Benedict, Francis, and Dominic, but by God.[60] This official recognition of the goodness of marriage did not seek to put an end to traditional views of marriage's third-place status on the three-rung ladder of Christian lifestyles (priests, religious, and laity). In the minds of most Christians, however, this recognition did not put marriage on a par with religious life as a way to evangelical perfection.

Family Responsibilities

In its long and arduous journey to gain ecclesiastical acceptance, marriage has always been tied to family life. Spouses are meant to become parents. Children are the desired outcome of wedded union. Penitential manuals and homilies from the period help the modern scholar catch a glimpse of what it meant to be a member of a family.

The Role of Husband

When perusing books about the Middle Ages, we find that many of them have chapters dedicated to women in medieval society, yet they do not specifically deal with men as a separate category. Until recently, it would seem that history has always been written by men, about men, and for men with the "implicit cultural supposition" that male gender and masculinity are readily understandable, while female gender and femininity need to be explained. Yet, in reality, most history books do not speak of men in general in the Middle Ages; rather, they speak of particular men: those who fight, those who pray, and those who work the land. Men in general disappear, leaving historians to speak about kings, knights, popes, bishops, priests, monks, lepers, and serfs without considering what makes a male.[61] It has been presupposed that what it meant to be a male, a husband, and a father was explained in speaking of medieval "hu-man-ity."

Men in medieval studies have been defined according to their role within society—not within the family. Thus, they were rulers, soldiers, prelates, monks, or laborers. They were defined according to function and not according to masculinity. But, apart from their tasks in society, there were also the functions that made men male: impregnating women, protecting one's dependents, and providing for one's family.[62] The male represented the rational part of the human being to the point that it was believed that the soul was given to a child in the genitor's[63] semen. Because of his rational nature, the male was encouraged to care not only for his offspring, but also for his wife, educating them, providing for them, and making sure that their emotional nature would not bring ruin to the family unit.[64]

As marriage became established in the sacramental life of the Church in the twelfth and thirteenth centuries, the pastoral work of the Church gave increasing attention to the role of the spouses. The pastoral writings of this time, in penitential manuals and sermons, took to heart the reciprocal duties of the spouses in the areas of love, sex, and fidelity. Though much more attention seems to have been given to the role of the wife, the role of the husband was not completely ignored.

Augustine implied in *De sermone Domini in monti* that a good Christian husband will love his wife in as much as she is a fellow human being and will desire to see her saved and transformed in heaven, but he will hate her "under the aspect of wifehood."[65] Even in marriages where the couple has chosen to live without sexual intercourse, or when the wife is spiritually stronger than her spouse, the woman needed to remember that she is subjugated to her husband. This subordination of the wife to the husband was seen as a divinely established hierarchy, representative of the hierarchy of God, Christ, and humanity.[66] Christian theologians found in the Scriptures a confirmation of the husband's authority over his wife (especially in Gen 3:16 and I Cor 11:3).

EQUALITY OF HUSBANDS AND WIVES

While both Church and society affirmed the superiority of man over woman, the Church began insisting on the need for both a man's and a woman's consent in their coming together as husband and wife. It was in this consent that man and woman are seen as equals and not just in the moment of their coming together in matrimony but all throughout their married life. It meant that, while the husband was his wife's head and she owed him obedience, he was to treat her as a sister and therefore not only could not force her to satisfy his sexual needs but also had an obligation to fulfill hers.

Husbands were encouraged not to forget that their wives were also their sisters in faith and the spousal relationship of Tobit and Sara was proposed to them as an ideal. According to the Scriptures, Tobit married Sara, a woman who had lost several husbands. He spent his first night with her in prayer, begging God's mercy upon them. In the Middle Ages, however, the Vulgate contained only a shortened version of this prayer: "You are blessed, O God of our fathers; blessed too is your name for ever and ever. Let the heavens bless you and all things you have made forevermore. You it was who created Adam, you who created Eve his wife to be his help and support; . . . . And so I take my sister not for any lustful motive, but I do it in singleness of heart. Be kind enough to have pity on her and on me and bring us to old age together" (Tb 8:5b–7).[67]

The Latin version removes the allusion to procreation and rather alludes to man's need for a helpmate. These changes make the prayer more fraternal, especially with Tobit's referring to Sara as his sister and to the relationship of Adam and Eve as being one of help and support.

This "fraternal" equality of the spouses could be said to exist only in the marriage bed and in a few Church documents idealizing marriage. At a time when European women were beginning to experience some autonomy from men, especially in religious life, Gratian undercut the Christian idea that men and women were the same before God. He did so by "sacrificing the spiritual to the natural, the invisible to the visible" in order to assert male supremacy in the Christian household. His message was reinforced in confessors' manuals. The husband was presented as the vicar of God in the Christian family.

Although the Church proclaimed the equality of the spouses in marriage, the natural inferiority of a woman and the teachings of St. Paul (Eph 5:22–24; Col 3:18)[68] made the wife necessarily submissive to her husband so that his task would not be that hard to fulfill.[69] Therefore, a husband's duties necessarily involved three areas: sustenance, instruction, and correction. These three were primarily intended to pertain to his wife and were eventually extended to their offspring.

A HUSBAND'S RESPONSIBILITIES

First and foremost, the husband was bound to maintain his wife, who in turn cared for the means of sustenance provided by the husband. Since most wives were usually about ten years younger than their spouses,[70] they needed to learn practically everything from their husbands. He was to be her spiritual guide and teacher, providing her religious and moral instruction. In reality, the instruction given a wife was more a means of controlling her than of giving her culture and education. As to morality, again, there was more repression than pedagogy.[71]

Because of a typical man's lack of pedagogical skills, instruction more often than not gave way to correction. Correction was considered a sign of love and showed interest in the betterment of the wife. We must not think that correction took the form of physical abuse either. Preachers encouraged correction of wives by husbands but warned that aggression and severity were a man's biggest faults in this area and caused problems in family life.

These three areas—sustenance, instruction, and correction—were seen as a husband's way of demonstrating his love for his wife. Wives were encouraged to love their husbands to the point of adoration, considering him the strongest, handsomest, and wisest person in their lives.[72] A man, on the other hand, who had the capacity to love rationally, was encouraged never to allow passion for his wife to cloud his judgment and thus spoil her: "The blindness and lack of measure which is proposed for the wife is exactly that which is denied the husband: his love should not be too ardent, rather it should be measured and tempered, . . . likening excessive love for one's wife to adultery . . . a man must love with judgement, not with affection, without ever losing control of his own rationality and without letting himself be carried away by emotion."[73]

THREATS TO MANHOOD

In this and many other ways, men in the Middle Ages had to constantly prove their masculinity. Both Church and society discouraged men from any semblance of femininity. While women who wanted to improve their lot were encouraged to take on masculine characteristics,[74] female characteristics in a male were seen as infirmity.

One very real danger to masculinity was emotional love. Love as a strong emotion, ungoverned by reason, was seen as "womanly."[75] Much to the Church's chagrin, society recommended sexual intercourse as the remedy for unmeasured love. Love-sickness led to the feminine feelings of helplessness and inadequacy. Through sexual intercourse, a husband reasserted his authority and regained control over the situation. At the same time it was maintained that sexual intercourse would keep women healthy.[76]

Unfortunately, the very remedy for love-sickness was itself a threat. Sexual intercourse with the pressure of impregnating one's wife and keeping her healthy was an added burden to the male role. Women were thought to be more humid than men, and in order to remain healthy they had to remain moist. Sexual intercourse was thought to be a useful way of keeping a woman from drying up.[77] While we in this century might consider this as a male rationalization for sexual pleasure, in the Middle Ages, this insistence on sexual intercourse was far from "machismo"; it was a way of caring for one's wife. In reality, this insistence on sexual intercourse was also physcologically stressful for a man. If he did not do his job well, it was thought that his wife could dry up and fall into hysteria or worse.

To this stress of having to keep a woman healthy was added the Church's teaching that every sexual act must be open to procreation. The only way to assure procreation, it was thought at the time, was to bring the woman to the point of orgasm, which would expel the female seed[78] into the uterus. The male role in conception was seen to be of the utmost importance even to the point of determining the sex of the child to be born. Everything depended on the strengths and temperature of the male sperm. Thus, a female child was proof of a man's weak sperm. When a daughter was born to a man, his only consolation would be if she looked like him. Although the child's female sex meant that the wife's sperm had conquered, the child's features could prove that the father's sperm was not completely weak. If a female child resembled her mother, everyone knew that her father was a fragile and weak man.[79]

The Good Wife

Sara, the wife of Tobit (Tb 10:12–13), was the model proposed by both Church and society for the wife in the pastoral writing and preaching of the thirteenth century. Sara's parents took leave of Sara on her wedding day and exhorted her to (1) honor her in-laws, (2) love her husband, (3) bear children, (4) govern her household, and (5) be above reproach. These five counsels to Sara became the general counsels for a good wife in the Middle Ages. A wife was to be a loyal daughter-in-law, a faithful wife, an attentive mother, a prudent matron, and an exemplary woman.

Honor Your In-Laws

Having established the role of father, society then defined the mother's role as being that of a woman who, having abandoned her family home, is destined to live among strangers. Most women would move in with the husband's family as part of the marriage contract. Honoring one's in-laws was therefore understandably considered an essential factor in keeping the peace within the household—and within society. The thirteenth-century Franciscan, Gilberto di Tournai, describes that in honoring her in-laws a woman treats them with reverence in word and with "acts of deference and in concrete ways of helping them in their need; this means avoiding all aggression, even verbally, smoothing out any eventual conflict with sweetness and kindness. Reverence, sweetness, sustenance . . . . Honoring one's in-laws means to extend to the husband's parents the attention owed to one's own parents, to assimilate to the bonds of blood the new bonds that are instituted by the marriage contract."[80]

Love Your Husband

Gilberto di Tournai further suggested that, in marriage, there are two types of love: carnal love and true conjugal love. The first is fed by lust and is characterized by excess. It is likened to adultery even in married couples because it produces lasciviousness, jealousy, and madness. On the other hand, true conjugal love is social love, since it establishes a relationship of equals in the couple.

The twelfth century saw a number of debates by theologians and canonists as to how to define marriage. These influenced the Lateran IV Council's decision to make marriage a sacrament and implied the mutual consent and equality of husband and wife.[81] But even though theologians, preachers, and canonists insisted on the equality of the marriage partners in matters of consent and the conjugal debt, and called them to love each other, in reality, this love was not seen as equal. Jacopo de Varazze clearly expressed the inequality of this love when he called the wife to have perfect love for her husband while his love must be moderated (*discretus*). Giovanni Buridiano described a husband's love as being nobler than the wife's not only because he is her superior but also because he gives her offspring as well.[82]

In the twelfth century, although theologians like Peter Lombard admitted that beauty was a determinant factor in marriage,[83] a woman's beauty was seen as something dangerous for both the woman and the man—for her, because it could lead to narcissistic pride, for him because it could lead to lust. Yet, with the new respect for marriage and conjugal love of the thirteenth century, a woman was invited to beautify herself for her husband. She was to make herself loved by her husband but not to excess. In this way, she helped him keep his love moderated and his thoughts away from adultery. An important aspect of a woman's beauty was her interior disposition to love her husband through voluntary submission in humility and obedience.

As a way of loving her husband, a wife was encouraged by preachers to be a preacher to her own husband: with sweetness and discretion she could invite him to be merciful, more generous, and to reproach his sins. A wife showed her husband love by caring for his soul and seeking to convert him.[84]

BEAR CHILDREN

A wife's primary obligation to her husband and his family was to give them children, especially male children. In an era when perfection was closely tied to virginity, bringing many children into the world was the road to salvation for the married woman. In Genesis, pregnancy and childbirth were ordained by God as a punishment for the sin of Eve, yet the Scriptures also showed that sterility was an even greater punishment, for it kept a wife from fulfilling her task in the family and risked her salvation.

Thanks to Eve, women were destined to be child-bearers, something that was a life-threatening ordeal in the Middle Ages. Fertile women and women with child were seen as precious commodities, especially given the real danger of losing them in the process of giving birth. Childbirth in the Middle Ages was truly a terrible ordeal, and, during it, the woman risked both her physical and spiritual well-being. The "danger of childbirth in the Middle Ages met with a 'curious mixture of folklore, obstetrics, religion and common sense.'"[85] It was a common belief that female blood attracted demons and a woman who died in childbirth before she could be purified was not allowed a Christian burial. Because childbirth meant pain, bodily damage, and frequently even death, medieval women turned to St. Michael the Archangel for protection.[86]

Pregnancy and childbirth are described by Innocent III in *De contemptu mundi* under the experience of pain and the specter of death. Women were encouraged to survive this bothersome and anxious moment by avoiding heavy physical activity, by eating and drinking in moderation, living as friends of God, and abstaining from sexual union. After childbirth, if it so pleased God and the child, she herself was to nurse the child. If anything went wrong during the pregnancy, the fault was conveniently deemed to be the mother's.

GOVERN THE HOUSEHOLD

Sara's—and all wives'—fourth responsibility was to govern the household—that is to say, to care for children and servants. Besides procreating and educating offspring, the matron had a generic duty to instruct and control the morality of the servants. A wife's space was primarily that of the household, and she was expected to conserve and administer that which the male produced, earned, and accumulated. During the end of the feudal era, as city-states and nations developed, many of these clans placed their men, as warriors, at the service of the state. This led to families in which the male was nothing more than an occasional visitor in the home. In these cases, the women assumed the responsibility of running the family household in the name of her husband or the father of the clan. These responsibilities ranged from cultivating the land to influencing military, political, and religious decisions—depending on the family's influence in the state.

Depending on her status in society, the principal tasks of the wife were to knit and sew, to clean the living space, to tend the domestic animals, to render hospitality to her husband's friends, and to educate and care for the children and servants. Moreover, because there were no grocery stores, women had to tend vegetable and fruit gardens and make their own wine, beer, cheese, and other products.

For noble women, this was always done acting on behalf of the lord of the house, her husband or his father. Hers was the task of management. Noble women were also expected to do works of charity and to help the poor. Usually, works of charity and religious exercises were the only times in which a noble woman, especially a young one, was allowed outside the confines of her house.

While noble women had to concern themselves with supervising their lord's household, merchants' wives of the new middle class in the High Middle Ages had to take on freedoms and responsibilities of which noble women could only dream. Merchants' wives, like Francis's mother, not only had to do the household tasks, but also oftentimes had to run the family business while the husband was away. Like noble women, they too were soon expected to undertake works of charity and to assist the poor.

BE ABOVE REPROACH

In this strict culture, honor had a very high price and a damsel's reputation was of supreme importance. A woman was not only to fulfill all of her obligations and act with honesty; she was also to avoid any hint of insinuation or gossip against her in order to safeguard the reputation of her family. Young noble women in that period could inherit land and were expected to marry well to expand the family's wealth.

The wedding of Cana was used by Giacomo di Vitry to show that in marriage the water of sin is transformed into the wine of virtue. Fidelity was essential to this virtue, especially since it assured that any offspring of marriage were legitimate heirs. Because of her very visible and physical relationship to a child in the womb, a woman can easily be identified as the child's mother. A man, however, has no such visible union with a child during its prenatal development and therefore is not readily identifiable as the child's father. The mother, who received the father's aid in the child's conception, is the only one who can truly identify him as such. Because of this reality, in the Middle Ages the fidelity of the wife was much more prized than that of her husband and her adultery much more punishable. With a wife's fidelity in mind, she was encouraged to cultivate the virtues of modesty, chastity, abstinence, sobriety, silence, and stability.[87]

As a daughter of one of the families of the *maiores*, Clare would have received a very strict education, one that would prepare her to be the respectable wife of a noble lord. Starting with the eleventh century, Europe formed a culture of chivalry and courtly love, which was at its height at the turn of the twelfth and thirteenth centuries. Poetry, song, and prose dealing with the likes of Charlemagne, King Arthur, and the young Parcifal were important in spreading this culture. Like many others, these heroes had adventures that would typically bring them into contact with a lovely princess who was always above reproach. These mythical princesses, like Parcifal's Blanche Fleur, were meant to be the example of how noble women should behave. They were to be pure, chaste, and righteous if they were to merit a strong and valiant lord as a spouse. This chivalrous culture exalted love and placed women on a pedestal, at least in legend and song.

The noble and chivalrous environment of Clare's family had to have instilled in her, as it did in the other young noblewomen of her era, such virtues of valor, nobility, detachment, discipline, self-control, silence, prudence, and humility. These virtues were meant to give the young ladies a sense of duty and justice that would be expressed in courteous behavior with their equals, magnanimity with the weak, and generosity towards the poor.[88]

CHILDREN: A QUESTION OF LOVE

We have already seen that bearing offspring for her husband and his family was a wife's principal obligation. In the book of Genesis, God commanded Adam and Eve to multiply and preserve the human species. Like all other species, humans were to join sexually and beget offspring. However, because their offspring require a prolonged period of care and training due to their immaturity and helplessness, the mating done by human beings necessarily becomes parenthood. *Parenthood* is a socially defined word, however, that can be understood in a variety of ways depending on the culture, circumstances, and historical period that defines it. Despite Christianity's preference for virginity, the Middle Ages saw parenthood as an essential task for married partners, who far outnumbered the celibates. Thus, parenthood was something that needed to be defined and cultivated.

In the early 1960s, the social historian, Philippe Aries, speaking of parenthood, proclaimed that parents did not love their children in the Middle Ages and that medieval society had no concept of childhood as a separate category of persons.[89] His study led him to believe that medieval adults saw and treated children as short adults. With this statement, he all but does away with any concept of parenthood in the Middle Ages. As defense for his thesis, he cites the large number of medieval illustrations in which children appear as short adults. His theory contradicts Harris's study of human parenthood, however, which speaks of the "bio-psychological component" found in human nature as being the underlying cause of begetting offspring. According to Harris, human beings beget children, not simply in order to reproduce the species, but primarily to meet a need for intimate, affective, and emotive relationships, which will sustain them and give them attention.[90] Aries would make it seem that the only reason people bothered bringing children into the world during the Middle Ages was because they were useful in agriculture and defense—that it had nothing to do with love.

Medievalists, today roundly refute Aries' thesis that parents in the Middle Ages did not love their children and that the concepts of infancy and childhood were unknown. According to Shulamith Shahar, there is much evidence in medieval sources and art to refute Aries' theory.[91] Manuscript illuminations of the period show children acting as children and doing what children do. There are images of children playing ball, swinging, and participating in a wide range of childhood activities that children across the centuries have enjoyed.

Speaking for and to his era, the lawyer and chronicler, Philippe of Navarre (1206–60) claimed, "Children should be allowed to play since nature demands it."[92] He also saw childhood as the foundation for life and insisted that it was imperative that the child be given a good foundation for the good of civilization.[93] The Middle Ages divided initial human development into three seven-year periods: infancy, early childhood, and later childhood. Unfortunately, medieval authors did not clearly define the characteristics of each stage.

Did parents love their children? Medieval texts, especially hagiographies, suggest that they did. It is true that, in noble households, all children, but especially girls, were seen as a means to ensure or strengthen the household's power and wealth, but this should not be judged as evidence of a lack of parental love. Affection is hard to measure from a historical distance, but evidence shows that parents wept at the illnesses and misfortunes of their children, that parents implored saints and Jesus for the health of their children, or even interceded for their resurrection. Nevertheless, hagiographic works also show the indifference that saints' parents had for their children, even to the point of abandoning them.[94] At the same time, poverty and misery seemed to harden parents or to push some parents to the point of selling or giving their children away.[95]

EDUCATING THE CHILD

There were fewer women in the eleventh and twelfth centuries than there were men. Yet there is no evidence that infanticide or lack of care for baby girls was the reason for this phenomenon. What we do know is that boys were preferred to girls, and that girls were a heavier responsibility than boys were. Parents needed to watch over them more, and educate them well in housework, courtesy, and modesty in order to find them husbands.[96] Education of children—of both girls and boys—usually turned more to punishment than to actual instruction.

Chastisement was seen as the means of guiding and teaching children. The sense of the word does not necessarily indicate corporal punishment in the Middle Ages, although physical punishment was encouraged as a pedagogical tool. Such punishment was encouraged only as a last recourse and with great moderation. Word and example were the preferred pedagogical tools.[97]

Although the mother was very present in educating the child, it is a false assumption to believe that only the mother took part in the rearing of a child. The father also helped raise the children and even the babies, especially when the mother had had a difficult childbirth that might have left her disabled in some way. In medieval Europe, a mother was called upon to birth and nurture a child until age seven, thus ensuring the child's survival. After that point, the father would gradually enter the child's world as an educator and protector.[98] Among the working classes, children typically became involved in or even apprenticed to their father's craft or manual labor to the extent that their age would permit. We can presume that there was more cohesion and warmth in families where the children were involved in the family business and that relationships between such parents and children were more informal than those of noble parents and their children.

Both parents were certainly more involved in raising their children in poorer families than they were in noble families. Medieval imagery shows the presence of the father with the children even as the children grow older, defending them from animals, teaching them to work, and gathering food. All of these things lead to one conclusion: Parents were not only involved in raising their children, they also loved them. Tender scenes of familial love were not uncommon.[99]

A Mother's Love

A mother's love (maternal love), more than a duty, is a fact; that a mother loves her children is evident to the eyes of all and derives from the immediate physical relationship that she has with each of them from the beginning. The mother, observed Jacopo da Varazze, finds in the child a part of herself, a creature for whom she suffers and works so much more than the father, and whom she absolutely recognizes as her own; the mother, affirms St. Thomas (Aquinas), loves the son more than the father does and she is pleased with loving more than being loved.[100]

Clerics saw the greatness of a mother's love and yet considered it a fault. They thought affection needed to be tempered with reason; for them, the intensity of a mother's love is its weakness. A mother's love was considered greater and more evident than that of a father and yet it was less noble and rational. A mother naturally and passionately loves the child of her womb because, as Giacomo De Varagine (1228–98) explained, "a mother gives more of her substance to her child," and she labors more for her child than does the father. Yet, it was felt that this same love could lead her to pamper and spoil her child.[101]

Mothers were allowed to give moral and religious education to their children only if they could control and temper the natural love that they had for them. Hers was a role that dealt more with controlling the morality and religious practices of her children than it did with real instruction. This was especially true with her daughters. She was required to especially care for their femininity and control their sexuality.

A Father's Love

According to Giacomo De Varagine, a child "naturally" loves his father more than his mother because the father is the active agent in the carnal generation of the child, the child stands to inherit the father's goods, the father and not the mother bestows titles and honors on the child.[102] Yet this natural love for the father does not exclude a communal love for the mother. For while the father has caused the child's procreation and gives the child his/her dignity and sustenance, the child initially spends much more time with the mother than with the father. This time spent with the mother, who nurtures the child with her own blood (milk),[103] was seen as a time of building a communal bond of friendship between the child and the mother. As the male child left infancy however, he was called to slowly wean himself from his mother: "The love of sons tends to become less carnal and more rational and move gradually from the mother to the father."[104]

A father's love was considered to be less intense than that of the mother, but his love was considered to be intrinsically virtuous because it cared for the perfection of the soul and the well-being of the body of the child. Children were required to love their parents and especially to love their fathers more than their mothers.

If the above was true of the generative father in most medieval families, it was especially true of the paterfamilias of the noble family. Love of the father was stressed for the good of the whole household. Noble families in the High Middle Ages lived a patriarchal worldview that stressed the importance of the household over and above the rights of the individual. Each member of the family was considered a vassal of the paterfamilias, who decided how each one was to contribute to the well-being of the family. In this classical worldview, the concept of a person as an individual, it would seem, did not exist. Nevertheless, like the rest of the feudal system, this worldview, and others that "stressed universal and abstract qualities were giving way to a new emphasis on the importance of the individual."[105]

The Wandering Years

Young males, especially, felt this new importance of the individual in medieval Europe. Until recently, historians and other scholars had taken for granted that "adolescence" was, for all practical purposes, unknown in medieval Europe. New research is revealing that, while women tended to come of age early in the Middle Ages,[106] most men seem to have postponed coming of age until after an extended period of psychological moratorium.[107] Economic factors and an upsurge of paternal authority in the twelfth and thirteenth centuries did not allow most noblemen to marry until they were in their twenties—and, in some cases, not until they were almost thirty years old.[108] Since they were without a wife, they were left to wander Europe in search of the adventure and wealth that could not be had at home.

Certainly, we are not claiming that the medieval male lived adolescence as it is lived today. While it is true that a type of adolescence was lived primarily by noble sons, many boys of different social classes had to leave home for a period of training, education, or wandering.[109] They had adult capacities without all the benefits or responsibilities of a married man. It was a period in which they were no longer children, yet they were not able to economically afford marriage, or they purposely chose to postpone it.

The sons of nobles and wealthy merchants seem to have had a longer time of psychological moratorium than did the sons of the lower classes. They extended their youth with a time of searching and adventuring, "waiting to be installed into a fief, to have inherited, or to have found an heiress that would permit them a proper establishment."[110] In the High Middle Ages, these young men divided their interests between chivalry and war.

When one considers the vitae of Francis, one discovers how close the description of his youth comes to what historians have discovered about medieval adolescents and young adults. Francis and his friends most certainly fit into the description of the wandering youth devoid of responsibility. Although it would seem that Francis helped his father in the cloth business, his manner of squandering his earnings certainly manifested a lack of responsibility on his part. Filled with the songs of troubadours and stories of chivalry and courtly love, Francis had a wanderlust that led him to war. Fortini attests that while the *maiores* had a hard time accepting the rising merchant class in Assisi, they did tempt the sons of merchants with titles of knighthood and chivalry.[111] It was in war that Francis hoped to find fortune and fame, like any other noble or merchant-class youth of his day. And this was for good reason; his father certainly seemed in no hurry to hand over control of the family business to his son.

Final Thoughts on Marriage and Family

No text can be extraneous to the culture or the time (*cotidianidad*) from which it came. In the Franciscan sources, we are challenged to discover the religious, cultural, and social systems within the text. In order to do this, we have sought to look at the period in which Francis, Clare, and their biographers lived and wrote and to glimpse the earlier influences that formed it.

Although many Christians did marry and raise families, marriage and family in the first Christian millennium seemed to be of dubious evangelical value. It is not surprising that early Christians would have given little importance to family life and, as a result, to marriage (after all, Jesus was born of a virgin, and his earthly father, Joseph all but disappears in the story of his life). Jesus' family, lacking a father, siblings, a wife, and offspring, did not inspire early Christians to develop a theology of family life. Rather, early Christians sought to justify virginity as a valid state of life in direct opposition to Jewish and Pagan societies.

It would seem that, although marriage did have some supporters, and even though many Christians did indeed marry and raise children, it was considered a lower stage of Christian living, not even meriting Church intervention during the first few centuries. If the Church did get involved in marriage, it was at the request of a growing feudal society that could not govern by itself after the fall of the Roman Empire. Even if the Church had doubts about the validity of marriage, secular society considered marriage important in the administration and handing on of its economic, political, and cultural goods.

As time moved closer to the period of Francis and Clare, marriage became a subject that increasingly interested canonists, theologians, and preachers. In the Church's struggle against heretical groups that espoused dualistic notions, its position on marriage and family life had to be reevaluated and cleansed of dualism. Marriage began to gain acceptance in orthodox Christianity, not only as the lesser of two evils and the way to combat fornication, but also as something sacramental. Marriage eventually came to be regarded by many preachers as a worthy institution, begun by God the Father in Paradise and consecrated by Christ at Cana. This worthy institution was the foundation for family life and the roles that it involved. Even Christ's strained relationship with His own family was forgotten, and the fact that he was part of a family at all became an aid in the defense of, and education for, marriage and family life.

It is not difficult to see that the struggle for the definition of marriage and family touched the lives of Francis and Clare, since it was during their own lifetime, in 1215, that the Church finally added marriage to the list of sacraments. These two saints were persons of their time and lived in families of their era. The next two chapters look specifically at their families and how they fit into the family structures of the period.

True to the hagiographies of the era, Francis and Clare had no choice but to abandon their families for the cause of Christ at a time when the Church was reaffirming the sanctity of family life. Nevertheless, they did not forget what they had learned about spouses and families in their early upbringing. Imagery of betrothal, marriage, parenting, and childhood are very much a part of their vitae and opuscula.

CHAPTER II:

FRANCIS, SON OF A MERCHANT FAMILY

While we are able to find references to marriage and family life in law books, confessors' manuals, and sermons, these are always set down as norms and ideals and not necessarily lived experience. Only limited biographies and hagiographies make reference to *lo cotidiano* of family experience, but, more often than not, they do so to make a point of theological, spiritual, or social value, rather than to explain or describe actual life. It is with this in mind that we turn to look at the family life of Francis of Assisi.

For this purpose we turn to the Franciscan sources that contain the life of Francis prior to his conversion. The Franciscan sources disregard Francis's family completely after the early days of his converted life. Therefore, the scope of our study is limited by the sources themselves (see Appendix D).

When one places these vitae in a synopsis, one is amazed at how similar yet different the material is. The material is similar in that all the authors agree on who Francis was and where he came from. He was the son of a wealthy merchant from the town of Assisi in the Italian region known as Umbria. They also agree that his father persecuted him for his desire to live the Gospel and that the rift between them was a violent one that ended in a total breakdown of the father-son relationship. The differences in the materials are regarding Francis's mother and how Francis lived his life in the "age" or "world."

The material gathered in our synopsis will be dealt with in sections moving from the context of Francis's life and Thomas of Celano's impressions of family life to Francis's final break with his family—in the person of his father, Pietro di Bernardone. We will look at Francis's upbringing, at his mother, his father, his family's reputation, the break with his father, and, finally, his relationship to his brother.

THE CONTEXT OF FRANCIS'S LIFE

In comparing the various vitae of St. Francis, we notice that they do not always agree among themselves as to the events surrounding his life. Some give importance to certain events while others totally ignore or change them. One thing they all agree on is the importance of situating Francis within the city of Assisi in the Spoleto Valley.[1] He came from a fixed location, which is to say, from a specific context.

Assisi was a medium-size town on the trade route between Rome and France with between ten and eleven thousand inhabitants.[2] It lay in the Spoleto region and was under the political influence of Perugia, which meant that, until the early part of Francis's life, it had been under imperial control and was the birthplace of Frederick II.[3] With the destruction of the fortress of La Rocca, symbol of the empire's control over Assisi, it was caught up in the struggle between the pope and the emperor and a civil war that would establish it as a free commune. All of this had a profound impact on *lo cotidiano* of Francis's family.

CELANO'S VIEW OF FAMILY

One of the main sources for the study of the medieval family is hagiography. The only general description of Francis's family life is in the first chapter of Thomas of Celano's *First Life of St. Francis*, which he wrote at the request of Pope Gregory IX in 1229. He began this section on the pure life of Francis by describing the impure manner in which he and other children were raised in medieval Europe.

Beginning with a brief description of Francis, who was brought up to be vain and frivoulous, Celano moves on to paint a disturbing picture of family life (1Cel 1.1–12). One wonders if he was referring more to his own upbringing. Yet, Celano didn't claim that this type of upbringing was reserved only to the family of Pietro di Bernardone or families in central Italy where both he and Francis grew up contemporaneously.[4] Rather, he claimed that this type of dangerous and ruinous child rearing was so widespread among those who claimed to be Christians that it seemed to be a normal and acceptable way of doing things.

One can accuse Celano of exaggerating in his description of family life at the time of Francis. Nevertheless, his is the only description we have in the Franciscan sources, which therefore makes it quite valuable. He is obviously overstating his case to make a point. Yet this embellishment does not negate the value of his caricature of family life. Since he traveled and lived in various areas of Italy and Germany during his life as a friar minor, he certainly would have been aware of the child-rearing practices of various areas of Europe.[5]

Celano, who twice mentioned "nominal" Christians, certainly bemoaned the fact that these people did not live up to the Gospel way of life. In an era whose prejudice it was that only religious could live the perfection of the Gospel, it is easy to understand why he would accuse all parents of not knowing how to raise their children in a Christian manner. After all, in order to have children, parents had to perform the lustful act of copulation; thus they were predisposed to lustful and lascivious practices and, he maintained, they raised their children to be the same.

Celano manifested an awareness of child development in his description of how a child grows from infancy to early adulthood. He speaks of the infant moving from the cradle through the weaning process into childhood and then speaks of this same child moving into an adolescent stage. In the beginning, the child, who is dependent on his parents, is taught to do shameful and detestable things. Though it would seem that the child's true nature would be one of innocence, the child is, in fact, constrained by his or her parents to go contrary to his or her nature. This constraint takes the form of harsh punishments, which the child fears and seeks to avoid by conforming to the parents' evil desires.

Eventually, the child becomes so accustomed to sin that she or he eagerly follows such desires. By this time, the visciated or infirm root has produced an infirm tree that "can hardly be brought into line with the rules of righteousness." As children grow, they become more and more independent of their parents in adolescence. Thus the parents should not be surprised that these same children will "float about in every kind of debauchery that is permitted them, satisfying their every desire, zealously giving themselves in service to shameful things."[6] The wording of this move into adolescence is reminiscent of every older generation's complaint about and misunderstanding of the younger generation. Celano questioned this misunderstanding by accusing parents of having raised their young to move in this direction, almost as if to say, "You should not marvel at the work of your own hands."

Celano described adolescence as the period in which human beings willingly give themselves over to the "slavery of sin," serving it with great efficacy. It is also the period in which they, like their parents, show themselves to be Christian in name only. At the same time, it would seem that he is also aware of the peer pressure that accompanies a child's growing independence from his or her parents. He claims that these young people boast of having done "even more worthless things, so as not to be humiliated by showing themselves to be too innocent."[7] Who, besides their peers, would seek to humiliate them for still having a residue of the natural innocence of childhood?

Celano does not include a general introduction to family life in his *Second Life of St. Francis*. He begins by speaking of the young Francis in a manner that, without denying his initial position, goes to some lengths to portray Francis's mother as a good woman who sought to raise her son as best she could given the brutal nature of her husband.

FRANCIS'S BIRTH

Dreams and visions foretelling the sanctity of a saint about to be born were commonplace in medieval hagiography. These prophecies usually were said to have happened during the mother's pregnancy or just after the child's birth.[8] The lives of the saints are filled with these prophetic omens. St. Bernard of Clairvaux's mother dreamt that she gave birth to a barking white dog covered with red spots. She was told that she would give birth to a formidable preacher and defender of the Church. St. Dominic's mother saw her child with a moon or a sun on his forehead indicating his great spirituality. In the case of St. Francis, his earliest vitae have not chosen to include this hagiographic aspect. It is only in later centuries that attempts are made to fill this lacuna.

With the exception of the *Legend of the Three Companions* (3Soc: *Three Companions*), the thirteenth-century sources do not mention Francis's birth as such; they are satisfied with simply situating him as a citizen of Assisi. The legend mentions Francis's birth as having occurred during his father's absence. Pietro di Bernardone's absence on the day of his first-born son's birth was probably only the first of many absences in the life of his son. This absence gives Francis's mother the opportunity to name her child when she has him baptized. She called him Giovanni (John), a name that his father quickly changed to Francesco upon his return.

The manuscripts of the *Legend of the Three Companions* mention these two points without giving any details of the wondrous events that are often said to have surrounded the birth of a future saint in hagiographic works. There is, however, one small exception—a manuscript found in the Vatican library called Ms Vaticanus 7739. It adds to this section on Francis's birth the story about a beggar who desires to see the child Francis and who prophesies his greatness.[9] The fact that other manuscripts of this *Legend* do not include this story makes it appear to be a later addition. It does, however, seem to be based on the supposed testimony of the thirteenth-century friar, Nicolas of Assisi, who attests to his having heard it from his mother.

> My father's house, he said, was adjacent to the home of blessed Francis. My mother also told me: When blessed Francis's mother lay postpartum upon her bed, as women are accustomed to do after childbirth, some neighboring women were near to her. Behold, a pilgrim came to the door as if to ask for alms, but when he had taken the piece of chicken that Francis's mother had sent to him, he began to insist that he desired to see the newborn child. And the women tried to get rid of him, but he kept insisting that he would in no way leave until he had seen the little boy. Then Lady Pica, his mother, said, 'Take the baby boy out so he can see it.' As soon as he saw the boy, he embraced it and said, 'Two baby boys were born in this neighborhood, this one and another. One of them, this one, will be one of the best men in the world and the other one will be among the worst.' And the procession of time has revealed as truth what he said.[10]

Whether the story is true or not is of little relevance to our purpose. What is important is that it tries to make up for the lack of prophecy regarding Francis's birth. This addition to the *Legend of the Three Companions* demonstrates a later century's attempt to make Francis's life conform to a hagiographic tool. This is not the only attempt. The late fourteenth-century document, *De conformitate vitae Beati Francisci ad vitam Domini Iesu*, attempts to demonstrate that Francis conformed to Jesus Christ in everything, including his birth. It would seem that its author, Bartholomew of Pisa, set to writing the oral traditions that surrounded Francis's birth.

These fanciful traditions included such things as angels being heard singing over the Porziuncola and mysterious men passing through the town of Assisi wanting to see the child.[11]

One of the most famous of these stories concerning Francis's birth is his mother's bringing him into the world in a *stalleta* (stable).[12] The story goes that Francis's mother, a devout woman, implored a son from God, which God granted. When finally she went into labor, it was a long and difficult one. She remembered that Jesus had been born in a stable, and so she was taken to one in which she gave birth to Francis. It is interesting to note that Bartholomew of Pisa, who most certainly would have used it in his *De conformitate*, did not know the story about Francis's birth in a stable.[13] This story adds little if anything to the study of Francis's family. It does, however, reveal knowledge of the travails of childbirth that were so frightening in the Middle Ages because of the grave possibility of death. That Francis's mother would attempt to give birth in a stable should come as no surprise in that she was a woman in a prolonged process of childbirth facing the possibility of death. In a society where culture and religion are so blended, it is only natural that a person in danger would find comfort and hope in the proximity to a holy memory like that of Mary giving birth to Jesus. It is also interesting to note that Francis's father is nowhere to be found in this story. It may be that he was away on business or that, following the custom of the day, he left the job of comforting his wife and easing her labor to other women.

FRANCIS'S YOUTH

Despite *First Celano*'s description of the child-rearing practices of Francis's day, none of the vitae offers a detailed explanation of how Francis was raised or of the child-rearing practices of his parents. This was not within the scope of these texts, nor was it of any interest to the readers of that era. The original audience would have been quite aware of the child-rearing practices of their day, having experienced them firsthand. We, on the other hand, are familiar only with our child-rearing practices and can do no more than read about those of Francis's time. When it comes to how Francis was raised, the vitae simply give us a glimpse of what he was raised to be. For our purposes, however, this and whatever else we know of child-rearing practices of the day are all we have to help us surmise how he was raised.

It would have been important that he, as the son of a merchant, be raised and educated in such a way that he would be able to work in the family business[14] and inherit it someday. According to *First Celano*, Francis was buried in that place where he was educated, which is to say the Church of St. George (ICel 23.4–5). In the atrium or portico of that church, he would have received "some knowledge of letters" (*aliqualem litterarum notitiam*) as is attested to in the first chapter of Bonaventure's *Major Life of St. Francis* (LegMai; *Major Life*). Along with reading and writing, he would have had to learn the mathematical skills that would be of service to his trade. As in all parochial schools of the time, Francis would also have learned Latin and how to serve at the altar.[15] From the vitae, we also know that Francis spoke French,[16] yet they do not tell us when or how he learned it.

In his film, *Brother Sun, Sister Moon*, Franco Zeffirelli portrays Francis's mother and Francis speaking to each other in French so as to leave Pietro out of their intimacies. There are many who, like Zeffirelli, would like to think that Francis learned French from his mother.[17] But he probably learned it from his father.[18] Once weaned from his mother, the child Francis would have begun spending increasing time with his father, helping him to the extent the limits of his young mind and body would have permitted. By the time he was fourteen, as Bonaventure clearly points out, Francis would have been spending most of each day in his father's shop. It would have been there that he learned French, since that was the business language in Western Europe at that time. More than likely, as he grew, he would have accompanied his father on trips to the south of France to the international fairs of the time, thus getting the opportunity to perfect his knowledge of the language.

By the time Francis was a teenager, he would have been working full time in his father's shop, and so, as Bonaventure describes, he would have spent much time "among avaricious merchants" (*inter cupidos mercatores*; LegMai I:I.2). Nevertheless, Pietro di Bernardone was not the type of man who would have allowed his mature son very much responsibility in a business that was still at the heart of his own life. Although most people of the time were socially and politically mature by the age of twenty, Francis, like many noble and wealthy middle-class youth whose father's greedily held on to responsibility, was afforded a rather lengthy adolescence or "psychological moratorium."[19]

It is probably this lengthy adolescence that Celano was attacking in chapter one of *First Celano*. Adolescence was a period during which youth would band together in search of adventure, glory, profit, and women. How long this period lasted depended on the power of the father, the number of siblings, the indivisibility of the inheritance, and the socio-economic situation of the family.[20]

FRANCIS *IN PECCATIS* [21]

After his tirade about the pitiful child-rearing practices of his day, Celano gives us a description of the end result in Francis's life. The other vitae join Celano in trying to describe what Francis was like up to age twenty-five. How he is described varies from "instigator of evil" (*incentor malorum*; 1Cel 2.2) to one who, despite being surrounded by "lascivious youth" and "avaricious merchants" (*lascivos iuvenes . . . cupidos mercatores*; LegMai 1:1.2), was still able to maintain his innocence. Francis, himself, described that period of his life as the time when he was "in sin" (*in peccatis*; Test 1), although he gave no indication what he meant by that specifically.

Julian of Speyer's *Life of St. Francis* (JulSpi; *Julian of Speyer*) and Henry of Avranches' *Legend of St. Francis*, written in verse (HenAv; *Versified Legend*), remained faithful to Celano's first version of Francis's youth, but in different ways. Julian basically reiterates what Celano had already written about Francis outdoing the rest in "the vanities of this world" (*in mundi vanitatibus*; JulSpi 1.2), while Henry poetically insists that Francis's downfall was following his father's example rather than his mother's. He insists that Francis "chose" this path (HenAv 1:41–49).

Although painted with different allusions, Henry's portrait of the young Francis is similar to Celano's. He does not elaborate on the young merchant's vices, as did Celano and Julian. Rather, he bemoans Francis's choice of abandoning the path set out for him by his mother. It was a choice that Henry says made him like his father: depraved. This depravity is manifested in a love that is not love. This love that is not love is the desire to satisfy the appetite, an appetite stirred by his father's lessons in greed.

Lest we think Francis completely depraved as a youth, Henry, like Celano before him, claims that there were traces of gentleness, generosity, kindness, and affability in the adolescent Francis (HenAv 1:67). Yet, in

Celano, these same virtues do not seem like virtues, but a way of showing himself off among evildoers. In Julian, these same virtues seem to be taken advantage of by the iniquitous tail of peers that he dragged behind him and who made him their leader.

Three Companions agrees with Celano's portrait of a young Francis who is similar to his peers in youthful extravagance. They add to this portrait a few nuances that are worth our attention. First, that Francis was not just a spoiled brat who loved to waste his time in pomp and vainglory. Celano mentions Francis's work in passing, while *Three Companions* begins with his being a hard worker. They knew that merchant fathers spent a lot of time and effort educating their sons for the family business. Di Bernardone would have been no different. Francis, it would seem, learned quickly, yet his love for the family business was not in the interest of greed, like his father. Adolescent that he was, he earned in order to spend (3Soc 2.2–8).

In the midst of all of this youthful passion, we need to find Francis's parents. Celano tells us that Francis did not know how to tame himself. This formation normally would have come from his parents. Celano and Julian mention neither of them at this point. Henry seems to refer to their contrasting opinions as to the formation given their son. Where the mother pulled to the right, the father pulled to the left. Apparently the father naturally had a stronger draw on his son. Yet the mother's influence was not to be completely disregarded.

A GLIMPSE AT HIS PARENTS

The vitae often present Francis's parents as a single unit. The picture painted in *First Celano* (1Cel I.1) and *Julian of Speyer* (JulSpi I.2) of Francis's parents was that they were arrogant and extravagant in the vanities of the world. This is not claimed directly, but indirectly, in comparing the son's extravagance to theirs and stating that he had surpassed them in this. Even the *Major Life* claims that Francis was *nutritus in vanis*, an allusion to the vain character of his nurturers, which is to say his parents. This attack on the persons of his parents lumps both mother and father together, although it was probably meant more as an attack on the merchant father—an attack that, given their being from the merchant class, was probably in keeping with the religious stereotypes against avaricious merchants or usurers.

While Celano and the other writers of the *Legendae* take care to eventually present Francis's mother in a good light, it is only the *Three Companions* that in any way alludes to both of Francis's parents being concerned with his vain and extravagant demeanor.

Another particularity added by the *Three Companions* to the portrait of Francis's parents is their trying to approach their son in a united front. They apparently tried to reprimand his youthful extravagances, concerned that he was going too far and living beyond his means. Yet even their united front was not strong enough to properly educate their son. Two things got in the way of giving him a good formation: their wealth and their love for him.

The prejudice of the *Three Companions* is that the wealthy are given to vanity and Francis's living like a prince fed the vanity of his parents. The love of the parents as a hindrance to his education may seem strange to us. Yet as we have seen in our first chapter, love in the Middle Ages was regarded as a weakness when it was not tempered with reason—which is why a mother's love was always suspect. According to the picture we get from the *Three Companions*, Francis was not used to a father's love because both parents loved their son like a mother who pampers her child. This love that depends more on feeling than on reason leads to the parents not being able to control their son, a fact that the *Three Companions* made evident in telling how Francis would abandon his parents at a moment's notice in order to run off with his peers, leaving his parents in affliction.

Up to this point, we have a portrait of Francis as a pretty normal adolescent of his day. He was raised and educated to work in the family business—a business that he took to, and yet a business that was seen as a means to an end and not an end in itself. Although his virtues manifested themselves at that time, they usually did so in ways that were either self-serving or easily taken advantage of. His parents seem to have been normal parents trying to raise an adolescent and rein him in, a job that they did not do well. Being male, Francis was naturally drawn to imitating his father and not his mother, which (according to the vitae) led him further and further into the vanity of the world.

YOUNG FRANCIS CLEANED UP

Thomas of Celano's *Second Life of St. Francis* (2Cel; *Second*

Celano) and Bonaventure's *Major Life* were written at the request of two different General Chapters of Order of Friars Minor; they were official texts written about the founder of the Franciscan family. Naturally, neither of these authors wanted to say anything that would make the saint look bad. Still, they did not completely overturn the image of Francis painted by the earlier vitae. They give us a picture of an adolescent who seems to remain unstained by the vanity that surrounds him. According to Celano's *Second Life of St. Francis,* he stayed away from what could be injurious to others and had refined manners. This fact is what caused others to say that Francis couldn't possibly be the son of his parents—the implication being that they had no problem injuring others and were not refined. This might have been an accurate assumption.[22] *Second Celano* (2Cel 3.4–5) isn't the only source to mention Francis's refined manner. Bonaventure most certainly made this his primary reflection on Francis's youth (LegMai 1:1.2–2.1), and even the *Three Companions* (3Soc 2.2–8; 9.4) alludes to this aspect of his character.

There is quite a difference between *First Celano* and *Second Celano*. As we have seen, *First Celano* goes to great lengths to explain how Francis's upbringing led to a Francis who was no different from his peers. Francis outdid his own parents and his contemporaries in arrogance, vanity, evil, foolishness, pomp, and vainglory (1Cel 1.1–2; 2.2–3).

In *Second Celano*, however, Celano saw no need to situate the young Francis in the allegedly "corrupt family system" that had penetrated Christianity, perhaps because he trusted that his readers would be familiar with his first work or with the "corrupt family system" itself. The Francis of *Second Celano* seems to be a young man who went untouched by the child-rearing practices of his day. He is an adolescent, admired for his refined manner, who kept away from anything that might seem injurious to others.[23] Yet one indication that Francis was raised corruptly is Celano's pointing out that Francis, as a refined and good man, does not seem to be the child of his parents, whom we assume could not have raised him in a noble and chivalrous manner.

Celano's second adolescent Francis is only a fleeting shadow of the adolescent Francis he first wrote about. The only thing left of that vain and arrogant Francis is a scene in which his former companions make him prepare a feast for them as he used to do in the past (2Cel 7.1–8).[24]

This scene contrasts the young Francis (on his way toward perfection) with his gluttonous and drunken friends.[25] In this one banquet, Francis's peers are shown for who they are: lascivious youth, children of Babylon (*filii Babylonis*) whose only desire is to get a free meal, get drunk, and cause a ruckus on the streets, while Francis is shown as one who offers the meal as a sign of courtesy and generosity. Yet, in Celano's words we find allusions to the fact that, prior to the beginning of his conversion, Francis was also one of the "children of Babylon" who would feast to the point of vomiting, defiling the streets of Assisi with drunken singing. In this passage, Francis, in the process of conversion, gives in to peer pressure. Henry of Avranches mentioned that, at this time of Francis's life, he would be "easily sidetracked . . . falling back on what he is used to" (*in avia pernix . . . tamen ad consueta recurrit*; LegMai 1:172–79). As with many, it was Francis's peers who got the best of him. As has been noted previously in the *Three Companions*, Francis was quite fond of being with his peers. *First Celano* (1Cel 9.5) also mentions Francis making merry with "family and friends" (*cognatos et notos*) up to the day prior to that on which he tried to give money to the priest at San Damiano.

Despite the fact that *Three Companions* (3Soc 3.1–10) extols the virtues of Francis in his youth, it cannot be considered an intense clean-up process for the young Francis, since it continues to present his faults. True, one can't help but notice that these memoirs insist on Francis's being "naturally courteous" (*naturaliter curialis*) in his conduct and in his words despite the fact that he was a "mischievous and lascivious youth" (*iuvenis iocosus et lascivus*). This insistence on his natural goodness connected with his being playful and lewd is probably tied to the young Francis's desire for knighthood and his attraction to courtly love and chivalry.

Bonaventure went further than Celano in cleaning up the image of Francis. While *Second Celano* (2Cel 3.4–5) and *Three Companions* (3Soc 3.1–10) both refer to Francis's virtues in the context of the process of his conversion, Bonaventure highlighted this virtue as growing with him since infancy (LegMai 1:1.3–8). Without denying Francis's being raised in the world with and by worldly people, Bonaventure had our hero living in the world without being a part of it. Nevertheless, Bonaventure's young Francis has fallen victim to a natural hagiographic process, the process of purifying and aggrandizing the image of the saint.[26] We can see that the closer a source is to the actual life of Francis, the less likely it is to present Francis as an ideal youth struggling against being contaminated by the sins of his peers or the bad example of his merchant family.

The process of purifying Francis's youth seems to focus on the person of his mother as the parent who spurred her son toward holiness in the absence of his father. Let us now consider this woman, known to us as Pica.

Lady Pica

What Franciscan does not know the name of Francis's mother? The name Pica is so well known to us that the realization that it is nowhere to be found in the official vitae of the thirteenth century comes as a shock. Her name, Pica, appears only in a sixteenth-century manuscript, Vaticanus 7739, and in a thirteenth-century testimony on Francis's birth left by Friar Nicolas of Assisi.[27] As we have seen, this testimony is the supposed basis for the same story (found in Ms Vat 7739) that was added to the *Three Companions.*

Who was Pica and where did she come from? While present Franciscan myth would like to think of her as a French woman of minor nobility who taught her son to speak her mother tongue, there is no real proof to sustain such thinking. Fortini has traced this unfounded idea to the sixteenth century. According to the *Vita* by Anonymous of Brussels, Francis's mother was named Iohanam (Joan or Joanna) and thus Pica has to have been a nickname[28]—perhaps deriving from Picardy, her region of origin. Picardy is situated in southern France near two of that time period's most famous international cloth fairs.[29] *Pica* is also the Italian name for the chattering magpie,[30] and the word *pica* also indicated at the time a "yen" or a strange desire brought on by pregnancy[31]—similar to pregnant women today craving pickles and peanut butter. Besides her coming from Picardy, could any of these have been reasons for calling her Pica?

The Franciscan sources remain silent about her origins. She is simply Francis's mother—strangely enough, not even worth naming, much less describing in detail in the vitae. When she is talked about, she is described in terms of her son. She is usually lumped together with her husband, which should come as no surprise in a society and period where the wife was seen as subservient to her husband. She is merely mentioned as part of the parental unit that raised Francis in such a vain manner. When she is "lumped in" with her husband, she does not seem to be any different from him, but when she is singled out, she appears as a heroine. When singled out, her role in the vitae seems to be as namer and liberator of her son.

MATERNAL LOVE

Francis's parents truly loved their son. Preachers of the time would probably say that it was because of their unfiltered love and devotion that they spoiled the young Francis. A mother's love was regarded with particular suspicion because it was not tempered by right judgment. A good example of a mother's permissive love is found in the story of Francis preparing bread for alms:

> Whenever his father was absent and Francis remained at home, even if he were to eat alone with his mother, he would fill the table with bread as if he were preparing it for the whole family. When his mother asked him why he placed so much bread on the table, he would respond that he did so in order to give alms to the poor because he proposed to give alms to anyone who begged for God's sake. His mother, who loved him more than her other children, tolerated Francis in these things, observing all that he did and pondering them in her heart (3Soc 9.1–3).

Despite this unflattering vision of maternal love, the *Three Companions* insists on how much his parents loved him. This *Legend*, however, singles out Pica's love for Francis as being greater than her love for any of her other children.[32] Her love tied her to her son in a way that excluded his father at both a ritual and a consanguinal level. At the level of ritual, *Three Companions* seems to use the story of the meal shared between the mother and the son to indicate a symbolic union that, at the exclusion of the authority figure and the traditional family, opened itself to those most in need. At a consanguinal level, however, we cannot imagine that this meal was the first or only occasion on which the mother and son waited for the father to leave so as to bond without him. This type of secretive action could indicate that when Francis was left alone with Pica he could do what his father would not allow. In doing so, he was taking advantage of the "supposed" weakness of maternal love. Yet, the story does not seem to be criticizing this maternal love that allowed her son to get away with strange behavior. On the contrary, the story (in chapter 9) insists that Francis's actions would often leave her "pondering them in her heart" (*in corde suo admirans*). This seems to hint at Pica's being like the mother of Jesus who meditated on the events of her child's life in her heart (Lk 2:19, 51).

ANOTHER ELIZABETH?

While Pica is only alluded to as being like the Virgin Mary, there is a scriptural woman to whom Pica is explicitly compared in the vitae, and that is St. Elizabeth, who is one of the strong women in the Sacred Scriptures. These comparisons to the Virgin Mary and St. Elizabeth should come as no surprise. Hagiographers were well versed in the Scriptures and used mothers like Hannah, Elizabeth, and the Virgin Mary to speak of the strong mother figures in the lives of the saints. In their minds, these women had the audacity to usurp the paternal role in the naming and rearing of their children.[33]

The bonding nature of Pica and Francis's relationship at the expense of Pietro di Bernardone began at the outset of Francis's life. According to the *Three Companions*, Francis was born while his father was away on business. Our modern sensibilities cannot imagine that a man would not be present at the birth of his children, especially his firstborn. But, those were other times, and Pietro was a businessman bent on making riches. The vitae also point out Pietro's absence from home in Francis's youth. As a merchant, he was not one to stay at home,[34] especially during the period of the French fairs. With the father's absence, Pica takes the reins and names her son Giovanni (John). If her name was truly Iohanam (Giovanna in Italian), she seems to have named her son after herself.

This naming of the child by the mother brings Pica into the circle of strong women found in the sacred Scriptures and in Christian tradition. Celano, in his *Second Life of St. Francis*, ties Pica to St. Elizabeth, the mother of John the Baptist. Elizabeth is one of the few women in the Scriptures who specifically name their children. She does so despite the resistance of her family, which justly turns to her husband thinking that he will do the right thing and put his wife back in her place. Zechariah, as we know, does quite the opposite and approves of his wife's choice (Lk 1: 59–63). Elizabeth (with Zechariah) and Mary (with Joseph) are good examples of how the mother's virility[35] places her husband in a minor role in the life of their holy child. Despite Pica's being depicted as a strong woman, however, she is not strong enough to overshadow her husband.

Judging by Pietro's decision to nickname his son Francesco upon his return, it is fair to imagine he must not have agreed with his wife about the infant's name. It is here that the comparison with Elizabeth breaks down. Pica, like Elizabeth, named her son. She named him John, like the son of Elizabeth, and, like Elizabeth, she had a spirit of prophecy. Unlike Elizabeth, however, Pica did not receive her husband's approval. Naming a child was not something taken lightly in the Middle Ages, for in a person's name was seen the life project of the person. It was the first social indicator of who the person was and what his parents's aspirations were for him.[36] Celano knew this when he wrote: "John referred to the work of ministry that he would undertake; the name Francis referred to the spread of his fame" (2Cel 3.6).[37] Pica's choice of the name *John* was tied to religion, while Di Bernardone's choice of *Francis* was tied to fame. Their son lived up to both names.

According to J. M. Charron in his book *Da Narciso a Gesù*, Pica must have named her son Giovanni (John) after the ascetic John the Baptist in a secret desire for a religious adventure for her son.[38] This may very well be true. We know that, at that time, many wealthy women were uncomfortable with their newfound wealth and tried in many ways to make amends for it. Pica was the wife of a merchant who, if he was like most merchants of the time, was also a moneylender.[39] Christianity had always condemned usury, and merchants were looked upon with suspicion because they made their fortune at the expense of others. Dominated by the instinct for lucre, a merchant/usurer was a master of cheating; he was considered treacherous and violent, not sparing even family or friends in order to make money (HenAv 1:33; 3:125–130). It is no wonder that, according to homilies of the period, the usurer not only damned his own soul but also that of his children. Jacques de Vitry, a contemporary of Francis, spoke about a priest who condemned his own father to hell, asking that no one pray for the salvation of his soul because he had been a usurer;[40] such was the strength of the Christian prejudice against merchants and usurers. And such was the need to make amends by those in merchant families who felt guilty because of the way their fortune was made. In giving him the name John, Pica might have desired that her son not turn out like his father; she may have hoped that her son would set out on a path that would purify the family name.

WHAT'S IN A NAME?

By re-naming his son *Francis*, Di Bernardone was indicating his desire to have a son follow in his footsteps and take over the family business, making it even more prosperous. France was the land where merchants traded their wares; it was the land that espoused wealth, nobility, and courtly love. So, by naming his son Francis, Pietro was preparing the way for his son to become like him and, perhaps, even more intent on making a fortune. It should come as no surprise that the authors of the vitae would see a need to show that Francis had been destined for something better than the name Francesco suggested. *Three Companions* (3Soc 2.1) indicates honestly that the name Francesco is tied to France, the land where Pietro di Bernardone got his merchandise and where he was, on business, at the birth of his first-born son. Even *First Celano* (1Cel 9.5–7), which gives no indication of Francis's having been called *John* at baptism, sees a need to cleanse the name *Francesco* by affirming that France became filled with Francis's followers and that the name Francis is a derivative of frankness.

Whatever Pica or Di Bernardone's desires might have been in naming their son *John* or *Francis*, one cannot help but notice that most people today have no idea who Giovanni di Bernardone was, yet so many have heard of Francesco d'Assisi. Though he broke with his father, Francis saw no need to give up the name his father gave him and revert to the one given him by his mother. For his father, France was a land of opportunity and wealth, but Francis saw in France the things that his father did not. For Francis, it was a land of chivalry and devotion. The French language was not used just for making money, it was a language used in troubadors' songs, and for Francis, God's troubador, French became the language of his prayer and praise.[41]

Francesco was not Francis's baptismal name. John could have easily given up his father's nickname for him at his conversion and reverted to the name that his mother gave him, but he didn't. Evangelically, it would make more sense to use his baptismal name than to use a name connected with a desire for fame and fortune. So why didn't he? Could it be that Francis loved his father more than his mother? Although it would be interesting to try to answer that question, it would always remain pure conjecture, so I will leave it, as it is—an unanswered question.

Pica's baby John grew into Pietro's young Francis, and yet, according to *Second Celano* (2Cel 3.3) and *Three Companions* (3Soc 2.6), she never seemed to have given up hope that her child would fulfill his baptismal name. As she saw him grow, she saw in him the virtues that led others to ask what would become of him. She prophesied his becoming a "child of God by grace" (*filius Dei per gratiam*). If this is true, she seems to have had no idea what kind of *filius Dei* he would become.

FREEING HER SON

Though Pica has been counted among the strong women of the Christian tradition, her strength was evident not just in the naming of her son. Much more than just a hagiographic metaphor, Pica, according to the vitae, was truly a strong woman. The last reference in the Franciscan sources to Francis's mother is in the famous story of Pietro imprisoning his son at home.

The prison episode seems to be a strange punishment for our contemporary mind, but in the Middle Ages, the head of the family had the right to have a family member imprisoned in the jail of the commune if that person had squandered the family fortune or in any way disobeyed him. Such imprisonment—either at the city jail or simply at home—usually required the consent of two blood relatives.[42]

In this story, despite Pica's disapproval, Pietro excercises his rights as a father. She waits for her husband to go away on business and then frees their son. Five of Francis's vitae refer to her having liberated Francis from his father's prison, at risk to herself (1Cel 13.1–5; JulSpi 8.4–7; 3Soc 18.2–5; LegMai 2:3.1–3; HenAv 3:79–96).

A MIND OF HER OWN

Of the five sources, only the *Versified Legend* does not mention that Francis's mother did not approve of her husband imprisoning Francis. Though she did not understand her son's strange behavior, she most certainly did not approve of her husband's reaction. The vitae do not tell us if she ever spoke up to Pietro as he beat his son, but judging from her love for Francis and her freeing him despite Pietro's violent personality, she must have done so. We cannot believe that she would have been the demure wife, hiding while her offspring was being abused.

TRYING TO DISSUADE HER BOY

Pica had a mind of her own. Unfortunately her strength was probably only in her personality; she had to wait for her husband to leave town before acting. This action continues to demonstrate that she was a thinking woman. If she did not agree with her husband's actions, she seems to have agreed with his reasoning, for the story indicates that she tried to lure Francis away from his new purpose. *First Celano*, *Julian of Speyer*, and *Three Companions* all state that she, with "flattering discourse" (*blandis sermonibus*), tried to sway her son and get him to reason. The *Major Life* simply states that she "intuited that she could not hope to break the inflexibility of her son" (*inflexibilem filii constantiam emolliri posse non sperans*).

The *Versified Legend* (HenAv 3:78–79) does not clearly speak about her not agreeing to her husband's actions or trying to persuade her son to give up his purpose; it simply refers to her tears as being the final blow in the list of things that conspired against Francis's determination to serve God. These things are the derision of his countrymen, his father's ire, the severe beatings he received, and the horrors of prison. The *Versified Legend's* having placed maternal tears in this dreadful list shows knowledge of the strength not just of a woman's tears, but of a mother's tears for the son she tenderly loves. These tears must have come with *blandis sermonibus*, and that is why they conspire against Francis's purpose. More than the beatings and the derision, these must have been the hardest thing for Francis to face.

OVERCOME BY MATERNAL SENTIMENT

Yet Pica's tears and soft words could not weaken her son's resolve. Finally the strength of a mother's words and tears gave way to the "weakness" of maternal love. The vitae speak beautifully of this weakness and strength. Both *First Celano* and *Three Companions* refer to *materna viscera*. *Viscera*, in romance language, indicates not just the physical bowels of a person but the very depths of one's person. Pica's *pietate* (devotion, compassion, dutifulness) for her son comes from the deepest part of her being, from what she identifies most with, "being his mother." This is the weakness that, according to the *Versified Legend*, God used in order to have Francis freed from prison. Thus, her weakness in the *Legendae* is hailed as her strength, and eventually, it is what enabled her to take her husband's punishment upon his return.

SUFFERING THE CONSEQUENCES

She knew that the weakness of her *materna viscera* would not go unpunished. She had lived with her husband long enough to know that he was not a man to be crossed. She was willing to suffer for the sake of her son; she took the consequences. These consequences are in keeping with Pietro's violent nature. He, "adding sin upon sin, hurled chastisement at his wife" (*peccata peccatis accumulans, intorquet convicia in uxorem*). But we cannot take this to mean that Pietro beat his wife, because all the vitae agree that if he "struck his wife" (*uxorem . . . lacessivit*) it was with insults and chastisement, not physical blows. What these insults were, we can only surmise, but presumably they were filled with cursing and blasphemy as is reported in the *Versified Legend*.

PIETRO DI BERNARDONE

Francis's father has been the shadow figure in this story for centuries, and Franciscans everywhere look at him as the archetype of whatever gets in the way of Gospel living. To many Franciscans through the centuries, Pietro di Bernardone had little if anything worth redeeming about him. But contemporary Franciscans would like to think that, sometime after his conversion, when things had settled down, Francis at least attempted some kind of reconciliation with his father. This, however, is a wish born out of our contemporary view of the family as a Christian institution. It is hard for us to accept a Francis who would not reconcile with his father, but he probably never did.

The Franciscan Sources address the person of Francis's father without contemporary Franciscan prejudices or needs in regard to Pietro di Bernardone. They have their own prejudices and those of their intended audience to contend with. Hagiographically speaking, we do not have an exact portrait of Pietro di Bernardone. Rather, he enters Francis's story as an archetype that acts against his son's soul and eventual vocation. Despite Pietro being the archetype of worldly vanity and seduction, however, traces of Pietro the father peek out at us from behind the archetypal mask placed on him by the vitae.

Let us first look at where the portrait of the bad father comes from. As we have already seen in Celano's first chapter, Pietro di Bernardone was not alone in being a bad father. Parents in general were looked upon as not knowing how to raise their children properly. Pietro's image, however, goes way beyond the portrait of the ignorant father; thanks to the way in which he reacted to his son's conversion process, his portrait was painted with the colors of violence and wickedness.[43]

The words used by the vitae to describe the actions of Pietro in this scenario have become the words used to describe Pietro himself. In the passing of the centuries, he has become the wicked wolf who mercilessly berates and persecutes his son with insults, blows, whippings, and incarceration. While the other vitae tie Pietro's wickedness to his mistreatment of his son in the process of conversion, the *Versified Legend* goes beyond the other vitae in casting an impenetrable shadow over Pietro. There, Pietro is called "sly and violent" (*subdolus et violentus*) right from the very start. Wickedness is his nature and not just a reaction.

Yet even the *Versified Legend* has to admit that Francis's father did not want to harm his son; he just wanted to punish him. In the other vitae, this desire not to hurt his son is tied to love, whereas in the *Versified Legend* it is tied to deception. The father was not so much concerned about losing a son but a business partner, it suggests. In a moving speech, Francis himself accuses his father of seeking his soul's corruption and of enticing him to continue cheating family and friends in order to make money (HenAv 3:128–30).

First Celano, Three Companions, and the *Major Life* accuse the father, when faced with a crowd that jeered at Francis's conversion, of not acting like a father. With the words, "not to free him from the affronts but to obliterate him,"[44] they manifest a great disappointment with Pietro di Bernardone, almost as if they were revealing Francis's own sorrow at his father's action. Obviously they expected that a true father would defend and liberate his son from the taunting crowd. Julian of Speyer also accuses him of acting "not in a fatherly but in a beastly way" (*non paterno sed ferali modo*). A father is expected to be one who generates life, not one who destroys it. Pietro, however, not only joined the crowd in taunting his son; he outdid them. He sought to crush, ruin, waste, and chastise; in a word, he sought to destroy the fruit of his loins. It is no wonder that both *First Celano* and *Three Companions* accuse him of acting like a "wolf among sheep" (*lupus ad ovem*) in describing the anger transforming his countenance with glaring eyes (*torvo oculo*). Bonaventure, in the *Major Life*, puts it less dramatically, simply stating the fact that Pietro acted with "all commiseration removed" (*omni miseratione subtracta*).

A FATHER'S LOVE

Before we join the *Versified Legend* in totally negating the humanity of Pietro di Bernardone, we do well to remember that one event cannot determine the total character of a person. Franciscans have judged and condemned Pietro di Bernardone over the centuries as a merciless beast who persecuted their blessed founder. And even though it is, for the most part, thanks to the thirteenth-century sources that we have this image of Francis's father, we cannot deny that they also spoke of Pietro's love and concern for his son.[45]

With painful words, the vitae seek to explain the love of Francis's father. They present a sorrowful man who has lost his son and cannot find him. He is "disturbed, deeply upset, and has a sorrowful heart."[46] One cannot help but think of the father of the prodigal son when the vitae speak of Pietro as a "diligent explorer going about looking earnestly for his son."[47] Yet just as the prodigal son knew his father and went home, Francis also knew his father—and hid. When he was crossed, Pietro di Bernardone's love manifested itself not in tenderness, but in punishment—and his son had crossed him. His was a violent love.

Pietro's search for his son was probably a true manifestation of his love and concern for him, yet this search did not end in a tender scene of reunion. Unfortunately, love was not the only thing that motivated his search for Francis. The vitae do not hide the fact that Pietro was a greedy and avaricious man. More than likely, he was "a domineering and vain burgher; he was fond of his gold, liked to be in the public eye, and was desirous of rising in the social scale."[48] He was a self-made man who had amassed a fortune that he meant to leave his sons. He could not bear to see Francis throw it all away. And so, it is highly likely that a mixture of love and greed motivated Pietro's search for his son. Added to that mixture was fear, as Di Bernadone saw Francis moving towards his own greatest fear— poverty.

FRANCIS CONFRONTS HIS FATHER

Celano and Bonaventure present Francis, who with "a free voice cried out" (*libera voce clamans*), as one who, fortified by God, no longer needed to fear his father's abuse. Neither author says what Francis shouted at his father. The *Versified Legend*, on the other hand, gives us a detailed verbatim report of Francis's clamor. This soliloquy is interesting, not because of what Francis is reported to have said, which is probably not factual, but because it has Francis shouting out the period's prejudice against greedy merchants. In this narrative, Francis faces his father much in the same way the early Christian martyrs faced their persecutors.[49]

Francis's soliloquy addresses his father (or "step-father," as he calls him). He addresses him not as father but as one who is trying to seduce him and lure him away from God. Francis preaches to his father, pointing out God's love and his own desire to no longer cheat people by means of the "merchant's art" (*ars mercatorum*). In doing this, Francis, like the early martyrs, is giving testimony to his faith in the presence of his accuser in hopes of aiding his conversion. Francis presents his father with the choice: Believe or remain incredulous. Francis himself, however, will not go back to his old ways.

Humanly speaking, Celano, Bonaventure, and Henry present Francis as a young adult who had come to a decision, a decision that placed him at odds with his father. The vitae present him as the son of a violent man and their Francis responds to a father's physical violence with oral violence. This should come as no surprise; Francis was in the process of conversion, sliding back and forth between his old self and the start of sainthood. This standing up to his father was essential to Francis's process of maturation if his conversion was to take hold and mature. The *Versified Legend* points out that

Francis had naturally preferred to follow his father's example and not that of his mother. It also goes to great lengths to describe the power of Francis's father over his son. Francis had to confront his father, and especially his father's example, if he was to be freed of Pietro di Bernardone's influence in his life.

SAN DAMIANO

Just how much influence Pietro di Bernardone had over his son can be seen in this episode of Francis's conversion. It speaks of the di Bernardone family reputation, which influenced the priest at San Damiano to not take Francis's conversion seriously. What's more, it also speaks of Francis acting like his father

First, let us consider the family reputation. Six of the vitae describe this episode in Francis's life (1Cel 8.6; 9.2–7; JulSpi 6.5–9; HenAv 2:160–69; 3Soc 16.1–5; LegMai 2:1.7–8; AnPer 7.3). The authors must have seen it as a critical moment in Francis's conversion—as a turning point. Neither *First Celano* nor *Julian of Speyer* mentions the words of the Crucifix at San Damiano, yet they are the first to mention the episode of Francis's trying to give money to the priest for its repair. As to why he did so, they simply explain that Francis felt pity for the miserable condition of the little church.

Anonymous of Perugia, in *The Beginning or Founding of the Order* (AnPer; *Anonymous of Perugia*), returns to this original story, where the gift of money has nothing to do with a response to the voice of the Crucifix. It also makes no reference to the pitiful conditions of San Damiano. Francis simply wanted to get rid of his gains and impulsively gave it to the priest, who refused it for lack of a safe place in which to keep it.

First Celano, Julian of Speyer, Three Companions, and the *Major Life* all agree, however, that the reason the priest did not want Francis's money was due to his family's reputation. This was a reputation that set fear in the heart of the priest. None of these vitae seek to explain what this reputation was. For them, it is enough to state that Francis's was a family to be feared. Given the episodes dealing with Pietro di Bernardone's violence and with Francis's brother taunting him, it must have been violence that tainted the family's reputation. At the same time, *First Celano* testifies that the priest did not trust Francis's sudden conversion because he had seen him just one day earlier "living irregularly among his relatives and friends and outdoing all of them in foolishness."[50] According to the *Versified Legend*, the priest had seen Francis "intent on his merchandise and burning with desire to make profit."[51] Perhaps Francis's family also had a reputation for—besides avarice—taunting people by playing mean tricks on them.

This episode, especially as a response to the words of the Crucifix, also shows how Francis was a chip off his father's block. He responded to the request for Church renewal, not by physically rebuilding the church himself, but by gifting the church with money. He expected the priest to use the money for the materials and laborers needed. In the *Versified Legend*, he did not even offer the money to the priest; rather, he offered to have the place reconstructed. Francis acted like a "vain burgher" just like his father, thinking that money solves everything. Why get your hands dirty when you can pay someone else to do it? Even in this generous donation to the priest at San Damiano, the influence of Francis's father on his life manifested itself.

BREAK WITH THE FAMILY

If Pietro di Bernardone has become the shadow figure in Franciscan Spirituality, it is because of his role in his son's conversion process. Pietro is the one who brought everything to a head. Let us consider how this came about and why.

Probably the most famous episode in Francis's conversion process is the scene of his stripping naked before Bishop Guido and returning everything to his father. This episode presents us with a Francis who is strong in his desire for God and who has reached valiantly the apex of his conversion process. On the other hand, it also presents us with an evil father who must be abandoned by his son. He is the greedy force of commerce that had threatened to consume Francis's soul.

This episode can be found retold with great detail in all but one of our vitae (1Cel 14.1–15.2; JulSpi 8.8–9.3; HenAv 3:153–199; 3Soc 19.1–20.6; 2Cel 12.4–5; LegMai 2:3.3 –4.8; AnPer 8.2). It was one which gave the authors free reign of expression in their admiration for Francis and their disregard for his father. Such was the disregard for Francis's father that both Celano and Bonaventure mention his name only once in their vitae, and that is in the context of Francis's self-deprecation (1Cel 53.7; LegMai 4:1.10). When people began to praise Francis's holiness, he ordered a friar to revile him, calling him "a boor, a hired servant, an ignorant and worthless being."[52] To this, Francis responded, "May the Lord bless you, because you speak the truth! Such are the things that the son of Pietro di Bernardone needs to hear!"[53] It was only in this context of Francis's self-deprecation that these two friars dared to reveal the name of Pietro di Bernardone. In so doing, they revealed their total disregard for this man; his was a name that was good only to remind the saint of his humble and worthless origins.

Second Celano adds the name of Pietro di Bernardone in a new detail added to the episode at the Bishop's palace: "Now I can freely say: Our Father who art in heaven and not father Pietro di Bernardone."[54] This detail probably came from the testimony gathered by command of the Chapter of 1244. Francis's words to his father continue to ring in our ears even today. But before we reflect on this phrase any further, let us first consider the events that led Francis to proclaim it and perform the ritual stripping that accompanied it.

Celano, in his First Life of St. Francis, established the outline for the process of Francis's conversion: his bad formation as a youth, his life as a merchant, his military plans, his illness, his prayer in the caves, his time at San Damiano, his mother's freeing him, and so on. Henry of Avranches gives us a good understanding of the struggle—between virtue and vice, between customary ways and the call of the Gospel—that went on within Francis. If we are to believe the Versified Legend, Francis naturally vacillated in his purpose, being sometimes hot, sometimes cold. And, above all, Francis feared that his parents would get in the way of his purpose.

This vacillation on Francis's part is only partially alluded to by the other vitae, especially since it took an act by Pietro di Bernardone to spur Francis to make the final break with his old self. This act was, of course, citing his son before the Bishop. Only Second Celano and the Anonymous of Perugia do not indicate that it was Pietro who led, forced, or compelled his son to the bishop's palace in order to have him tried. If we are to believe the vitae, he did so motivated by greed, desirous of getting back what his son had taken from him. Yet, according to the same vitae, Pietro had already gotten the San Damiano money back from his son.

The *Major Life* claims that the reason Pietro dragged his son before the bishop was to have him "renounce his paternal inheritance and return all that he had into his hands."[55] According to Arnaldo Fortini, the city statutes of that period could have allowed Pietro to have his son banished from the city for his crimes against him. Banishment was the punishment given to murderers, traitors, and bad offspring. It entailed being kicked out of town to die in shame. The banned citizen would lose all civil rights and inheritance. Relatives and friends were prohibited from giving him food or drink. The banned person could be hunted down and killed without retaliation.[56]

According to the *Three Companions*, this banishment from the town of Assisi seems to be the reason that Francis was first dragged before the city council. Pietro was excercising his power as head of the family in what he saw as the family's best interest. He could not afford to have Francis squander his hard earned wealth. The *Versified Legend* claims that Pietro was determined that Francis would not receive a penny of the paternal inheritance and that Pietro no longer wanted Francis to call him father.

According to the *Three Companions*, the city council refused to judge the case, claiming that it was a matter for the bishop, since Francis was in the "service of God" (*servitium Deo*). Pietro had no choice but to take his claim to the bishop. According to *Second Celano* and the *Three Companions* the bishop admitted that Pietro had a case against his son. This does not mean that he refused Francis. Quite the contrary is true; all the vitae agree that the bishop greatly admired the young man's conversion. This notwithstanding, he advised Francis to give back to his father anything he might still have.

It was before the bishop that Francis ritually broke with his father in particular and his family in general. Francis apparently knew the norms set up by the town for rejecting family membership, norms that meant he would lose any claim to his father's inheritance or to family protection. His self-imposed banishment would also mean that he would lose any rights as a citizen. For the same reason, however, it also meant that Francis had the right to go undisturbed to another town with the prospect of eventually returning when the matter had calmed down or had been forgotten.[57] But Francis went beyond the prescription established by the community; he added a ritual stripping because he wanted to make sure that his father knew that he had absolutely no more claims on him.

According to *Three Companions, Second Celano,* and the *Major Life,* this ritual stripping included the now famous quotation: "Listen everyone and understand. Up until now I called Pietro Bernardone my father, . . . from now on I want to say, 'Our Father who art in heaven' and not 'father Pietro di Bernardone.'"[58]

It was thanks to Pietro that Francis was able to do this. The vitae claim that even though the father had brought him to the bishop's palace, Francis had gone gladly. If Pietro constrained his son and forced him before the presence of the bishop, that was what Francis wanted to make his conversion complete. And as the *Versified Legend* underscores, Francis had become a self-imposed exile "who naked takes his leave of his father, the prelate, and all his fellow citizens of Assisi"[59] (HenAv 3:204–5).

A FATHER'S HEARTBREAK

What started out as a common procedure of a father who demanded his rights against a disobedient son before the Bishop ended up in Francis's stripping ritual (3Soc 20.5–6; 23.1–5; AnPer 9.2–3). This ritual revealed Francis's intrepid idealism, impressed Bishop Guido, and did not leave his fellow citizens unmoved. Yet, what did it do for Pietro di Bernardone who had set off this series of events? What were his original motives? Had he expected that his son, when faced with being disinherited and exiled, would be shocked into reality and abandon his foolishness? Answers to these questions would be helpful, but Francis's hagiographers do not have any.

Only *Three Companions* and the *Anonymous of Perugia* give any indication as to how Francis's action affected his father. As far as the other vitae were concerned, the father's reaction was not important. The father was lost to the son and the son lost to his father. What further need was there to speak of Pietro di Bernardone? The hagiographers turned to a new page in Francis's life, his being "embraced" (*amplexatus*) by the Church in the person of the Bishop of Assisi who, with tears, gathered him "into his arms" (*inter braccia sua*).[60]

On the other hand, the *Three Companions* and the *Anonymous of Perugia* speak of Pietro's sorrow at the loss of his son. They did not let him

simply slip away unnoticed. They take the episode of the father cursing his
son, which *Second Celano* (2Cel 12.1–3) placed prior to Francis's stripping
in the presence of the bishop, and put it after the stripping ritual. *Second
Celano* makes this story part of Pietro's persecution of his son during the
conversion process, indicating Francis's initial move towards abandoning his
father. Francis realizes that his father's education in wealth has truly cursed
him and that only in poverty will he be truly blessed. For this reason, he
counters his father's maledictions with a poor person's benedictions.

The *Three Companions* and the *Anonymous of Perugia* situate this
story as happening after the episode at the bishop's palace. The story was
not portrayed as occurring immediately; rather it seems that it was something
that occurred often in the days of Francis's initial freedom from his family.
Pietro would curse his estranged son every time he ran into him. It seems
strange that a father would curse a son, yet we must understand that, as far
as Pietro was concerned, Francis had completely dishonored the family, and
honor was highly prized in the Middle Ages.

Besides dishonor, another reason lay at the root of Pietro's maledictions for his son. It was his love for him. We are accustomed to regarding
di Bernardone as a heartless man who repudiated his son. According to the
Three Companions, however, Pietro loved his son and had loved him greatly
(*multum dilexerat ipsum*).

It was love wronged that led Pietro to react so harshly to his son.[61]
There is no anger so bitter as that which is produced by unrequited love.
And Francis no longer accepted Pietro's love for him. Pietro's love for Francis
showed itself to have been possessive, and Francis's newfound freedom had
been at the cost of that love. *Three Companions* tells twice about Pietro's
sadness at his son's rejection of him. The initial dolor came immediately as
a result of Francis's stripping ritual and his proclaiming for all to hear that
he would no longer call Pietro di Bernardone his father. This grief was accompanied by anger as Pietro, with money and clothing in hand, went home
without his son. Eventually, Pietro expressed this potent mixture of dolor
and furor in curses.

AN ABSENT MOTHER

During Francis's birth, youth, and adolescence, Pietro had often been absent and Pica had taken up the slack by being very present to her son. In the episode before the bishop, however, it was Pietro who was very present and Pica who was noticeably absent. The total lack of the name Pica or the reference to Francis's mother is quite striking, especially in the *Three Companions*, which specifically makes reference to Pietro's sorrow.

Franco Zeffirelli's movie, *Brother Sun, Sister Moon*, dramatically plays out the episode at the bishop's palace and, in a moving scene, focuses the camera on the mother as she sadly realizes what her son is doing. She gently raises her hand to her face and weeps. This scene is founded on the very human concept of maternal affection, something seen as a weakness by medieval authors and preachers—a weakness which had a power all its own, as Henry of Avranches mentioned when he claimed that one of the things that assailed Francis during his conversion process was his mother's tears (HenAv 3:76–79).

The concluding mention of Pica in her role as Francis's mother was her freeing her son from his father's prison. She had done so because, even though she did not agree with her son's folly, she also did not agree with her husband's reaction to that folly. She was mentioned once more in her role as the wife abused by her angry husband. These two things may indicate why she is not mentioned after that point: she has done what was hers to do— free her son not just from his father's chains but, more importantly, from the emotional bonds that tied him to the family. She did so at great cost.

Pietro's violence against his wife only served to emphasize their lack of agreement. She could hardly be expected to accompany her husband in a trial against her son. In order for the child to be sentenced, the courts needed two blood relatives to consent to imprisonment or exile. Perhaps Pica's noticeable absence is meant to underscore her refusal to condemn her son. Her absence may also have been the hagiographer's way of making sure that the medieval reader knew that Francis's exile was self-imposed since Pietro lacked another relative who would join him in making sure Francis was exiled. Or, did he?

FRANCIS'S BROTHER

Little can be said about Francis's brother except that, according to the *Three Companions*, Pica loved Francis more than him (3Soc 9.3). In the story of Francis's setting the table with extra bread, *Three Companions* refers to "other children" (*ceteris filiis*) indicating more than one sibling for Francis. But the only two vitae (3Soc 23.7–8; 2Cel 12.8–10) that specify a sibling mention only the brother *perversus*. A note for *Three Companions*, found in the *English Omnibus of the Sources for the Life of St. Francis*, claims that Francis did indeed have two brothers.[62] One of these would have been the perverse brother, and the other would have been the brother called Angelo. It is much more probable, however, that Angelo and the perverse brother were one and the same person.[63] Arnaldo Fortini insists that Francis must have had only one brother, who in the city records is referred to as Angelo di Pica or Angelo son of Pica.[64]

Angelo was probably younger than Francis, and most likely lived in his older brother's shadow. Jealousy and sibling rivalry were commonplace among noble families, especially regarding the rights of the eldest son to the family fortune and inheritance.[65] We can only imagine that, given Pietro's wealth and prestige, Angelo must have lived a type of sibling rivalry with Francis, even though they were not a noble family. As has been mentioned in *Three Companions*, Francis was Pica's preferred child and the vitae certainly point out that Pietro had loved him very much. How did Angelo react to this love? He certainly would have had everything to gain from Francis's being cast out of the family and giving up his claim to the paternal inheritance.

Despite Fortini's work in hunting down Angelo in the Assisi archives, this younger brother remains a figure on paper with very little life. Questions about his relationship with Francis prior to 1206 remain unanswered. What we do know about him is little: His name was "Angelo di Pica; he named his offspring Giovannetto [Johnny] and Piccardo (after his brother and his mother it would seem); he was named Seneschal by the city of Assisi and was charged with providing for the Franciscan Chapter of Mats held at the Porziuncola in 1221. All these things raise questions about his relationship with his father.

Why wasn't he called Angelo di Pietro di Bernardone? Why did he name his children after his mother and his brother and neither one of them after his father?[66] Why did he end up assisting the Friars, even prior to Francis's death? Did Angelo break to some degree with his father? Perhaps, after

Francis abandoned the di Bernardone family, Pietro became an embittered man, someone hard to live with. Certainly his relationship with his wife would have suffered greatly after the loss of the eldest son, with her probably blaming her husband for having pushed Francis to reject his home. If, according to the vitae, Pietro and Angelo would run into Francis on the streets of Assisi, who's to say that Pica didn't also have to suffer the sight of her emaciated son? She presumably would have blamed Pietro for her son's condition. Life in the di Bernardone household likely never recovered after the loss of Francis, and Angelo most certainly would have had to live through this tragic turn of events.

It seems that Angelo's first reaction was to hate his brother, to taunt him. This teasing took a cruel turn when he asked Francis to sell him some sweat. Showing that he knew well the vanity and weak points of his brother, Angelo taunted Francis's ability as a merchant. He must have known just how good his brother was at selling, and it was this that he taunted, reminding Francis of his past reputation. There must have been a point in Francis's life where he was so concerned with making money that he would have willingly sold his own sweat—and Angelo knew this. When taunting each other, siblings have an added advantage that strangers don't: They know each other all too well, and Angelo certainly knew Francis.

At some point, Angelo must have given up taunting his brother. Eventually, he became involved somewhat in the affairs of his brother's Order, for he was sent to be provider for the Chapter of 1221. At that same time, the city of Assisi had built a house for the friars, a house that Francis wanted destroyed. Angelo was sent along with some knights to make sure that his brother left the house as it was.[67] This involvement with Francis's order continued in Angelo's son, Piccardo, who became procurator and treasurer for the Sacro Convento in Assisi. Piccardo was very devoted to his saintly uncle and helped to insure the beauty and grandeur of his basilica. Other descendants of Angelo (who died soon after Francis, just prior to 1229) became either Friars Minor or Poor Clares.[68]

FINAL REFLECTIONS ON FRANCIS'S STRUGGLE

Francis's struggle with his family has to be seen in the context of his conversion process. This was a process that made him face himself and what he had been brought up to be—the typical elder son of a wealthy merchant. Although he had relished that way of life, he eventually saw through it and made a radical life change—a change that put him at odds with the family he loved, a family who loved him.

Despite *First Celano*'s horrid description of family life, the other vitae give us the impression that, initially, Francis was raised in a loving family environment. They also confirm that he was raised for a specific career. Given this information, we can deduce that Francis's parents were typical of his period and his social class. Their not agreeing with his vocational choice is part of the typical family setting in which he was raised. He had been raised to inherit his father's business, wealth, and the responsibilities that came with it. Although many parents who raised their children for a military, political, or mercantile career accepted their child's choice of a religious vocation, many others did not. "Some wielded emotional blackmail, reminded the son of all they had done for him since childhood, and reproached him for abandoning them in their old age."[69] This was especially true of those who opted for a less established way of religious life, like the mendicant orders.

This emotional blackmail is the context for Pica's tears and her trying to talk sense into her son before finally releasing him. This emotional blackmail is also the context for Pietro's violence and his pushing his son to renouncing his inheritance. More than likely, Pietro was in his own way trying to do what he felt his wife had failed to do—talk some sense into the boy.

Francis's way of life eventually attracted many followers, who in turn would have had to face their own families. And if what we know about families wielding emotional clout against sons who chose a mendicant order is true, they would have needed Francis's support in coming to terms with the loss of their loved ones. It is no wonder that the thirteenth-century vitae placed such importance on portraying Pietro di Bernardone as the villainous archetype of all that would keep a son from following the Gospel. Francis's story was the story of so many of his early followers, and, no doubt, his example gave them courage.

The story of Francis's family paints the struggle that following Christ placed on so many disciples throughout the centuries. Francis lived in a setting that made martyrdom practically impossible, yet the struggle with his father is portrayed as similar to that of the martyrs who were brought to court for their faith. The story of his family moved from lived experience to hagiographic legend as the centuries took hold of it. The myth surrounding his birth tried to add the prophetic element that the thirteenth-century narratives were missing. Francis became the archetype of the medieval martyrs who, although brought up in a Christian environment, found themselves surrounded by new ways of life with which *Christianitas* was uncomfortable. Regarding the Christian misgivings about merchants and the usury they practiced, Francis became the saint who put them in their place by breaking with his own father and not allowing himself to be overcome by his mother's tears or the taunts of his brother.

Chapter III:

Clare's Noble Family

Like Francis of Bernardone, Clare of Favarone was born in Assisi. Unlike Francis, she was born to a noble family, a fact that was to condition her upbringing and her family's aspirations for her. The daughter of Messere Favarone and Madonna Ortulana, she was probably born around 1193–94. While little is truly known about Francis's home life, thanks to the sources (Appendix D), we have a good idea of the life that Clare led in her paternal home, a life that prepared her for the decisive moment of fleeing her father's house.

This information can help us answer questions about this saintly woman. Who and what were her parents like? How did her mother, Lady Ortulana raise her and influence her faith? How and when did she meet Francis? Why did she break with her family? Did she really move a heavy door all by herself when she fled from home? What happened to her inheritance?

The Nobility of Clare's Parents

Regarding Clare's family, the *Bull of Canonization for St. Clare* (BuCl: *Bull*), the *Legend of St. Clare*, written in verse (LegVer; *Clare's Versified Legend*), and the *Legend of St. Clare of Assisi* (LegCl; *Clare's Legend*) contained a lacuna which has been somewhat filled by the discovery of the *Process of Canonization for St. Clare of Assisi* (Proc; *Process*) in the early part of this century. Neither the *Legendae* nor the *Bull* mentions the name of Clare's father, limiting their references to Clare's mother, Ortulana, her uncle, Monaldo, and her sister, Agnes.

The discovery of the *Process* has been fortuitous in many ways for our understanding of Clare and of her lineage. Until the discovery of this document, scholars had erroneously regarded Clare to be a member of the Scifi household. It was commonly held that Ortulana had been from the Fiumi family of Strepeto and that Favarone had been the son of a certain Bernardo di Paolo Scifi.

It would seem that Clare's connection to the Scifi family came about due to her kinship with Friar Rufino. Rufino's father was Scipione d'Offreduccio and his name is found in various documents from Assisi's archives of the period. Rufino is often referred to as Rufino Cipii (or Scipii) in documentation of the thirteenth and fourteenth centuries. In time, Scipii was transformed into Scifi and Clare came to be associated with that family.[1]

Scholars in later centuries went to great lengths to establish the nobility of many saints, creating genealogies tying them to well-known noble families. In the sixteenth, seventeenth, and eighteenth centuries, scholars—including Tossignano, Wadding, and Salvatore Vitali—created genealogies for Clare.[2]. These are so fantastic that they are not to be taken seriously, especially after the revelations of the *Process* and the discoveries made by Arnaldo and Gemma Fortini.

According to the Fortinis, Clare was of Germanic descent deriving from a fusion of Franks and Lombards. Gemma Fortini traced Clare's maternal family back to Bernard, Charlemagne's grandson who was given the Italian kingdom by his father Pepin. Her paternal family can be traced back to Rapizone I of Assisi, who was the grandfather of Offredo, grandfather of Offreduccio de Bernardino (c.1145–77), father of Favarone. Just like the secular witnesses for the process of canonization, both Fortinis convincingly seek to assure us that Clare did indeed come from a very noble lineage on both her father's and her mother's side. Clare's parents not only came from noble lineages, they, in fact, shared the same lineage; like many noble couples, they were distant cousins.[3] Clare's genealogy is as follows:[4]

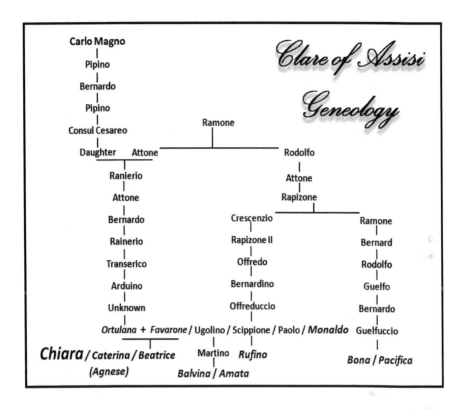

Before looking at either of Clare's parents, however, we will first consider what the sources have to say about the nobility of her family. While Madonna Bona de Guelfuccio de Assesi makes no mention of the nobility of Clare's family, the four male witnesses in the *Process*, Alexander IV in the *Bull*, and her two biographers gave it special importance. According to Messere Ugolino, Clare was from "the noblest lineage" (*nobilissima progiene*). Ioanni de Ventura declared that she was of Assisi's "most noble parentage" (*più nobile parentado*). The *Legendae* state that she was of a "distinguished blood line" (*sanguine conspicua*) and that her "father was a soldier and (her) relatives from both sides came from military lineages."[5]

With the exception of the four or five years in which her family sought refuge in Perugia during Assisi's civil war, Clare spent the greater part of her childhood and adolescence in Assisi[6] as a member of the *maiores* of the city. Ioanni described the house of the sons of Offreduccio in these terms: "The court of her house was one of the best in the city" (Proc 20:3).[7] Pietro di Damiano, a neighbor of Favarone, testified that Favarone and the other six knights[8] of his house were part of Assisi's noble, great, and powerful families, thus confirming the military lineage mentioned in *Clare's Legend.*

Except for Sister Pacifica, it seems that the Poor Ladies gave little, if any, importance to Clare's noble family background. Still, we cannot underestimate the importance of Clare's lineage. She was born to one of Assisi's most noble families in a time when the feudal system was crumbling and nobles were struggling to keep their status. More than likely, she was raised in a traditional household with her uncle Monaldo, Offreduccio's first-born son,[9] acting as the paterfamilias. Monaldo, the violent Lord, was one of the seven knights in a typical aristocratic urban domus, which was compact, organized, and rigidly centered on male heirs. An obvious sign of this household's importance in the city of Assisi was their home's location. For over fifty years, they had lived in the area of San Rufino, the aristocratic center of the city's noble families.[10] Being one of about twenty noble families that dominated Assisi,[11] Monaldo's household would have been part of the consortium, which maintained and protected the Basilica San Rufino.

Despite their power, even Monaldo's household had its share of woes in the war that set the scene for Francis's conversion. Desiring to establish a commune, the *minores* fought against the *maiores;* Clare and her family knew the perils of civil war. When Clare was seven years old, she and her family were forced to flee Assisi and take refuge in Perugia during Assisi's conflict. Monaldo, as head of the Offreduccio household, took citizenship in Perugia and swore to join the Perugian nobles in their battle against Assisi. Subsequently, Clare's house was attacked and severely damaged by the *minores.*[12]

In 1205, the Mayor of Perugia forced the Assisians to return confiscated property to the noble families and to repair whatever damage they may have caused them. It was probably at this time that Monaldo and his family returned to Assisi. The war that so touched the *cotidianidad* of Clare's family had a profound effect on Francis's life, and it figures prominently in the *Legendae* that speak of his conversion. Strangely, Clare's biographers and witnesses made no mention of the war or of Clare's flight to Perugia, but this violent set of events must have colored her life. She could not have lived with seven knights and not have been affected by war, especially when her own father, Favarone, was one of the knights.

MESSERE FAVARONE

Neither the *Bull* nor her two *Legendae* give any indication as to the name of Clare's father or his lineage. Ignoring him, they instead highlight the person and role of Ortulana, her mother. *Clare's Legend* refers to Clare's father in passing, only to say that he was a knight. It is thanks to the *Process*, however, that we have some knowledge of Messere Favarone and his ancestry.[13]

Five witnesses speak of Favarone. Sister Pacifica de Gelfutio de Assise (*sic*) was the first to reveal his name and mention his being a knight. On the other hand, Messere Ugolino de Pietro Girardone, Pietro de Damiano, and Ioanni de Ventura refer to the fact that her father was from an important family in Assisi. Of these witnesses, Ugolino and Ioanni stress the importance of this family by making direct references to its lineage.

Lineage was especially important for noble families in the High Middle Ages. It was a means of solidarity, and was especially important in dealing with matters of controlling an estate and handing on that power—usually to the eldest son.[14] Given the domination of lineage in medieval culture, the witnesses also give the names of Favarone's nearest ancestor, his father Offreduccio of Bernardino, one of Assisi's old nobles.[15] They underscore with certitude that Offreduccio was Clare's grandfather, probably to assure persons familiar with Assisi's noble families that hers was truly a rich and powerful family.[16] This underscoring of Offreduccio, tied to the fact that only three of the witnesses actually mention the name of Favarone, is probably a good indication that Favarone alone was not a good guarantee of Clare's nobility. Recourse had to be taken to her grandfather, as the patriarch of a household in which Favarone was more than likely of lesser importance.

Other than his lineage and his being a knight in the Offreduccio household, we have no information about Favarone. There is, however, an obscure reference in the Assisi archives to a certain Favarone who, in 1229, was the patron of three servants who had been condemned by the city.[17] This Favarone might have been Clare's father. Some scholars hold that, given Ortulana's late entry into the Poor Ladies, Favarone would not have died until after the death of Francis of Assisi.[18] Sister Pacifica's testimony, on the other hand, raises questions about this late date. She claims that, although she had seen Ortulana, she had never seen Favarone. Most readers take this to mean that he was dead.

It is hard to account for the fact that Pacifica, who lived across the plaza from Clare's house, had not seen (*non vidde*)[19] Favarone, despite the fact that she had close ties to Ortulana.[20] Even with feudal society's strict norms regarding the honor of a young woman, her never having seen Favarone is hard to explain. It might be that Favarone was never home—always away at some war. On the other hand, as often happened with men who went off to war, he may never have come back. His death would certainly have been a convenient answer to the question about Pacifica's never having seen Favarone. Yet, according to Pietro, who had seen (*vidde*) and known (*cognobbe*) Favarone, he was alive when Clare was seventeen years old (Proc 19:2).

The issue of the death of Clare's father is a question with which Franciscan scholars have struggled throughout the centuries. Her biographers in the latter half of the nineteenth century and the early part of the twentieth century would have us believe that Favarone died sometime around the death of St. Francis of Assisi. They based their assumption on the work of Tossignano, placing his death between 1224 and 1229.[21]

The basis of an argument for a later death is the late entry of Ortulana to the Order of the Poor Ladies. Yet, some scholars would argue that Favarone had to have died before Clare's flight from home since she was able to sell her inheritance. In order for her to have had access to her inheritance, her father must have been dead. This, to the modern reader, would seem to be an obvious conclusion. Yet, in the time of St. Clare, an inheritance was a right given by virtue of birth and not the parents' wishes. Thus, offspring had the right to their inheritance even during the parents' lifetime.[22] Clare's having sold her inheritance does not necessarily mean that Favarone was dead. And, just when did she sell her inheritance? Was it before or after her conversion? This is a question I will deal with later in this chapter. For now, let us turn our attention to Clare's mother.

MADONNA ORTULANA

While Favarone all but disappears from the life of St. Clare, her mother Ortulana shines as a model of faith and the real cultivator of Clare's holiness. The *Legendae* place her in the list of great women who headed matrilineal families according to the works of hagiography and scripture. We cannot, however, understand Clare as coming from a matriarchy as is understood within modern anthropology or sociology because it is quite clear from the *Process* that she is a product of a patriarchy.

Both Ortulana and Clare lived in a period which considered the Holy Family to be made up of St. Anne, the Virgin Mary, and Jesus. The *Legendae* of St. Clare were written in this same period. In minimizing and ignoring the paternal figure of Favarone, the authors of these *Legendae* unconsciously exalt Ortulana as the founding parent of Clare's religious family. "Like St. Anne, Ortulana was the mother who functioned to mediate tradition, who represented kinship and family connections, and who symbolized the conviction that new institutional formations would cohere and produce even richer benefits than traditional forms."[23]

In an age that finally began to accept marriage and parenthood as valid Christian lifestyles, it is not surprising to find a figure such as Ortulana being exalted in the *Legendae* of St. Clare. In an age that was not sure if the Gospel could be lived to perfection outside of religious life, Ortulana represented a bridge between two contradictory lifestyles: marriage and monasticism.

ORTULANA'S SANCTITY

The *Bull* and the *Legendae* name Ortulana and give us a glimpse of this saintly woman. Contrary to *First Celano's* horrid description of parents, Clare's *Legendae* speak well of parenthood—thanks to Ortulana's efforts in raising her "little plant." All of the sources agree on the personality of Ortulana. She is not just portrayed as simply a woman of prayer and devotion, but also as a strong and magnanimous woman, aiding the poor and going on pilgrimages.

The authors of the *Legendae* were quite faithful to the witnesses in the *Process* in their testimony regarding Ortulana. She is mentioned, either by name or by role, by nine of the twenty witnesses. The secular witnesses mentioned her, but their patriarchal mindset caused them to quickly ignore her on behalf of Favarone. They simply acknowledge that she, too, came from a noble family, and that, like her husband, she was a good and honest person. Aside from hinting at her agreeing with the family's desire that Clare marry, they offer no other information, not even her name. And they certainly never mention that she, too, ended up at San Damiano.

Only four of the Poor Ladies mention her, giving us her name and some details about her piety, prayer, and nobility of spirit. Of these, Pacifica, who admitted to having had close ties with her, gives us a more complete picture of Ortulana (Proc 1:4–5). The other sisters spoke of the Clare–Ortulana miracle (Proc 4:11) and of Ortulana's prophecy (Proc 3:28; 6:12). It is this well from which the author of *Clare's Legend* took much of his information for the portrait of Madonna Ortulana.

Of all the sources, *Clare's Legend* does the most for outlining a matrilineal tradition regarding Ortulana's role in the development of Clare's faith and personality. Whereas neither the *Bull* nor *Clare's Versified Legend* mention Clare's father, *Clare's Legend* begins the section describing Clare's family background with the nameless father and quickly drops him in favor of Ortulana. This move on the part of the author speaks unconsciously of the importance of Clare's mother and the insignificance of her father. If the author had simply ignored the father as was done in the *Bull* and *Clare's Versified Legend*, Ortulana would not have had anyone to be compared with. The role of the noble yet nameless father seems to act as a point of contrast to that of the mother.

Clare's Legend was written in a time soon after marriage was consecrated as a sacrament. The author seeks to describe that Ortulana, despite her being a wife and mother, was still able to live a holy life. He openly admits to this almost impossible task by claiming that "even though she was bound by the yoke of matrimony and even though she was taken up with all the cares of a family" (LegCl 1.4),[24] she was still dedicated to the "things of God," but only in as much as she was able. In other words, Ortulana was limited in how much she could do for the Lord, because she had accepted the yoke (*iugum*) of marriage along with all of its burdens.

ORTULANA'S PREGNANCY

The witnesses of the *Process* gave a special role to the Holy Spirit in the formation of the young Clare, to the point that Madonna Bona and Messere Ranieri claim that Clare had been sanctified in her mother's womb (Proc 17:1; 18:1). In their minds, Ortulana had joined the ranks of those holy mothers whose children were great in holiness—mothers like Hannah, Elizabeth, and the Virgin Mary. These women had the audacity to usurp the paternal role in the naming of their children. In their stories, the husband/father is a lesser figure overshadowed by the mother's virility.

In considering the sources,[25] we find that most the Poor Ladies completely ignored the fear and danger Ortulana faced during her pregnancy. Only two witnesses, Philippa and Cecilia, speak of it. Taking their cue from them, the male writers assign great importance to Ortulana's fear and to the real dangers that accompanied childbirth. This might have been the biographers' attempt to point out to female readers just how wise the option for virginity truly is. It also might be that the cloistered women were so impressed by the prophecy of Clare's birth, and the danger of childbirth was so well-known, that they chose simply to concentrate on the marvelous revelation of Clare's name.

According to the witnesses, Ortulana, praying before a crucifix, was told not to worry about her pregnancy for she would "give birth to a light that would greatly enlighten the world" (Proc 3:28).[26] Both *Legendae* add the detail of the light being "clear" (*clarius*), which inspired Ortulana to name her daughter Clare.

In her book on Clare, Ingrid Peterson tied Ortulana's pilgrimages to St. Michael the Archangel to the period of her pregnancy,[27] but none of the sources seems to indicate this. Peterson's reason for connecting the pregnancy to the pilgrimage to St. Michael is based on the medieval belief that the archangel was the patron saint of women in childbirth (and of soldiers on the battlefield). Childbirth in the Middle Ages was truly a terrible ordeal, during which the woman risked both her physical and spiritual well-being. It was commonly believed that female blood attracted demons and a woman who died in childbirth before she could be purified was not allowed a Christian burial. It is no wonder that Peterson claims that Ortulana turned to Michael, the archangel who fights demons, for protection. The sources state, however, that she turned to the Crucified Lord instead. This may also be an allusion to Francis before the Crucifix of San Damiano.

ORTULANA'S ENTRY INTO SAN DAMIANO

As we have seen above, *Clare's Legend* recognized Ortulana's predisposition to holiness in this married woman's pilgrimages and in her visits to the poor. This holiness, however, was eventually tied to her becoming a Poor Lady and living as a widow among virgins.

Although some would indicate that Ortulana was already at San Damiano when Francis died, there is nothing in the sources that confirms this. There is, however, an early sixteenth-century source, *Libro delle dignità et excellentie del ordine della seraphica madre delle povere donne sancta Chiara da Asisi* (*Book on the Dignity and Excellence of the Order of the Seraphic Mother of the Poor Ladies, St. Clare of Assisi*),[28] written by Friar Mariano da Firenze (Mariano da Firenze, *Libro delle dignità et excellentie*), which affirms that Ortulana was received into the community of San Damiano by St. Francis himself. Although we cannot be sure of the historical accuracy of this late source, it is worth considering, since it is the only source that speaks of Ortulana's entry into religious life.

> After her husband Messere Favarone died, Blessed Ortulana did not remain long with her three holy daughters persevering in the works of piety and mercy, giving alms to the poor for love of God, frequenting churches and the divine office, and conversing with her two eldest daughters *and* St. Francis. Being finally abandoned by these two daughters, however, she remained with her little daughter Beatrice. She pondered and deliberated about following her daughters' holy footsteps. Upon deciding, she gave her daughter Beatrice into the care of Messere Monaldo. The part of her inheritance which remained—from when St. Clare had sold her birthright and distribuited the proceeds to the poor—she distributed for the love of God. She was then vested and veiled by St. Francis and enclosed with her daughters in San Damiano.[29]

Mariano gives no date for Ortulana's joining the community at San Damiano, but does give an interesting picture of how she joined. Mariano's description of Ortulana's leaving home is in sharp contrast with how Clare and Agnes left. As a widow, Ortulana did not have to abandon her family, as did Clare, in order to give herself to the religious life. Given the care and acceptance of both Francis and Clare by the Papal Curia, by the time Ortulana left the family, the Poor Ladies of San Damiano had a certain amount of acceptability. The hostile reaction of Monaldo and the rest of the family would not have been her lot as it had been for Clare and Agnes. On the contrary, Monaldo helped her ease into religious life by caring for her remaining daughter, Beatrice.

The responsibility of caring for her child had kept her from following her elder daughters sooner. Her family assumed this task, however, and she was free to go. She, who had been abandoned by her two older daughters, in turn, abandoned her youngest daughter. Not that Ortulana took her decision lightly. Mariano's description of the events carefully points out that she "pondered and deliberated" (*pensò et deliberò*) prior to her decision, but in the end, the love she had for her youngest daughter could not keep her from following her other daughters into religious life.

Ortulana became a Damianite, under Clare's leadership. It must have been strange for mother and daughter to switch roles. With Clare as Mother Abbess, Ortulana would have been subject to her, just like all the other sisters. Still, in at least one miracle story of Clare, we find Ortulana being invited to participate in a way that none of the other sisters did. She was asked to bless the person in need of liberation.

THE CURE OF THE PERUGIAN

Among the many liberation miracles[30] performed by Clare is a curious story about Clare and her mother healing a child from Perugia.[31] It has its roots in the testimony of Clare's niece, Amata de meser Martino da Cocorano, and it is the only instance of a miracle performed by Sister Ortulana. Aside from the shared nature of this miracle, this story is important when we consider the possible identity of the child who was liberated from an eye ailment.

This miracle involved a child from Perugia, where Ortulana's family spent time during Assisi's civil war. Thanks to the work of the Fortini, we know that Clare had relatives in Perugia. And, although the sources give no indication as to the identity of the child, one has to wonder if this child was a member of Clare's extended family or the child of friends of the family. If such were the case, then it could explain why the child was sent to Ortulana: they would have known each other.

If, as we would like to think, the child was a relative of Clare's, the inclusion of her mother in this miracle can be taken as an indication of Clare's continued closeness to her family. It is true that Clare had to abandon her family in order to live an evangelical life. However, it would seem from the number of female relatives who followed her into the Order that this break with the family was not as drastic as that of Francis. Where Francis and his family severed all ties, Clare and her family seem to have continued some contact. Clare, it would seem, invited her family to share in her new lifestyle, perhaps in imitation of an invitation she received from her own cousin, Rufino. In this way, Clare mirrors a changing attitude toward the family in hagiography and Church teaching.

CLARE'S UPBRINGING

Although the sources do not go into detail about Clare's upbringing, the comments they make about her holiness, her love of the poor, and her virtues indicate a *cotidianidad* that prepared her for the religious life. The agents of this upbringing, as we will see, are Ortulana and the Holy Spirit.

A SAINT FROM THE START

Like many of the female saints,[32] Clare manifested signs of sanctity from very early on.[33] Four of the five secular witnesses give the impression that Clare was a saint from the very beginning of her life. Madonna Bona and Messere Ranieri de Bernardo de Assisi even claim, "It seemed that she had been sanctified in her mother's womb" (Proc 17:1; 18:1).[34] This belief was based on the apparent and great sanctity of Clare's life.

To our modern mentality, a declaration that a person has been sanctified in her mother's womb may seem exaggerated. But to the medieval mentality, accustomed to Francis's *Legendae* and legends of the prophets and saints, this idea was far from absurd. The witnesses were simply explaining that the child Clare had, early on, given herself to pious and holy works so as to live a spiritual and holy life. It was the common opinion that Clare was a saint, and, given that, the hand of God should be recognized in the events of her life.

In their testimony, neither Pietro nor Ioanni mention that she had been sanctified in her mother's womb. Rather, they claim that the general opinion was different. According to Pietro, Clare "lived spiritually as it was believed" (Proc 19:2).[35] The Umbrian phrase can be translated in one of two ways: Clare lived a spiritual life in accord with the faith, or Clare lived a spiritual life, as was believed. This second translation goes quite well with the Ioanni's belief that the Holy Spirit inspired Clare from her very beginnings. The general opinion presented by the male witnesses adds nuance to that of Madonna Bona. Where she affirmed that Clare had most certainly been sanctified in the womb of her mother, they declared that she acted as if she had probably been sanctified in her mother's womb.

Sister Philippa added to the testimony of the secular witnesses. She recalled that prior to her entering the religious life, Clare was considered a saint by all those who had witnessed the honesty of her life and her many virtues and graces. However, she also recognized the origin of Clare's holiness when she testified that these virtues and graces are those "which the Lord God had placed in her" (Proc 3:2).[36]

Her two biographers followed Pietro's and Phillippa's lead by ignoring the references to Clare's being sanctified in her mother's womb and stressing instead the workings of the Holy Spirit in her youth. *Clare's Versified Legend* (LegVer 196) states, "thus the Spirit breathes upon her" (*eam sic Spiritus*[37] *afflabat*), while *Clare's Legend* states that it is "by/with/to the spirit simultaneously melting and molding her interiorly" (LegCl 3.2).[38] This use of the ablative, *spirito*, by *Clare's Legend* might have been referring more to Clare's interior disposition than to the action of God's Spirit. Yet, it would be highly unlikely that the infant Clare's spirit would melt and mold her; so the author must have been referring to the Spirit of God either as agent or goal.

In referring to God's Spirit, the author ties the spiritual to the anthropological. He joins the action of God's Spirit to Ortulana's action of giving Clare the faith from her very mouth, much like a mother bird feeding her young.[39] This image of Ortulana giving Clare the faith from her very mouth is also found in *Clare's Versified Legend* in a reference that ties the work of the mother to the work of the Spirit. It was the Spirit who prepared the child Clare to follow her mother's footsteps by making her "alert in mind, with a docile soul, with shining understanding" (LegVer 198)[40] to better receive the faith from her mother's mouth.

LOVE FOR THE POOR

Clare's Versified Legend stresses that the child Clare followed the footsteps of her mother, who, like the noblewomen of her time, practiced charity. Clare certainly must have learned from her mother that *dominae*[41] were expected to care for the needs of the unfortunate. We know that Ortulana voluntarily visited the poor, but did she care for them? If Clare's love and care is any indication, she certainly must have acted more out of real concern than mere social practice.

War and violence marked the era in which Clare lived. In her youth, she herself had joined her family in exile, fleeing to Perugia to escape civil war in Assisi. It was during this exile that she would have come to know firsthand, as well as from friends of her family, the harsh reality of economic need. She would have met Philippa de Messere Leonardo de Gislerii[42] at this time. Messere Leonardo was the captain of the castle known as Sasso Rosso, which was destroyed in Assisi's civil war. Philippa's family was one of the first noble families obliged to seek refuge in Perugia. From her, Clare would have learned of the tragedy suffered in war and the destitution of those who lost everything due to economic necessity.[43] The *Bull* (BuCl 17) declares "while she was still a child of 'the age' . . . she dedicated herself to pious and luminous works."[44] Exactly what these works were is never really mentioned.

In order to explain why he believed that the Holy Spirit had inspired Clare, Ioanni declares that it was because "she fasted and was in prayer and did other pious works" (Proc 20:5).[45] These three reasons come at the tail end of his description of the type of life that she led as a youth—a life of charity and penitence in which she would deprive herself in order to feed the poor. He marveled at how she would send them the very food she was given to eat and describes it as being "the food that was given to eat, like that of great households" (Proc 20:3),[46] obviously impressed by the wealth of her family and the magnanimity of her action.

Madonna Bona also testified that Clare would send to the poor "the food which she claimed to eat" (Proc 17:1).[47] While Ioanni refers to the refined nature of the food, Bona underlines the fact that Clare claimed to have eaten it, when in fact she did not. The author of *Clare's Legend* neatly joined these two testimonies in his description of how Clare would "deprive her own little body of refined foods and—sending them secretly, by way of messengers—would restore the flesh of orphans" (LegCl 3.4).[48] He also ties this fact to her being molded interiorly by the "spirit."

Clare would secretly send this food to the needy. She herself was not able to take it to them, probably out of fear of her family's reaction to such a gesture. Not that her family did not practice generosity. Quite the contrary was true—as Arnaldo Fortini discovered in the Archives of San Rufino. Clare's family had a tradition of being generous with that particular church.[49] But there is a marked difference between giving property to a church, probably in the interest of indulgences and social recognition, and giving food to those who can in no way repay you. It's not that the wealthy were generous only out of self-interest. Noblewomen were encouraged to give alms, but this was to be done from their surplus, not from the very food with which they were to feed themselves.

Messere Ranieri and the sources attest that Clare would willingly give as many alms as she could (Proc 18:3). She would deprive herself of her own nourishment to feed others. In her compassion, Clare was probably embarrassed by the great abundance in her family's house while so many around her were suffering from hunger.[50] As Sister Pacifica tells us, Clare loved the poor (Proc 1:3), and most assuredly this love wanted to transform itself into solidarity. In solidarity with the poor, she could not eat while others went hungry.

A VIRTUOUS YOUTH

Bringing together all of the witnesses lets us see what kind of a youth Clare was. She was a girl of good conduct and of good reputation; she led a life that was "almost angelic" (*quasi angelicha*; Proc 12:1) since her childhood, as we are told by her carnal sister, Beatrice. Sister Pacifica (Proc 1:1–3) tells us that she was known for her "great honesty" which showed itself in her "loving greatly the poor" and her involvement "with the works of piety" (Proc 1:1.3).[51] Sister Benvenuta da Peroscia described her as being of "great honesty, goodness and humility" (Proc 2:2). Sister Philippa affirmed that "great was the sanctity of her life and the honesty of her manners" (Proc 3:2).[52] While declaring that God had placed many virtues and graces in the young maiden, she specified only the virtue of honesty. Sister Amata recognized and affirmed that Clare manifested the virtues and graces "which God had given her" (Proc 4:2).[53]

The witnesses tried in various ways to explain that Clare's sanctity did not simply manifest itself in her charity for the poor but could also be seen in her virtues. In the testimony of the secular witnesses, these virtues take the form of adjectives used to describe the young woman from Assisi and to speak of her life. Besides speaking of the young woman's virtues, they also gave concrete examples of how these virtues were manifested in her.

Madonna Bona declared that Clare "was a prudent youth of about eighteen years of age, and she was always at home, in her room, not wanting to be seen by those who passed by her house. She was also very good and attended to other good works" (Proc 17:4).[54]

Messere Ugolino recalled that Clare "in her father's house was of very honest conversation and gracious towards everyone" (Proc 16:2).[55]

Messere Ranieri testified that the young girl "fasted, prayed . . . [and] would willingly give as many alms as she could. And, whenever she was seated with those of her house, she always spoke of the things of God" (Proc 18:3).[56]

Ioanni explained "that at that time the child was of such honesty in life and custom, as if she had already spent many years in the monastery . . . . She wore a white *stamigna* (woven of rough wool) under her other garments" (Proc 20:2.4).[57]

Together, the testimony of the various witnesses paints a picture of a Clare who was prudent, kind, and honest both in custom and in conversation. She was always at home and avoided being seen by those who passed by her home. She lived a semi-cloistered life at home, attending to good works and being gracious and kind towards all.

This picture could seem a bit exaggerated, especially when it paints a semi-cloistered life for a young secular woman. We need to remember, however, that Clare was not a woman of our century and her witnesses describe a Clare who lived perfectly society's expectations for young noblewomen of her day. Ioanni described Clare as a little girl who lived as if in a monastery, a fact that lady Bona better explained, describing Clare as a serious young woman who knew how to care for her reputation. A woman who was too visible risked being considered a woman of ill repute and ruining her family's honor, and would never have been able to enter a good marriage. Thus, it is no wonder that her family raised Clare in a semi-cloistered environment. We also need to keep in mind that, unbeknown to her family, Clare had decided to remain a virgin and thus had no reason to display herself to the men of Assisi.

BREAK WITH THE FAMILY

From the story of St. Francis of Assisi, we have already learned that in order to live a truly evangelical life, one had no choice but to abandon one's family. This hagiographic topos did not escape the author's of Clare's *Legendae* or Clare herself, as is pointed out by the witnesses in the *Process*. Pressured by the demands of a noble family, and desirous to serve the Lord, Clare found herself needing to run away from her father's house.

The Poor Ladies clearly affirm that Clare had been a virgin since her infancy, and the secular witnesses did the same.[58] Messeres Ugolino and Ranieri affirmed that Clare was and had been a virgin. Ioanni united his testimony to theirs by declaring that he had known her as a "child and a virgin" (*mammola et vergine*), while Madonna Bona declared that everyone considered her to be a "most pure virgin" (*vergine purissima*) underscoring the fame of Clare's virginity.

REFUSAL TO MARRY

Her family must have certainly appreciated this fame. The young Clare was beautiful, as is noted by the witness Ranieri (Proc 18:2), and her family intended to take advantage of her beauty and good reputation. Like all noble families of the period, they knew that a good marriage for Clare would increase the influence and power of the family by establishing or strengthening a political alliance. During her adolescence, Clare's family must have certainly begun to pressure her into marriage. Given the custom of her day, a groom would probably already have been chosen for her, a groom who, according to the laws of the Church, could not have taken her as bride without her consent.[59] According to her witnesses, Clare would not consent to a marriage, yet her *Legendae* insist that she did not openly reveal her desire to remain a virgin (LegVer 214–19; LegCl 4.5). *Clare's Legend* claims that she would pretend to consider marriage in the future, all the while dedicating her virginity to the Lord.

Madonna Bona stressed how, as a youth, Clare already sought the will of God for her life. Clare's witnesses and biographers reveal an adolescent struggling to be faithful to God. While she aspired to give herself totally to God, her relatives pressured her to consent to marriage—maybe even to marry the witness Messere Ranieri[60]—and to follow the normal path set out for her since the day of her birth.

Clare, however, had encountered God, who sanctified her while she was still in Ortulana's womb, and she had encountered the poor Christ in the needy whom she assisted. These encounters with God in her *cotidiano* led her to have to encounter herself as well. Upon seeing herself in the mirror of the poor and crucified Lord, she discovered that she was a rich woman living in the vanity of the age. She was faced with being a member of a family that spent vast sums of money on itself fighting to defend its social position from the rising middle class *minores* who sought to establish themselves through money and social power. She lived as a prized member of an institution that pressured her to consent to an arranged marriage meant to turn her into the *domina* of an important household. As she gazed into the mirror, she felt Christ invite her to do as many young women had done in the past and were doing in her own era: struggle against her family's ambitions. Her struggle increased as she learned of Francis, the young man who had abandoned his own family in order to live the Gospel.

Encounters with Francis

Clare must have been about twelve or thirteen years old when Francis of Assisi returned money, clothing, and name to his father. She most certainly heard of this event; such a thing would hardly have gone without comment and derision in her father's house. Ioanni confirmed this probability when he declared that she "heard that Saint Francis had chosen the way of poverty" (Proc 20:6).[61] At the time of this testimony, Ioanni was speaking of one who had been accepted as a saint, yet at the time of Francis's conversion, he would have been considered more of a fool than a saint.[62] The first news that Clare would have received about Francis would have been about his sudden insanity. But, judging by Ioanni's testimony, she ignored this explanation of his conversion and "decided in her heart that she would do exactly the same thing."[63] That which both *maiores* and *minores* judged as insanity, she recognized as wisdom.

RUFINO, HER COUSIN

Clare felt called to imitate Francis, who had become poor for the love of Christ because Christ had become poor for the love of humanity. She was not, however, the only member of her family to see the life of Francis as an example to be followed. We know that her cousin Rufino also followed the example of Francis and went to live among the first companions.[64]

We are not sure exactly what kind of relationship Clare and Rufino had before or after his abandoning the family to live as a *frate minore*. Given the close-knit nature of the feudal family, however, news of his conversion and the family's reaction to it would most certainly have reached her ears and touched her heart. She would have been about sixteen years of age and would already have nurtured her desire to "remain in virginity and live in poverty" (Proc 19:2).[65] Rufino's conversion to Francis's way of life would have only encouraged her to do as he had done.[66]

During that period of her life, as Madonna Bona related, Clare would send money "to those who worked at Santa Maria della Portiuncola" (Proc 17:7).[67] We cannot say with certainty that these workers were Francis and his companions, but taking into account the abandoned condition of the chapel when the first brothers arrived there, we cannot think that it would have been anyone else. Clare's concern for the workers of the Portiuncola may have been inspired by her natural love for the poor, yet it also might show a concern for her cousin Rufino. It is thought that Rufino joined the Friars around the year 1210 when they were still in Rivo Torto, before their move to the Portiuncola.[68] We have no news of Clare's having sent money to the friars in Rivo Torto. We can however state that she sent money to the friars at the Portiuncola. Keeping in mind Francis's prejudice against money, Clare probably had not yet met him or must not have known him very well, during that time.

THE MEETINGS WITH FRANCIS

Francis of Assisi received papal approval for his style of life around 1209–10, along with permission to preach a life of penance.[69] At that time, he and his friars began to preach penance in Assisi and the surrounding area. According to St. Bonaventure, one of the places where Francis used to preach was the church of San Rufino.[70] Clare's house, as is well known, was on the plaza of San Rufino. The witnesses affirmed that Clare "came to," "took on," or "entered" (*venne, haveva presa, intrò*) "religion" thanks to the "preaching of St. Francis," but they do not mention the context of this preaching.[71] We can only suppose that Clare must have had the opportunity to hear him at San Rufino—as Friar Mariano affirmed in his *Libro delle dignità et excellentie.*

To this preaching, Sister Amata and Messere Ugolino added the exhortation and admonition of Francis (Proc 4:2; 16:3). While the word *predicatione* conjures up images of Francis publicly preaching to groups of people in a church or plaza, the words *exortatione* and *admonitione* seem to connote a more private context. While it is true that one can exhort and admonish even during public preaching, these do not bear as much fruit as do exhortation and admonition given in a more private and personal way.

If we consider everything that the witnesses said about Clare's encountering Francis,[72] we can imagine that she probably had the opportunity to hear him preach at San Rufino. But how did this young noblewoman ever get to meet with Francis—a *minore*—privately? It is thanks to the intervention of Madonna Bona that Clare was able to meet secretly with Francis for private instruction. Judging by the information we have in the *Process*, we conclude that, like Madonna Ortulana, Bona and her sister Pacifica belonged to the Consortium of San Rufino (Proc I:1.4; 17:1).[73] Having traveled with Ortulana on some of her pilgrimages, they were probably somewhat older than Clare was—maybe even old enough to have been Clare's wet nurses.[74] Given her age, Madonna Bona was certainly freer than Clare was and would have been able to take food and money to the poor for Clare. Her age and her being trusted by the Offreduccio family would also have permitted her to accompany Clare on walks through Assisi, making it possible for her to meet with Francis.

According to Madonna Bona, Clare "would go secretly (to speak with St. Francis) so as not to be seen by her relatives" (Proc 17:3).[75] Certainly, Francis, who desired to meet Clare because of her holy reputation, took care to ensure that that reputation remained untarnished, and so he met with her in secret. Clare, on the other hand, had other motivations for meeting secretly. She desired to serve God, which meant leaving "this age" and entering the religious life. Knowing of her family's desires for her future, she took care that her talks with Francis would remain undiscovered until she could come under the protection of the Church.[76] Had her family come to know of Clare's meetings with Francis, she would have been quickly forced into a marriage. Clare's fear of her family made her take precautions against being discovered. As long as Clare was in her father's house, her plans could be overturned and she could be forced to comply with her family's wishes.

FRANCIS'S MESSAGE

Given the results of Clare's encounters with Francis, one is curious as to the content of their discussions. From the very beginning of his life of penance, Francis had designated himself as the herald of the great King,[77] and in his encounters with Clare, he must have behaved as such. As the messenger of the great King, Francis brought the nuptial invitation of his Lord to the young damsel. What did this invitation consist of? What words could move a noble lady to a life of poverty? The answer to these questions comes from Madonna Bona who had the opportunity to hear this message, since she was present at these meetings. Unfortunately, all Bona told the tribunal was that Francis spoke to Clare of conversion to Jesus Christ.

To deduce what this conversion to Jesus Christ meant, we need to consider what the other sources have to say (Proc 3:1; 4:1; 18:2).

In speaking of their encounters with Clare, these witnesses use a variety of verbs; Clare "proposed" (*propuse*) to Philippa, spoke to Amata with *admonitione* and *exortatione*, and she "would preach" (*predicava*) to Ranieri. These different words used to explain Clare's action in her meetings with the witnesses are the same words used to describe Francis's action in his meetings with Clare.[78] Together, these testimonies indicate the content of Clare's message to the witnesses: a presentation of the passion and cross of Jesus Christ along with an invitation to respond to His salvific action by not allowing themselves to be fooled by the world, by renouncing this age, and by hating the world in order to enter religious life and practice penance. Could this have been Francis's message to her?

Clare's little sister, Beatrice, declared that Clare's reaction to the preaching of Francis was the renunciation of the world and all earthly things in order to serve God as quickly as possible (Proc 12:2). None of the witnesses tell us what Francis actually preached to Clare. We have to remember that they were speaking in 1253 about an event that had occurred some 42 years earlier. But when we gather together Beatrice's testimony along with that of Bona, Philippa, Amata, and Ranieri, we can deduce that Francis's message was (1) the passion and crucifixion of Jesus Christ, (2) the deception of the world which needs to be hated, (3) the invitation to renounce the world and earthly things, and (4) the invitation to enter into the service of God in the religious life.

What the witnesses of the *Process* have to say about Francis's discourses with Clare, and then her own with others, was summed up as follows by the author of *Clare's Legend* who claimed that "Father Francis encouraged her to have contempt for the world. With a living sermon, he demonstrated the arid hope of this age and its deceptive beauty. Sweet marriage with Christ he instilled in her ears, convincing her to guard the pearl of her virginal chastity for the blessed spouse, whom love made human" (LegCl 5.5–6).

In her meetings with Francis, Clare encountered Jesus and the world. She came face to face with the reality of her family's social condition and her own desire to serve the Lord in virginity and in poverty. She had to free herself of the chains of the marriage that her family desired for her and of the social barriers that kept her from encountering the poor as her equals. It was in these encounters with Francis that Clare began to prepare herself for her break with her family and her flight from her father's house.

CLARE'S FLIGHT FROM HOME

The fruit of Clare's meetings with Francis was the decision to abandon her paternal home in order to follow the poor and crucified Christ. The witnesses recalled the events of Clare's passage from the riches of her family to the poverty of Christ, from the security of her family to Francis's evangelical adventure.[79]

Sister Cristiana was amazed at the "marvelous way" (*modo meraviglioso*) in which Clare escaped her paternal home. She insisted that many marveled at how she could have done it. The "it" in question here is Clare's opening of a heavily reinforced door. But, at the same time, the members of her household must have wondered how Clare could abandon her home and family emotionally. Her desire to flee from her father's house must have caused both astonishment and scandal.

As we have seen, nobles of Clare's era treated their daughters as precious commodities, utilized to make advantageous alliances for the sake of power and fortune. Women simply did not question or challenge such a system, and losing Clare would not have been taken lightly by the sons of Offreduccio. Clare knew this, and so, in keeping with the secrecy of her meetings with Francis, she secretly left her home by a back door.[80] The house of nobles had one main entrance that was always guarded by armed men, and it is only natural that Clare would have avoided that door. Clare's desire to serve the Lord was so intense that she did not want anyone to hinder her, especially her kin. So strong was her desire to flee from home that the Lord gave her the power needed to remove all obstacles, the fortified door, her social condition, and even her family.

By removing the heavy logs and stone column that barred the door, Clare was removing the social conditions and family expectations that barred her way. With all the vigor of her youth, she gave herself over to the service of Christ. *Clare's Legend* proclaimed her break with all earthly things to be a final separation. She gave the world a bill of divorce (*libellum repudii*). These earthly things, referred to as "the ruckus of this age" (*saeculi strepitu*) by the *Bull*, included her house, her city, and her blood relatives. *Strepitu* is an appropriate word in that it contains all the negative feelings of churchmen towards the responsibilities having to do with family life—responsibilities that keep one from dedicating oneself, completely and without diturbance, to the things of God.

Moreover, if we keep in mind the Palm Sunday liturgy in which Bishop Guido seeks Clare to give her a blessed palm (LegVer 268–79; LegCl 7.3–5), we see that this churchman seems to have approved Clare's decision to flee her family. The witnesses of the *Process* make no mention of this incident, and yet both *Legendae* describe it beautifully. *Clare's Legend* adds that, on the night of Palm Sunday, Clare fled from home "with honest company" (*cum honesta societate*)—not stating, however, who that was. It might have been someone assigned by the Bishop so that all would proceed well. If we are to believe Sister Pacifica's testimony that she entered the Order at the same time as Clare (Proc I:3), then it might have been Pacifica herself. Yet we will never know who accompanied the young Clare in her flight from home. Given Francis's concern for her reputation, we have to agree with the author of *Clare's Legend* that someone has to have accompanied her to the Portiuncola.

THE VIOLENT RESPONSE OF THE FAMILY

The morning after Palm Sunday must have been a noisy one indeed. We can only begin to imagine the anger felt by Monaldo and his household. Having already lost one family member, Rufino, to Francis's folly, they would not have been happy to see this beautiful young woman follow in her cousin's footsteps. All the sources agree that her decision, coming so soon after that of her cousin, greatly disturbed her relatives. The witnesses for the *Process of Canonization* and the authors of the *Bull* and the *Legendae* all describe the violent reaction of Clare's family to her flight from home.[81]

Like other damsels of her period, Clare could have left her family home through the front door during the light of day. She could have entered a wealthy monastery as a choir nun with the dowry that her family could have given her for such a thing. It would not have been exactly what her family had planned, but it undoubtedly would have been better than what she did. The fact that she rejected an arranged marriage, and the way in which she left her home were both an embarrassment and a scandal for the honor of the Offreduccio family.

Rather than enhancing her family's honor by becoming a choir nun in a wealthy and influential Benedictine monastery, Clare served at San Paolo as a servant.[82] As far as her family was concerned, Clare had done everything wrong. She had fled her father's house as if escaping from a prison in the middle of the night. She then went to a man of questionable reputation who, despising his father's honor, had challenged his own family's reputation. It is no wonder that Monaldo and the rest of the Offreduccio household reacted as violently as they did.

Only three witnesses in the *Process*, mentioned that her family went to get her from San Paolo.[83] The witnesses used strong and descriptive verbs to speak of the reaction of Clare's family and to show the confidence with which she faced them. Sister Beatrice used eight verbs in one small phrase to describe the event, while Messere Ranieri used five and Ioanni de Ventura used four. The verbs common to the three witnesses are *volere* (desire), *cavare* (remove; yank), *remenare* (return) and *mostrare* (show). The first three verbs are used to express the wrath of the family that had presented itself at the monastery of San Paolo. These verbs create a violent image of a family that sought to yank a determined young woman away from her chosen way of life in order to drag her back to her previous one.

The *Legendae* also paint a picture of a family wanting to take back the daughter they had lost. This desire is motivated by a "lacerated heart" (*corde lacero: dilacerato corde*). They were acting out of a love that had been wounded. They were probably asking themselves where they had gone wrong in her upbringing. They were most likely mortified by her future possibilities. All of these things they seem to have shared with Clare in the form of "counsels," "soft words," and "promises" (*consiliorum, blanditias, promissionum*). Clare rejected all of these, and their love and concern turned into a resentful violence that demonstrated a jealousy of losing something that belonged to them.

The verb, *mostrare*, indicated Clare's reaction to the violence of her family: she quite simply had to show them her "tonsured head" (*capo tondito*) in order to stop them. Clare confronted the violent Monaldo and took control of that dramatic encounter. She who was the intended object of the verbs describing her family's wrath became the subject of the verbs explaining her action: she took hold of (*prese*) the altar cloth and uncovered (*scoperse*) her head, showing them (*mostrandoli*) that it was tonsured; she in no way consented (*aconsentì*) to her family's desire; she did not allow herself to be removed (*lassò cavare*) from there or to return (*remenare*) with them. The family's reaction was, quite simply, that they let her be (*lassarono stare*). The family, which sought to break her will, was broken itself instead.

Clare could in no way be conquered by her family's violence. She took control of the situation, and faced them, without the help of Francis of Assisi, the Bishop, or the Benedictine nuns. She found herself alone at the altar of her Lord, revealing the one thing that guaranteed her ecclesial protection: her tonsured head. Seeing that symbol of her determination, her relatives left her. She had all the opportunities that a young woman of her time could dream of: A prestigious marriage had been arranged for her, she had a rich inheritance, and she belonged to the social class that everyone aspired to. Clare despised all of this and abandoned it in the name of her spouse, the poor and crucified Christ.

A Question of Inheritance

With her family retreating to Assisi, we have the transformation of a young noble maiden into a poor woman. Part of this transformation included the selling of her inheritance, which would have consisted of land and properties. She, who had been born into one of Assisi's better families, had taken the condition of a poor serving girl, stripped of status and without rights. She who had had everything was without anything. Having used her inheritance for the poor, she found herself sharing their lot.

In reference to this sale, Sister Benvenuta da Peroscia used the verb form *fece vendere*, thus indicating that, although Clare took the initiative of selling her inheritance, she did not do so in person. Of the witnesses who spoke of Clare's selling her inheritance and distributing the gain to the poor, she is the only one to indicate this. *Clare's Legend* concurs with this witness's testimony. As can be seen in the synopsis above, the other witnesses used the active verbs *vendecte* (sold), *decte* (gave) or *distribuì* (distributed) which seem to indicate that Clare personally sold her inheritance and gave it to the poor.

Whether Clare sold her inheritance before or after her "conversion,"[84] we have to agree with Sister Benvenuta that she would have had to do so through intermediaries. If the other witnesses use verb forms that seem to indicate otherwise, it would be to underscore the fact that it was Clare's right to do what she willed with the inheritance she received from the family's wealth and that it was her desire to use it for the poor.

So as Not to Cheat the Poor

While the other witnesses simply declared that Clare had sold her inheritance and given it to the poor, Sister Cristiana revealed Clare's solidarity with those of her new social class. In order to assure her complete poverty and her following the Gospel, while Francis had given everything back to his father, Clare sold her inheritance in a way that could truly help the poor.

Clare demonstrated that she had completely broken with her family by destroying her family's patrimony on behalf of the poor. She demonstrated that she had been well educated in her knowledge of the feudal system and the military strategy of the time. Said strategy needed a family's patrimony to remain intact in order for it to dominate or to join other families in dominating a certain region. A family's patrimony was primarily in land that was strategically situated in order to form a line of defense against an attacking enemy. When we speak of Clare's inheritance, we are speaking of land and properties. In selling them, Clare did not desire to cheat the poor. To our way of thinking, it would seem only natural that Clare would sell her property to the highest bidder in order to have more money to give to the poor. In the case of Clare's inheritance, however, the highest bidders were the members of her own family. But she chose to avoid selling to her family because this would have simply perpetuated her family's social condition and the subjugation of the poor. More than likely, she divided her land into small portions, affordable to those poor who had some money (but not enough to afford land). In selling to them, she bettered their situation and then gave to the destitute whatever price she had received.[85]

THE QUESTION OF WHEN

The sale of Clare's inheritance[86] raises the question of when she would have had the opportunity to arrange and complete the transactions. If, as has been indicated by Madonna Bona, Clare did everything in secret to avoid her family's interference, she could not have done so prior to leaving her father's house. Cristiana's testimony that her family had discovered her desire to sell her inheritance and their desire to buy it would indicate that they had given up any hope that she would eventually marry. Having already lost Clare, they chose to attempt to keep her inheritance in the family's name by buying it. This all indicates that the sale of her inheritance took place after Clare's arrival at San Damiano.

The other witnesses give little if any indication as to the time of the sale. Pietro de Damiano related that Clare demonstrated the sincerity of her desire to live in virginity and poverty by selling her inheritance and giving it[87] to the poor (Proc 19:2). Sister Benvenuta joined her testimony of the sale of the inheritance to the fact that Clare declined Pope Gregory IX's desire to give her property (Proc 2:2). Sister Philippa spoke of this sale among some of the final news regarding Clare's life and miracles mentioning her love of poverty (Proc 3:31). None of these witnesses further clarifies the time of this sale.

But Sister Beatrice (Clare's little sister) does give us another bit of information regarding the sale of the inheritance. When Clare sold her own inheritance, she also sold some of Beatrice's (Proc 12:3). This is described before the mention of Clare's tonsure, which would make it likely that the sale happened while she was still at home. The problem with this testimony is not the sale of Clare's inheritance, but the sale of Beatrice's. Having reached the age of seventeen, Clare was already of legal age and had the right to dispose of her inheritance[88] as she desired. Beatrice, however, would have still been considered a minor, and, as such, had no rights over her inheritance. Clare could not have sold part of Beatrice's inheritance until her little sister had reached legal age.

Even though the *Legendae* would have us believe that Clare sold her inheritance and gave the gain to the poor prior to her having fled from home, the testimony of the *Process* questions the validity of that time line. Clare probably took a few years in order to sell all her inheritance[89] in a way that would be beneficial to the poor and the destitute. If she did indeed sell part of Beatrice's inheritance along with hers, then it was probably because in some way these two inheritances were connected and needed to be sold together.

SPLITTING UP HER FAMILY

Unlike Francis, who broke completely with his family, Clare had the joy of being followed by some of her kinfolk. Where family was a conflict of interests in Francis's following of the Gospels, family seems to have been in Clare's life a means of connecting people to the Gospel. We have already seen that her mother's Christian practice greatly influenced the child. Furthermore, her cousin Rufino most probably eased the way for her connection to Francis, whom she visited with the aid of her kinswoman Madonna Bona. These family members assisted her in her search for a Gospel way of life, and, eventually, Ortulana and other kinfolk followed her too.

Following the lead of her cousin Rufino, it seems that Clare did not so much break with her familyas she, rather, *broke up* her family. Rather than condemn Rufino for dishonoring the family, she joined him in his dishonor and invited relatives and friends to flee "the age" with her. Thus, she and Rufino divided the family into those who remained in "the age" and those who chose to live the Gospel. As we have seen, her mother, Ortulana, joined Clare at San Damiano. When she did so, she was not just following Clare's example, she was also following the example of her second daughter, Agnes, and maybe that of her third daughter, Beatrice.[90] Besides Ortulana, Agnes, and Beatrice, other relatives—Pacifica,[91] Amata, and Balvina de Messere Martino da Cocorano[92]—also followed Clare.

CATHERINE (AGNES) OF ASSISI

> For she had a sister of a tender age, a sister in flesh and purity for whom she desired conversion. Among the first prayers she ardently offered to God, she resolutely implored that just as in this age she had a coherence of soul with her sister, so now in God's service there might be among them a unity of will. Therefore she prayed insistently to the Father of mercies that the sister she had left at home might consider the world foolish and God sweet, and so exchange her proposal of a carnal marriage to unite with his love to the point that one with her she might be married to the Spouse of glory (LegCl 24.2–7).

Of all the relatives who followed Clare into religion, none is more famous than her saintly sister Catherine, better known as Agnese de Messere Favarone de Assise (Agnes). Agnes is especially of interest to us in that she, like Beatrice, was Clare's blood sister, and yet she was more than just a sister in the flesh. She was a sister in "perfection of life" and in the "union of wills in (God's) holy service."[93] Their affection became the archetype of sisterhood in the family of the Poor Ladies. They shared life experiences, such as the flight from Assisi during the period of its civil war, that bonded them closely together in ways that their little sister, Beatrice, could not share— she was so much younger.[94] For Clare and Agnes, Beatrice was probably more like a daughter than a sister.

Born in 1297, Catherine,[95] as she was known in "the age," was only four years younger than Clare and, therefore, practically grew up with her. When Clare fled from home, she found herself in the Church of San Paolo, where she prayed for Catherine's conversion. The author of *Clare's Legend* (LegCl 24.8) explains Clare's desire for her sister's conversion: "In fact, an extraordinary mutual love had come to rest upon each of them, which although for different dispositions, made this new separation so painful."[96]

Given the closed nature of a noblewoman's domain, it is only natural that relationships established within a household would turn into bonds of mutual affection that could not be easily forgotten, especially when those bonds were founded on blood ties. The story of Catherine's conversion demonstrates the power of sibling love in a medieval household. As the author of *Clare's Legend* indicates, this mutual affection does not necessarily mean similarity of disposition. According to the sources,[97] it seems that, although the two sisters were very close and shared many common desires, Catherine, unlike Clare, wanted to wed and raise a family.

Catherine's desire for marriage should come as no surprise; after all, she had been prepared for it since birth. She had been raised within a noble family, and had been expected to establish a marriage contract that would insure the growth of her family's power and prestige. Her own mother, Ortulana had demonstrated that for a noble woman, marriage did not have to mean the limitation of her freedom to travel or even give herself to works of piety and charity. Ortulana had inspired Clare to a life of virginity, while she had inspired Catherine to a married life. It was conversion from this desire that Clare sought for her sister.

Clare's flight from home probably came as no surprise to Catherine, who, given their closeness, must have known of her sister's plans. We can hypothesize that Clare might even have invited her to join her in her flight, but that, given her disposition, Catherine was not ready to make such a break with the family. One thing that we can be certain about is that she did not remain indifferent to Clare's affront to the family. Where Messere Monaldo and others reacted with anger and hatred, she must have reacted with sorrow and wonder. Given her eventual decision to flee from home, it seems that Clare's absence left Catherine with a pain and a sorrow that could only be eased by joining her sister in espousing Jesus.

Catherine's decision to abandon carnal marriage was a decision *for* Christ and Clare, a decision *against* the power and prestige of her family. Two events must have been very present in her mind and heart when she, inspired by the Holy Spirit, fled from her father's house: Clare's flight and her relatives' violent reaction. She must have responded with admiration to Clare's decision and must have felt disdain for her family's mistreatment of the young woman whose only crime was to follow Jesus. Catherine most certainly knew what she was getting herself into when she fled to the Church of San Paolo, and thus the violence of Messere Monaldo and his twelve knights should have caused her no surprise. Bearing the name of Catherine, she was prepared to undergo martyrdom in order to espouse Christ.

What we know of Catherine's conversion and ordeal is thanks to *Clare's Legend* (LegCl 24.1–28.8),[98] and *The Chronicles of the Twenty-Four Generals* (24Gen).[99] These take care to present her ordeal as a martyrdom, basing themselves on the martyrdom of the virgin and martyr St. Agnes.[100] This is not to say that her ordeal was completely invented. Given the family's reaction to Clare's affront, Agnes's action would be seen as an even greater affront. It would mean that not only did she not care for the family's dignity, she was not afraid of their violence. Theirs was a violence that had already been expressed against Clare and of which she would certainly have been aware. Hers would have been seen as a premeditated affront that could not go unanswered. She had offended the family in a way that Clare had not, in a way that, if the events written down in the sources are to be believed, led to greater violence than had been used with Clare. Although the sources mention violence against Clare, it would seem this violence was more in the form of verbal attacks and threats than the actual kicks, slaps, and other forms of physical violence used against Catherine. Catherine was attacked physically to the point that her uncle Monaldo was willing to kill her. The physical nature of Catherine's ordeal led Francis to change her name to Agnes in memory of the innocent lamb, Jesus Christ, who had suffered so much for us (24Gen 175.10–13).

Unlike Francis, who was absent from Clare's confrontation with her family, Clare was very much present at Agnes's ordeal. It only makes sense that Clare would be present. After all, it was in response to her prayers that Agnes had broken with the family. And, once again, Clare's prayers showed their efficacy in that, through divine intervention, Agnes became immovable, and the head of the family, Messere Monaldo, was punished by God (LegCl 26.5). Clare was able to convince her family that they should leave Agnes to her care, and the two sisters returned to the Church of San Paolo (LegCl 26.6). Eventually, the two sisters moved to San Damiano.

After having dealt with Agnes's conversion, the author of *Clare's Legend* claims that words will not suffice to explain the holiness of her life.

He then leaves Agnes's story in order to return to his subject, Clare. *The Chronicles* (24Gen), however, continue to give us some information about her life, death, and miracles. They refer to her having been sent by Francis as abbess to Monticello, just outside of Florence,[101] and to the letter (24Gen 175.25–177.2) that she with "great tribulation and immense sorrow"[102] (24Gen 173.31), wrote to her sister Clare. This letter, written within a year of her arrival in Monticello, expresses the depth of sibling love that joined Agnes to Clare.

AGNES'S LETTER TO HER SISTER CLARE

Due to the pathetic tenor of Agnes's letter, there are those, like Cadderi, who doubt its authenticity, yet others (Lazzeri and Omaechevarria) have no problem in accepting this as Agnes's letter to Clare. They do, however, caution that the version handed down to us in *The Chronicles* is more than likely a Latin translation of an Umbrian original, a translation that has been embellished. *The Chronicles* does not claim that the letter, as written, is the actual letter written by Agnes. Rather, it introduces the letter as follows: "Because of the physical separation from her most holy sister, Clare, afflicted beyond measure, she herself wrote a letter from Florence in the following manner" (24Gen 175.21–22).

Whether or not it is an embellishment, the pathetic tenor of Agnes's letter reveals the depth of sibling love that united the two sisters. Most likely the tenor of the Latin letter is based on the original Umbrian writing, which must have indicated the deeply felt sorrow of separation. This separation was not just a separation from her blood sister, but also from "her whole community" at San Damiano to whom the letter is addressed.

The sorrow expressed in Agnes's letter went beyond that of a younger sibling who is overly dependent on an older sibling. Agnes's sorrow was not due to her blood ties or sibling relationship with Clare, whom she called mother and *domina*, but to her physical separation from all the sisters at San Damiano—thus it transcended the familial bonds established by blood ties. She included all the sisters into the love and affection she had for Clare. Although the letter specifically mentions Clare—by name or as mother—Agnes never ceases to call upon all the sisters, whom she fears she will never see again. Included in the group of sisters is her own mother, Ortulana,[103] and her other blood sister, Beatrice, whom she never mentions by name. In Agnes's mindset, they had all been absorbed into a new family structure that recognized no blood ties or engendering roles, only unity of wills and a common vocation.

BEATRICE

As we have previously noted, Beatrice was about two years old when Clare and Agnes fled the house of their father. Because of this, she was not to develop the normal sibling relationship that Clare and Agnes shared. For her, the betrayals by Clare and Agnes were probably a family taboo that, as she grew, piqued her curiosity. What she must have heard about her sisters was likely conflicting, since from her mother she would have received a portrait of her sisters that would have been quite different from that offered by her uncle Monaldo. Given that girls had little if any contact with the men of the family, Ortulana's portrait of Clare and Agnes likely prevailed. Added to this was the fact that Madonna Bona was part of the circle of women who would have had frequent contact with the young Beatrice.

Given her testimony, it appears that Beatrice had had the opportunity to get to know her sister, Clare, firsthand. She claims that Clare had been angelic since her youth and was known by all to be a virtuous youth who gave herself to works of holiness (Proc 12:1). She briefly described the events of Clare's flight from home in a manner that indicated she had learned of these things from others. When asked how she knew what she testified about, she responded that she had seen some things and others she had heard about from Clare and others.

One thing that strikes the reader about Beatrice's testimony is her insistence that she was Clare's blood sister. Given her young age, she must have felt a need to reassure herself and others that Clare was truly tied to her by traditional consanguinity and not just a common vocation. This contrasted greatly with Agnes's having arrived at a spiritual definition of sisterhood that went beyond blood ties. We will never know if Beatrice was able to move beyond consanguinity, as her blood sisters had done. Unfortunately, we have no other testimony by Beatrice. She became the forgotten sister, left behind with family ties that do nothing to aid growth in sanctity. Her insistence on being Clare's blood sister went unheard by the author of *Clare's*

Legend who chose to ignore and forget her along with her father Favarone.

Beatrice is mentioned as one of the sisters who, later, left San Damiano in order to form or reform other monasteries. Tradition has it that she went to form the monastery of Santa Lucia in Rieti.[104] She died in 1260 and was buried with her sisters.

FINAL REFLECTIONS ON CLARE'S STRUGGLE

A series of events prepared Clare for her struggle with her family: her name, her mother's example, the penitential life she lived at home, Francis and Rufino's conversions, and Francis's exhortations. Clare encountered the reality of her *cotidianidad*, a reality which dealt with social conflict, a reality of economic difference which permitted her family to make grand expenditures (Proc 20:3) while others went hungry, a reality of women being used as barter to extend a family's prestige and power. In facing the reality of her age, she encountered the reality of the poor and crucified Lord, who invited her to follow His Gospel. These realities led her to abandon her family as a worldly institution that kept her from serving God.

In describing Clare's upbringing, the *Process* and the *Legendae* mention her youthful sanctity, her generous love for the poor, and her virtues. Aside from sanctity, concern for the poor and the development of virtues were commonly an integral part of any noblewoman's education. As a young *maiore*, Clare would have received an education meant to prepare her to be a *domina*, which is to say, a wife, mother, and a governess—charged with caring for the children and the servants of a household.

Besides the well-defined virtues of her social class, Clare also reflected the virtues which she saw in her mother and which she encountered in hagiography: devotion, prayer, and interior asceticism, accompanied by external penance and care for the poor. Messere Ranieri and Ioanni de Ventura show themselves as people of their day in giving much importance to Clare's ascetical practices. In an age where martyrdom was highly unlikely, she martyred her own flesh with fasting and mortification and eventually fled this age by breaking with her family.

We cannot see Clare's break with the family in terms of Francis's own break. Socially speaking, she had so much more to lose in opting for a life of poverty, because women suffered more from poverty than men did.

Clare, who had been educated to be a *domina*, knew this truth. Yet, enflamed and guided by the Holy Spirit, she abandoned her father's house in order to live in poverty. Unlike Francis, who was forced into a decision, Clare's break with the family was a deliberate, knowledgeable, and unpressured choice.

Clare, taking seriously her name as *light*, seems to have built upon the Gospel of John's image of the struggle between darkness and light. She recognized in her family the elements of darkness that spurred her towards the light as she fled from her father's house, leaving behind the people she loved most. She experienced the darkness of her family's outrage as it poured out on her in the form of promises, reasoning, and (finally) rage at San Paolo—a rage that she countered with her love for Christ. The split with her family cannot be seen as an indication of hatred towards them, but rather as her espousing Christ.

Clare not only broke with her family, she also eventually broke it apart by drawing Agnes and others to her way of life. Splitting her natural family was an indication of her love for them, a love that desired to move them from carnal to spiritual bonds and a union of wills, not blood. Her love for Agnes certainly could not have been exclusive. Rather, it has to be taken as an indication of how she felt for other relatives. Given this love for her family, it is amazing that she was able to break with her family, and it is no surprise that she would pray for Agnes's conversion and preach the love of God to Amata. Moreover, she did not allow the love she felt for her family to keep her from the service of God. It is in this service that she would fulfill what the voice of God had revealed to her mother about her—that she would greatly illuminate the world. Clare had no choice but to break with her family and, eventually, to split her family into those who remained in the darkness of "the age" and those who moved into the light of the Gospel.

Chapter IV:

Kinship in the Opuscula of Francis

Francis's opuscula demonstrate that he is a theologian, one who—in the *cotidiano*—ponders, lives, and proclaims his faith. As such, his theology is not limited to scholastic study but rather desires to erupt into the lives of others: "Francis's theology is intimately tied to life."[1] This life, however, is culturally bound to Europe of the High Middle Ages. His opuscula were written and read against the backdrop of this *cotidiano*. The lived experience of medieval Europe pervades his writings, as does his faith. It conditioned what he wrote and added life to it by recalling in the minds of his initial readers cultural elements with which they were quite familiar. One of these cultural elements is kinship language and imagery. Before considering the kinship elements found in Francis's opuscula, however, I begin with a quick survey of the texts.

Francis's Opuscula

Francis's opuscula are composed of works in different literary genres, including prayers, songs of praise, blessings, missives, letters, rules, exhortations, and testaments (Appendix B).[2] With the exception of the "Canticle of Brother Sun" and the "Listen, Poor Little Ones,"[3] which were written in thirteenth-century Umbrian, Francis's opuscula were primarily written in Italianized Latin.

Francis described himself as an uneducated and simple person (*ignorans et idiota*; Cf. EpOrd 39; Test 19) and probably turned to a number of friar secretaries to assist him in his writing.[4] We have seen that, like many children of well-to-do parents in an urban setting, Francis received some education, including a rudimentary knowledge of Latin. Judging by the many run-on "phrases, clauses and thoughts as well as poor grammatical construction"[5] in his writings, however, he probably never took the time to refine this knowledge of Latin. Since French was the primary business and cultural language of the era, the young Francis was probably content to learn only enough Latin to get by, preferring to master French instead.

Francis's Use of the Sacred Scriptures

Francis gave a great deal of importance to his own writings, demanding that they be read, learned, copied, and handed on to others.[6] So great was his conviction that God himself had inspired his writing that he did not want his writings to be changed by commentary, omission, or addition (Test 35–39). Rather than this being a sign of Francis's arrogance, it was instead a manifestation of his profound trust in God's guidance and providence. Francis himself testified that it was God who told him what he should do (Test 14).[7] This is not to be taken as a veiled reference to the voice coming from the Cross of San Damiano, for nowhere in his writings does Francis make reference to overtly "mystical" visions, voices, or revelations. Rather, Francis's testimony probably meant that he found God's will in the Sacred Scriptures, especially in the Gospels. This trust in finding the voice of God in the Scriptures led him to repeatedly turn to them in his own writings.

"One of the chief characteristics of medieval piety was that it was deeply biblical."[8] This is certainly true of Francis who quotes the Scriptures, explicitly or by reference, some 434 times (the New Testament 266 times and the Old Testament 168 times) in his opuscula. The single book that he quoted most often was the Psalms (120 times), which, given his recitation of the Roman Office, should come as no surprise. As a group, he most often quoted the Gospels (Mt, 71 times; Lk, 57; Jn, 38; and Mk, 14; for a total of 180 times).[9]

His use of the Scriptures is quite impressive, just in numbers alone. But even more impressive is how these texts impregnated Francis's writings. Matura would say that "Francis's theological vision expressed in his opuscula has Johannine traits; his anthropology is Pauline and his ethics are owed above all to the Synoptic Gospels."[10] This varied use of the Sacred Scriptures[11] in his writings is probably due to Francis's wanting to lend his own words a certain authority that comes from the conviction that the word of God is "spirit and life" (Jn 6:64; RnB 22.39). He was doing as Jesus had done before him, handing on to others what he had received, the "word" which God had given him (Jn 17:8; RnB 22.42). Such was his love for the word of God that he asked priests, friars, and all Christians to reverently respect God's written word. This was to be done not only by keeping the Scriptures in appropriate places but also by collecting and keeping anything that contained God's word in appropriate places as well. For Francis, it seems, one of the best places to keep the word of God was interspersed in his own writings.

KINSHIP IN THE SACRED SCRIPTURES USED BY FRANCIS

A number of themes arise from or can be found in the Scripture texts that Francis used or alluded to in his writings. For our purposes, we need to consider if kinship is one of these. Kinship is certainly not the most important theme in the biblical texts that Francis used in his writings, but kinship language is to be found in several of them. Kinship terminology, such as *father* and *son*, is nearly unavoidable in quoting the Scriptures, especially the New Testament, which speaks of the Sonship of Jesus to the Father. Francis was so fond of this kinship bond between the Father and Jesus that he introduced it into the Hebrew Scripture that he used for his "Office of the Lord's Passion."[12] There he takes the title Lord in the psalms and adds to it texts from the Gospels. For example, in Psalm 14:1, Francis combines Is 12:1 and Mt 11:25 to read, "I salute (praise) you Lord, Most Holy Father, King of heaven and earth, for you have consoled me."

Besides the use of kinship terminology to describe the relationship between the Father and the Son, Francis also used the Scriptures to speak of either the believers' or the friars' kinship relationship with the various persons of the Trinity. He described the Father as being a paterfamilias whose family is both in heaven and on earth and whose first-born Son, Jesus Christ, is both the savior and a model for all those who believe.[13] This family is comprised not only of believers (1EpFid 1.7–14)[14] and spiritual beings (2EpFid 4),[15] but also of all creatures, whom Francis calls brothers and sisters (CSol).[16] In addition, Francis turned to the Sacred Scriptures to describe what the friars' relationship with the family of origin should be and what their relationships should be in the religious family called the Order of Friars Minor (RnB 1.4–5; 9.11; 11.3; 22.18, 33–37).

RELATIONSHIP WITH THE FAMILY OF ORIGIN

Like many other saints before and after him, Francis had to break with his family in order to live the Gospel of Jesus Christ. He experienced firsthand the pressures that a human family can place on one who is trying to live according to the Spirit of the Lord. He also experienced the struggle of those who, like Clare and Agnes of Assisi, were confronted violently by their family because of the Gospel. Consequently, he begins the "Non-Bulled Rule" (RnB) with a reminder to those who wish to follow the teaching and footsteps of the Lord Jesus Christ that they must do so in obedience, in chastity, and without anything of their own (*sine proprio*). Besides having to sell all their possessions and give the proceeds to the poor, the friars were to stop being possessions themselves by breaking with their families. In medieval Europe, offspring, no matter their age, were considered the possessions of their families, especially of the father as head of the family.

FAMILY PRESSURE AGAINST THE MENDICANT ORDERS

While noble and well-to-do families even encouraged their children to join monasteries or the clergy, most did not want their children leaving the household in order to join the new mendicant or begging orders of the time. Having a relative in a prestigious and wealthy monastery was considered, by most, an advantage for the family. On the other hand, to have a relative join a mendicant order, such as the Friars Minor, was to lose a family asset. It seems that most members of the new mendicant orders cut themselves off completely from their families.[17] It is no wonder that many families used considerable emotional pressure to keep their children from joining this new form of religious life. Some families even resorted to physical violence. Others, like the father of Friar Salimbene, made recourse to civil and ecclesiastical authorities, though without success.[18]

While the hagiographies of monastic saints sometimes went to some lengths to demonstrate a saint's sanctity from the very onset of childhood, a new topos was created in the hagiographies of the mendicant saints. These usually followed the passions of the early martyrs, but with a new element: the persecutors were no longer faithless pagans, but nominal Christian parents. Nor should we think that it was only the father or mother who persecuted the offspring who desired a religious life. Many times the future saint's siblings and other kinfolk joined in trying to keep the person from conversion.[19]

It was in this *cotidianidad* that Francis wrote his Rule, and it should come as no surprise that he insisted on the break with the family. He defends this break as Christian by turning to the synoptic Gospels and quoting directly from them Jesus' injunction: "If one comes to me and does not hate his father and mother, his wife and children and brothers and sisters and even his own life, that one cannot be my disciple" (Lk 14:26). To this statement, Francis adds his own reworked version of Mt 19:29; Mk 10:29; and Lk 18:29: "Everyone who has left father or mother, brothers or sisters, wife or children, houses or lands because of me, shall receive a hundredfold and shall possess eternal life" (RnB 1.5).[20] It is worth comparing this version with those of the synoptic Gospels that place the parents in the middle of the list of those to be left behind. Francis's list seems to reflect his own experience; the first three family members named are exactly those Francis abandoned.

It seems Francis encouraged the friars to follow his own example. He desired that the friars model their relationship with their families on Jesus' pronouncement on radical discipleship to the rich young man in the Gospel who, when invited, walked away and did not leave everything in order to follow Jesus. It might be that Francis could identify his former self with the rich young man. He could understand that, for him, leaving his riches would have meant a break with those who had given him his riches and who would inherit it from him:[21] his family.

Yet the identification of Francis with the rich young man breaks down in that Francis was willing to give up everything in order to follow Jesus. Refusing his own family, Jesus had proclaimed a new family, the family of those who do His Father's will (Mt 12:46–50). Francis invited his friars to join that family. It would seem that if Salimbene's Chronicles (*Cronaca*) are any indication of the attitude and practice of the thirteenth-century friars, then the friars adhered to Francis's teaching on abandoning the family of origin. In fact, Salimbene's description of his response to his father begins by quoting the synoptic Gospel passages used already by Francis in the "Non-Bulled Rule." Salimbene then adds a reminder of Jesus' pronouncement that he had come to divide families and set children against their parents (Mt 10:35–36; Lk 12:53).[22]

THE FAMILY AS AN OBSTACLE TO GOD'S WORD

Besides these two verses, the "Non-Bulled Rule" also contains another passage of Jesus' injunctions regarding leaving the family behind.[23] Francis ends his exposition on the "Parable of the Sower and the Seed" (RnB 22.11–18)[24] with Jesus' response to the disciple who wanted to go home and bury his father. Having explained the different ways in which one can respond to the word of God, he concludes by saying that the friars should do as the Lord says and "let the dead bury their dead" (Mt 8:22). Francis understood and desired that his friars recognize that trying to be the good soil, on which the word of God fell (Lk 8:11), meant a break with one's past. This break was with anything, even family, that could take the word from their hearts (RnB 22.13) and cause them to falter and fail (RnB 22.15), or could choke the word and cause them to remain without fruit (RnB 22.16).

For Francis, this trying to be good soil had manifested itself in his radical break with his family. His was a break that was probably never repaired, a wound that probably never healed. For, though Francis loved his family and was loved by them, he mistrusted this love, seeing it as counterproductive to Gospel life. His choice of ending his exposition of the "Parable of the Sower and the Seed" might also indicate Francis's having refused to go to his own father's funeral. Francis's stay at the Portiuncola would certainly have meant that eventually he would have been faced with what to do about his aging and dying parents, although this is never mentioned in the Franciscan sources. When you break with the family for the sake of Jesus, reconciliation with them is often considered to be a turning back after you have placed your hand on the plow (Lk 9:62).

Most of the early friars probably did break with their families[25] as we see in Salimbene's break with his father. We cannot but help think that Rufino met a reaction from the Offreduccio household similar to the one his cousins Clare and Catherine (Agnes) received. The wealthy noble, Bernard of Quintavalle, certainly must have had to deal with his family's anger at not leaving them his wealth, but (to their minds) squandering it on the poor.[26] In contrast, Francis rejected the vocation of someone from the Marca Anconitana for having given all his wealth to his kinfolk.[27] *Three Companions* (3Soc 11) describes the type of life the early friars led and the love that bound them. The authors point out that the friars did not want to be sta-tioned anywhere near their hometown so as to avoid running into their kin-folk and fraternizing with them.[28] This may have been to avoid further repercussions for their having abandoned their families of origin, as well as to avoid being tempted to return to the household of their fathers. In either case, the author of the *Anonymous of Perugia* certainly insisted on the friars leaving their families as a way of recalling that Jesus had come to divide fam-ilies (Mt 10:34–35).[29]

Francis and the early friars considered the family of origin to be an obstacle to living the Gospel. As such, it should be refuted. The Gospel texts dealing with the break with one's family are nowhere to be found in the "Bulled Rule" (RB), however. In their work on the "Non-Bulled Rule," Ac-crocca and Ciceri take notice of the omission—from the subsequent "Bulled Rule"—of the evangelical texts in question, and they exclaim that this is not an indication that these texts no longer had any weight in the community of friars.[30] Although many of the early friars had broken with their families, most of the friars in the succeeding generations did not see this break as being an absolute requirement for religious life.[31]

Kinship with God: Trinity and Unity

If radically breaking with one's family was not an absolute necessity for living the Gospel, establishing kinship ties with God was. Francis de-scribed these ties as being with each individual person of the Trinity. Francis's use of trinitarian formulas was both traditional and innovative. He used the formula of *Pater(ris) et Filius(i) et Spiritus Sanctus(i)*[32] or made reference to the *Gloria Patri et Filio et Spiritui Sancto*[33] some twenty-one times in his writings. He commingled the three persons of the Trinity in a variety of ways and relationships among themselves as well as with creation and the faithful.

The whole of the Trinity is the focus of Francis's spiritual adventure. His is not a scholastic endeavor, but rather an experiential one.[34] In his opus-cula we find that he referred to God in the plan of salvation: creation, re-demption, and the eschaton.[35] This is his primary experience of God. But besides the leitmotif of the Trinity as Creator, Redeemer, Consoler, and Sav-ior, Francis also describes the Trinity sociologically in terms of kinship roles: Father, Brother, Son, and Spouse.

In his writings, Francis used traditional mystical themes, such as divine filiation, being espoused to Christ, and the birth of Christ in the soul.[36] Worth noting about these themes is that Francis brought them together in a text addressed not to the Damianites or the Friars but to all Christians. In an age of various religious and chivalrous movements that strove to keep the Gospel and the Church in the hands of an elite caste system,[37] Francis, in his redactions of the Letter to the Faithful (1EpFid, 2EpFid), democratized and secularized mysticism.[38] In what Paolazzi calls the "Hymn of 'the children of the heavenly Father, whose works they do,'",[39] Francis encouraged all the faithful to enter a kinship relationship with the Triune God. The two versions are practically the same. They are worth considering as the main source of Francis's vision of the faithful soul's kinship to God.[40]

1EpFid

1.5. Oh how happy and blessed are the men and women who do these things and persevere in them,
6. for the spirit of the Lord shall rest upon them and make its habitation and mansion among them

7. and they are children of the celestial father whose work they do

and they are spouses, brothers (sisters) and mothers of our Lord Jesus Christ.
8. We are spouses, when the Holy Spirit unites the faithful soul to our Lord Jesus Christ.

9. We are his brothers (sisters), when we do the will of the father who is in heaven.

2EpFid

48. And the spirit of the Lord shall rest upon them and make its habitation and mansion in all these men and women, who do such things and persevere in them till the end.

49. And they will be children of the celestial Father, whose work they do

50. And they are spouses, brothers (sisters) and mothers of our Lord Jesus Christ.
51. We are spouses, when the Holy Spirit unites the faithful soul to our Lord Jesus Christ.

52. We are his brothers (sisters), when we do the will of his father who is in heaven.

10. Mothers, when we carry him in our heart and body through divine love and pure and sincere conscience; we birth him through holy works which should be light and example for others.

53. Mothers, when we carry him in our heart and body through divine love and pure and sincere conscience; we birth him through holy works which should be light and example for others.

11. Oh how glorious, holy and magnificent it is to have a Father in heaven!
12. Oh how holy, consoling, beautiful, and admirable it is to have such a Spouse.
13. Oh how holy, and how delightful, pleasing, humble, peaceful, sweet, loving, and above all desirable it is to have such a Brother and such a Son: Our Lord Jesus Christ,
14. who laid down his life for his sheep and prayed to the Father . . . .

54. Oh how glorious, holy and magnificent it is to have a Father in heaven! Oh how holy, consoling, beautiful, and admirable it is to have a Spouse.
55. Oh how holy, and how delightful, pleasing, humble, peaceful, sweet, loving, and above all desirable it is to have such a Brother and Son who laid down his life for his sheep and prayed to the Father for us . . . .

MEN AND WOMEN

The first thing that strikes the contemporary reader of this text is Francis's use of gender-inclusive language. He makes it a point to explicitly mention both men and women as the recipients of God's grace.[41] This is especially important because he will be using the kinship terminology of *sponsi, fratres, et matres* (spouses, brothers, and mothers) that is usually gender-specific. In the case of *sponsi*, given that the bridegroom, Jesus, is male, one would expect this term to be applied only to brides (*sponsae*). Francis, however, cleverly leaves *sponsi* in the masculine plural. As for *fratres*, despite our contemporary sensibilities, this word was normally understood to mean both brothers and sisters, unless otherwise specified by its context. Finally, the word *matres* always denotes women, because of male/female biological functions for procreation.

This invitation to cross gender roles reveals a Francis who had integrated his anima and animus. In his writings and in his life, he had no problem using feminine roles or symbols either for himself or for other males.[42] Francis was not alone in the use of role reversals that may seem like gender confusion to our contemporary sensibilities. One has only to peruse the writers of the Middle Ages to realize that it was a common practice in both male and female writers, although with different points of view in men and women. Men saw the male/female dichotomy as part of the divine/human, cleric/lay, and spirit/flesh dichotomy.[43] While women seem to have accepted the male/female dichotomies defined by men, they do not seem to have completely internalized them. To the medieval mind, the male gender came to symbolically represent God, authority, and intelligence, while the female gender came to represent humanity, submission, and emotion.[44]

Francis certainly was influenced by the male/female and divine/human dichotomy and symbolism in which God is male while the human soul is female. Important here is the place of the *cotidiano* in Francis's spirituality, for he was a visual and practical man.[45] He saw and experienced all of humanity's (male and female) concrete need for redemption in his own life and the daily lives of the people he met. In his writings, the feminine nature of humanity is not a negative or passive reality; rather it is considered active and fruitful availability to God's redemptive grace.[46] Humanity's masculine nature becomes a creative force that struggles and battles to go to God.[47] In other words, the whole human person actively seeks God—knowing full well that ultimately it is God who will come to the receptive soul. Francis's symbolic patterns reflected a need to redeem the male element of humanity through the female, and vice versa. In this, he is no different than twelfth-century religious leaders who desired to temper their paternal authority with maternal references and symbols.[48] The great difference that Francis offers is moving this role reversal outside the monastery and into the world. He takes it out of the hands of bishops and abbots and places it in the hands of everyone, male and female.

Francis's experience of the Triune God can be had by anyone. God does not care about a person's social or religious status, nor does God care about a person's gender. Divine filiation, espousal, fraternity, and maternity can all be experienced by all who "love the Lord . . . love their neighbor . . . hate their bodies' vices and sins, receive the Body and Blood of our Lord Jesus Christ, and produce fruits of penance" (IEpFid I.1–4).[49]

CHILDREN OF THE CELESTIAL FATHER

The first kinship relationship found in the Hymn within the Letter to the Faithful is that of being children of the heavenly Father. The Father is at the heart of Francis's trinitarian experience. He considers the first person of the Trinity to be the origin of all things *ad intra* and *ad extra* the Trinity. The Father is the source of every will for creation, which is to say that the "creative will"[50] belongs to the Father who, through the Son and the Spirit, has created all things (RnB 23.1). The importance of the Father can be seen in Francis's abundant use of the term; after the term *frater*,[51] the term *pater*[52] is the most commonly found kinship term in his writings. It is often on the lips of Jesus (1EpFid 1.14),[53] whose prayers for us are quoted repeatedly in Francis's opuscula. Other times, it flows from Francis in the many prayers and expressions of praise and supplication (EpOrd 38)[54] that he spontaneously directs to God. Many of the other times that he uses the term *Father* it was to denote God's paternity of his Son (1EpFid 1.14)[55] or of the faithful (1EpFid 1.7).[56]

FRANCIS'S DESCRIPTION OF THE FATHER

In order to discover what Francis thought of the Father, we have only to peruse his opuscula to discover the abundance of titles and adjectives that he ascribes to Him. Of all his writings, however, none is more privileged in this regard than his "Explanation of the 'Our Father'" (ExPat). It is in this exposition or commentary that he, with his own and with borrowed words,[57] describes the Father's role and the filial response of the faithful.

He begins by ascribing to the Father all of the roles of the Trinity in the plan of salvation: "Oh most holy Father of ours: our creator, redeemer, consoler and savior" (ExPat 1).[58] This formula is curious because it breaks with Francis's trinitarian motifs in that, rather than keeping the traditional trinitarian concept of God as creator, redeemer, and consoler, Francis felt a need to add the fourth element of savior. At first glance, since savior and redeemer are normally considered to be synonymous, it seems that he is being redundant. But Francis's use of these words indicates that redemption and salvation are two distinct moments in God's plan for humanity.[59] The one, redemption, occurred in Christ's paschal mystery, while the other, salvation, is destined to occur with his coming in glory to judge the living and the dead (OffPass 6.15–19; RnB 23.8).

Our interest here is not to consider Francis's theology of the Father's role in the plan of salvation but rather to consider his description of the Father. This first passage adds adjectives to the word Father, which recur often in Francis's opuscula: *sanctissime* and *noster*. For Francis, the Father is not just holy (*sanctus*),[60] but the Most Holy (*sanctissimus*).[61] It is because of this that He is in heaven[62] living in inaccessible light (Adm I.5). The Father is *lux* and, as such, is to be found in His heavenly household that is made up of "angels and saints" whom He enlightens. He is *amor* and, thus, he enflames his household to love. The Father is the Most High,[63] who can only be revealed by and discovered in His Son (Adm I). This is how Francis discovered the Father and found that the Father is "the highest good, the eternal, from whom all good comes, without whom there is nothing good" (ExPat 2).[64]

ONE IS YOUR FATHER, WHO IS IN HEAVEN

Thanks to the Son who redeems us (ExPat 6–7), we can call the Father "our" (*noster*). Nowhere in His writings does Francis dare to use the term *meus* (mine) in referring to the Father (ExPat I). Only Jesus can singularly call the Father *meus*;[65] all others call the Father *noster* (RnB 22.34) because response to the Father must be a joint one. As children of a royal Father, the faithful must know, serve, and love their paterfamilias (ExPat 3–5).[66] They must also know how to be brothers and sisters to one another and love their neighbors (ExPat 5, 8).

It would seem that Francis accepted the role assigned by his society to children vis-à-vis their parents. A child had to come to the recognition of his father as distinct from his mother. Already in classical Latin, the words *pater* and *mater* carried with them the truth that, while a mother was known from birth, a father had to be accepted. Thus, while a mother was readily recognized by her child, she had to bring the child to recognize and accept his/her father.

Once the child had recognized the father, he or she had to learn to allow the father to govern his/her life to the point of serving him as one would a Lord. The child was to love the father over and above the mother, for, while she had given life to the child, the father was the one who could give her or him the teaching and correction needed for life. Francis himself had experienced this through his own parents.[67] Although there had probably been a special bond with his mother, he knew that it was his father who, ultimately, had taught him how to live and work. If this was true of the human father, how much more was it true of the Father who is *omnipotens, summe Deus, rex,* and *Domine* (omnipotent, most high God, King, and Lord).[68]

Surely Francis's own filial love for God the Father had its seeds in the love, awe, and admiration that he once had for Pietro di Bernardone. Indubitably, he had experienced what it meant to turn to his father for protection and safety in war-torn Assisi, and on the long and arduous trips to the merchant fairs in the south of France. Despite the final break with his father, Francis could not but turn to the childhood and adolescent experience of his father to find the adjectives that he used in his rejoicing over being a son of the only Father. In his "Praises of God Most High" (LDei), he calls the Father strong and great. In addition, when speaking of the whole Trinity, he uses the paternal ascriptions of protector and defender in his list of God's attributes. In his "Exhortation to the Praise of God" (ExhLD), he invites all of God's children to praise Him, because, like a father, God is to be feared and given honor.

Jesus Prays to His Father for Us (Jn 17:6–26)

The Hymn in his Letter to the Faithful leads into Jesus' prayer to the Father on behalf of the faithful (1EpFid 1.14–19; 2EpFid 57–60). Along with Jesus' prayer in "Non-Bulled Rule" (RnB 22.41–55), it demonstrates Francis's extraordinary freedom in quoting the Sacred Scriptures.[69] In the "Non-Bulled Rule," it is part of a section of Gospel quotations that invites the friars to be on their guard against Satan who uses every form of malice and subtlety (RnB 22.19–26), even one's own family (RnB 22.18), to cause one to turn one's mind and heart away from the Lord. He adds that the friars are to (1) make a home and dwelling place for the Trinity; (2) have recourse to the Good Shepherd who reveals to us that there is only one Father and we are all brothers; and (3) hold on to Jesus' words, life, teaching, and Gospel because he humbled himself for us and prayed to His Father for us (RnB 22.27–31, 32–40, 41–54).

In Jn 17, Jesus prayed for the glorification of the Father and for His own glorification as well. This glorification process engulfs all of humanity, because Jesus' prayer is that His followers have a share in His Sonship. In Francis's "Non-Bulled Rule," Jesus prayed that the Friars would be (1) protected in the name of the Father, (2) infused with joy, (3) preserved from evil while in a world that hates them, (4) sanctified in the Father's truth, which is His word, (5) completely one in testimony to the world of Jesus' having been sent by the Father, (6) loved like the Son, and (7) present where the Son is, so as to see the Father's glory.

In the versions in both redactions of the Letter to the Faithful, Jesus prayed for all Christians, that they would be (1) protected in the name of the Father, (2) sanctified, (3) holy in being one as the Son and the Father are one, and (4) present where the Son is, so as to see the Father's glory.

In comparing both versions, one discovers that there is an overall concern that the friars and all Christians realize that Jesus desires that they share in his divine filiation to the Father. In all three cases of his use of John 17:6–26, Francis has joined this prayer of Jesus to the theme of kinship with the Triune God—and, in the "Non-Bulled Rule" version, specifically to the fraternal kinship of the friars.

The version of this prayer in the "Non-Bulled Rule" is much more complete than that contained in the redactions of the Letter to the Faithful. Its emphasis is more centered on the struggle between the world and the faithful. In this text, Francis is writing to the Friars, who, according to the mindset of the time, had left the world (*mundus*). In the Letter to the Faithful, however, he is writing to all Christians, most of whom were, by the standards of their day, still in the world. It is interesting to note that, in both cases, Francis insists that Jesus is praying not just for the present audience but also for those who would come to believe because of them. Thus, Francis expects that all Christians, regardless of their being in or out of the world, will bring others to the faith because they are God's children.

Daughters and Servants of God

In both versions of the Hymn in his Letter to the Faithful, Francis describes the faithful as being God's children. Although he alludes to the friars being God's children, he never explicitly claims such a title for them. He does do this for Clare and her sisters, however, by claiming for them a title that he gives the Virgin Mary in the antiphon of the "Office of the

Lord's Passion." In the "Form of Life" (FormViv) that he gave to Clare and her sisters, Francis describes them as having made themselves "daughters and handmaidens of the most high King the celestial Father" (FormViv I).[70] His choice of *handmaidens* (*ancillas*) alongside of *daughters* (*filias*) might come as a surprise to the contemporary reader. But in the Middle Ages, the servant was on a par with the underage members of the blood family and very much a part of the family unit. Thus, in Francis's "Form of Life," the Father is not simply a father in the generative role contemporary society gives the male parent in a nuclear family, but is the paterfamilias in the sense of one who governs a huge household where offspring and servants are considered his children and responsibility.

Nowhere in Francis's opuscula[71] is this paternal love made more manifest than in the person of the Blessed Mother. She is the model, par excellence, for divine kinship, to which Francis will turn in order to explain the believer's kinship with God. Although she is honored by Francis above all for being the mother of the Son, he does not ignore her being daughter and handmaiden of the most high King, the celestial Father.[72] This is the same title he gives to Clare and her sisters.

CALL NO ONE FATHER

Jesus' kinship role with humanity was to do the will of the Father in order to redeem it and, at the same time, reveal to people that they have no other Father than the most high King in Heaven. Francis was unwilling to have God share this paternal role with anyone, not even with Francis. He took seriously Jesus' injunction to call no one on earth father (Mt 23:9; RnB 22.34)—so seriously, in fact, that when Brother Pacifico addressed Francis, he referred to him as mother (2Cel 137.3, 8).

Why would the friars refer to Francis by the title mother? The role of mother is one that Francis ascribes to himself. He uses it for himself in telling the pope that he has given birth to many sons for God (2Cel 16–17). It is also one that Francis assigns to the friars in the hermitages who are called upon to protect their children from distractions. Given this, we can imagine that when people called Francis "'father," as was the custom in addressing a holy man, he insisted that God was the only Father—which left him with the title *mother*.

Nowhere in his writings does Francis ever use the term *father* to refer to anyone other than God, not even the Lord Pope.[73] With the exception of the *Sacrum commercium*, all the Franciscan sources go against Francis's desire to be called mother and his repetition of Jesus' injunction to call no earthly person father. They refer to him by the title *father*, which was the one traditionally given to a patristic writer, pope or bishop, founder of an order, abbot, one's personal confessor, or an elderly and venerable monk.[74] Priests were traditionally called *don* or *lord*. Not only do the Franciscan sources call Francis father; they also add adjectives (*holy, most holy, good,* and so on) of which he would certainly not have approved.[75] Francis reserved these titles for God and God alone.

Despite the authors having gone against Francis's wishes in calling him "father," they seem to have at least respected his desire that *he* call no one but God father. The *Legendae* have Francis, after his conversion, use the title or role of *father* for a human person only in eight instances. Most of these refer to father as a role and not as a title. For example, he supposedly asked the friars to remind a bishop that he is "father and lord of souls" (*pater et dominus animarum*) before asking his permission to set up house in his territory.[76] Judging from the maternal–fraternal imagery in Francis's writings, his referring to himself as a woman and mother,[77] and the *Assisi Compilation* (CompAs) reminder that he desired to reserve the title *father* to God alone,[78] seven of these eight occurrences are probably literary inventions of the authors.

The one occurrence in which Francis is said to have used the title father for a human being that just might have actually happened is his calling a poor man father. Just after his conversion, while his father continued to persecute him, Francis took a poor man and called him father. This event is referred to only in three *Legendae*: in *Second Celano* (2Cel 12.1–3), Francis gives a poor man the role of father prior to his final break with his family; in *Anonymous of Perugia* (AnPer 9,2–3) the event occurs after Francis's conversion, but the role or title of father is never mentioned; only *Three Companions* (3Soc 23.1–5) has this event occur just after Francis's conversion and has Francis use the title *father* in reference to the poor man he asks to bless him.

If this event did occur as reported in *Three Companions*, it must have happened before Francis became familiar with Jesus' injunction against calling anyone father. It seems that once Francis did come to know Jesus' injunction, he took it to heart and invited the friars to do the same (CompAs 100.4; RnB 22.34). Judging by the sources, with the exception of Friar Pacifico (2Cel 137.3, 8),[79] the friars and the sisters did not consider Francis's invitation worth taking, at least as regards the title they gave him. In his *Legendae*, they call him "father," but during his lifetime, they must have referred to him as "brother."

SPOUSES, BROTHERS, SISTERS, AND MOTHERS OF OUR LORD JESUS CHRIST

Francis joins the role of brother to that of mother and spouse of the Lord. A renewed appreciation for the humanity of Jesus worked its way into the spirituality of the High Middle Ages moving both men and women to develop a spirituality of mystical union with God. During the previous centuries, mystical union took on the spousal imagery of the Church as bride of Christ in Christian Scripture. Bernard of Clairvaux had invited Christians to share in the Passion of Christ by letting his suffering evoke compassion in them as they prayed. So, for many believers, prayer became a way of emotionally connecting with the Suffering Servant whom they claimed as Spouse and Lord.

Although an accent on the Passion of Jesus is found in Francis's writings, he really stresses the Incarnation. By means of the Incarnation, the Son of God has entered a kinship relationship with the faithful, whose brother he became. This stress leads Francis to formulate his own understanding of mystical union with Christ. His is a union that moves beyond that of spousal imagery, to the believer being Christ's *frater* and *mater* as well. These two additional unions are important because they move the believer from the realm of prayer to that of ministry.

The idea of being brother and mother of the Lord Jesus is one Francis took from the synoptic Gospels (Mt 12:49–50; Mk 3:34–35; and Lk 8:21). The passage in which Jesus refuses to see his mother, brothers, and sisters who have come looking for him gives Francis the words he needs to establish his concept of a Christian's divine kinship. When we compare the three versions of the event, it is abundantly clear that Francis must have consciously chosen to use Matthew's version. Mark's and Luke's versions claim that those who do God's will are Jesus' brothers (and sisters) and mothers, while Mathew's version adds that this God is Jesus' Father. Francis deliberately chose to use Matthew's version because of God's paternal role in it. Thus, besides being Jesus' brother and mother, the faithful person is first of all the Father's child.

Francis claims that the faithful take on (*sunt*, they are) the roles of spouses, brothers, and mothers. At the same time, in spelling out how this is done, he stresses his (*sumus*, we are) being involved in these roles as well. He has no desire to invite the faithful to experience something that he does not experience himself. He is not writing about a theological truth; he is expounding on the *cotidianidad* of lived experience. Francis is inviting the faithful to experience for themselves his kinship relationship with Jesus, a relationship that involves "the tenderness of a spouse, the strength of a brother, the secret love and fecundity of a mother."[80] These relationships all happen in and through the Holy Spirit.

THE HOLY SPIRIT, THE FAITHFUL SOUL, AND JESUS

In Francis's experience, it is the Holy Spirit's coming to rest on the faithful that allows for any kind of kinship with God. The Spirit joins or weds (*coniungitur*) the faithful to Jesus Christ. In order to understand how and why mystical union can be likened to a spousal relationship, medieval authors turned to the Song of Songs. When speaking of the soul's union with God, the Song of Songs was undoubtedly the most discussed book of the Old Testament during that time period.[81] It is worth noting that, despite the fact that Francis used the symbol, spouses of Christ, he never once quoted the Song of Songs in his writings.[82]

Nevertheless, the love-sickness, languor, and even anguish of the bride-to-be in the canticle[83] is important for understanding Francis's use of the image. The Song of Songs reflected for both the female and the male mystics of the Middle Ages an ultimate source of love imagery to express their love and yearning for God.[84] In it, the bride-to-be anxiously awaits the return of her fiancé. She awaits his erotic embraces and the kisses of his mouth. For Christians, this book from the Hebrew Scriptures became an expression of the relationship of the Church to Christ—and the relationship of the individual soul to Christ.

Traditionally, the image of spouses of Christ had become almost exclusively bound to the Virgin Mary and to consecrated (female) virgins. If the bridegroom is the masculine Jesus, then His spouse naturally is feminine. Francis, however, did not use the term sponsae (brides) but sponsi (grooms) in the Hymn in his Letter to the Faithful despite the fact that it was meant as a feminine symbol. In attributing a masculine noun to a feminine role, Francis combined both the masculine and the feminine nature of the person and generalized the term to include both male and female believers. He broke open a role that had been traditionally applied to consecrated women; he invited all Christians to enter.

In the Hymn, the soul is espoused to Christ as part of its kinship with the Trinity. Francis did not feel a need to limit the soul's spousal relationship to Christ, however. This spousal relationship is the work of the Holy Spirit, who, according to Francis, is the spouse of the Virgin Mary and the spouse of Clare and her sisters (OffPass Ant. 2; FormViv I). We will consider this intervention of the Holy Spirit further on. For now it is enough to note that Francis's followers took up this spousal imagery and applied it to both Christ and the Holy Spirit. Bonaventure, the mystical theologian, regarded the Holy Spirit as the spouse of the soul in the third book of his *Sentence Commentary*.[85] Angela of Foligno also related that she heard the Holy Spirit call her his "daughter and sweet bride." Yet it is difficult to discern in most of her spousal mysticism whether she considered herself the spouse of Christ or of the Holy Spirit.

BETROTHAL TO THE HOLY SPIRIT

In the Hymn in his Letter to the Faithful, Francis explains that becoming spouses of Christ is only possible through the Holy Spirit, whose work it is to "unite/wed the faithful soul to our Lord Jesus Christ."[86] He says nothing more about the matter in either redaction. In order to understand what he means, we must turn to those who were traditionally associated with this kinship role: consecrated virgins.

As previously noted, Francis invited Clare and her sisters to a filial relationship with God. In the "Form of Life" given to Clare and her sisters (FormViv I), he tied the filial role to that of spouse, saying, "You have betrothed yourselves to (*vos desponsastis*) the Holy Spirit." Francis explicitly placed the Damianites into a kinship relationship with God, in terms of the Father and the Holy Spirit. A relationship with the Son is not explicitly mentioned, but it is implied. Francis claimed that the women "made themselves" the Father's daughters and servants. They "betrothed" themselves to the Holy Spirit. The verbs, *fecistis* (you have made yourselves) and *desponsastis* (you have betrothed yourselves) are both active verbs. Francis did not see the Damianites as the passive recipients of God's intervention. These were women who took the initiative and, as such, were examples to all the faithful who are called to be spouses (brides and grooms) of Christ in the Spirit.

Francis calls Mary the "spouse of the Holy Spirit" (*sponsa Spiritus Sancti*) and claims that the Damianites had betrothed the Holy Spirit; he also encourages the faithful to be spouses of Christ. He probably held the traditional view that Christ is the spouse of the Church and the faithful soul. Nonetheless, it is interesting to note that, for Mary and the Sisters, he felt a need to stress a spousal relationship with the Holy Spirit. But there is a notable difference in this spousal relationship, for while Mary is already the bride of the Holy Spirit, the Damianites are merely betrothed (fiancées). They have been promised to the Holy Spirit, and, as was the custom of the time, engagement came with the firm promise of marriage. Their betrothal to the Spirit was unusual because, as Francis indicates, it was they and not their relatives who had established this contractual relationship. Though this personal consent was something for which the Church strove and which it taught, it was not a socially accepted reality. The Damianites then truly follow the example of Mary who, at least in Luke's account of the Annunciation, gave personal consent to what Francis saw as her marriage to the Holy Spirit.

The Franciscan scholar, Thadée Matura, grapples with why Francis might have chosen the title "Spouse of the Holy Spirit" for Mary.[87] He believes that it had to do with Luke's account of the Annunciation, where it is explained that Mary will conceive a Son thanks to the Holy Spirit overshadowing her (Lk 1:35).[88] In my opinion, Matura is only partially correct. He does not consider that, to Francis, this interpretation would have made absolute sense considering the marriage patterns of his day, especially among the nobility. Francis would have seen the Father as the Paterfamilias who chose a bride for a member of His household so that His household could be enriched with an heir.[89]

In this perception, Gabriel would be the herald sent to court the Lady (Mary) and receive her consent. Since the Father is the Lord and Christ is the Son born of Mary, then it is obvious that the Spouse has to be the Holy Spirit. What is not obvious is why Francis indirectly attributes this same role of spouses (albeit future spouses) of the Holy Spirit to Clare and her sisters and not to all the faithful. It may be that in claiming that they have betrothed the Holy Spirit, he is honoring each as an *altera Maria* because of her religious consecration.[90] Not that Francis was trying to get them to see themselves as identical to Mary, for Mary had been specifically chosen and consecrated. The Damianites, on the other hand, took the initiative and betrothed themselves to the Holy Spirit—choosing for themselves the role for which Mary had been chosen.

Where did these women get the desire, the strength, and the audacity to initiate such a relationship with the Father and the Holy Spirit? The answer is the *perfectionem sancti Evangelii.* This is where the relationship with the Son can be found. For Francis, the Gospel belongs to and comes from Jesus (RnB Pro. I).[91] It is his word and his life because he is the Word. It is almost as if Jesus is the herald who brings to Clare and her sisters God's declaration of love and his request that they marry his Spirit. In this, Francis ascribes to Jesus the role that the Poor Ladies had ascribed to Frances when he invited Clare to espouse Christ: the role of Gabriel. If these women entered filial and spousal relationships with the Father and the Holy Spirit, it was thanks to their contact with the Word/Son in their "choosing to live according to the perfection of the Holy Gospel" (FormViv I).[92] Jesus, in His Gospel, inspired them to become the daughters and servants of His heavenly Father and spouses of the Holy Spirit. The kinship relationship to which Francis calls the Damianites and the faithful is always trinitarian.

Francis as Spouse of God

Francis's understanding of the kinship relationships of the Damianites with God is the source for his "diligent care and special solicitude" (FormViv I)[93] for them. This is the same care and solicitude he had for the friars. In the "diligent care and special solicitude" Francis promised that he (and his friars) would have for the sisters, one can see the influence of the medieval family. For it was the job of the wife and mother to care and have solicitude for the children, servants, and eventually the spouses of the children. In describing his care and solicitude for the sisters in the "Form of Life," Francis took on a spousal relationship with God as well.

The words *curam* and *sollicitudinem* can be found together in other writings. In his Letter to the Rulers of Peoples (EpRect) Francis encourages the rulers not to allow "the cares and solicitudes of this age"[94] to keep them from serving God (EpRect 3, 6). In the "Bulled Rule" (RB 10.7), he admonishes the friars to avoid a number of dangers to the soul; he includes "the cares and solicitudes of this age" as a part of this list. In the "Non-Bulled Rule" (RnB 22.26), he claims that leaving behind (*postposita*) every care and concern (*cura et sollicitudine*) is a precondition to loving, serving, honoring, and adoring God. Finally, in both versions of the Letter to the Faithful (1EpFid 2.5–6; 2EpFid 65–66) he explains that those who experience "the cares and solicitudes of this age and the cares of this life"[95] are those who do not do penance. These persons, Francis wrote, belong to the Devil, "whose children they are" (*cuius filii sunt*). They belong to another household and thus have cares and concerns that are different from those who belong to the household of God.

In the "Form of Life," Francis takes up the words *curam* and *sollicitudinem* to contrast the children of God with the children of the Devil. These terms expressed the relationship that Francis had with Jesus' brothers and sisters. As spouse of Christ or the Spirit, Francis was taken from one household into another. He who had been in the household of Satan was espoused to Christ in the Holy Spirit and changed allegiance, as any bride of the period had to do. He no longer cared for the things of his family of origin, but rather gave "diligent care and special solicitude" to the things of his spouse's family. His new status as spouse in God's household was at odds with the household of Satan. For while Satan's children care for the things of this world, Francis, like all the children of God, cares for the members of God's Family.

THE FAITHFUL AND THE SPIRIT OF THE LORD

Although Francis saw the efforts of the faithful as essential to their entering kinship with God, he never saw this process as a merely human endeavor. In both the "Form of Life" given to Clare and her sisters and the two redactions of the Letter to the Faithful, Francis turned to the Spirit of the Lord. Clare and her sisters had acted under divine inspiration. The men and women who persevere in penance are happy and blessed, according to Francis, because the Spirit of the Lord will rest upon them and inhabit them.

According to him, a faithful person will have the Spirit of the Lord rest upon him or her and the Spirit will espouse them to Jesus. It is here that Francis returns to the traditional spousal language of the Church. Christ is the spouse of the faithful soul, thanks to the operation of the Holy Spirit. It is in this Spirit-guided espousal that the faithful person will also be brother and mother to Jesus in doing the will of the Father and in giving birth to Jesus through their good example. The Spirit allows one to call Jesus Lord (Adm 8.1) and the Spirit makes one recognize Him in the Eucharist (Adm 1.8–13). Moreover, the Spirit weds the soul to Jesus Christ.

The Spirit's marrying the faithful soul to the Lord Jesus is another way in which Francis calls the faithful to an intimate union with God. Yet he recognizes that the presider of this union, or perhaps the matchmaker, is the Holy Spirit. The operation of the Holy Spirit in the human soul is something that Francis could not stress enough in his writings. He challenged his brothers to desire nothing more in this life than to "have the Spirit of the Lord and his holy operations" (RB 10.8),[96] and he admonished the Damianites to avoid the exterior life by looking to the life of the Spirit, which is better (AudPov 3). This same Spirit joyfully caused them to treat each other with respect and filled them with the desire to be together (RnB 7.15). He asked that the brothers take care to admonish and correct those brothers who preferred to "walk in the flesh and not spiritually" (RnB 5.4–6).[97] This *spiritualiter ambulare* (walking according to the Spirit) is contrary to the spirit of the flesh or the spirit of the age. The spirit of the flesh and age is a possessive spirit that desires and wants to bring everything to itself (RnB 17.11; Adm 7). This spirit is definitely at odds with the spirit of poverty that Francis espoused as the means to best live the Gospel of Jesus Christ.

The spirit of poverty, of being poor in spirit, does not allow anyone to possess even the good and pious works that they do for God and others. Those who do good works and possess them are easily scandalized by the sins of others or by an attack on their person (Adm 14).[98] These people will never be able to care for and nurture other Christians. Thus their spousal union to Christ in the Spirit will be a barren one, and they will not be able to give children to the Father.

THE SON'S BROTHERS AND SISTERS

The spousal and maternal relationship to Christ is also a fraternal one. In the Hymn in his Letter to the Faithful, Francis rejoices at Jesus' being our brother and son. This rejoicing is part of his overall rejoicing at the faithful soul's kinship with God. It takes on an undeniable crescendo (three adjectives for the Father,[99] four adjectives for the spouse,[100] and finally, eight adjectives for the brother and son). The adjectives, *holy, delightful, pleasing, humble, peaceful, sweet, loving,* and *above all desirable,*[101] used to describe being the Son's brother and mother, indicate that these roles supersede the other two combined. It is obvious that, for Francis, these are the two main roles for Christians.

In the view of medieval medical authors, a parent's love for his or her children is greater than the reverse, because the children carry the parent's substance and not the other way around. These writers went on to conclude that, as time goes on, a parent's love for his or her child grows. Yet the reverse is not true, because the child's love for the parent naturally diminishes so that he or she can grow in independence, especially in view of the parent's eventual death. If this is so, then, for most people, sibling and marital bonds remain the primary expressions of familial love—that is, prior to generating offspring. In Francis, we have seen how the love for his carnal father was overwhelmed by his love for the only Father—to the point where he was able to leave his parents. In this break, however, he not only lost his parents, he also lost his brother. It is only natural that if he replaced Pietro with God the Father, then he would replace Angelo with God's beloved Son and the brothers given him by the Lord (Test 14).

Angelo showed Francis no love after his break with the family. In fact, he mocked him, imitating his father's disgust with Francis. Nevertheless, Francis found in Jesus a brother who showed no signs of sibling rivalry. According to Francis, Jesus demonstrated his being a true brother in giving his life for humanity and in praying for the faithful (RnB 22).

THE INCARNATION OF THE SON

Referring to Mt 12:50, Francis describes the faithful person who does the will of the Father as being Jesus' brother. It seems that Francis insisted on this kinship tie with Jesus to the point that Thomas of Celano and Bonaventure both attached it to Francis's Marian devotion. His love for the Mother of Jesus was due to her having made the Lord of Majesty our brother.[102] Nevertheless, Francis himself never explicitly states this in his opuscula. At best, he alludes to it by saying that one of the reasons for thanking God the Father was for his having brought about the birth of His Son, "true God and true human by the glorious ever virgin, the blessed St. Mary" (RnB 23.3).[103]

For Francis, the Son who was sent to give us life (1 Jn 4:9) is not just the Son sent by the Father; he is the Son who was born of the Virgin Mary (OffPass 15.3). He, Jesus Christ, is the one through whom humanity is the image and likeness of God (Gen 1:26), for God created humanity in "the image of His beloved Son according to the body and to His likeness according to the spirit" (Adm 5.1).[104] Obviously, in keeping with Francis's anthropology, this image and likeness of the Son was broken by sin (2EpFid 46; RnB 23.1). Still, for Francis, the pre-existent Word and Son of God was definitely moving toward a fraternal relationship with humanity. His active role in creation was to be a model for the human creature. In the kenosis (self-emptying) of the second person of the Most Holy Trinity and His being born of Mary, the Son became humanity's brother in the flesh.[105]

In His fraternal love for humanity, the Son desired that humans become His brothers and sisters in the spirit. Consequently, He modeled obedience to the Father's will. The whole "Office of the Lord's Passion" is Francis's attempt to explore the mind of Christ moving toward the Passion. The whole of the Office is made up of a series of reworked Psalms that reflect various points of Jesus' human reality and divine Sonship. These Psalms manifest a Christ who has hoped in God since his mother's womb (OffPass 2.4–5), who cries out to his Father for assistance, and who accepts suffering for Him who vindicates Him (OffPass 3.3-5). Jesus gave in to the will of the Father and underwent passion and death (2EpFid 8–15). It is this obedience to the Father's will that makes Jesus "the way, the truth and the life" (Jn 14:6), the only One who can reveal the Father, because anyone who sees the Son sees the Father (Jn 14:9). It is no wonder that Francis rejoiced at having such a Brother.

BROTHERS FROM THE LORD

> And when the Lord gave me brothers, no one showed me what I should do. Rather, the Most High revealed to me that we should live according to the form of the Holy Gospel. And I had it written in few and simple words and the Lord Pope confirmed it for me. And those who came and received life gave away everything they had to the poor, and they were content to have one tunic, patched inside and out, with a cord and shorts. And we did not want to have anything else (Test 14–17).[106]

In his "Testament" (Test), Francis describes his initial conversion, and goes on to explain that he began to do what all Christians should do (respect the clergy and theologians, and honor the Eucharist and the word of God). Having done this, he interrupts the account of his life with these words: "And when the Lord gave me brothers . . . ." It is with these words that he explains how he and the brothers began living a more evangelical life in poverty. For Francis, poverty is modeled after the life of Jesus, his mother, and the disciples. Poverty is a way of entering a deeper brotherhood with Jesus in community. Being Jesus' brother is not an individual endeavor. Francis states that we are His brothers. This *we* is a very important word in Francis's vision of kinship with the Trinity. Just as the faithful can only refer to God as Father with the communal *Pater noster*, no one can claim brotherhood with Jesus except in communion with others.

Francis's explanation—that it was the Most High alone who showed him what he should do—is intimately tied to his having received brothers from the Lord. We cannot be sure whether *Lord* (in Test 14) refers to Jesus Christ, or the Father, or the Trinity.[107] His immediately referring to the Gospel in the following phrase could indicate, however, that it was the Lord Jesus who gave him brothers. This certainly would be in keeping with his usage of Mt 12:50, in which Jesus claims as brothers those who perform the will of His Father. It seems that Francis saw his early companions as those who had been brought into a fraternal relationship with Christ. These men had been given him as brothers by that same Christ.

It certainly is the case that, if Francis came to realize what it was God wanted him to do, it was thanks to his trying to understand the will of God in the lives of Bernard of Quintavalle and the first brothers.[108] When

Bernard came to him, Francis immediately turned to the Scriptures to discover what Bernard should do. When a small group had gathered around him, the sources claim that they turned to the Scriptures in order to learn to live the Gospel. The Gospel became the source of the lost Rule presented in 1209 to Pope Innocent III. The Prologue of the "Non-Bulled Rule" (1221 CE) declares that Francis asked the Pope to confirm the life of the Gospel for him and his brothers. The whole of the Rule is filled to overflowing with direct quotations from and references to the Gospels. In the "Bulled Rule" (1223 CE), Francis proclaims that the Rule and life of the Friars Minor is to live the *sanctum Evangelium* of our Lord Jesus Christ[109] in obedience, chastity, and without anything of one's own.

OBEDIENCE

Obedience is just one of the virtues that Francis praises in his "Salutation of the Virtues" as turning the faithless into faithful souls. This becoming faithful through the virtues (SalBVM 6) is tied to the praises of the Blessed Virgin Mary in Francis's text.[110] Certainly, no one can deny that these virtues were found in Mary, just as no one can deny that they were found in her Son, Jesus.

Obedience is the sister of charity, and, like all virtues, she comes from the Lord. Like all the virtues, she destroys the body and the flesh (Satan, the ways of the world, the cares of this age, and the like). Obedience binds the mortified body to the obedience of the Spirit and to one's brother. Francis immediately ties this obedience—to the Spirit and to one's brother—to submission to all persons in the world and to every creature as well.

This is an interesting portrait of obedience, especially if we keep in mind that Jesus is the model par excellence of holy obedience. In the "Non-Bulled Rule," Francis refers to the "obedience of Jesus" as that of being able to serve and obey the brothers through the charity of the spirit (RnB 6.14–15). Jesus, in his obedience, lived in a spiritual and fraternal obedience. Obedience subjected Jesus to all creatures, especially to the human creature whose brother He became in the flesh. Because of this, Jesus fulfilled the will of the Father and died to redeem humankind, to make the faithful his brothers and sisters in the Spirit.

This connection of fraternal love and obedience is quite enlightening. Francis, in his writings, refers to obedience in the traditional sense of doing the will of a prelate,[111] yet he limits the scope of that prelate's power and authority. He does so by rejecting the titles of prior, abbot, superior, father, and prelate. Instead, he calls his Order's leaders by new titles: minister and guardian/custodian. At the same time, he insists on the servile nature of their office. He also recognizes that the individual person is capable of judging as to whether or not an order from a minister is in keeping with the way of life he has espoused. If it is harmful to his soul and conscience, he is not bound to obey (RnB 5.2).[112]

Obedience can even compel a person to die for his brothers or to serve them as local, provincial, or general minister—as in the case of the minister to whom he wrote his Letter to a Minister (EpMin). This letter was written to offer encouragement to a minister who had apparently tired of serving the brothers and wanted to retire to a hermitage. Francis reminded him that true obedience is to endure the struggles brought about by the brothers or others. In other writings, Francis ties obedience to providing for the friar's material and spiritual needs (RnB 5; Adm 3). He stressed obedience as a fraternal relationship. The brothers are to obey each other in mutuality (RnB 5.13). Obedience is a way of going beyond one's self and opening up to Jesus and others (2EpFid 40).

CHASTITY

In his writings, Francis explicitly used the word *obedience* forty-seven times, and *poverty* sixteen times, while he explicitly refers to the word *chastity* only four times. He did not even see fit to name chastity as a virtue, however, as he does obedience and poverty. Where Francis felt a need to explain his position on obedience and poverty, it seems that, given the teachings of Christian morality, chastity needed no such explanation.

Although it could be said that Francis considered the vow of chastity as self-explanatory, he did caution the friars about dealings with women. In both versions of his Rule, Francis refers to Jesus' injunction against looking at a woman with lust (Mt 5:28) and to Paul's reference to the body as the "temple of the Holy Spirit" (1 Cor 6:19; 3:17). Concerning dealings with women, chapter 12 of the "Non-Bulled Rule" shows a fraternal concern for the spiritual well-being of the friars.

It is worth noting that Francis's concern for the friars in their dealings with women shows none of the misogynist tendencies of the time.[113] It was not because women are temptresses that the friars should be careful of their relationships with them. In fact, it seems the women in question were pious women seeking spiritual advice, confession, and a penitential life. Francis did not at all condemn dealing with them.[114] They could be looked at as long as it was done without impure glances (*malu visu*); they could be counseled as long as they were sent to go and act on their own without having to depend on the friars.

What Francis does seem to consider, in the matter of keeping the body pure and undefiled, is the weakness and fragility of male flesh. Like an older brother, who has probably had brushes with impurity,[115] Francis counsels and advises his brothers for their own good.[116]

Francis's concern for the sexual purity of the brothers also manifests a concern that scandal not be laid upon the brothers because of one man's sin. Brushes with impurity can lead a fragile man to commit the sin of fornication—a sin that Francis absolutely rejects as contrary to the way of the Gospel.

In chapter 13 of the "Non-Bulled Rule," Francis, in a surprising display of mercilessness toward a friar who has fornicated, condemns him to expulsion from "our religion" (*nostra religione*). That friar is sent away to do penance for his sins. Francis does not mention any possibility of readmission to the brotherhood, however. Fornication, it seems, is the only sin that breaks fraternal union, probably because of the bad reputation it would bring a group of brothers who were already held suspect (by many) because of their radical poverty.

In most normal families, marriage and the generation of offspring determine a family and its continuation. In religious families, however, this is not possible. This was true in the Middle Ages just as it is today. Francis takes this matter to heart, and where sexual intercourse is the way of insuring the continuity of a natural family, for Francis, chastity is the way of assuring the continuity of the religious family. By setting a good example and avoiding scandal, the friars could draw new members to the household of God.

Without Anything of One's Own

In his "Salutation of the Virtues" and in "Admonitions" (Adm 27),

Francis names poverty as the sister of humility and claims that she destroys the desire for riches, avarice, and the cares of this world. His references to poverty are usually tied to the person of Jesus Christ (RnB 9.1). One cannot help but think of Francis's father as the exact opposite of Francis's definition of poverty. Before his conversion, he used to serve his father in the desire for wealth, in avarice, and in the cares of the age. After his conversion, he learned to serve his heavenly Father in the same way that Jesus did—in poverty. And yet, although Francis and his followers were intimately tied to poverty, in his opuscula, poverty does not seem to be the most important part of his identity or that of his brothers.[117] In fact, while Clare repeatedly makes references to poverty in her opuscula, Francis does not. He prefers stressing *minoritas*, calling poverty the vow of living "without anything of one's own" (*sine proprio*).[118] In this way, poverty goes beyond simply being an economic reference and becomes a way of living in simplicity and without earthly attachments.

What Francis refers to as *proprio* (one's own) is worth noting. In his opuscula, we find him use *proprium* as an adjective in various references. He speaks of the God of Israel having saved His servants with his "own blood" (*proprio sangue*) (OffPass 6.15; cf. 2EpFid 11). The *proprium* is as close to oneself as one's own hand, one's own person (EpFran 1; Test 32). In his "Admonitions," Francis warns the friars to truly live *sine proprio*, which is to say without one's will (*voluntatis*) (Adm 2; 3.10).[119] In this way, they will not be angered or disturbed by the sins of others. Ultimately, poverty is tied to giving up everything of one's own, especially one's own person. This form of poverty becomes the ultimate expression of obedient sonship, for this obedience needs to be directed toward the only Father.

In chapter 9 of the "Non-Bulled Rule," Francis invites the friars to imitate the way in which the Lord Jesus Christ lived this obedient Sonship. Like the poor children in the Parable of Francis as a poor mother,[120] Jesus had also taken *sine proprio* as his lifestyle. His being the Son of God did not inhibit him from being "poor and alien" (*pauper et hospes*) and from living off "alms" (*eleemosynam*). In this poverty, he was joined by his mother and his disciples (the evangelical family of those who do the Father's will). It is worth noting that this chapter on begging alms contains the passage (RnB 9.10–11) that is at the heart of maternal–fraternal love among the friars.

MOTHERS WHEN WE CARRY HIM AND GIVE BIRTH TO HIM

Turning our attention once again to the Hymn in the Letter to the Faithful, we note that Jesus is not just the brother of the faithful soul. The numerous adjectives used to rejoice at His being the soul's brother are also tied to his being the son of the soul. This mothering the Son of God is nothing new in Christian spirituality. Ireneus, Ambrose, and other patristic writers had already used the theme of mothering Christ.[121] In the century before Francis, the Cistercians had popularized the image of the leader in monastic circles as a maternal figure.[122] Francis, however, describes maternity in real terms of gestation, the birthing process, and nourishment.

Francis's love of the Feast of Christmas is very well known.[123] We do well to consider his re-creation of the Bethlehem stable at Greccio in light of his own writings. When he meditates on the birth of the Son of God, he does not hesitate to consider the concrete manner in which He came into the world between an ox and a donkey. Francis did not spiritualize the carnal birth of Jesus in Bethlehem and he certainly was not spiritualizing the birth that every faithful soul must give God's Son. Francis knew from experience that birthing Jesus, like birthing any child, is a labor of love, but it is just that—labor. [124] It is a maternal labor that he himself did not shy away from and one that he invited the faithful to undertake.

According to the Greccio story, a virtuous man saw Francis approach and awaken a child who appeared to sleep in the hay. In this vision, Francis is assigned a maternal role. Christian art had, since the middle of the eleventh century, begun to popularize imagery of the Madonna and child,[125] yet there are no images of Joseph (a father) having any direct contact with the infant Jesus. In images of the Christmas story, if Joseph was represented at all, he was usually sitting off to the side, not participating in the event. Socially, infants were outside the realm of paternal care, so that any contact Francis had with the infant Jesus would have been considered maternal, perhaps in imitation of Mary.

PARTICIPATION IN THE MATERNITY OF MARY

Different scholars over the centuries have tried in various ways to explain Francis's devotion to the Mother of the Christ.[126] Despite all the pages that have gone into such attempts, however, I believe the best explanation is the earliest one, given us by Thomas of Celano. Francis's devotion to Mary is tightly bound up with her role as the one who "made the Lord of Majesty our brother" (2Cel 198).[127] This explanation resonates with Francis's wonderment and awe at the God, King, Judge, and Pantocrator,[128] who, out of love for sinful humanity, became human. His devotion to Mary springs from this amazement about the Lord's Incarnation and his being thankful for her role in this process,[129] a role that he desired to imitate and call others to.[130]

Celano's description of Francis's devotion to the Virgin is very much in tune with what Francis himself wrote in this regard:

> This Word (Verb) of the Father so worthy, so holy and glorious, was announced by the most high Father of heaven through his angel St. Gabriel in the holy uterus of the glorious virgin Mary, and in her uterus He received our human flesh and fragility (2EpFid 4).[131]

> And we give you thanks because, just as through your Son you created us, so too, through the holy love with which you loved us (cf. Jn 17:26), you caused Him, true God and true human, to be born of the most blessed Virgin St. Mary and desired that, through His cross and blood and death, he might redeem us captives (RnB 23.3).[132]

> Listen my brothers: if the blessed Virgin is honored, [it is] as it should be, because she carried him in her most holy uterus (EpOrd 21).[133]

Mary made the Son of God one of us, the brother of our human nature, flesh of our flesh and blood of our blood, sharing in our human flesh and fragility. This emphasis on Mary's having enfleshed the second person of the Trinity stands in sharp contrast to the Manichean and Docetist heresies against human flesh that the Cathari espoused in Francis's day. Pope Innocent III had called for a crusade against heretical teachings—teachings that condemned the body as material and evil, claiming the Son of God had only pretended to take on human flesh.[134] Dominic of Guzman and others took up this crusade, but Francis neither crusaded nor wrote theological treatises in defense of the orthodox position. He did, however, emphasize Jesus' having come among us in our flesh thanks to Mary and the Son's continuing to come to us in bread and wine thanks to the clergy and the Holy Roman Church (Test 6–10).

Mary, whom Francis also calls "the Virgin," is always to be found at the head of the list of God's household (RnB 23.6; EpOrd 38). In his "Explanation of the 'Our Father,'" she is the only one of the elect who is named directly as interceding for the faithful to God the Father. She is portrayed as a favorite daughter, or *ancilla* (SalBVM 5), who, because of her having been chosen by the Father, has influence on Him. She shared in the Sonship of Jesus Christ and his disciples by begging as they did (RnB 9.5; 2EpFid 5). But her being the daughter of the divine King or the spouse of the Holy Spirit did not make her expect a rich inheritance or a well-to-do household. Rather, she was content to share in the inheritance of all God's children who are still in the world (RnB 6.1–6).[135]

Francis honors Mary, as he asks his friars to do, not by placing her so far from human reach that she becomes someone to be adored rather than imitated. He places her as the first in God's household and outlines her kinship to the Trinity. What's more, he invites all the faithful to participate in this very kinship. The faithful are invited by Francis, each and every one, to become not just a child of the Father and spouse and brother of the Son, but also His mother.

Mary was Christ's mother in the natural order because she physically conceived and generated Him, making Him flesh of her flesh and blood of her blood. In the Patristic Era, Mary came to be seen as the spiritual mother of Christians. Her natural maternity was a sign of the supernatural maternity[136] she was destined for in generating the Body of Christ, the Church. The faithful believer who is invited to share Mary's spiritual maternity, on the other hand, is to be Christ's mother in the supernatural order of things.

Francis ends his "Salutation of the Blessed Virgin Mary" with a greeting to the virtues, by which the unfaithful are made faithful and able to share in Mary's maternity.[137] Their hearts are infused with faith thanks to the Holy Spirit; thus, their maternity is spiritual. Spiritual maternity does not mean maternity through adoption or friendship, however. In Francis, it keeps the generative aspects of natural maternity: "We carry Him in our hearts and bodies"; "We birth him."[138]

Francis does not shy away from the physical allusions to gestation and childbirth with all the discomforts, pains, and joys that are associated with these two periods of maternity. But, consciously or unconsciously, Francis does avoid juridical maternity, based on recognized responsibilities and promised inheritance established by law.[139] He stresses instead the natural bond of love and affection that he presupposes to exist between a mother and her child, a natural bond that he himself had experienced with his own mother. In this maternal process, Christ becomes our Son, a son to rejoice in, a son to love because of lived experience, not because of doctrines, law, or inheritance.

Mary's natural maternity became spiritual, thanks to the redemption of humanity by Christ's Paschal Mystery. Human beings became God's children and siblings of Mary's son, Jesus, because he birthed them on the cross and in baptism and because he nourishes them with his body and blood, which of course he received from Mary.[140] In all of this, Mary's natural maternity of the Child Jesus is extended over time to include the spiritual maternity of God's children[141]—children who, in turn, are called to become mothers of Christ.

PRIESTS AS *ALTER MARIA*

St. Mary may have birthed Jesus in a unique and unrepeatable fashion, but her maternity of God's Son is meant to be shared by the Christian faithful, especially by those who bring him physically into the world. Francis admits that Mary had incarnated Jesus in His humanity. Jesus alone gives us access to the Father; he is "the way, the truth and the life" and he is, in Francis's thought, our Master, our Wisdom, and our Light.[142] Consequently, the faithful need to see Him, experience Him, taste, and receive Him. But Christians can no longer see Him as the Apostles had done, in the body that Mary had given Him. So the Church needs other mothers who can continue to incarnate Him.

The person whom Francis places as closest imitator of Mary in this task is the priest[143] in the sacrament of the Eucharist. In his first "Admonition," Francis pours out on paper his love for this astonishing sacrament and miracle of Incarnation. While all Christians are able to spiritually bear Jesus, the priest alone is able to incarnate Him in a visible and concrete manner. The only way to see the Lord Jesus is in the bread and wine which "are sanctified through the Lord's words upon the altar at the hands of the priest" (Adm I.9).[144] It is not because of the holiness of the priest[145] but rather because Jesus "reveals Himself to us in the sacred bread" (Adm I.19).[146]

This is the marvel that Francis beheld in his worship and which he sought to describe in his writings. To his delight and wonder, he saw Jesus humble Himself and, "just as when He came from the royal throne into the womb of the Virgin, . . . daily He descends from the bosom of the Father upon the altar in the hands of the priest" (Adm I.16, 18).[147]

There are many cases in the Middle Ages of people reportedly seeing the Eucharistic bread turn into the child Jesus. The medieval mind seems to have associated the Eucharist not just with Christ's Passion but with his initial Incarnation. Mary herself was tied to the Eucharistic symbolism as the one who administered Jesus to the world. Francis called her the tabernacle of God.[148] Altar *retablos* and tabernacle doors were decorated with her image either in the Annunciation, or the Christmas story, or as the Madonna who becomes the throne for the Prince of Peace whom she holds out to the world for adoration and reception.[149] The priest, faced with this image of the Madonna, understood that, at least during the consecration and distribution of communion, he was a mother.[150] Judging from the account of mystical visions, the laity also saw the priest as another Mary (mother of Christ) to the point that, during the consecration, priests where seen to swell in pregnancy.[151].

According to Carolyn Walker Bynum, Francis of Assisi was one of two men in the High Middle Ages whose spirituality was most feminine.[152] Yet, she claims that Francis did not use the food metaphors that thirteenth-century women used.[153] What Bynum seems to ignore is Francis's repeated insistence on the priests administering the Body and Blood of Jesus and especially his insistence on the Blood. By her own definition, she claims that in the mystic experience, Jesus' crucifixion is a type of symbolic gender reversal whereby he becomes a mother who births and nurses others. She also ascribes this reversal to priests at Mass.[154]

This is Francis's experience as spelled out in his writings. He definitely tied the clergy to the Body and Blood of Christ, insisting that it was only they who could consecrate the bread and wine, thus acting like Mary in the process of Incarnation. He furthermore insisted that it was only they who could administer the Body and Blood to the faithful. The priest in Francis's mind is the one who feeds the children of God. He is a mother figure who nourishes and cares for the faithful.[155] Following the example of Mary, the maternal relationship that priests have with Jesus necessarily spells itself out in a maternal relationship with the faithful.

JESUS AS BROTHER AND MOTHER

If the faithful come to this recognition and acceptance of God as the only Father, it is thanks to Jesus, His only begotten Son who reveals Him (RnB 22.33–34; Adm I.1–7). It would not be far from the truth to say that in the medieval mindset, Jesus took on the maternal role of bringing the children to the Father. The medieval concept of Jesus' maternity[156] has its roots in the second century when Clement of Alexandria made use of the Eucharistic image of Christ as a mother breastfeeding the soul.[157]

In the twelfth century, Anselm of Canterbury had made the distinction between God the Father and the maternity of Jesus. At that time, a father was thought to be more active in the generation of offspring than a mother, because the male semen was then considered to contribute most to the begetting of a child. Anselm recognized that the mother imperils her life in order to birth that same child, oftentimes dying in the process—as Christ did when he gave birth to the Church. Anselm compares both Jesus and St. Paul as mothers, but he insists that they are also fathers: fathers by result, authority, and protection; mothers by affection, kindness, and compassion.[158]

Francis may or may not have been aware of the devotion to the maternity of Jesus. One thing is certain: he had no problem assigning Jesus the maternal role of bringing children to the Father. This certainly would have been in keeping with Francis's assigning all brothers a maternal role (RnB 9.11).[159]

Another way in which Francis assigns maternal–fraternal tension to Jesus is through nourishment. Nourishment, as we have noted, is a maternal activity, especially in the period of infancy, when the Church insisted that the natural mother should be the one to breastfeed her own children. In the celebration of the Eucharist, the priest consecrates the Body and Blood of the Lord, and then feeds it to the faithful. We saw earlier that this Body and Blood of Christ were the way in which Christ himself fed and nourished the soul from his own flesh—much like a lactating mother.

Francis's insistence on the blood of Christ as essential to salvation is reminiscent of breastfeeding. In his writings, Francis usually ties the Blood of Christ to the Body of Christ and insists that both be received by the faithful.[160] Even so, Francis explicitly singles out the Blood of Christ as that which was poured out in sacrifice for our redemption and salvation (2EpFid 11); as Jesus prayed on the night before He died, His sweat turned into Blood (2EpFid 9); Christ's words and His Blood are the only salvation (2EpFid 34); and the Lord has washed us in His Blood (EpOrd 3). Francis also warns that Priests should be careful not to contaminate His Blood (EpOrd 18).

To the medieval mind, the milk that flowed from a mother's breast was nothing more than reconstituted blood. In this blood–made–milk, the mother passed on her characteristics to her baby, just as the father had previously done with his sperm. I am not saying that Francis singled out the Lord's Blood as a veiled reference to mother's milk. However, knowing the biological beliefs of the time and the faithful's taste for mystical milk,[161] it would not be far-fetched. Given Francis's maternal–fraternal view of Jesus as the big Brother/Mother who takes the faithful to the Father, he might have made an unconscious reference to the Blood of Christ as maternal milk. Certainly, Francis insists that it is thanks to the Blood of Christ that one is redeemed and saved. In feeding the faithful with His Blood, He not only passes on redemption; He passes on His characteristics/virtues, as mothers were thought to do with their milk.

AS A MOTHER LOVES AND NOURISHES

Having considered the maternity of Mary, the faithful, Priests, and Jesus, I now turn to the maternity of the friars. Francis, as we have seen, took a maternal role in his relationship with the brothers.[162] He did not want to be called father, for there is only one Father. If only one is Father, then everyone else is spouse, brother (or sister), child, or mother, just as in the households of medieval nobility.

In the "Non-Bulled Rule" (RnB 9.11), Francis invites the brothers to "love and nourish his brother, as a mother loves and nourishes her son."[163] The two verbs *diligere* (to greatly prize, to esteem, to love) and *nutrire* (to nourish, to nurse, to suckle, or to rear) are strong affective verbs that Francis associates with maternal care. If the authors of his *Legendae* are correct, Francis most certainly knew this type of maternal love. His mother, Pica, was depicted as one who delighted in her son—although she did not always understand him. Francis must have encountered the mothers of the various men and women who sought to imitate his way of following the poor Christ. In these encounters, at least according to the *Legendae*, he developed a special view of maternal love. We know that he was insistent that those who live the Gospel in religious life should break with their families. Yet, we also know that he felt sorry for the poor mothers of various brothers and that he declared that the mother of one brother was the mother of all brothers. In addition, although he was not willing to give mothers back their children, he did take pity on them in their material needs.

In both Rules, Francis refers to the maternal–fraternal vocation of the Friar Minor, in the context of material need. After explaining his position regarding ownership and begging, he insists that the brothers give testimony to the fact that they belong to one family. This testimony takes on the concrete manifestation of making known one's needs to each other. The result of this manifestation is that the brothers will love each other maternally. The mother in the medieval family was the one who most directly met the corporal needs of her children. Not only did she feed them from her very body; the manner of holding them close to her breast as they fed also responded to the child's emotional need for affection and closeness.

Initially the brothers were to take care of each other's material and emotional needs, making sure that the brothers had what they needed and that brothers did not criticize each other in their need (RnB 9.12). Francis knew that these needs were different in each brother and did not pretend that all brothers were the same. Because of this, he ends his section on maternal–fraternal care in the "Non-Bulled Rule" with an injunction against judging each other specifically in the need to eat or not to eat. In the "Bulled

Rule," this section is ended with an injunction on caring for the infirm brothers and treating others as one would want to be treated. Maternal care, it would seem, is tied to understanding or trying to understand the physical and material needs of one's brothers and not expecting them to be like oneself.

In the "Bulled Rule," Francis had to drop or change many of the things he had written into his earlier Rule. Yet there are certain points that remain. These were probably points that Francis was truly convinced came directly from the Lord. One of these is the maternal–fraternal vocation and tension of the Friar Minor. He does however show a new understanding of this vocation. It is probably due to lived experience that he changed the original text to read, "If a mother nourishes and loves her son in the flesh, how much more lovingly should one love and nourish his spiritual brother" (RB 6.8).[164]

The spiritual element is the profound key to the understanding of the maternal–fraternal vocation and tension. Where a mother and child share a natural kinship, the Friars Minor share a spiritual kinship as brothers in the Spirit, not in the flesh. Francis's profound devotion to the Holy Spirit had been lacking in his "Non-Bulled Rule" (RnB 9.11); in the "Bulled Rule" (RB 6.9), he corrects this lacuna. Just as the flesh gives children to the mother, the Spirit gives brothers to the brother. In the medieval household, carnal/natural brothers did not choose each other but were brothers because of a shared paterfamilias. Being in the same household translated itself into a fraternal bond with the obligation to care for each other. Unfortunately, in many noble households, it also translated into sibling rivalry with brothers vying against each other for the father's favor.

In Francis's mind, just as with natural brothers, spiritual brothers do not choose each other but are brothers because of a shared Father, whose will they do. Because they are all the children of one Father, Francis sees no need for paternalism in his Order. He warns the brothers who are ministers to act as if they are servants, not priors, and not to seek to hold on to their position in the community. The other brothers are given the right to keep a minister's power in check. Both the ministers and the brothers subject to them are to keep watch over each other so as to correct each other if one happens to act according to the flesh and not the Spirit, or in a manner not in keeping with the integrity of the life they have professed.

In his writings, he recognizes the potential for sibling rivalry among his brothers and goes to some lengths to caution against this and to describe the love that each one should have for the other. Just because this love has a spiritual foundation does not mean that it should be an abstract form of love. Concrete person that he was, Francis puts into writing the authentic manifestations of maternal–fraternal love. The friars are to love each other by considering themselves worthless servants, by being modest, and by reflecting on their own faults. This, he suggests, will keep them from slandering the other, from arguing, from gossip or murmuring against each other and from judging or condemning each other (RnB 11).

Francis calls all Christians to be spouses, brothers, and mothers of Jesus as a way of underlining the importance of familiarity with Christ.[165] This familiarity was based on the believer's living out the kenosis of the Son of God through penance, obedience, and humility. All three of these keys to kenosis are found in the maternal–fraternal vocation of the Friar Minor. Their love for each other is part and parcel of the penance, obedience, and humility, which is their evangelical life. To love one's brother like a mother, or even more than a mother, is not an easy task, especially when this means caring for each other's needs which are so varied and not always understandable. Open and honest communication is key to the maternal–fraternal life Francis proposed.

Francis explicitly referred to the maternal–fraternal love of the brothers in two other writings: his Letter to Brother Leo (EpLeo) and the "Rule for Hermitages" (RegEr). These are worth looking at if we are to understand the nuances of this type of vocation and especially of this type of tension in community life. In the "Rule for Hermitages," Francis refers to the maternal–filial care of Martha and Mary as a model for Gospel life in a specific context. His Letter to Brother Leo reveals the way in which he himself lived the maternal–fraternal vocation and tension with a specific brother, Leo.

Although none of the *Legendae* mentions this letter, no one can deny its authenticity, because it is preserved in the saint's own handwriting. It is more of a brief note than it is a letter, and it refers to Francis and Leo's having been on the road together. While they journeyed together, apparently they were discussing matters that regarded their way of life. We know from

"On True and Perfect Joy" that this was something they were in the habit of doing.

Although the matter they were discussing is not mentioned, we can deduce from Francis's comments that it involved how to best please God and follow His footsteps and poverty, which is to say, how to live the Gospel life. The letter leads one to think that they, as friars sometimes do, must have disagreed as to how this was best done. What is of interest to us, however, is not the subject of their discussion, but rather the attitude with which Francis handled the matter: "I speak to you, my son, as a mother" (EpLeo 2).[166]

In his living out of the maternal–fraternal tension, Francis calls Leo his son. In the Letter to the Entire Order (EpOrd 5), along with calling the friars his lords and brothers, he calls them his sons. Francis had no problem with calling the friars sons. This however, does not get lived out in an attitude of paternalism; rather, as Francis specifies, it is with a maternal attitude that he regards his brothers as his sons.

This maternal attitude, at least in the Letter to Brother Leo, shows itself to be based on the love that Pica had for him. Francis and Leo had been discussing how best to live the Gospel, as Francis and his mother might have done when he was imprisoned by his father. And, although Pica had tried to convince him that his way was exaggerated or at least incomprehensible to herself, she set him free to do as he saw best. Francis seems to have learned that this type of maternal liberation was essential to letting the brothers decide how best to live the Gospel.[167]

In the "Rule for Hermitages" (RegEr 2), Francis shows himself a gifted interpreter of the Sacred Scriptures. He takes what is the story of two sisters caught in a bout of sibling rivalry (Lk 10:38–42) and turns it into a model for maternal–filial love. It is worth noting that in Luke's version, Martha—whom Francis assigns the task of mother—does not understand Mary's decision to sit at the feet of Jesus. To Mary, Francis assigns the role of son. Again, we are met with a mother who does not understand the son's desire or manner of living the Gospel. In the original story, she complains to the Lord, but in Francis's "Rule for Hermitages" (RegEr 8), Martha is redeemed by becoming a loving and nurturing mother, who seeks to protect the way Mary has chosen to sit at the Lord's feet. Understanding is not a necessary virtue when dealing with a spiritual son or brother; rather, non-judgmental acceptance is what is needed.

Finally, in his "Rule for Hermitages," Francis underscores his belief that, just as obedience should be reciprocal, so too should be the maternal–filial roles. The son should periodically become the mother, and vice versa. I believe that Francis saw this as an important element of mutuality in the maternal–fraternal relationship to keep the mother from becoming paternalistic in caring for the needs of the brother or son. The reversal of roles from time to time in the hermitages was also an astute way of getting the brothers to enter into each other's shoes (or rather, sandals) so as to better understand each other's needs and concerns. Friars who become general, provincial, and local ministers should never be allowed to keep that role for long or to jump from one leadership role to another. Rather, they should step down and become one among the many friars while another friar takes the lead for a while.

In both the "Non-Bulled Rule" and the "Bulled Rule," the famous invitation—to live community life as modeled on and far surpassing the kinship ties of a mother and son—came in the context of Francis's concern for poverty. Poverty, which is to say material necessity, forms the basis for the fraternal life of the Friar Minor. Francis realized, however, that material necessity is not the only type of necessity that a person has. Based on his experience of his own mother (I believe), Francis chose the maternal archetype as a means to help the friars meet each other's affective needs. But Francis did not stop there. He wanted the friars to love and nourish each other in ways that are greater than a natural mother's love. They were to love each other in ways that cared for one another's spiritual needs while forgetting neither material needs nor the need for affection.

It is said that, for Bernard of Clairvaux, "all the obligations of the Rule are ordered and subordinated to the primacy of charity."[168] The same thing could be said of Francis—with one difference: For Francis of Assisi, all the obligations of the Rule are ordered and subordinated to the primacy of *maternal* charity, where friars help each other by meeting each other's material, emotional, and spiritual needs, taking turns filling leadership positions and roles.

FINAL REFLECTIONS ON KINSHIP IN FRANCIS'S OPUSCULA

From Francis's opuscula, we discover that, despite the fact that his initial concern was for the brothers and sisters who followed his way of living the Gospel, he was also concerned that all the faithful live the Gospel. He spelled out this living of the Gospel in very concrete ways in his writings, and he spiritualized this way of life by attributing to it a kinship factor. Kinship becomes the way of internalizing the Christian commitment of all the faithful.

As we have seen, this kinship is vertical; it is a belonging to the family of those who do the Father's will. Nevertheless, this kinship would not be Christian if it did not have *cotidiano* and horizontal ramifications in kinship among those who do the Father's will. Francis saw the brothers, the sisters, and all the faithful as children of the Father, spouses of Christ and/or the Holy Spirit, and brothers and mothers of the Lord Jesus Christ. This in turn extends itself to all the faithful being brothers and sisters to each other as well as to their being reciprocally mothers and children to each other. The maternal–fraternal tension that Francis lived he also proclaimed and offered as a model to all believers.

The maternal–fraternal tension and vocation is so strong in Francis that he attributes it to everyone except God the Father. In presenting Jesus, he hints at His living this maternal–fraternal tension as well. Jesus is our Lord and Brother, yet he is also the Mother who brings the children to the Father and who feeds them with his body and, especially, with his blood. True to Francis's view that the roles of mother and child should be interchangeable, Francis invites the faithful to consider mothering the Lord Jesus Christ. This maternity is a direct result of their being children of the Father, Spouses of Christ in the Spirit, and brothers and sisters of Christ. Maternity is a natural result of having been brought into a new household as spouses. The spouse, who is brother or sister to the Spouse, is also child to the Father whose household she or he must bless with a Son. This mothering of the Son is done through good example by which the faithful not only mother the Son of God but birth others into the Gospel life.

This mothering of others is bringing them to the point where they can glorify the Father. In a romance language, such as Spanish, an expression concerning the birthing process is *dar a luz* (bring to light). Through good example, mothers of Jesus are called to bring Him who is the Light to others. In this way, they live out Jesus' injunction that believers be "the light of the world. . . . Let your light shine so that other's will see the good that you do and glorify your Father in heaven" (Mt 5:14–16). When a mother births a son, the kinfolk glorify the father, especially in cultures where the birth of a son is a sign of male dominance and the father's genes are considered stronger than those of the mother. As sexist as this might seem, Christians are called to birth a Son (Jesus) to the glory of God the Father who is certainly stronger than the human soul.

This certainly was true of Mary, Jesus' natural mother. She gave birth to the Son of God, and, even in her human frailty, she was able to join the evangelical family that does the will of the Father. Consequently, she is not just the mother of the Faithful as the Church had defined her; she is also the sister of the faithful. She walked side by side with the disciples as they joined Jesus in his mendicant life and his begging for alms. In inviting Christians to imitate her maternity, Francis invites them to consider her as a sister in the task of birthing the Son. (This is especially true of priests, who continue to incarnate the Son in the bread and the wine.)

Although kinship language and imagery abounds in all of Francis's opuscula, nowhere is it more manifest than in his Hymn in the Letter to All the Faithful, where he describes how the faithful soul enters a kinship relationship with God and with others. Considering the reality of the medieval family to which Francis belonged, it is easier to understand why Francis virtually breaks out into song after this explanation. The only way to truly understand this exuberant and affective manifestation on the part of Francis, however, is to experience for ourselves what it means to be children, spouses, brothers, sisters, and mothers of the Triune God—and brothers, sisters, mothers, and children of each other.

CHAPTER V:

KINSHIP IN CLARE'S OPUSCULA

Of Francis's early followers, none was more insistent on keeping his ideals burning in the heart of his evangelical family than Clare of Assisi. In Francis, Clare found an emissary who brought Christ's invitation to liberate herself from traditional kinship roles in order to espouse the eternal King. In Clare, Francis found a *plantulam* (little plant) that kept his ideal of evangelical poverty alive in the Franciscan family tree as it grew after his death.

Yet we do well to recall that Clare had a life and formation before Francis and outlived him by about twenty-six years. Although she insisted on being his *plantula*, she was a person in her own right and made her presence known within the Franciscan family of her time and on into the present. We recall the wisdom and teaching found in her opuscula as a source of inspiration. Although that inspiration was originally written down for one or more of her daughters, with the passing of the centuries, it has become public domain for the Franciscan family and the Christian faithful of our time.

CLARE'S OPUSCULA

Keeping in mind that Clare loved Francis because of his involvement in her vocation, we now turn to her opuscula (Appendix C). It comes as a great surprise that a general interest in Clare's opuscula[1] has been expressed in the Franciscan family only after the seventh centenary of her death.[2] The Italian Franciscans added her sources to the Fonti Francescane in 1977.[3] Eventually other language groups began to print Francis and Clare's opuscula together,[4] but it was only in 1982 that an English edition brought Francis and Clare's opuscula together into one volume: Regis Armstrong and Ignatius Brady's *Francis and Clare: The Complete Works*.[5]

Perhaps only now is the Franciscan family able to truly grasp and cultivate her teaching. For her opuscula cannot be said to be a mere imitation of Francis's teaching. They not only reflect the influence that Francis and his opuscula had on her, but also manifest her capacity to turn her *cotidianidad* into mystical theology. But Clare is not a theologian in the scientific understanding of the word. Rather, she is one who lived and breathed theology in such a way as to inspire others. Hers is a theology written down for life and the *cotidiano*; it is not dogma. Her opuscula do not present a systematic explanation of her thought; they are occasional writings meant to comfort, encourage, sustain, and challenge. In this way, hers is a theology infused in her through contemplation and service.

Clare's writings reveal an excellent education, in keeping with her upbringing in a noble family, which prepared her for life as a matron.[6] They also reveal her as a woman of her age. Clare's language has a certain nobility that suggests a "regal spirituality."[7]

CLARE'S USE OF THE SACRED SCRIPTURES

Like the European writers of her day, Clare turned to the Scriptures as a primary source for her inspiration. Her opuscula make conscious and unconscious reference to biblical passages and reveal her constant turning to God's word as a source of hope and a means of exhortation. (Her use of scriptural texts in the opuscula can be divided as follows[8]: references in 3EpAgn, 33; in 1EpAgn, 30; in RCl, 30; in 4EpAgn, 29; in TestCl, 25; in 2EpAgn, 24; in EpErm, 19; and in BenCl, 7.) All together, she used some 146 references from the Christian Scriptures and some 51 references from the Hebrew Scriptures. Of the 197 times she quoted or alluded to the Sacred Scriptures[9] in her opuscula, the single book quoted most oftenis the Gospel of Matthew, which she used thirty-six times. She quoted Luke seventeen times and John nine times, never once referring to the Gospel of Mark. She quoted the Gospels 62 times in total, while she referred to the rest of the Christian Scriptures 84 times. She quoted the Psalms 18 times and the rest of the Old Testament 33 times. She alluded most often to 2 Cor 11:2 (nine times).

Her use of the Scriptures should not be considered a mere imitation of Francis's use. When we compare Clare's scriptural references to those of Francis, we may be surprised surprised by her extensive use of the Scriptures. In his thirty-seven opuscula, Francis cited the Sacred Scripture some 434 times, which is an average of 15.5 times per work. Clare on the other hand cited them 197 times for an average of 24.6 times per work, significantly more often Francis.

Nor did Clare simply repeat the same Scripture passages used by Francis. Only 38 of the Scripture passages used by Clare can be found in 69 passages from Francis' opuscula. These she used in 56 passages of her own opuscula.[10] During her struggle with the Roman Curia, which bounced her and her sisters from one Rule and set of Constitutions to the next, Clare seems to have turned primarily to Francis's Rules and his Second redaction of the Letter to the Faithful, together, as a beacon in the storm. The importance she attached to these particular writings of Francis can be guaged by the number of times she alludes to them or directly quotes them in her own writings. Many of the scriptural passages that she echoed from Francis can be found in them: eighteen passages from the "Non-Bulled Rule," fourteen from the Second redaction of the Letter to the Faithful, and nine from the "Bulled Rule." She quotes some Scriptures found in his other opuscula as well, but this does not mean that Clare actually had access to all of those texts.[11] She may not even have consciously borrowed from these texts. Her use of the verses quoted by him may simply be an indicator of her familiarity with his thinking and her affinity for his spirituality.

Kinship in the Sacred Scriptures Used by Clare

Although Clare did not specifically turn to the Song of Songs until her last letter to Agnes, spousal language and imagery are a very important factor in her opuscula. Clare's frequent use of the word *sponsa* alludes to 2 Cor 11:2. This verse—in which St. Paul admits wanting to jealously guard the Corinthians because he has promised them as a chaste virgin to the only Spouse, who is Christ—seems to be the thought behind Clare's spousal references. It makes sense that Clare refers to this passage of Scripture[12] because her opuscula reveal a certain preoccupation with the perseverance and constancy of the Poor Sisters.

Sponsa also alludes to Rev 5:6; 14:1–4 and 19:9, however, in which she is espoused to the Lamb of God who is also King. These passages from Revelations refer to the Lamb as the one who has been slain and who sits upon the throne. He is the one who, because of his suffering, has redeemed the faithful and is worthy to receive their worship. Clare ties her spousal reference to both the humanity and divinity of the Spouse who is Christ. She insists that the sisters need to stick by their Spouse in both his suffering and his glory. They are to be with him through thick and thin or, as wedding vows state, "for better or for worse, in sickness and in health."

Unlike the other foundations that came from San Damiano, the Poor Sisters at San Damiano were never under Cistercian Visitators.[13] Nevertheless, Clare's writings reflect the influence that she received from Cistercian spirituality. While Francis never once quoted or alluded to the popular Song of Songs, Clare makes remarkable use of this book in her Fourth Letter to St. Agnes. One can only suppose that Cardinal Hugolino must have introduced her to the thought of Bernard of Clairvaux and other Cistercians.[14] Bernard of Clairvaux and other Cistercian writers in the twelfth century had taken what the patristic writers had begun and further developed it as a spousal mysticism based on the Song of Songs.[15]

Spiritual writers of the twelfth century brought the language of the Song of Songs into the mystical writings of the High Middle Ages—especially with respect to virgins. In Clare's writings, we see that, like the many women who chose to live in chastity, she saw herself as "destined for a higher consumption. She scintillated with fertility and power. Into her body, as into the Eucharistic bread on the altar, poured the inspiration of the Holy Spirit and the fullness of the humanity of Christ."[16] Male mystics were also sensitive to this imagery of the Song of Songs, but these nuptial themes, first articulated by men, become in women's writings more erotic and affective.

The other kinship references from the Scriptures used most often by Clare is Mt 12:50 (four times) to which can be added her reference to Mt 19:21 and Mt 19:29. These three passages from the Gospel of Matthew she probably borrowed from Francis's Letter to the Faithful, "Non-Bulled Rule," and "Bulled Rule." They refer to the need to break with one's family in order to be able to sell what one has and give it to the poor. This break with family is necessary in order to follow Jesus Christ, live the Gospel, and thus be Jesus' sisters and mothers. Clare's use of these texts manifests a complete adherence to Francis's teachings about family relationships—with the family of origin and with the evangelical family of God.

Another kinship passage from the Scriptures that Clare refers to is

Lk 17:10, in which Jesus calls "useless servants" those who do only what is necessary. Clare's use of this passage shows a noble concept of servanthood in which a servant was a part of the family or household. At the time, there are three titles for the female servants which serve a noble household:[17] *serva*, *famula*, and *ancilla*. She uses all three.[18]

RELATIONSHIP WITH THE FAMILY

Clare took to heart Francis's evangelical call to break with family in order to enter a kinship relationship with Jesus Christ. Yet she added a different twist to Francis's call. As a woman, she was not interested only in a break with the family of origin. A woman, especially a noble woman, was raised with this break in mind as she was prepared to marry and leave her father's household to enter the household of her husband. Like the noble women of her time, Clare had been prepared for such a break with her family of origin. Thus, the break that she stressed was a break with the family of destination, which is to say a refusal of earthly marriage.

SACRUM COMMERCIUM [19]

Clare's interest in the breaking of familial ties is manifested in a particular way in her letters to Agnes of Prague. Agnes, daughter of King Ottocar I of Bohemia and Queen Constance of Hungary, was destined for a royal marriage. From age three, Agnes had several suitors who desired her hand in marriage. These were the prince of Slesia, King Henry III of England, King Henry VII of Germany, and the widower, Emperor Frederick II.[20] She came to know about Francis and Clare of Assisi, however, and chose a life of poverty and virginity. She did not have the same trouble with her family of origin as Clare and Francis had had.[21] But she did have to seek the aid of Pope Gregory IX in order to break the cultural and political schemas of her day. This need for aid was probably due to ties and treaties that her father might have made with the possible suitors.

Clare's letters to Agnes reflect certain knowledge of Agnes's social and personal reality. Having come from a noble family herself, albeit not a princely one, Clare knew what Agnes must have gone through in her training to be a royal wife and matron. The marriage of nobility in the Middle Ages was a business deal, a *commercium*. Clare also understood "marriage with

Christ, or spiritual union with Christ, as an economic deal."[22] She also has to have understood at what cost Agnes had taken the veil. After all, Agnes could have become an empress. Clare does not belittle this cost, but rather exalts Agnes's *sacrum commercium*. Agnes, like Clare and Francis before her, had traded a life of comfort for a life of austerity, a life of wealth for a life of poverty, an earthly promise for a celestial one. In Agnes's case, she had traded a royal spouse, the "illustrious emperor" (*inclito Caesari*) for Jesus Christ—a "spouse of even greater origin" (*sponsum nobilioris generis*; IEpAgn 5–7).

While the male religious tended to give up one family, the female in reality gave up two families. She broke with the family of origin, and (what was even more important) she broke with the family of destination. Clare's letters to Agnes show this turning from an earthly fiancée to be a *sacrum commercium* by which one leaves behind earthly marriage and the possibility of offspring for a divine Spouse in the eternal household of God the Father. This "sacred exchange" is a reason to rejoice, and Clare invites Agnes to do so because she has chosen the better part. Agnes has cast off her precious garments to enter the kingdom of heaven through the narrow gate (IEpAgn 21–29). In doing so, she has become the spouse, mother, and sister/daughter of Jesus Christ (IEpAgn 12);[23] she is able to carry him spiritually in her body as the Virgin of virgins had carried him materially in hers. She has not allowed herself to be deceived as are the kings and queens of this world. She had broken free of the vicious cycle of breeding that goes on in royal families, choosing to mother Christ instead. She traded the transitory for the eternal—Him by whom all things are held.[24]

In Clare's writings, as in the rest of Franciscan tradition, the *sacrum commercium* is a kinship relationship for it is a marriage by which offspring are brought into the household of God. But in Clare's opuscula, poverty is not a poor and battered woman. Rather, the spouse in question is the poor and naked Christ. The heavenly Spouse incarnated poverty, becoming poor so that the faithful might be rich (2 Cor 8:9). Yet Clare's love for the Spouse was not interested only in the treasures the Spouse could give her. She proposes a spousal relationship that is "for better or for worse." The *sacrum commercium* that she proposes as a spousal union is one based on earthly marriage where a bride/wife has to share her husband's lot in life.[25] She has to stand by him according to social convention and, being much younger than him, she has to learn from him how to deal with life and the people around her. The faithful *sponsa* learns from her *Sponsus* and she desires to share his lot. It is for this reason that Clare invites Agnes to this "sacred exchange": "Because if your suffer with him, you will reign with him, if your suffer with him, you will rejoice with him, if you die with him on the cross of tribulation, you possess holy, splendid, eternal mansions and your name, inscribed in the book (of life), will be glorious among humans. In this way, you will come to possess in eternity and age upon age the gloriouos celestial Reign in place of earthly and transitory honor. You will participate in eternal goods in exchange for corruptible ones and you will live age upon age" (2EpAgn 21–23).[26]

CONCERN FOR PERSEVERANCE

Clare's writings manifest a real concern for perseverance.[27] It seems that, having seen and heard what was happening in the Order of Friars Minor after Francis's death, she wanted to insure that her sisters would remain faithful to Francis and to Clare's original inspiration. Thus, the poverty of the Spouse in his incarnation became central to her spirituality. Her stress on poverty and minority seem to be even stronger than Francis's in his opuscula.[28]

Clare was well aware that Francis, like other medieval men, saw her and her sisters as naturally weak and fragile women. Yet she insists that they had proven themselves to Francis who examined them in light of the saints and his own brothers. Seeing their ability to endure hardship and trials, he took it upon himself to care for them with "special care and solicitude" (TestCl 27–29).[29] For Francis, this "special care and solicitude" was a part of the struggle of God's household over and against the household of Satan. Clare and her sisters had espoused Christ and had become members of God's household.

God is the Father with whom one needs to be reconciled because of the "transgression of our first parent" (1EpAgn 14).[30] In her first letter to Agnes, Clare invites her to be strengthened in the service of the "poor crucified one" (*pauper Crucifixus*). He it was who underwent the Passion so as to rescue us from the Prince of Darkness. Clare places the rescue in terms of one household against another. The Prince of Darkness is set up in a tug of war with the Father.

Yet Clare knew that living in poverty was not an easy thing. She must have seen any number of sisters return to their families of origin. Clare's uncle Monaldo had likewise tried to force her and Catherine (Agnes) to return to the household. Many other heads of families had probably done the same for the other noble women who had joined them at San Damiano and elsewhere. Many families used emotional pressure to convince their sons not to join the mendicant orders. It is only reasonable to expect that the Poor Ladies would have received the same treatment. A mother's tears must have tempted many a Damianite to turn back from Christ, the Spouse.

She realized that the temptation to flee the Spouse in order to return to the family of origin is great. Manifesting the same jealousy that Paul showed the Corinthians, Clare insists that one should know one's vocation. Her own lifestyle became her pedagogy for the Damianites and other Poor Sisters.[31] You should never let go; be wary of those who would place stumbling blocks in the way or who would persecute you; bring to completion and fulfill the mystery that you have embraced; take up your cross and hold fast to the path of Christ.[32]

Clare blesses those sisters and daughters who persevere until the end with the same blessing that Francis had given Leo (Num 36:24–26; BenCl 2–5):[33]

> I Clare, handmaiden of Christ, little plant of our most blessed father St. Francis, your sister and mother and of all the poor sisters, although unworthy, beg our Lord Jesus Christ through his mercy and the intercession of his most holy mother Saint Mary and Blessed Michael archangel and all the holy angels of God, Blessed Francis our father and all male and female saints, may the same clestial Father give you and confirm this his most holy blessing in heaven and on earth: on earth may he multiply grace and his virtues in you among his servants and handmaidens in his mililtant Church; and in heaven, exhalt you and glorify you in the Church triumphant among his male and female saints (BenCl 6–10).[34]

In Clare's self-definition, we find a woman who saw herself in the light of others as if reflected in a mirror.[35] She called herself *ancilla* of Christ, "father" Francis's *plantulam*, and the *soror et mater* of the Poor Ladies. We will use these self-definitions in order to consider the kinship language found in Clare's opuscula.

ANCILLA CHRISTI [36]

Jesus Christ is ever present in Clare's opuscula.[37] She refers to him as Lord some sixty-eight times.[38] He is truly her God and King,[39] her all, and she is his *famula*, his *ancilla*.[40] Although Clare developed a regal spousal spirituality, she never once attributed the title "spouse of Christ" (*sponsa Christi*) to herself or referred to Christ as her spouse in her writings, preferring the role of beloved servant girl. Yet, despite Clare's insistence on being the *ancilla* of Christ, we cannot forget that she worshipped a God who is Three in One. For this reason, we will consider her relationship with each member of the Trinity as part of her being *ancilla Christi*.

Clare referred to God twenty-eight times without expressly tying the title to God the Father. She also used the word *God* another four times in a way that makes it clear that by *God* she meant the Father.[41] We can only conclude that when Clare used the word *God*, she was referring to the Triune Godhead,[42] as she had no trouble in singling out the individual Persons of the Trinity on other occasions. We have already noted the number of times she referred to Jesus Christ (124 times). She also singled out the Father seventeen times and the Holy Spirit five times.[43] Although the numbers manifest an emphasis on the Son, Clare did not ignore the Father or the Holy Spirit.

CLARE'S DESCRIPTION OF THE FATHER

The witnesses to Clare's life of holiness all attest to her having developed a life of intense prayer.[44] Unfortunately, she did not leave behind any written prayers except for the blessing she gave to all of her present and future sisters. Because of this, it is hard to put together an image of God the Father in the spirituality of St. Clare. She left us only small glimpses of God as the Father of the Spouse and Lord.

FATHER OF THE SPOUSE

If we try to piece together Clare's portrait of God the Father, we have to begin with Jesus Christ. Where Francis turned continually to the Father, Clare turned to the Spouse, who is the Son of the Father.[45] She did not even dare to call the Father of Jesus, "our" Father, except when using the title "Pater noster" for the Lord's Prayer which the sisters were required to say (in a Rule patterned after the Rule of St. Francis).

This may seem strange, yet Clare's relationship with the Trinity is a familial and not an individualistic one. She modeled her relationship to the Trinity on the patterns of the noble families. In this pattern, the bride would leave her father's house to become a vassal in the household of her husband's father. Preachers of the period insisted that the wife was to honor and respect her in-laws. This is not to say that the bride's familial relationships were lacking in warmth or emotion in the household of the husband. There are many testimonies to the fact that husbands and wives in the arranged marriages of the nobility did indeed come to love each other.[46] There is even testimony of brides coming to love and feel a part of the husband's family. Yet, the love that was expected of these brides was not one based on emotion, but on commitment and fidelity to a new household, that of her husband. This commitment, even when it was a loving one, was based on hierarchical norms and principles. When a bride's father-in-law was the paterfamilias of a great and noble family, he was to be treated with all due respect as her husband's father.

Clare had been raised to leave home and become a matron in the household of her husband's father. This reality was etched into her psyche. But her bridegroom was not an earthly noble, so her bridegroom's Father was no ordinary paterfamilias. He was, as Francis had told them in his "Form of Life," the highest supreme King (FormViv in RCl 6.3). Her respect for so great a King could only bring her to her knees before him who is the Father of her *Sponsus*,[47] our Lord Jesus Christ (TestCl 77).

FATHER OF MERCIES

Clare's description of her bridegroom's father shows the noble nature of her attachment to God. She has no terms of endearment for the Father. Rather, the Father is *altissimus* (RCl 6.1),[48] he is *perfectus* (2EpAgn 4), he is *caelestis* (RCl 6.1),[49] he is *gloriosus* (TestCl 2), and he is *summus Rex* (RCl 6.3).[50] This does not mean that Clare did not love God the Father. She obviously did. Yet, her love for him was expressed with the noblest form of respect that she could give him.

For Clare, the Most High, perfect, heavenly, glorious Father and greatest King is, above all, the *Pater misericordiarum*[51] (TestCl 2, 58; BenCl 12). Clare took this rather peculiar title from Paul's hymn of consolation in

2 Cor 1:3–7. In the Vulgate, the word *misericordiarum* can also be found in 2 Chr 6:42; 32:32; 35:26; Ps 24:6; Is 63:7; and Lam 3:32. In these verses, it is used to mean "favor," "pious works," and "faithfulness"—as well as "mercy." It is only in 2 Cor 1:3, however, that *misericordiarum* is specifically tied to the title *Pater*.[52]

God is Clare's primary consolation.[53] She turns to God for consolation as Father of mercies in Paul's hymn, in which consolation is given by God to Christians so that they might console others in turn. Clare saw her vocation as having been just that. She had received consolation from Francis who had received Divine consolation at San Damiano during the process of his conversion (TestCl 9). She, in turn, became consolation for the Poor Sisters. Specifically, she realized that her words to Agnes of Prague were a consolation for her, whom she had never met (2EpAgn 10). This vocation of consolation she specifically assigned to the abbess, especially in caring for the afflicted sisters (RCl 4.11). Thus, just as in Paul's hymn, consolation received must become consolation given.

Besides the Pauline connection with consolation, Clare connects the title, *Father of mercies*, to mercy, grace, and the benefits received from Him, who is the Father of mercies. The greatest benefit is that of the vocation by which the sisters are called from their families into the evangelical family. This family was founded by Jesus Christ, yet, in the lives of Clare and her sisters, it was Francis who in word and example showed them that Jesus was the "way" of their vocation.

The vocation to which God called the sisters must give consolation even outside the monastery walls. This consolation must extend itself from one generation to the next. Clare's interest in God's household seems not to know the limits of time and space. She sees that the Father of mercies works in her sisters, gifting them and making them so fragrant that their aroma reaches far beyond San Damiano (TestCl 58). This fragrance extends itself even into our age as Clare blesses both in life and in death (BenCl 11).

HEAVENLY FATHER

Clare learned from Francis that God is no ordinary paterfamilias. He is the *Pater caelestis* or heavenly Father (TestCl 14). In addition, the Damianites are meant to glorify the Father within his Church by the holiness of their lives. While a mother was supposed to give the infant its primary education, it was the responsibility of the father to educate his children for life. In her opuscula, Clare turns from Francis to God the heavenly Father, for she understands that she and the sisters must learn directly from him if they are to persevere in their vocation and thus glorify him within the family of the Church.

Clare insisted on perseverance. She did not want shame brought upon the family of God, so she turned to several saints as models and instructors for her sisters. Francis, in word and example, had begun their education (3EpAgn 30).[54] The sisters were to model themselves after the mother of the Divine Spouse (3EpAgn 18).[55] Agnes of Prague was to turn to Rachael and St. Agnes, the virgin martyr, as models, too. In the Middle Ages, Rachael was proposed as a model of contemplative life.[56] From early Christian times, women like the martyr Agnes had chosen to reject marriage and remain virgins for the heavenly Spouse. In fact, St. Agnes was one of the favorite saints of the medieval period and was often used as a role model for virgins.[57]

For Clare, however, these role models were not enough. Knowing the educative role of both fathers and husbands, Clare also turned to God as teacher of holiness. The Father who forgives is called heavenly by Clare and is placed as a model for the sisters in the monastery. The sisters were to forgive each other. Otherwise, how could they expect the heavenly Father to forgive them? Perhaps this notion of the *heavenly* Father is meant to point up the contrast with the earthly fathers who do not always forgive their children nor teach their offspring to forgive their own siblings. God, on the other hand, does everything possible to forgive his children and to teach them how to love and serve each other.

Finally, the heavenly Father is the one whom Clare asks to give and confirm her blessing (BenCl 8). He is, after all, the celestial Paterfamilias on whom the family is founded and centered and from whom the family receives its vocation and blessing.

THE MOST BEAUTIFUL AMONG THE CHILDREN OF HUMANITY

In her "Blessing for the Sisters, Present and to Come" (BenCl 7), Clare calls upon the Father's household to intercede to the Father for the sisters. Clare asks the rest of God's household—Mary, Michael the Archangel and the other angels, Francis, and the male and female saints—for intercession. In this blessing, the Lord Jesus Christ is invoked as the first of God's household. She does not request Jesus' intercession but his mercy. Jesus Christ is the "mercy" of whom God is Father.

Jesus is the absolute center of Clare's attention and devotion. She is his *ancilla* and *famula*, his spokesperson and instrument. He is the spouse and mirror that she recommends to Agnes of Prague—and to us, through our appropriation of her Letters to Agnes.

SPOUSE

Although we have run into Jesus Christ at every turn of our study of Clare's opuscula, it is imperative that we consider him specifically under the category of Spouse. For Clare, Jesus Christ is the reason for abandoning the family in order to live in poverty. He is the reason for persevering in the way of life which she and the sisters have chosen. He is their final reward. In all this, he is, first and foremost, Spouse and Mirror.

Francis of Assisi had invited Clare to wed Christ (LegCl 5.6). Both Innocent III and Gregory IX refer to the daughters of Clare as having renounced everything to follow him who became poor—the Way, the Truth, and the Life. They go on to insist that He, the *sponsus caelestis*, has reclined the sisters' heads upon his shoulders so that he can sustain their frail bodies through the turmoil of poverty. It seems that Clare took to heart these spousal references in the description of her vocation and that of the sisters. Nowhere is this better seen than in her letters to Agnes of Prague, especially in her final letter, where Clare exuberantly speaks of being taken into the nuptial chamber where the Lord will hold her in his arms kissing her with the kisses of his mouth (4EpAgn 30–32).

There was little room for spousal language in the "Form of Life for the Poor Sisters," the "Testament of the Virgin Saint Clare," and the "Blessing for the Sisters Present and to Come." In those texts, Clare had other matters to attend to, especially insuring that Francis's ideal of poverty not be lost. This ideal of poverty, however, seems to give rise to and be nourished by Clare's spousal language, a language that, in her letters, expresses a spousal spirituality.[58]

Clare's spousal language is tied to the negation of "matrimony" (*co-niugium, connubium*; 2EpAgn 6–7) and the acceptance of "betrothal" (*de-spondere*;[59] 1EpAgn 5), and being a "bride" (*sponsa*;[60] 1EpAgn 12) of the divine "groom" (*sponsum*;[61] 1EpAgn 7). Not once does Clare refer to the roles of wife (*uxor*) or husband (*maritus*) in her writings.[62] It seems Clare is not interested in contrasting the difference between ordinary wives and the spouses of Christ. Rather, she limits her discussion to Agnes of Prague as the model of what the spouse of Christ is to be.

She is to be the one who has rejected earthly marriage for a heavenly betrothal. This rejection is best seen in Agnes, for while Clare and the others may have rejected ordinary noblemen, she rejected the Emperor. Hers is a demonstration of just how far one should go in breaking ties with the families of origin and destination when choosing to betroth a "spouse of more noble origin" (*sponsum nobilioris generis*; 1EpAgn 7). The spouse has to consider that she or he is betrothed to the Lamb, who is the King, Jesus Christ.[63] Clare's insistence on the royal dignity of the *Sponsus*, although alluded to in her First Letter to Agnes, is only explicitly announced in her final letter. It seems that Clare had been holding on to this mystery as the best part, the final wonder of wonders. The husband, whom one has followed in poverty and hardship, is the supreme, celestial, and eternal King (4EpAgn 1, 4, 17, 27). He is the Lamb who was slain and now reigns forever and ever.

How wonderful it is to have such a Spouse and to hold on to him. How extremely desirous it is to spend eternity in his loving embraces and be kissed with the kisses of his mouth (4EpAgn 30). The thought of it seems to send Clare into an ecstatic and almost erotic state. One could say that the Fourth Letter to Agness seems to be Clare's "Swan Song" and she desires to sing it for her daughter, mother, and sister—Agnes. Clare has transcended the family of origin. Moreover, in singing of the desire for her Spouse, she sings to Agnes as if to the whole evangelical family of which she has become mother and sister.

The betrothal becomes a process of contemplation, reflection, and imitation. It leads to the realization that final consumption with the Spouse can only happen through a joining of oneself to the evangelical family of which the Father of the Spouse is Paterfamilias and where the spouse of the lamb is also mother, sister, and daughter.[64] The spouse is to follow the

Spouse (2EpAgn 7) by being mother, sister, brother, son, and daughter of the King in the lives of those around her or him.

Mirror

Spousal spirituality in Clare is very much tied to gazing into the mirror, which is the Spouse. In the High Middle Ages, European noble marriages were usually made up of older men and younger women. Because of this, the husband often found himself having to educate his young wife. In being handed over by the father, she moved from one tutelage to another. Clare continually insists on this educative role of the Spouse, for if the mortal husband could be teacher of his wife, how much more should the eternal Bridegroom educate and form his brides.But how?

In Clare's letters to Agnes, the Groom's pedagogy is that of the speculum (mirror).[65] Clare invites Agnes to observe, consider, contemplate, and desire to imitate "your Spouse, the most beautiful among the sons of men" (2EpAgn 19–20)[66] who for her salvation had become the vilest of men. This kenosis is the way in which the Son of God became our mirror. The bride then is to *speculare* (reflect) her wealth and beauty in the mirror, that is, in the Groom.[67]

Clare's interest in having Agnes reflect her wealth and beauty in the mirror may sound vain to our contemporary ear. Yet, we need to read Clare's writing in the context of her day. With a growing interest in governing family life on the part of the Church, women were invited to beautify themselves inwardly and externally for the pleasure of their husbands.[68] Mirrors were certainly essential tools in the task of beautification. Stereotypically, the mirror has always been considered a woman's instrument.[69]

Clare's insistence on the mirror in her letters to Agnes manifests the medieval concern that the bride be pleasing to the groom's eyes, especially when the groom in question is the Lord. In Clare's era, literary mirrors abounded for the expressed purpose of helping both men and women, but especially women, beautify themselves inwardly.

We find the word *speculum* twelve times and the verb *speculare* twice in Clare's opuscula. Most of these are in the Fourth Letter to Agnes, where Clare specifically describes the act of looking at oneself in the mirror as a task belonging to the bride of Jesus Christ.[70]

Look into this mirror everyday, o queen, spouse of Jesus Christ, and
constantly examine your face in it. In this way you will be able to interiorly and exteriorly adorn yourself completely wrapping yourself with
a variety of dresses and with the flowers and vestments of all virtues
adorned as is proper to the daughter and the most beloved spouse of
the Exalted King. Moreover, blessed poverty, holy humilty, and ineffable
charity shine in this mirror, and you can contemplate them throughout
the whole mirror with the grace of God.

I say focus in the beginning of this reflection on the poverty of
him who is laid in a manger and wrapped in diapers. Oh surprising humilty, oh stupendous poverty! The King of angels, the Lord of heaven
and earth is put to rest in a manger. Then, in the middle of your reflection, consider the humilty or at least the blessed poverty, innumer-
able labors, and penalties which he sustained for the redemption of
humankind. Then, at the end of this reflection, contemplate the inef-
fible charity that caused him to want to suffer on the stake of the cross
and on it die a most reprehensible death (4EpAgn 15–23).[71]

Although it is only in the Fourth Letter to Agnes that Clare ex-
pounds her thoughts on the mirror, it is not the first time she mentions it
in her letters to Agnes. Already in the Third Letter to Agnes (3EpAgn 12–
15), she invites Agnes to rejoice and not to be saddened. Clare tells her to
look into God. Clare invites Agnes to do this with her "mind, soul, and
heart" as if into an eternal mirror that shines forth the image of the "divine
substance." Clare is not referring to a quick glance at the mirror. Rather, she
intends a long hard look that is meant to transform Agnes and all brides
into an image of God's divinity and, in this way, to experience what God's
friends and lovers experience.

This long hard look is meant to show Agnes and all brides how they
need to beautify themselves to be pleasing to the Groom. Ultimately, Clare
considers three areas in which the human "mind, soul, and heart" need to
beautify themselves: poverty, humility, and charity. Once again, Clare shows
herself a noble woman of her time, she understands that the bride must be
formed by the groom and the Groom in question is hung upon the cross as
a mirror for the bride (4EpAgn 24). This Groom is not a resplendent and
luxurious mirror, as those found in the homes of queens. Rather, in his kenosis, he is poor, humble, and charitable, naked upon a cross (TestCl 45).

In the kenosis, which leads to the cross, Clare sees that the bride must be moved by pity for Him whose suffering knows no equal (4EpAgn 25).

This pity becomes the intense craving of the bride in the Song of Songs, who yearns to the point of suffering for her heavenly Groom. Obviously, although Clare refers to the Groom/Mirror hanging on the cross, she understands that he reigns triumphantly in heaven, where he prepares his wine cellar for the faithful bride. Before arriving there to be with Him, however, the bride must beautify herself in the poverty, humility, and charity she sees in the Groom/Mirror.

CHRIST AS BROTHER

Although Clare never explicitly refers to Christ as brother, she does explicitly call Agnes his sister. This fraternal relationship of Agnes and Christ is always couched in other kinship references. Agnes is called *sponsa, mater, et soror* (spouse, mother, and sister) of Jesus Christ, or simply *soror et sponsa* of the highest King of Heaven (1EpAgn 12, 24; 3EpAgn 1).

Clare's vision of the betrothed as spouse and brother does not come as a surprise in a time when the paterfamilias still reigned in the noble household. For when a paterfamilias jealously held on to his power, even married sons remained as vassals. Being under a head of household strengthened sibling bonds among vassals who had come together as the result of marriage. The often-quoted book of Tobit served as support for the sibling bond between marriage partners.

Husbands were encouraged not to forget that their wives were also their sisters in faith, and we have seen that the spousal relationship of Tobit and Sara was proposed to them as an ideal. The Vulgate story of Tobit and Sara emphasizes man's need for a helpmate. This ascribes a more fraternal role[72] to spouses.

Clare adds the fraternal relationship dimension expected of married couples in thirteenth-century Christendom to her spousal references. As daughters of the Father, she and the other Damianites are the sisters of Christ, their spouse. It is a spousal sisterhood that Clare wants to transmit to Agnes. She is not just the promised bride of the King; she is also his sister. This fraternal relationship in earthly marriages was meant often to remind husbands that their wives were to be treated with respect and with as much equality as their limited nature allowed. In Clare, however, it would seem that Christ had no need for such a reminder. The fraternal reference may have served instead as a reminder to Agnes of her dignity as partner and *sponsa* of Jesus Christ. This certainly would be in keeping with Clare's referring to Agnes as God's helper (*adiutricem*)[73] in sustaining the frail members of his body (3EpAgn 8).

THE CALL OF THE HOLY SPIRIT

Although the witnesses in the *Process* gave a special role to the Holy Spirit in the formation of the young Clare, Clare herself hardly ever mentions the Holy Spirit in her opuscula. In fact, she explicitly refers to the Holy Spirit only three times: once when quoting Francis, once when speaking about Francis, and finally as a part of the trinitarian formula (RCl 6.3; TestCl 11; BenCl 1). In two other passages, she refers to the Spirit of the Lord: one time in quoting Francis and another in referring to God's call (RCl 9.9; 2EpAgn 14). She refers vaguely to the Spirit another three times: each time as the unifying agent who joins the brides of Christ in a common and joyful response to the divine Sponsus (4EpAgn 7, 26, 36).

In considering Clare's usage of the Holy Spirit in her opuscula, one cannot help but notice how the Spirit is intimately connected with Francis. This close connection of Francis and the Spirit is reminiscent of Luke's connection of the Virgin Mary and the Spirit.[74] It seems that, for Clare, Francis was an instrument of the Holy Spirit. Francis foresaw the coming of the poor Ladies and invited them to divine nuptials. He challenged them and his friars to seek nothing more than the Spirit of the Lord and his operation (cf. RB 10.8), which is to say that the Spirit and the Spirit alone can take a person to perfection in the living of her or his vows.

For Clare, the perfection in living the vows is what binds the bride to the Bridegroom. In her Second Letter to Agnes, Clare insists on this perfection as being made manifest in Agnes by her refusal of the emperor's marriage proposal to eventually join Christ in the heavenly bridal chamber (2EpAgn 5–7). Agnes, because the Spirit of the Lord has called her to them, cannot allow anyone to impede her in perfectly living her vows.

Curiously, Clare quotes Francis's "Form of Life," given to Clare and her sisters, in which he states that she and the other Damianites have betrothed themselves to the Holy Spirit, yet she never once speaks of this be-trothal.[75] Rather, she insists repeatedly on betrothal to Christ. When Clare wrestled with understanding Francis's "Form of Life," she probably came to understand betrothal to the Holy Spirit as betrothal *through* the Holy Spirit. Certainly, the witnesses in the *Process of Canonization* agree that, if Clare had lived her vows to perfection, it was due to the Holy Spirit's operation. She herself claims that it was the heavenly Father who enlightened her through the words and actions of Francis (RCl 6.1; TestCl 24) who in turn was enlightened by the Holy Spirit (TestCl 11).

PLANT OF OUR MOST BLESSED FATHER

Clare, as a medieval noblewoman, knew that her life was meant to be defined by the role she would take in her husband's family. In espousing Christ, she needed to come to learn what her role was in light of Christ's paterfamilias. Although she referred to Francis as father, she knew that he was not the father of Christ. Francis himself reserved the title *Pater* only to God (RnB 22.34). In the Middle Ages, *father* was a gender-specific title for a male authority figure in a household. He was over and above the family. Francis did not see himself as such an authority. Rather, he saw himself as the spouse of the Son. Consequently, he and his offspring were under the one *Pater*, who is the God and Father of the Lord Jesus Christ. Why then did Clare ignore Francis's wishes and refer to him as father?

FATHER FRANCIS?

> And just as the Lord gave us our most blessed father Francis as our founder, planter and helper in the service of Christ and in those things we have promised our Lord and blessed father, who while he was still alive was sollicitous in word and deed to always cultivate and foster us his plant, in the same way I recommend and relinquish my sisters who are present and who are still to come to the successor of our most blessed father Francis and (to his) whole religion, that they may always help us to make better progress in the service of God and especially to better observe most holy poverty (TestCl 48–51).[76]

Clare referred to Francis thirty-two times in her opuscula. To these she added the title *father* twenty-three times. Most of the references to *father*

Francis are in her Testament (TestCl) and Blessing (BenCl),[77] which many consider to be of dubious origin in their present form. Copyists may have added *father* to these two writings, yet the title is also found twice in her "Form of Life for the Poor Sisters" (RCl 1.1; 6.1) and once in her Letters to Agnes (3EpAgn 30). In any case, Francis's frequent presence in Clare's opuscula testifies to the unique position he had in her human and spiritual experience.[78] Most of the references dealing with Francis recall that it was he who taught the Poor Ladies how they were to live their vocation in poverty.

Unlike Pacifico, Clare did not refer to Francis by using the title mother, at least not in her opuscula. She gave in to the mentality of her age, which saw founders and spiritual directors as fathers. In calling him father, she was referring to the spiritual authority God had given him to teach a specific way of living the Gospel. Her use of that title seems to stress the dignity of the way of life she was defending against those who wanted her to live it less radically. This way of life, after all, was given her by Francis, whom the Church had canonized a saint and recognized as a founder on a par with Augustine, Benedict, and others who had written rules for religious communities.

For the community of sisters at San Damiano, Francis was not just any saint; he was their founder, gardener, and helper in the way of poverty. Clare's use of the title *father* certainly could have come from her affection for him, yet her use of the title seems to be more of a polemical tool in defense of the poverty she and Francis had espoused. She seems to have used *father* Francis as the most powerful weapon with which to fight for his ideal and his original insight into Gospel living.[79] Yet, Clare did not want Francis to replace God. She clearly proclaims that if Francis founded, planted, and aided them in the service of Christ, it was because of God. Divine intervention is the source of all that Francis said and did in order to cultivate and foster[80] his *plantula* (the sisters at San Damiano). His planting and cultivating them had one end: the service of God in Christ.

MOTHER FRANCIS!

Her calling him "father" does not mean that Clare ignored Francis's maternity. In her opuscula, Clare adds a hint of his maternity. After all, it is the Lord Father who *genuit*[81] (grew) Clare's flock in the holy Church through the word and example of Francis (TestCl 46). Thus, God is the only true Father of Clare's flock and Francis was more than just the founder of her form of life. He was the instrument by which God's seed bore fruit.

HORTULANUS

Clare calls herself the *plantulam* of the most blessed father, Francis (TestCl 37).[82] However, the imagery used is not congruent. The wording would have been better as "*daughter* of the most beloved *father* Francis" or "*little plant* of the most beloved *gardener* Francis." As we have seen, Clare states in her Testament (TestCl) that Francis was their founder, gardener, and helper. Yet she goes on to describe Francis's role as gardener (*hortulanus*) but not his role as founder or helper. It would seem that it is with this in mind that Clare specifically chose to call herself and even her sisters Francis's little plant(s).

The wording hides a crossing of genders for the blessed Francis. Clare was the daughter of Ortulana whose name means gardener. One cannot help but think that, in her youth, Clare must have been referred to as Ortulana's little plant.[83] In calling herself Francis's *plantulam*, Clare is claiming him as a spiritual mother who replaces her material mother. That Clare imagined Francis as a substitute for Ortulana is witnessed to by the famous vision of nursing at his breast.

VISION OF FRANCIS'S BREAST

> Saint Clare also mentioned that once, in a vision, it seemed to her that she was taking a jar of warm water to saint Francis with a towel for drying his hands, and she was climbing a high staircase, but she walked so lightly, almost as if she were walking on flat earth. And when she came upon Saint Francis, this saint took from his chest a (female) breast and said to the virgin Clare: "Come, receive and suck." And when she had sucked, the saint admonished her to suck again. And when she sucked that which she sucked from there, it was so sweet and delectable that she could not in anyway explain it. And having sucked, the roundness or rather the mound of breast from which the milk came remained in between the lips of that blessed Clare. And taking it with her hands that which had remained in her mouth, it seemed to her that it was gold

so clear and lucid that she could see herself completely, almost as if in a mirror (Proc 3:29).[84]

Clare's strange dream/vision[85] apparently caused some embarrassment[86] in those who made use of the *Process of Canonization* for the first time, since it does not appear in any of the early *Legendae* or in the *Bull*. This embarrassment is strange in that breast imagery was not uncommon in the writings of medieval authors.[87] Thanks to the rediscovery of the *Process*, scholars in the twentieth century came to accept and deal with this vision. I feel that this vision was either the cause or result of some of Clare's references to herself as Francis's *plantulam* and her insistence on poverty as the special charism of the Damianites. For this reason, it would be good to briefly consider what some authors have said about it.

The first scholar to deal with this dream in any detail was Marco Bartoli.[88] Dividing it into six scenes or images,[89] Bartoli interprets the vision as Clare's feeling that she is charged with continuing the work that Francis had begun in order to guarantee that his original insight and spirit would not be lost. The vision mirrors the love that she had for him, a love that expresses itself in a faithful defense of the primordial Franciscan way of life.

In a historical-literal reading of Clare's vision, Peter Van Leeuwen affirms that Clare's vision shows that she saw Francis as the teacher of her evangelical lifestyle.[90] But it also reveals that Clare is much more than just a disciple of Francis of Assisi; she is his companion on a path that he pointed out to her, and she complements him.

Carol Carsten refers to Clare's vision as a vision of Francis's "androgynous persona" suggesting that Clare saw Francis as a man who was in touch with his own femininity. Clare might indeed have known of Francis's dream of his soul being a woman (2Cel 82).[91]

In her work on medieval women and food, Carolyn W. Bynum deals briefly with Clare's vision of Francis.[92] She ties it to the fact that while Francis renounced wealth to beg and preach, Clare renounced food in order to serve and nourish her sisters. In nursing her, Francis reflected or mirrored what Clare did for her sisters.

Basing his proposal on the title given the vision by the notary of the Process, Anton Rotzetter sees it as "a prediction of things to come"—

which is to say, death. He sees Clare's vision as an affirmation that her life of service would lead her to heaven. In the vision, Francis's breast is transformed into gold, which for medieval Europeans was a promise of eternal life. Clare's vision is a manifestation of a friendship that is so strong it transcends death.[93]

While other scholars place the vision practically at the end of Clare's life, María Victoria Triviño suggests that Clare had this vision as a form of consolation when Francis himself was dying.[94] The vision gave her the message that her friendship with Francis had taught and prepared her to go on without him. In it, the source of her wisdom was found in her own lips as a mirror of gold in which she was reflected.

Ingrid Peterson describes Clare's Francis as being tied to the "eucharistic man of sorrows" who offers his body as nourishment. She ties this vision to Pope Gregory's desire to keep the Friars Minor from acting as chaplains for the sisters. As far as Clare was concerned, that which she received from Francis and his friars was a spiritual food of which she would not be deprived. Peterson suggests that Clare's taking the golden breast in her mouth was meant to challenge her to make sure that Francis's spiritual drink would never be lacking for her sisters.[95]

Alfonso Marino and Felice Accrocca make a historical reading of Clare's vision situating it in the context of Gregory IX's Bull, *Angelis gaudium*. With this Bull, he declared to Agnes of Prague that the "Form of Life" (FormViv) given by Francis to Clare and her Poor Sisters was nothing more than "milk" for newborn children. The Papal Bull goes on to declare that the Constitutions, which he, Gregory IX, had written as a cardinal in 1219, were "solid food."[96] Accrocca affirms that this vision allows us to see the tenacity with which Clare reaffirmed her fidelity to Francis's original ideal.

Fernando Uribe, in his article on the various opinions about this curious vision, concludes by affirming that "substantially there is no opposition among the various interpretations." He insists that together they symbolize her spiritual itinerary in which she is in no way annulled or absorbed in her "mystical-fraternal" union with Francis. The vision is an expression of her love for Francis lived in the sphere of her love for God.[97]

Finally, in their introduction to Clare's Letters to Agnes, Giovanni

Pozzi and Beatrice Rima give a rather detailed analysis of each symbol found in Clare's vision.[98] Yet they insist on calling this vision the "Vision of the Mirror" rather that the "Vision of Francis's Breast." The breast-turned-mirror is the key to understanding a process by which Clare comes to realize that she, like Francis, is mirrored in Christ, the Mirror of her Letters to Agnes.

FRANCIS'S MILK

Most authors see Clare's vision as tied to her tenacious defense of Francis's ideal of poverty and the "Form of Life" given by him to her and her sisters. It designates Clare's filial sentiment in regards to Francis. As a gardener/mother, he has planted, cultivated, and fostered her.

Clare grew up in an era in which the Church (as well as physicians) advised against the pagan practice of using wet nurses. In order to impress on mothers the importance and dignity of breastfeeding their own children, Christian artists turned to the figure of the Madonna breastfeeding the baby Jesus.[99] In Clare's mind, Francis must have been more than just a wet nurse, for in feeding at his breast, she was taking his characteristics and values into herself just as a baby takes his mother's traits by drinking her milk.

Francis fed Clare on rich and sweet milk from his maternal breast. It was so indescribably delicious that she sucked hard at his breast and his nipple remained upon her lips. Francis's nipple is described as remaining in her mouth because what she had received from it as mother's milk she then had to proclaim aloud as true wisdom.

Recognizing that they had no institutional right to teach Church doctrine, the women of Clare's day turned to the mystical language of dreams, visions, and prophecy in order to educate the popular Church.[100] In responding to Pope Gregory IX's charge that what Francis had given them was good only for babies,[101] she came to Francis's defense with symbols filled with the wisdom of the Sacred Scriptures, patristic authors, and medieval mystics who referred to Christian teaching and doctrine as milk. Clare's source of this milk is Francis's breast, and in it, she sees herself as the one who could best interpret the desires of St. Francis, who presents himself as the mother of her way of life.

If God was Clare's Father, then Francis was her mother. This maternal vision of Francis should come as no surprise, since he himself used the maternal image of nurturing and caring for the son as the primordial image for his brotherhood (RB 6).[102] Clare insisted on the unity of the Friars Minor and the Damianites. She could not help but turn to "mother" Francis to receive his values and characteristics in the milk of wisdom that came from him.

Sister and Mother

Francis's maternity is just part of the most Franciscan theme used in the familial imagery of Clare's opuscula: maternal–fraternal tension. Clare used the words *sister, daughter,* and *mother* to express her relationship to Agnes and the other Poor Ladies. This language expresses a tension by which Clare saw herself charged with the care and nurturing of her sisters. As is well noted, Clare saw herself as a mother and did not desire the title of *Abbess* (Proc 1:6; LegCl 12.3–4).

Yet the term *abbess* appears forty-four times in Clare's opuscula, and all of these instances are found in her "Form of Life for the Poor Sisters," most likely at the insistence of those who helped her in its redaction.[103] The lack of the term *abbess* was more in keeping with her sense of sisterhood. She did not want to emphasize the paternalistic role of abbess. Instead, Clare referred to the head of the monastery as "she who is in the (responsible) service of the sisters" (TestCl 61).[104] The sisters and not the Abbess are at the heart of the community. She is one of them and one with them; she is not a paterfamilias who is over and above the sisters. At every turn in the "Form of Life for the Poor Sisters," Clare limits the power of the Abbess with the freedom of the sisters to the point that the Mother Abbess is more of an elder sister than a mother. This sisterhood on the part of the mother is further expressed as motherhood on the part of the sisters, who are called to imitate Mary's pregnancy, to love and nourish each other, and thus to take part in God's household.

The Mother of Christ

As Francis did before her, Clare manifests a devotion to the Blessed Virgin Mary that centers on a devotion to Mary's maternity.[105] Clare never calls Mary "my" or "our" mother, she is always considered as mother of

Christ. This in no way means that Clare did not consider Mary the mother of Christians. It might simply indicate that, for Clare, Mary's role was so intimately tied to mothering the Son of God that she did not want to distract from it. Clare also recognizes the special nature of Mary's relationship to the Trinity, and the rest of God's household. She is listed in God's household, just after her Son, and right before the Archangel Michael (TestCl 77; BenCl 7).

Clare refers to Mary's divine maternity to present her as a model for Christians.[106] The Mother of the Poor Christ Child is to be loved as he is loved (RCl 2.25). This love for the Mother of the Son was promoted by Francis, who insisted on following the life and poverty of Christ and his most holy Mother (RCl 6.7). Clare obviously internalized Francis's love for the Poor Christ and his Mother, and reminds her sisters that they share in the inheritance of God's Kingdom through poverty and other virtues (RCl 8.4–6).

Clare's love for Mary cannot be completely attributed to what she received from Francis. She considered Christ her betrothed, her fiancé—in a word, her *Sponsus*. In the Middle Ages, love for the groom included honor for his parents. This honor was a form of respectful love[107] that did not always translate into sentimental love, though in Clare's case it did.

Love for Christ and his Mother led Clare to advise Agnes to cling to the sweetest Mother (*dulcissimae Matri adhaereas*; 3EpAgn 18–19) who birthed such a Child (God's Son), for she contained in her body Him whom neither heaven nor earth can contain.[108] Clare speaks of Mary with the active verbs *genuit, contulit*, and *gestavit* (to birth, to contain, and to form). This does not mean that Mary took the active role in Christ's conception and birth. In fact, elsewhere Clare refers to the Son of God actively incarnating himself within the Virgin's womb (1EpAgn 19). In as much as it was God who acted within her, just as He can act within the human soul, Mary's greatness can be imitated. Clare's Marian message to Agnes needs to be seen in this light. She is asking Agnes to do what Francis has asked all the faithful to do, namely, carry within themselves the Son of God. Agnes, like Mary and all the faithful, is to be the mother of the Lord Jesus Christ (1EpAgn 12, 24; 4EpAgn 4).[109]

The insistence that the human soul is capable of doing what the

Virgin Mary had done does not keep Clare from acknowledging that there is a difference between what Mary did and what the faithful soul does. Mary, *Virgo virginum* (Virgin of virgins), had carried God materially while Agnes and the faithful soul do so spiritually (3EpAgn 24–25). Materially, Jesus Christ has only one mother, while spiritually—meaning in the Spirit—he has a multitude of mothers (male and female), thanks to God's grace (3EpAgn 21).

As a Mother Loves and Nourishes

The divine maternity of believers in Clare's letters to Agnes is intimately tied to her spousal imagery,[110] which is the predominant kinship symbol in Clare's spirituality.[111] Yet, we cannot ignore her maternal references. For any truly Christian spirituality cannot be so concentrated on the vertical ("God and me") dimension that it ignores the horizontal ("God and we") dimension of faith. Clare's vertical dimension of spousal union with Christ is fruitful only in the horizontal dimension of a maternity that is lived out in sorority.

Borrowing again from Francis's opuscula, she adds to her "Form of Life for the Poor Sisters": "And if a mother loves and nourishes her carnal child, how much more lovingly should a sister love and nourish her spiritual sister?" (RCl 8.16).[112] Clare places this phrase, taken directly from Francis's Rule, at the heart of her chapter on poverty and infirmity. It seems that in these two situations sisterhood is tested and found maternal. For the time in which one is in need is the time in which the mother is needed and looked for. According to the *Process*, Clare herself, while she lay on her deathbed, compared God to a mother.[113]

This symbol of the nurturing and caring mother becomes for Clare, as it had been for Francis, the symbol and tension of fraternal life. For Clare, however, the symbol of sister is much more important than that of mother.[114] This may be because, in Clare's upbringing, the mother who happened to be the spouse of the paterfamilias was expected to be the matron (or *domina*), which was the female counterpart of the paterfamilias.

Clare did not want the sisters in charge acting as matrons. She preferred that the abbesses act as generative mothers who, according to the scheme of familial power, had little if any power and were thus equal to the children they bore. This equality of sisterhood is the hallmark of her "Form of Life for the Poor Sisters." She acknowledges that the sisters need a mother, yet the mother needs to be a daughter and a sister. She recognizes herself as being both mother and daughter to Agnes of Prague and sister to the Poor Ladies (4EpAgn I, 36, 39; RCl I.5).[115]

Her description of life in community further enhances this sense of equality between the abbess and the sisters. Clare did not want the abbess of the Poor Ladies to be the feminine counterpart of the abbot.[116] Rather, the abbess and the sisters are called by Clare to be co-responsible for the life of the community[117] because they have all been equally inspired to become "daughters and handmaidens of the most high, supreme, heavenly Father" (RCl 6.3). This common vocation Clare insisted on to the point that, in speaking about her own profession, she claims to have made it together with "her sisters" (RCl 6.1).

Clare did not want to be separated from her sisters. Often, she refers to the sisters as being one with her (2EpAgn 25). She proclaims that the sisters have been given her by God (TestCl 25) and, as such, she guards them as a treasure, praying for them, blessing them, and teaching them by word and example. From them, she seeks fidelity to the way of life they have been called to.

She treats them not as children but as responsible adults, inviting them not to do what "they see" is against the Gospels (2EpAgn 17). The verb *videre* (to see)[118] is found often enough in her opuscula to make it probable that she valued the opinions and thoughts of her sisters. She also trusted them enough to allow them to receive gifts from their kinfolk, so that these might be shared with all the sisters. This trust in the sisters might indicate an optimistic view of human nature on Clare's part. Clare's optimism is founded not on human nature, however, but on the household of God. She understands that the Father of mercies has enlightened her sisters to become one in the Spirit as brides of the eternal Bridegroom. To the extent that the sisters participate in this being espoused into God's household, they will be able to mother each other.

GOD'S HOUSEHOLD

In the "Blessing for the Sisters, Present and to Come" (BenCl 6–

13) we find Clare's versions of Francis's list of God's Household.[119] The most obvious change is the mention of Francis as an officially recognized member of God's family on a par with Saints Mary (Mother of Jesus) and Michael (the Archangel). We have already noted Clare's devotion to the father/mother of her way of life, as well as her veneration of her Spouse's mother, so we will turn our attention to the other saint in her list of God's household, Michael the Archangel.

First, let us consider another obvious difference between Clare's and Francis's lists of God's family: where Francis refers to the generic (but nominally masculine) *sancti*, Clare insists on the gender-specific *sancti et sanctae*.

In her opuscula, Clare never explicitly uses the reversal of gender roles,[120] as Francis does in his. Her female audience would have had no need for gender reversal in understanding union with God. For the most part, medieval Europeans tended to see God as masculine and active while considering the human soul as feminine and passive in the language of union. For this reason, betrothal language came easier to women, as did the image of mothering Christ and others for the only Father, who is God.

In the Blessing, Clare uses explicitly gender-inclusive language. She refers to male and female saints, to sons and daughters, and to a spiritual father and mother. This gender-inclusive language is not found in the rest of her opuscula. Nevertheless, in her Blessing, she breaks into gender-specific language as her way of "democratizing" her blessing. Like Francis, she believed that the experience of God could be had by everyone, but unlike Francis, she insisted on the fact that there existed both male and female saints and founders of religious families.

Of the male and female saints that Clare refers to, she specifically namesSaint Michael the Archangel as part of God's household. Francis himself made sure to include Michael in each of his lists of God's family. Why did Clare and Francis both select Michael as the archangel and saint to be specifically named in their lists?

Clare took up Francis's concept of embattled households belonging to God and Satan. She manifests a determined preoccupation with the steadfastness of the sisters who have been espoused into God's household. The Blessing reveals to the sisters what Clare has always alluded to, that they belong to an immense and powerful household that will assist them in persevering until the end. This household is the family of the saints in heaven. Here it seems that Clare refers to all those members of God's household who will be of most use to her sisters in maintaining their perseverance. Francis is recalled as the founder of their way of life, Mary is recalled as model to be held onto, and finally, Michael is named (most probably) as warrior and protector against the Prince of Darkness.

A notable difference in Clare's vision of the battle between families is that for her, humanity seems to be a family of serfs caught in this battle. Noble families in Clare's day were used to having weaker families come under their control. Weaker families would bounce around from one noble family to the next depending on the whims of nobles or the debts that they incurred. In an age when families were used to alliances for survival in times of war, daughters knew that they were the very ones on whom these alliances depended. Their espousing the Poor and Crucified Son could change the alliance of the human family and bring it under the household of God.

Clare knew firsthand the precarious nature of peace in her own time and the need for knights and warriors to protect a household from those seeking to destroy it. It is in this vein that I believe Michael makes his presence felt in both Clare's and Francis's opuscula. After all, Saint Michael has always been universally accepted as the Archangel who defeats Satan and his minions. God, in his infinite goodness, sent Michael and his angels to protect the human household in these bloody ordeals.

Clare divides the Church in two. She sees the Church in heaven as the Church Triumphant, made up of both male and female saints, not the least of which is the Archangel-Knight Michael. The Church on earth she considers to be the Church Militant (BenCl 7, 10, 12, 13). It should not surprise us that this noblewoman, coming from a family of *milites* (knights), would allude to the Church as being militant. Having lived through war, she must have seen the men of her family prepare for and return from battle. She must have known what it meant to tend to the soldiers and give them consolation.

So we can see that the Church is here perceived as a military household under siege within which Clare and her sisters are called to console and edify others through the holiness of their lives modeled on the members of the Church Triumphant. This holiness of life was meant to keep the sisters from injuring and dishonoring Christ, his Mother, Francis, and the Church. Women in noble households were educated to be above reproach. A family's honor was a priceless treasure that was not to be touched or stained in any way. What was true of human families was certainly even truer of the family of God.

FINAL REFLECTIONS ON KINSHIP IN CLARE'S OPUSCULA

There are constant references to kinship language and imagery in Clare's opuscula. Her relationship to God could only be humanly expressed in the language of kinship. Thus, she plunges deeply into the image of bride and Bridegroom, anxiously anticipating the moment of union. Her thoughts turn to the promised Spouse, and from Him she moves to the Father in the Spirit and to the Father's household. She takes the spousal language that was present within the Christian tradition of her time and developed it into a royal spousal language. It seems that she was deeply impressed by Agnes of Prague's refusal of marriage to the emperor in order to live as a Poor Lady. This admiration, however, is not as much for Agnes as it is for the divine Bridegroom who offers so much more than a human emperor. Her royal spousal imagery takes on the connotation of the *Sacrum Commercium* of which the Franciscan family is so fond.

This *Sacrum Commercium* makes the betrothed woman a sister. The vertical relationship with the *Sponsus* takes on a horizontal life that compels sisters to live as one. Without simply imitating Francis, Clare takes on the maternal–fraternal tension she had found in Francis's Rules. She invites Agnes to conceive Christ within her own body, just as she invites her to care for and pray for the sisters. In her other writings, we see Clare's deep concern for the sisters, a concern that is not just maternal; it is sisterly. She sees her sisters as adults and treats them as adults—in her "Form of Life for the Poor Sisters" and in her "Testament." But she also sees them as daughters, and she blesses them, as a mother would, in her "Blessing for the Sisters, Present and to Come." She lives in her own flesh the maternal–fraternal tension that she writes down on paper.

Although Clare's writings cannot be read without thinking back to Francis, she deserves to be respected as an original thinker. She took the milk of Francis's teaching, and, with her love for the *Sponsus*, she ingested

it until it became a wellspring of wisdom. Clare incarnated Francis's promised care and concern for the sisters and, most probably, even for the brothers. She had found in Francis the Way of Christ, and she defended that way
as a manifestation of her love for God, for Francis, and for their brothers
and sisters. Theirs was not a love based on the traditional ties of kinship,
for the only blood that tied them to each other was that of the Lamb of
God. They were not vowed to each other by any other vow than that of being
espoused to Christ in the Spirit and being children of the Father.

CONCLUSION

Both Francis and Clare of Assisi encourage us, as brothers and sisters in Christ, to love each other with a love that is greater than a mother's love. What does this unusual challenge actually mean? Although Francis and Clare never met our mothers, in this book we have had a chance to catch glimpses of theirs. We have seen their fathers and examined the structure and relationships of the medieval family. We have attempted to enter into the "living personal images"[1] of mother, father, brothers, sisters, and spouses as experienced in the *cotidiano* of Francis, Clare, and their readers.

In the first part of this book, we learned of the implicit cultural presuppositions and specific cultural factors around the kinship language and imagery in Francis's and Clare's opuscula by looking for what they and their intended readers shared as common knowledge about medieval kinship ties and roles.

Neither of these saints wrote about their natural families, and with the exception of Catherine's (Agnes's) letter to her sister Clare, there is no correspondence to be found between either saint and original kin. So I turned to their vitae in hopes of discovering their societal expectations of family life and roles. Chapters 2 and 3 brought together what the writers of the vitae and contemporary authors have to say about the Bernardone and the Offreduccio families and their relationships with Francis and Clare, respectively.

By placing Clare's and Francis's family life against the backdrop of the European family of their day, I was able to highlight some differences and similarities in their experiences. There were social differences. Clare grew up in an established noble family of the town of Assisi, while Francis grew up in a merchant family that was struggling like other merchants to gain respectability in the commune. There were also gender-defined differences. Being a boy, Francis was raised for travel, adventure, and business. Being a

girl, Clare was raised to govern a household. Boys were expected to be bois-
terous, while girls were expected to be reserved and demure. Both Francis's
and Clare's vitae show just how these things were lived by each of them prior
to their conversions.

Another major difference in the family life of both Francis and Clare
is that of their own aspirations as regards the family. As a female in a noble
household, Clare's family expected her to marry well and thus help establish
an alliance with another noble family for both power and prestige. She was
expected to build a noble reputation and guard it well against any hint of
scandal. The witnesses in Clare's *Process of Canonization* go to some lengths
to demonstrate that Clare was already a saint in childhood. This early holiness demonstrated that she had indeed learned to protect her reputation as
a youth. Yet in doing so, she went over and beyond what was expected of
young noblewomen, to the point of seeking to go against her family's aspirations. Where her family sought to have her married, she secretly intended
a life of virginity for herself. While her family spent much money on itself,
Clare sought to help the poor by secretly giving them her portion. Enlightened by the Spirit, Clare seems to have desired nothing more than to abandon
her noble status from the outset of her life, and this meant breaking with
her family.

Francis, on the other hand, gave in to his family's desires for him.
As wealthy members of the *minori*, his family aspired to break free of its
social condition and join the ranks of the *maiori*. Francis bought into his
family's desire for power, fame, and prestige. He seems to have spent all of
his early years running after what Clare sought to renounce: a noble family.
His beloved father, Pietro, probably instilled this desire for nobility in him.
On the other hand, Clare's esteemed mother, Ortulana, probably instilled
an uneasiness with this very same notion of nobility. While Clare secretly
denied her family's plans for her, Francis openly and boisterously embraced
his family's desires for him. It was this desire to please his family, especially
his father, that eventually sent Francis off to war, where he hoped to gain a
noble title. Little did he know that it was this adventure that would mark
the beginning of the events that would lead him to break with his family—
a break done openly and boisterously, as his personality warranted, under
the radiant sun. It was Francis's open break with his family that eventually

inspired Clare to reveal her secret desire and to break with her own family. Clare's break, however, took place in the secret of the night, guided by the silent moon.

Yet for all their differences, Francis and Clare had striking similarities, too. Both had a special parent to whom they turned in their youth. While little is known of Messere Favarone, Clare's father, her mother, Madonna Ortulana stands out as Clare's favored and more influential parent. In Francis's life, although his hagiographers gave much importance to his mother, Pica, it seems it was Pietro whom Francis naturally considered his favored and more influential parent. Both Francis and Clare had to deal with the noble family structure, although their dealings were quite different. Clare lived uneasily in that structure which Francis so longed for. I mention this again because we cannot underestimate the importance of the structure of the noble family in both Clare's and Francis's "regal" spirituality.[2]

The above similarities and differences culled from our study of the saints' family experiences are not meant simply to satisfy historical curiosity. They are important in understanding the events that moved them to conversion and influenced their spirituality. They are part of the human nature that God's grace sanctified, and as such, their influence can be inferred in their opuscula.

So what does the unusual challenge of loving one another with more than a mother's love mean? I turn to several insights I gained during my study of Clare, Francis, and their families.

BELONGING TO GOD'S HOUSEHOLD

Having considered the implicit and specific cultural presuppositions and factors that had formed their use of kinship language, we turned in the next part of the book to see how these factors are present in their opuscula. I was especially interested in seeing how these cultural presuppositions and factors underwent a process of differentiation whereby Francis and Clare expressed the explicit spiritual intention of their work.

Yet the writings of the saints of Assisi like those of all spiritual writers "are not concerned with 'knowledge' in the sense of empirically verifiable facts, but rather with an 'awareness of God' in the sense of private or communal experiences of the encounter with God. . . . [Their writing] is concerned with the nature and content of the relationship between an individual and God."[3] As such, it was meant to help their readers see things in a spiritual way. Quite aware that Francis and Clare had several intentions for their writings, I chose to focus on that of their relationships with God and others. For each of them, these relationships are expressed in terms of belonging to the noble household of God—meaning the family of those who do the will of Jesus' Father (Mt 12:46–50).

Francis and Clare made great use of the Sacred Scriptures in their writing. Theirs was a spirituality that took seriously the words of the Gospel. Each one, in response to Jesus' call to radical discipleship (Lk 14:26), saw the importance of breaking with the family of origin (and destination) in order to give themselves completely to God's household. Both Francis and Clare broke with their families, but they also had to break with the medieval noble family structure in order to give themselves to a family of even nobler origin and condition.

In opting to imagine the spiritual family as a regal family, they had a lot to learn from each other's experiences and youthful desires. Francis seems to have learned from Clare that earthly nobility is not worth more than the empty titles it gives. Clare, on the other hand, learned from Francis that, if one abandons the emptiness of earthly nobility, it is to gain the fullness of divine nobility. Francis's desire for a noble family remains the key to understanding both his and Clare's use of kinship roles and ties in their "regal" spirituality. Consequently, his youthful desire for nobility, which was probably shared by many of the readers of his day, was transformed into an intense desire for the nobility of the family of God.

Many scholars have shown that Francis and Clare were people of their period. They were very concrete individuals who were not given to scholastic speculation. They and their spirituality were influenced by the European culture in which they lived. The kinship vocabulary and language which Francis and Clare used in their writing have little to do with the *cotidiano* of our twenty-first-century family imagery.

The contemporary family in western societies is in crisis. The sense of individuality that slowly began to develop in the western world around the time of Clare and Francis has turned into an individualism that tends to preclude the sense of family duty and group purpose that the medieval family fostered. Western cultures have moved from a traditional socio-centered emphasis to an ego-centered emphasis—stressing individualism and self-realization.

Still, a sense of individuality is not anti-Gospel. If Francis and Clare were able to break with their families in a period in which belonging to the clan was of the utmost importance, it was thanks to their feeling called by God to make an individual response to the Gospel. But their act of individuality was not an act of individualism. They soon found themselves surrounded by brothers and sisters who formed a spiritual family of which they could be a part. Moreover, as they grew in their sense of belonging to God's household, they began to see God, Jesus, the Holy Spirit, and their spiritual brothers and sisters in a way that their natural inclinations and social imaginations had not allowed them to see. Grace builds on nature; Francis and Clare moved from the limits of the natural family to the transcendence of the spiritual family, a socio-centered family headed by the God and Father of our Lord Jesus Christ.

GOD THE FATHER IS NOT A MOTHER

Today there is much talk about the maternity of God. Feminist theologians have justly noted that a strictly paternal God lacks the maternal warmth that today's Christian seems to need. While I agree that God is both father and mother, God is, in fact, neither father nor mother. But because *Creator* is such an impersonal term, lacking in warmth and commitment, humanity has tended to imagine God anthropomorphically as the Father in Heaven. Moreover, it seems from the Judeo-Christian Scriptures that this is an image that God himself has chosen, for these revealed texts are filled with references to God's paternity.[4] Nonetheless, God often chose to reveal God's self as Mother[5] and Spouse.[6] These images, however, did not capture the human imagination in the way that the image of Father did. For several millennia, Jews and Christians have preferred to image God as Father. Nonetheless, any anthropomorphic image like that of father used to describe the Godhead is just that: an image that runs the risk of becoming an idol, and an image through which we can only partially know God. In the past, many have turned the image of God the Father into an idol to put women down and keep them from leadership roles in the Church and in society. But the image of God the Mother can be just as idolatrous when proponents of God's maternity force such an image into the teachings of saints and writers of the past in order to idealize the feminine or to condemn the masculine.

It is true that the Sacred Scriptures and Christian authors of the past have made use of maternal imagery when speaking in general about God, and even when speaking of God the Father. However, it is also true that the title *Mother* was probably far from their minds when referring to God the Father. Francis certainly never seems to have used or alluded to it. Clare affirms that the Lord (*Domine*) acted like a mother in protecting her after having created and sanctified her (LegCl 46.3–5; Proc 3:20; 11:3). It is clear, however, by her use of the masculine *qui* and *Domine* that she was affirming God's paternity. She may have been able to compare God's actions to those of a mother with her child—using the image of mother as a simile— but she did not take the step to actually say that God is Mother.

We have seen why this is so. Although the Church promoted some equality between husbands and wives, in the noble family of the time, the husband/father was still unequivocally the head of the household. The wife/mother, along with her children and servants, was subject to his authority and discipline. In this scheme of things, it would be unthinkable that God the Father or head of the household could be God the Mother, a dependant of the head of the family.

As for most Christians of their time, for both Francis and Clare, God is the Father of our Lord Jesus Christ. And since it is through Jesus that we become members of the divine household, God is *our* Father as well. As such, God the Father remains in both saints' writings a patriarchal figure reminiscent of the noble or regal paterfamilias.

While the Father takes center stage in Francis's opuscula,[7] He all but disappears in Clare's. Used to her uncle Monaldo's probable misuse of the role of paterfamilias, Clare turned to Christ as Spouse as the center of her attention. Francis, unconsciously nostalgic for the father of his childhood, turned to the Father as the object of his desire. In this desire for God the Father, Jesus becomes a model and aid for Francis, and it seems that, for him, the Lord Jesus Christ becomes both brother and mother.

CHRIST AND MATERNAL–FRATERNAL TENSION

If God the Father is not a mother, then everyone else is a mother.[8]

In Francis's and Clare's spiritualities, the Father is the anthropomorphic paterfamilias. He is Father and King, and as such, he is the head of a vast and noble household. In this household, Jesus becomes the point of entry. Although Francis never outright proclaimed the maternity of Jesus, for him, it is clear that Jesus, our Brother, took the role of the Mother who birthed Francis into the family of God and nursed him with his own flesh and blood. This in no way denigrates the maternal role of Mary in the life of the faithful.[9] Still, in their opuscula, Francis and Clare never refer to her as their mother, but rather see her as a model of the generativity to which all Christians are called. Jesus remains for Francis and Clare the entry into God's family, just as he was for his mother, Mary.

While Francis gave maternal overtones to Jesus' role, Clare considered Jesus the Spouse who married her into the family of the Father and who educated her for her responsibilities within that family. Being male, the only way that Francis could enter into a family was through birth. He came naked into the family of Pietro di Bernardone, and in the presence of Bishop Guido, responding to the call of Christ, he came naked into the family of God. Francis's vision of Jesus as mother-brother seems to become the paradigm of fraternal relations not only in the lives of the Friars Minor, but also in those of the Poor Ladies. I will write about this maternal–fraternal love and tension further on, but first I'd like to consider the spousal language used by both saints.

Francis entered God's household through birth in Christ Jesus, and Clare seems to have entered through marriage—but marriage to whom?

BETROTHED TO AND IN THE SPIRIT

Saint Bernard speaks of monastic life as the school of Christ.[10] Francis and Clare would probably insist that it is the community—in the cotidianidad of both its internal and external relationships—that is the school of Christ. The Father is the one who teaches, His primary example is Jesus our Brother, and His pedagogy is the maternal–fraternal tension of Franciscan/Christian life in the Spirit.

The maternal–fraternal love that binds all of the followers of Francis and Clare nurtures us in the ways of Jesus and his Father. Moreover, this tension is one born of the Spirit. Thus, the image of the Holy Spirit cannot be lacking in their ascribing familial roles and descriptions in relationship with God. The Holy Spirit, being described as "a wind that blows where it will," is hard to pin down with anthropomorphic language and symbols. Francis does manage to make of the Spirit a Spouse for Clare and her sisters. Even though Clare received his spousal reference to the Holy Spirit directly from Francis, her writings do not seem to show that she accepted it. As I noted in chapter five, she preferred her spousal relationship to be with Christ, Jesus. What then of the Holy Spirit in our discussion of family imagery in the spirituality of Francis and Clare?

Spirituality by its very nature is tied to the Holy Spirit. Paul reminds the faithful that we are "temples of the Holy Spirit" (I Cor 3:16, 6:19). The indwelling of the Holy Spirit promised by Jesus (Jn 14:15–17, 16:7–15, 20:22) is the way Christians live the Gospel. More than a person to be encountered, the Spirit can be seen as a personified relational energy or bond. Thus, in Francis and Clare, the Holy Spirit is of supreme importance, binding them to the God and Father of our Lord Jesus Christ and to each other as brother and sister. Like Mary, whom Francis referred to as the "spouse of the Holy Spirit," (OffPass Ant. 2) they are called to be fruitful in birthing Jesus.

In Christian mysticism and spirituality, the generative task of the Holy Spirit in the faithful soul has traditionally been referred to using spousal terms and language.[11] It is the Spirit who brings the soul into union with God, thanks to the redemptive action of Christ. In this union, the soul is able to become the mother of Christ. Yet this generative union with the Christian person cannot be conditioned or forced. Francis insisted that it was Clare and her sisters who had betrothed themselves to the Holy Spirit of their own free will—without the usual coercion of the blood family.

By recalling the Damianite's espousal to the Holy Spirit, I am not inferring that betrothal to Christ or the Holy Spirit is reserved only to women. On the contrary, spousal and generative language needs to penetrate into the whole of the Franciscan family and to every Christian. Francis and Clare remind the faithful that the Gospel calls all who do the will of the Father to be mothers, brothers, and sisters of Christ (Mk 3:33–35; Mt 12:48–50; Lk 8:21)—and, they would add, of each other.

BROTHERS, SISTERS, AND MOTHERS OF THE SON

Francis and Clare's desire to belong to God's household seems to center on their relationship to the Son of God. We have seen that Jesus is the one who brings us into the Divine family. All Christians are to be the brothers, sisters, and mothers of Christ. How can one even imagine being a Christian without a relationship to Christ?

As members of the household of God in Christ, we are called to generate life. All households need new life if they are to continue and the Household of God continues in eternal life. As brothers and sisters of Christ, the faithful do the will of God. They are to be fruitful as the Son was. They are called to be pregnant with Christ in a pure and sincere conscience and to birth him in their good works (1EpFid 1.5–14; 1EpAgn 12, 24).[12] Birthing Christ is a task that priests do in imitation of Mary by materially producing Him on the altar in the Eucharist (Adm 1.16, 18).[13] Yet the faithful birth Christ spiritually in the *cotidiano*. As mothers of Christ, they bear him in their hearts and in their bodies.

In birthing Christ for all to see, Franciscans (and all the faithful) participate in generating new life for the family of God. It is through example more than through word that many are moved by compunction to seek God. This constant invitation of others into the household of God not only births Christ, but also brings men and women into spiritual brotherhood and sisterhood. Francis and Clare invite these brothers and sisters to imitate Christ and his maternal–fraternal tension.

MATERNAL–FRATERNAL TENSION

So what does it mean to love each other with a love that is greater than a mother's love? I believe it is to love each other as mothers, brothers, and sisters of Christ and each other. In brief, it is to live the Gospel in continual maternal–fraternal tension.

In their writing, Francis and Clare made use of traditional mystical themes: divine filiation, espousal to Christ/Spirit, and the birth of Christ in the soul. Their original contribution to the use of kinship language and imagery in Christian spirituality seems to be the maternal–fraternal tension. Nowhere is the maternal–fraternal vocation and tension of the Franciscan family seen more clearly that in Francis's Rules and Clare's own "Form of

Life" (RCl). The call to a love that is greater than a mother's love is placed in the section where the brothers and sisters are called to make their needs known to each other, to care for the infirm among them, and to not judge each other.

A mother naturally desires what is best for her child. Her internal love will manifest itself externally in what she believes is the best for that child. In many of our contemporary societies, it is believed that children are better off with their mothers than with their fathers. One has only to follow custody battles to see that this is so. Western courts are usually reluctant to gives fathers custody of their children unless a mother is proven to be truly unfit to raise her offspring. This contemporary bias was certainly not true for most of human history.

It is true that a mother has typically been the best parent to nurture an infant, but once weaned, the child was handed to the father to be educated as he considered best for the needs of the family. It was love that caused mothers of Francis and Clare's day to hand their children over to their fathers. They believed that it was best for their children. When the Saints of Assisi refer to maternal love, they meant a love that knew when to hand children over to the more powerful and influential parent, the father. It was a love that continued to attend to the child under the father's tutelage.[14]

As brothers and sisters, we are not called to love each other as thirteenth-century mothers would have loved. We are called to love more than that—to surpass the maternal strength necessary to fully love and nurture a child in thirteenth-century Europe. Mothers of that time turned over their children to the paterfamilias and continued to assist in raising the child. We, however, are to hand our brothers and sisters over to be educated through the grace of God the Father, the head of the household. We have to truly believe that God will train the brothers and sisters as God sees fit so that they themselves can come to know what they truly need.

Handing our brothers and sisters over to the spiritual formation that only God can give does not free us from the responsibility of continuing to assist and care for them. For once a brother or sister has learned from God what they need, they are to make their needs known—to us.

The hardest part of the maternal–fraternal love proposed by the Franciscan Rules, then, is being brothers and sisters to each other. I agree with Optatus van Asseldonk's conclusion that the fraternal-yet-more-than-maternal way of love cannot be specified in great theories, systems, plans, and spiritual or material programs. This way of love is made evident in concrete, personal, and fraternal help, incarnated here and now, where every person, brother or sister, finds himself/herself in suffering or in solitude, in identification with every human person or creature, in seeking to vivify—to give life.[15]

Older brothers and sisters have no trouble being mothers to younger members of the family, especially to those in their initial formation or in the catechumenate. But things don't remain that easy for long. They may insist that "we are all equal," but once a younger brother or sister tries to live the Gospel in a way they don't agree with, those same older brothers or sisters become "superiors" and no longer equals. Francis and his good friend, Brother Leo, might have had such a confrontation at the time that Francis felt the need to write his "Letter to Brother Leo." My guess is that Francis and Leo had a disagreement about how Leo could better live the Gospel. Leo might have felt God leading him in a way that Francis did not understand or appreciate. Francis apparently got into an argument with Leo wanting him to follow the Gospel as Francis did. But Francis had to love Leo more than a mother. Rather than merely letting Leo go to the Father, Francis had to remain with his brother as well and be willing to learn from Leo's understanding of what the Father wanted from him.

It is certainly true that the family of Friars that Francis birthed weaned themselves from him even before his death. Francis, like a mother, had to give his order over to the Father. But like a brother, he needed to continue walking with that Order as well. He had to allow others to mother him[16] and to be *his* brother in the family of God the Father.

If the sources are correct, Francis did not do this well. Francis obviously felt certain of his way of living out the Gospel and did not always agree with other ways of living it out. He saw the way in which certain members of the hierarchy were taking the brothers and he did not like it (2Cel 188; SpecPer 41). The hardest part of being both mother and brother is that, when we hand our brothers and sisters over to the Father's school, we have to continue to help them discern what is the Father's will. We have to continue walking together in the way of the Spirit, even when we do not understand how they are trying to live the Gospel.

Clare, for her part, seems to have managed to keep her daughters closer to her initial inspiration. Perhaps it was the enclosed space that aided her in being both mother and sister to her sisters. Or maybe it was the weekly chapters that she built into her "Form of Life for the Poor Sisters" so that the sisters could discern together the will of the Father for their monastery. Contemporary Franciscans are more apt to find themselves in smaller communities and thus have the opportunity to involve everyone in the process of local chapters (religious community meetings). This does not necessarily mean weekly chapters as long as brothers and sisters who live together do some form of faith sharing and talk to each other about their aspirations and their love of the Father, nurturing one another as mothers and more than mothers, living together as siblings, children of the one Father.

The genius of Francis was his insistence that no one be called father except for the God and Father of our Lord Jesus Christ. In this way, he desired to free his family from paternalistic superiors who would want things done their way and only their way. Francis chose to keep his family under the *only* Paterfamilias.

Spirituality and Family Language

Spirituality as an academic field is an interdisciplinary endeavor.[17] The so-called secular disciplines can be used by the faithful to learn about how our spiritual ancestors lived the Gospel and followed Christ in the way of the Spirit.[18] If these secular sciences are to be applied to Francis, Clare, and other spiritual ancestors, it should be members of the Christian (especially Franciscan) community who do it, using a socio-spiritual approach to these spiritual classics. We are their spiritual heirs, and as such, we are aware of the limitations the social and other sciences bring to the study of spirituality. Social sciences tend to reduce everything to human experience, where we as Christians know that God's Spirit works through, in, and despite human experience.

The human experience that I have sought to use in our study is that of medieval kinship. I have emphasized how Francis's and Clare's family experiences might have touched them spiritually and affected their writings. I have done so utterly aware of the work of the Spirit in their lives, a work that did not happen in a vacuum or on a tabula rasa. Francis and Clare came to the Gospel bringing with them their home and family experiences. The Spirit took this experience and built on it a spirituality of kinship.

As I finish writing this book I find myself remembering fondly the Mary-Martha experience I shared with my fellow novices. I began this book to answer my questions about the curious maternal language of Francis. I discovered a whole new maternal–fraternal language that raises in me even more musings and questions. I would like to leave you with some of these.

Franciscans, as well as most Christians today, have continued to make use of kinship language to speak of their relationships to God, to Francis, to Clare, and to each other. At the same time, Franciscans today continue to be influenced by a whole new set of cultural presuppositions based on the family models in which they grew up both personally and socially. Much of the language we use today to speak of Franciscan life has been borrowed from Francis and Clare, but it is not always reflective of their understanding. We certainly have ignored Francis's injunction against using the title father for anyone but God. We even call *him* father.

Is our widespread use of the title *father* for the brothers of the first order abusive? What does it do to our relationships with the brothers and sisters in the rest of the Christian community? What about the people we minister to in parishes, schools, and elsewhere—how does it affect *their* relationship with God the only Father?

And what about spousal and maternal language for today's spirituality? Is it still a valid way of describing the relationship that the brothers and sisters have with Jesus and the Holy Spirit? In a world of heightened sexual awareness, can gender-related terms such as *spouse* and *mother* still be applied to the human person (male and female) without fear of negative homosexual innuendo?

Finally, as Christians, we justly call each other brother and sister. Yet, what does this mean in cultures that are ego-centered rather than socio-centered? What does Franciscan kinship spirituality have to say to the family ties of today? What happens when our spiritual brothers and sisters cannot seem to break with their natural families in order to live the Gospel more fully? Should they have to do so?

Francis's and Clare's radical breaks with their families do not seem to be needed in most of our contemporary cultures. And yet contemporary

Franciscans and Christians may have much to learn from Clare's running away from home and Francis's dramatic break with his family. The Gospel radical injunction found in Mt 19:29 is still valid for all those born of the Spirit. Hence Francis and Clare's zeal for the Gospel and the desire to belong to the One Father and to God's household must be ours as well, albeit tempered by our own social preconceptions and spiritual imaginings.

Being born of the Spirit, all those who choose to do the will of the Father are mothers, brothers, and sisters of Christ and each other. Francis and Clare qualify the fraternal vocation with a maternal one. Their maternal role was an unconscious move on the part of the saints to qualify fraternal love with the mother's social function. People in Christian community are to nurture each other only to the point of bringing each other to the Father who truly educates the Friars Minor, the Poor Clares, the Franciscan sisters, the Secular Franciscans, and all Christians.

Brothers and sisters who love each other with a mother's love do not want to withhold each other from the Father by acting as "superiors" or by judging the other's way of Gospel living as unfounded. Any formation given in the Christian family is meant to prepare the brother or sister for life in the Father's household where God the Father is the only true formator, just as the Holy Spirit is the true general minister of the Order of Friars Minor.

Maternal–fraternal love and tension knows when to wean the brother and sister just as it knows when to nurture. Mothers who nurture without weaning do nothing more than raise a spoiled child who will never be ready for the Father to form them. Conversely, mothers who wean without nurturing leave their children looking for love in inappropriate places. Thus, a maternal–fraternal love needs to be affectionate, gentle, strong, passionate, mutual, challenging, and comforting; it calls for a blending of anima and animus, as well as a balancing of obligation, responsibility, and freedom in one's brothers and sisters in the Spirit.[19]

Family language will not simply disappear in a group of people who have no blood ties and yet refer to themselves as brothers and sisters. As children and spouses, Jesus Christ brought Francis and Clare into God's household. As fruitful spouses, they both mothered children for God, the Father—children who were their brothers and sisters in the Lord, thanks to the grace of the Holy Spirit. This incarnation of their spirituality has continued for almost eight hundred years, producing an abundant family of spouses, mothers, brothers, and sisters for Jesus Christ. Francis and Clare call all of these to a love that is greater than a mother's love, one that is maternal–fraternal.

Appendicies

Appendix A:
Abbreviations for the Opuscula and Vitae of Francis and Clare

Here, the abbreviations for the saints' opuscula and vitae are listed in alphabetical order for easy reference. Works authored by Francis are arranged by type (and chronologically within each type) in Appendix B: The Opuscula of Saint Francis. Works authored by Clare are similarly arranged in Appendix C: The Opuscula of Saint Clare. The rest of the works constitute the saints' vitae; these are listed chronologically for each saint in Appendix D: Sources for the Lives of Francis and Clare.

Abbr.	Author,	Title (Short title),	Date
Adm	Francis,	"Admonitions,"	undated
AnPer	Anonymous of Perugia, *The Beginning or Founding of the*		
		Order (Anonymous of Perugia),	after 1260
AudPov	Francis, "	Listen, Poor Little Ones,"	Sept. 1226
BenBer	Francis,	"Blessing Given to Brother Bernard,"	Oct. 1226
BenCl	Clare,	"Blessing for the Sisters, Present and to Come,"	1253
BenClara	Francis,	"Blessing Given to Clare and Her Sisters,"	Sept. 1226
BenLeo	Francis,	"Blessing Given to Brother Leo,"	Sept. 1224
BuCl	*Bull of Canonization for St. Clare (Bull),*		1255
1Cel	Thomas of Celano, *First Life of St. Francis (First Celano),*		1228
2Cel	Thomas of Celano, *Second Life of St. Francis*		
		(Second Celano),	1252/53
CompAs	*Assisi Compilation,*		1266–1318
CSol	Francis,	"Canticle of Brother Sun,"	Spring 1225
			/Oct. 1226
1EpAgn	Clare,	First Letter to Saint Agnes,	1234
2EpAgn	Clare,	Second Letter to Saint Agnes,	1238
3EpAgn	Clare,	Third Letter to Saint Agnes,	1238
4EpAgn	Clare,	Fourth Letter to Saint Agnes,	1253

EpAnt	Francis,	Letter to Brother Anthony,	1224
EpBon	Francis,	Letter to the City of Bologna,	1221–23
EpCl	Francis,	Letter to Clare on Fasting,	undated
EpCler	Francis,	Letter to All the Clerics,	1219
1EpCus	Francis,	First Letter to the Custodians,	1219
2EpCus	Francis,	Second Letter to the Custodians,	1219
EpErm	Clare,	Letter to Ermetrude,	undated
1EpFid	Francis,	First redaction of the Letter to the Faithful,	1213–21
2EpFid	Francis,	Second redaction of the Letter to the Faithful,	1219–21
EpFran	Francis,	Letter to the Friars in France,	undated
EpJac	Francis,	Letter to Lady Jacopa,	Oct. 1226
EpMin	Francis,	Letter to a Minister,	1223
EpLeo	Francis,	Letter to Brother Leo,	undated
EpOrd	Francis,	Letter to the Entire Order,	1225–26
EpRect	Francis,	Letter to the Rulers of Peoples,	1219
ExhLD	Francis,	"Exhortation to the Praise of God,"	undated
ExPat	Francis,	"Explanation of the 'Our Father,'"	undated
FormViv	Francis,	"Form of Life," given to Clare and her sisters,	1212
Fragm	Francis,	"Fragments of the Non-Bulled Rule,"	1209–21
24Gen		*The Chronicles of the Twenty-Four Generals* (*The Chronicles*),	1360
HenAv		Henry of Avranches, *Legend of St. Francis* (*Versified Legend*),	1232–34
JulSpi		Julian of Speyer, *Life of St. Francis* (*Julian of Speyer*),	1232–39
LDei	Francis,	"Praises of God Most High,"	Sept. 1224
LegCl		*Legend of St. Clare of Assisi* (*Clare's Legend*),	1255/56
LegMai		Bonaventure, *Major Life of St. Francis* (*Major Life*),	1260–63
LegPer		*Legend of Perugia*,	1266–1318
LegVer		*Legend of St. Clare* (*Clare's Versified Legend*),	1254/55
LHor	Francis,	"Praises to Be Said at All the Hours,"	undated
OffPass	Francis,	"Office of the Lord's Passion,"	undated
OrCru	Francis,	"Prayer before the Crucifix,"	1205–6
Proc		*Process of Canonization for St. Clare of Assisi* (*Process*),	1253
RB	Francis,	"Bulled Rule,"	1223
RCl	Clare,	"Form of Life for the Poor Sisters,"	1253
RegEr	Francis,	"Rule for Hermitages,"	1217–21
RnB	Francis,	"Non-Bulled Rule,"	1221
SalBVM	Francis,	"Salutation of the Blessed Virgin Mary,"	undated
SalVir	Francis,	"Salutation of the Virtues,"	undated
3Soc		*Legend of the Three Companions* (*Three Companions*),	1246
SpecPer		*The Mirror of Perfection*,	1318
Test	Francis,	"Testament,"	Oct. 1226
TestCl	Clare,	"Testament of the Virgin Saint Clare,"	1253

TSen	Francis,	"Testament Written in Siena,"	April 1226
UltVol	Francis,	"Last Will for Clare and Her Sisters,"	Sept. 1226
VPLaet	Francis,	"On True and Perfect Joy,"	undated

APPENDIX B:
THE OPUSCULA OF SAINT FRANCIS

According to Friars Kajetan Esser and Giovanni Boccali, thirty-seven of the writings attributed to Francis can be considered authentic.[1] Traditionally, following the division set up by Leonhard Lemmens,[2] these opuscula have been divided into legislative texts, letters, and prayers. Regis Armstrong pointed out this division's problems, however, concerning the importance of certain writings and the historical prejudices present in the development of the Order.[3] He proposed a threefold division of the opuscula based on their date of composition: writings 1205–23, undated writings, and writings 1224–26. This division is helpful in studying the development of Francis's thought and life experience, but it does not take into account the types of the writings. For my work, I have chosen to keep Armstrong's dates but use Matura's and Lemmens's threefold division as well: writings dealing with living an evangelical Christian life, prayers and praises, and missives in the form of letters.

ABBR.	TITLE[4]	ADDRESSED TO[5]	DATES
WRITINGS DEALING WITH LIVING AN EVANGELICAL CHRISTIAN LIFE:			
FormViv	"Form of Life," given to Clare and her sisters	Poor Ladies	1212
1EpFid	First redaction of the Letter to the Faithful	Christians	1213–21
2EpFid	Second redaction of the Letter to the Faithful	Christians	1219–21
Fragm	"Fragments of the Non-Bulled Rule"	Friars	1209–21
RegEr	"Rule for Hermitages"	Friars	1217–21
RnB	"Non-Bulled Rule"	Friars	1221
RB	"Bulled Rule"	Friars	1223
Adm	"Admonitions"	Christians	undated
SalVir	"Salutation of the Virtues"	Christians	undated
VPLaet	"On True and Perfect Joy"	Christians	undated
EpCl	Letter to Clare on Fasting	Poor Ladies	undated
EpOrd	Letter to the Entire Order	Friars	1225–26

TSen	"Testament Written in Siena"	Friars	1226 April
AudPov	"Listen, Poor Little Ones"	Poor Ladies	1226 Sept.
UltVol	"Last Will for Clare and Her Sisters"	Poor Ladies	1226 Sept.
Test	"Testament"	Friars	1226 Oct.

PRAYERS AND PRAISES:

OrCru	"Prayer before the Crucifix"	personal	1205–6
ExhLD	"Exhortation to the Praise of God"	Christians	undated
OffPass	"Office of the Lord's Passion"	Christians	undated
LHor	"Praises to Be Said at All the Hours"	Christians	undated
ExPat	"Explanation of the 'Our Father'"	Christians	undated
SalBVM	"Salutation of the Blessed Virgin Mary"	Christians	undated
BenLeo	"Blessing Given to Brother Leo"	personal	1224 Sept.
LDei	"Praises of God Most High"	personal	1224 Sept
CSol	"Canticle of Brother Sun"	Christians	1225 Spr / 1226 Oct
BenClara	"Blessing Given to Clare and Her Sisters"	Poor Ladies	1226 Sept.
BenBer	"Blessing Given to Brother Bernard"	personal	1226 Oct.

MISSIVES IN THE FORM OF LETTERS:

EpCler	Letter to All the Clerics	clergy	1219
1EpCus	First Letter to the Custodians	friars	1219
2EpCus	Second Letter to the Custodians	friars	1219
EpRect	Letter to the Rulers of Peoples	rulers	1219
EpBon	Letter to the City of Bologna	Christians	1221–23
EpMin	Letter to a Minister	personal	1223
EpLeo	Letter to Brother Leo	personal	undated
EpFran	Letter to the Friars in France	friars	undated
EpAnt	Letter to Brother Anthony	personal	1224
EpJac	Letter to Lady Jacopa	personal	1226 Oct.

Appendix C: The Opuscula of Saint Clare

Clare's opuscula are not as extensive as those of Francis; while thirty-seven texts are attributed to him by scholars, only eight are attributed to Clare. Of these, only five (her Rule and the four letters to Agnes of Prague) are universally accepted as authentic, while another two, "Testament" (TestCl) and "Blessing" (BenCl), are held in doubt by some and accepted by others. Finally, the Letter to Ermentrude is universally thought to be a mishmash of Clare's original letters to Ermentrude.[6] Like Francis's opuscula, these also follow a threefold division: writings dealing with living an evangelical Christian life, prayers and praises, and missives in the form of letters.

Abbr.	Title	Addressed to:	Dates
Writings dealing with living an evangelical Christian life:			
RCl	"Form of Life for the Poor Sisters"	Poor Sisters	1253
TestCl	"Testament of the Virgin Saint Clare"	Poor Sisters	1253
Prayers and praises			
BenCl	"Blessing for the Sisters, Present and to Come"	Poor Sisters	1253
Missives in the form of letters			
EpErm	Letter to Ermetrude	personal	undated
1EpAgn	First Letter to Saint Agnes	personal	1234
2EpAgn	Second Letter to Saint Agnes	personal	1238
3EpAgn	Third Letter to Saint Agnes	personal	1238
4EpAgn	Fourth Letter to Saint Agnes	personal	1253

APPENDIX D:
SOURCES FOR THE LIVES OF FRANCIS AND CLARE

For the sake of simplicity, I call all of these documents "vitae," even though some are actually *legendae*, testimonies, memoirs, *acta*, or papal bulls.[7] The vitae dealing with Francis include official Franciscan vitae (1Cel, 2Cel, and LegMai) as well as the material gathered from his witnesses (AnPer, 3Soc, CompAs, LegPer, and SpecPer) and personal reinterpretations (JulSpi and HenAv). The Versified Legend (LegVer) is especially interesting in that it comes from outside the Franciscan family. The section on Francis's family and life before his conversion reveals a secular writer's view of family. The vitae dealing with Clare are few and diverse. Clare's vitae include two *legendae* (LCl and LegVer) and two eyewitness testimonies (Proc and BuCl). The Process of Canonization for St. Clare of Assisi (Proc) gives interesting secular and religious views of family.

ABBR.	AUTHOR, TITLE (SHORT TITLE)	DATE[8]
1Cel	Thomas of Celano, *First Life of St. Francis* (*First Celano*)	1228
JulSpi	Julian of Speyer, *Life of St. Francis* (*Julian of Speyer*)	1232–39
HenAv	Henry of Avranches, *Legend of St. Francis* (*Versified Legend*)	1232–34
3Soc	*Legend of the Three Companions* (*Three Companions*)	1246
2Cel	Thomas of Celano, *Second Life of St. Francis* (*Second Celano*)	1252/53
LegMai	Bonaventure, *Major Life of St. Francis* (*Major Life*)	1260–63
AnPer	Anonymous of Perugia, *The Beginning or Founding of the Order* (*Anonymous of Perugia*)	After 1260
CompAs	*Assisi Compilation*	1266–1318
LegPer	*Legend of Perugia*[9]	1266–1318
SpecPer	*The Mirror of Perfection*	1318
Proc	*Process of Canonization for St. Clare of Assisi* (*Process*)	1253
BuCl	*Bull of Canonization for St. Clare* (*Bull*)	1255
LegVer	*Legend of St. Clare* (*Clare's Versified Legend*)	1254/55
LegCl	*Legend of St. Clare of Assisi* (*Clare's Legend*)	1255/56
24Gen	*The Chronicles of the Twenty-Four Generals* (*The Chronicles*)	1360

Appendix E:
"Hymn of 'The Children of the Heavenly Father, whose Works They Do.'"

This is a comparison of versions of this hymn in the first and second redactions of Francis's Letter to the Faithful.

1EpFid	1EpFid
1.5. O quam beati et benedicti sunt illi et illae, dum talia faciunt et in talibus perseverant, 6. quia requiescet super eos spiritus Domini et faciet apud eos habitaculum et mansionem,	48. Et omnes illi et illae, dum talia fecerint et perseveraverint usque in finem, requiescet super eos Spiritus Domini et faciet in eis habitaculum et mansionem.
7. et sunt filii patris caelestis, cuius opera faciunt,	49. Et erunt filii Patris caelestis, cuius opera faciunt.
et sunt sponsi, fratres et matres Domini nostri Jesu Christi. 8. Sponsi sumus, quando Spiritu Sancto coniungitur fidelis anima Domino nostro Jesu Christo.	50. Et sunt sponsi, fratres et matres Domini nostri Jesu Christi. 51. Sponsi sumus, quando Spiritu Sancto coniungitur fidelis anima Jesu Christo.
9. Fratres ei sumus, quando facimus voluntatem patris qui in caelis est.	52. Fratres enim sumus, quando facimus voluntatem patris eius, qui est in caelo;
10. Matres, quando portamus eum in corde et corpore nostro per divinum amorem et puram et sinceram conscientiam; parturimus eum per sanctam operationem, quae lucere debet aliis in exemplum.	53. matres quando portamus eum in corde et corpore nostro per amorem et puram et sinceram conscientiam; parturimus eum per sanctam operationem, quae lucere debet aliis in exemplum.

231

11. O quam gloriosum est, sanctum et magnum in caelis habere patrem!

12. O quam sanctum, paraclitum, pulchrum et admirabilem talem habere sponsum!

13. O quam sanctum et quam dilectum, beneplacitum, humilem, pacificum, dulcem, amabilem et super omnia desiderabilem habere talem fratrem et talem filium: Dominum nostrum Jesum Christum,

14. qui posuit animam pro ovibus suis et oravit patri . . . .

54. O quam gloriosum et sanctum et magnum habere in caelis Patrem!

55 O quam sanctum, paraclitum, pulchrum et admirabilem habere sponsum!

56 O quam sanctum et quam dilectum, beneplacitum, humilem, pacificum, dulcem et amabilem et super omnia desiderabilem habere talem fratrem et filium, qui posuit animam suam pro ovibus suis et oravit Patrem pro nobis . . . .

This is a comparison of the first and second redactions of Francis's Letter to the Faithful and his "Non-Bulled Rule."

2EpFid 57–60 (1EpFid 1.14–19)	RnB 22.41–54

56. O quam sanctum et quam dilectum, beneplacitum, humilem, pacificum, dulcem et amabilem et super omnia desiderabilem habere talem fratrem et (talem) filium, (Dominum nostrum Jesum Christum,) qui posuit animam suam pro ovibus suis et oravit patrem pro nobis dicens:

41. Teneamus ergo verba, vitam et doctrinam et sanctum eius evangelium, qui dignatus est pro nobis rogare Patrem suum et nobis eius nomen manifestare dicens:

Pater clarifica nomen tuum et clarifica Filium tuum, ut Filius tuus clarificet te.
42. Pater, manifestavi nomen tuum hominibus, quos dedisti mihi; quia verba quae dedisti mihi, dedi eis; et ipsi acceperunt et cognoverunt, quia a te exivi et crediderunt quia tu me misisti.
43. Ego pro eis rogo, non pro mundo,
44. sed pro his quos dedisti mihi, quia tui sunt et omnia mea tua sunt.

Pater sancte, serva eos in nomine tuo, quos dedisti mihi.

45. Pater sancte, serva eos in nomine tuo quos dedisti mihi, ut ipsi sint unum sicut et nos.

46. Haec loquor in mundo, ut habeant gaudium in semetipsis.

47. Ego dedi eis sermonem tuum; et mundus eos odio habuit, quia non sunt de mundo, sicut et ego non sum de mundo.

48. Non rogo ut tollas eos de mundo, sed ut serves eos a malo.

49. Mirifica eos in veritate.

50. Sermo tuus veritas est.

51. Sicut tu me misisti in mundum, et ego misi eos in mundum.

52. Et pro eis sanctifico meipsum, ut sint ipsi sanctificati in veritate.

57. Pater, omnes, quos dedisti mihi in mundo, tui erant et mihi eos dedisti.

58. Et verba, quae dedisti mihi, dedi eis; et ipsi acceperunt et cognoverunt vere, quia a te exivi et crediderunt, quia tu me misisti; rogo pro eis et non pro mundo; benedic et sanctifica eos.

59. Et pro eis sanctifico me ipsum,

(Non pro eis rogo tantum, sed pro eis qui credituri sunt per verbum illorum in me,) ut sint sanctificati in unum sicut et nos sumus.

53. Non pro eis rogo tantum, sed pro eis, qui credituri sunt propter verbum eorum in me, ut sint consummati in unum, et cognoscat mundus, quia tu me misisti et dilexisti eos, sicut me dilexisti.

54. Et notum faciam eis nomen tuum, ut dilectio, qua dilexisti me, sit in ipsis et ego in ipsis.

60. Et volo, pater, ut ubi ego sum et illi sint mecum, ut videant claritatem meam in regno tuo.

55. Pater, quos dedisti mihi, volo, ut ubi ego sum, et illi sunt mecum, ut videant claritatem tuam in regno tuo. Amen.

Notes

Abbreviations

(Abbreviations for the saints' opuscula and vitae can be found in Appendix A.)

Lat. Dict.   Lewis, Charlton T., and Charles Short, *A Latin Dictionary*, 2 ed. (Oxford: Clarendon, 1955).

PL   Migne, Jacques-Paul, ed., *Patrologiae cursus completus: series latina*, 221 vols. (Paris, 1841–1864).

Introduction

1. Luke Wadding called Francis's writings "opuscula" in order to indicate that these brief literary works are not necessarily in their original form; cf. Esser, ed., *Gli scritti di S. Francesco d'Assisi*, 24–25. I use the same term, *opuscula*, to refer to the writings attributed to Clare. I use the critical edition of both Francis's and Clare's opuscula found in Menestò and Brufani, eds., *Fontes Franciscani*, 23–245; 2262–2324. All translations of their opuscula and vitae used in this book are my own.

2. Optatus Van Asseldonk, OFM Cap, contributed much to the concept of Franciscan brotherhood when he coined the phrase "un amore (fraterno) più che materno" (a fraternal love that is more than maternal). My translation of his expression is quite simply "greater than a mother's love"; cf. Pyfferoen, and Van Asseldonk, "Maria Santissima e lo Spirito Santo in San Francesco d'Assisi"; Van Asseldonk, *Maria, Francesco e Chiara*, 444–70; Van Asseldonk, *Lo Spirito dà la vita*, 67–75; Van Asseldonk, "Madre."

3. In feudal Italy, the *maiores* were the nobles and knights. The only other social class was called *minores*.

4. Simply put, minority is the way of life that Francis and his movement espoused. The term comes from *minores*—indicating all those people who did not belong to the noble class. For Francis, who had always wanted to become a *maiore*, minority meant embracing the social class to which he was born. For Clare it meant rejecting her social status. And for both of them it was an imitation of Jesus' kenosis by climbing down the ladder, not up it.

5. In traditional Catholicism, monasteries and convents are not meant to be determined by the gender of those living within their walls, but rather by the type of religious life they are living. Monks and nuns traditionally live a contemplative life in monasteries, while brothers and sisters live an apostolic life in convents. It seems that only Anglophone usage relegates the term *convent* to the homes of women in apostolic communities and prefers the term *friaries* for the homes of mendicant men.

6. We cannot refer to the Poor Clares (as such) before the death of St. Clare. Francis referred to them as the Poor Ladies, while Clare called them the Poor Sisters. They seem to have been known as the Poor Sisters of San Damiano, or Damianites. I will primarily refer to them as the Damianites.

7. I have chosen to call my method a socio-spiritual method emphasizing the work of the Holy Spirit in and through social reality. It is based heavily but not exclusively on the method explained and used in Destro and Pesce, *Antropologia delle origini cristiane*. This section has been published in an altered form in the *Journal of Hispanic/Latino Theology* (online). Cf. Cavazos-González, "*La Cotidianidad Divina*: A Latin@ Method of Spirituality." For more information on Spirituality as a theological discipline and a socio-cultural reality please read Cavazos-González, "Spirituality," 749–60.

8. Latino is the normal manner in which U.S. citizens of Latin American and Hispanic descent refer to themselves as a cohesive group. This word however is masculine in gender and many Latinos are actually Latinas (women) therefore the @ at the end of Latino indicates both the Latina and the Latino person.

9. *Cotidianidad* or *lo cotidiano* are used by many U.S. Latin@ theologians as the locus of theological reflection and discussion. Cf. Nanko-Fernández, "Traditioning *Latinamente*: A Theological Discussion on *la Lengua Cotidiana*; Nanko-Fernández, "Lo Cotidiano," 158–60."

10. Cf. Espín, *Futuring Our Past: Explorations in the Theology of Tradition*, 1–22.

11. Cf. García, "Hispanic Theologians as Actors, Prophets and Poets of Their Communities," 11.

12. Cf. Frohlich, "Spiritual Discipline, Discipline of Spirituality: Revisiting Questions of Definition and Method."

13. By the term *socio-spiritual* I understand all of the aspects of human life. *Socio* = social, political, religious, economic, and material—in other words, the exterior life. *Spiritual* = spiritual, educational, cultural, affective, and psychological—in other words, the interior life.

14. Nanko-Fernández, "From *Pájaro* to Paraclete: Retrieving the Spirit of God in the Company of Mary."

15. Other works that speak of the application of social sciences to the study of theology and spirituality are Scroggs, "The Sociological Interpretation of the New Testament: The Present Stage of Research"; Brown, *The Cult of the Saints*; Weinstein and Bell, *Saints and Society: The Two Worlds of Western Christendom, 1000–1700*; Russell, "Sociology and the Study of Spirituality"; Secondin, *Spiritualità in dialogo. Nuovi scenari dell'esperienza spirituale*; Martin, *Reflections on Sociology and Theology*; and Flanagan, *A Sociology of Spirituality*.

16. Although the history of humanity is diverse in its origins and developments, depending on whether one looks at the history of Meso-America, Asia, Europe, or elsewhere, the terminology developed in Western Europe to divide its history has become the predominant terminology used for the study of history in the West. It is from this terminology that we use "the Middle Ages" as a way of designating the time lasting from the fifth to the fifteenth centuries of the Common Era (CE). Latin cultures tend to divide this period

into two major eras: the High Middle Ages and the Late Middle Ages. Germanic and Anglophonic peoples divide it into three periods: (1) the Early Middle Ages, from about the year 476 CE (with the fall of the last Roman Emperor in the West) to 1050 (with the division of Christianity between East and West); (2) the High Middle Ages, lasting from 1050 to anywhere from 1250 (with the death of the Emperor Frederic II) to 1350 and the Black Plague; and (3) the Late Middle Ages that go until 1453 (with the fall of Constantinople) or 1517 (the beginning of the Reformation); cf. McNally, "Middle Ages"; and Peters, "Middle Ages."

17. Cf. Duby, *The Three Orders: Feudal Society Imagined*, 81, 108, 209–10, 255–56; Le Goff, "Introduction: Medieval Man," 22; Klapisch-Zuber, "Women and the Family," 285; Peterson, *Clare of Assisi: A Biographical Study*, 8; Bynum, "Religious Women in the Late Middle Ages," 286.

18. A. Fortini, *Nova vita di San Francesco*; Helen Moak published a condensed translation of Fortini's work in 1981. She took what she considered most important to understanding Francis and indicated where one can find more information on certain topics in the Italian original; A. Fortini, *Francis of Assisi*, trans. Helen Moak. A few years before the life of Francis was published, Arnaldo Fortini had already published an article about his findings on Clare's family: "Nuove notizie intorno a S. Chiara d'Assisi."

19. G. Fortini, "The Noble Family of St Clare of Assisi."

20. Le Goff, *Saint Francis of Assisi*, 14.

21. Sabatier, *Vita di San Francesco d'Assisi*, 61–68; Sabatier, *The Road to Assisi: The Essential Biography of St. Francis*.

22. Ortolani da Pesaro, *La madre del Santo d'Assisi*.

23. Englebert, *St. Francis of Assisi: A Biography*, 1–21.

24. Manselli, *St. Francis of Assisi*, 28–61.

25. Cardini, *Francesco d'Assisi*, 27–28, 34–36, 45–47, 81–83.

26. Le Goff, *Saint Francis of Assisi*, 23–24, 87–88, 102, 126.

27. House, *Francis of Assisi: A Revolutionary Life*, 15–35, 68–70.

28. Rotzetter, *Chiara d'Assisi. La prima francescana*; Peterson, *Clare of Assisi*; Triviño, *Clara de Asís ante el espejo*; Bartoli, *Clare of Assisi*.

29. Zavalloni, *La personalità di Francesco d'Assisi*; Zavalloni, *La personalità di Chiara d'Assisi*.

30. Charron, *Da Narciso a Gesù*.

31. Cf. Kazantzakis, *Saint Francis*; Trettel, *Francis*; Larrañaga, *El hermano de Asís*; "Ulivi, *Le mura del cielo*.

32. Matura, *François d'Assise, "auteur spirituel." Le message de ses écrits*; Matura, *Francis of Assisi: Writer and Spiritual Master*.

33. Van Asseldonk, Maria, *Francesco e Chiara*; Van Asseldonk, *Lo Spirito dà la vita*.

34. Nguyên-Van-Khanh, *Teacher of His Heart: Jesus Christ in the Thought and Writings of St. Francis*.

35. Paolazzi, *Lettura degli "scritti" di Francesco d'Assisi*.

36. Cremaschi and Acquadro, *Scritti di Santa Chiara d'Assisi*, 111.

37. Bartoli, *Clare of Assisi*.

38. Dhont, *Chiara madre e sorella.*

39. Peterson, *Clare of Assisi.*

40. For more recent insight into the debate dealing with the Franciscan question, see Di Fonzo, "Questione Francescana"; Uribe, *Introduzione alle agiografie di S. Francesco e S. Chiara d'Assisi* (sec XIII–XIV), 9–42.

CHAPTER I: EUROPEAN FAMILY OF THE HIGH MIDDLE AGES

1. Cf. Harris, *Our Kind: Who We Are, Where We Came From, Where We Are Going,* 189–96.

2. Lenzen, *Alla riceca del padre, Dal patriarcato agli alimenti,* 45–63.

3. Ibid., 65–88.

4. Cf. ibid., 69–70, 72.

5. Cf. Guttmacher, "Family and Family Life," 336.

6. Cf. Gen 28:7; Dt 21:13; I Sam 22:1; 2 Sam 19:38; Jer 16:3ff; 20:14ff.

7. Cf. Gies and Gies, *Marriage and the Family in the Middle Ages,* 4.

8. Herlihy, *Medieval Households,* 3.

9. Osiek, "Family Matters," 215.

10. Cf. Lenzen, *Alla ricerca,* 109–28; Danieli, "La famiglia nel diritto romano e intermedio," 989–90.

11. Cf. Harris, *Our Kind,* 311–13; Danieli, "La famiglia," 989.

12. Osiek, "Family Matters," 211.

13. Cf. Danieli, "La famiglia," 989; Lospinoso, "Matrimonio," 208.

14. Elliott, *Spiritual Marriage: Sexual Abstinence in Medieval Wedlock,* 47.

15. Nuptiae sunt coniunctio maris et feminae, consortium omnis vitae, divina et iuria communicatio. Cf. Lospinoso "Matrimonio," 208. (This translation is my own.)

16. Cf. Destro and Pesce, *Antropologia,* 65–82, 162–69; Elliott, *Spiritual Marriage,* 17–19; Mt 12:48; 19:3–12, 22, 30; Mk 3:31–35; Lk 8:19–21, 14:26, 18:29–30, 21:30; Jn 2:1–5, 2:11; 7:1–10; 19:26–27.

17. For the most part in the Anglophonic world, the word *spouse* is used to indicate bride, wife, bridegroom, and husband. The Latin origin of that word (*sponsa, -ae* and *sponsum, -i*) specifically denoted the roles of fiancées, brides, and bridegrooms, and I have chosen to translate them as "spouse"; cf. Hames, "Bridal Mysticism," 106; Malatesta, "Marriage, Mystical," 631; Brunet, "Figures de l'Eglise"; and Adnès, "Mariage, spiritual."

18. Cf. Elliott, *Spiritual Marriage,* 3–4, 19–22, 39 n.

19. For a detailed explanation of the development of Christianity's view of marriage, sex, and family, see Elliott, *Spiritual Marriage;* Brooke, *The Medieval Idea of Marriage;* Goody, *The Development of the Family and Marriage in Europe;* Herlihy, "The Family and Religious Ideologies in Medieval Europe"; Parmisano, "Love and Marriage in the Middle Ages"; Sheehan, "Sexuality, Marriage, Celibacy, and the Family in Central and Northern Italy: Christian Legal and Moral Guides in the Early Middle Ages."

20. Elliott, *Spiritual Marriage,* 22.

21. Cf. Osiek, "Family Matters," 211; Herlihy, *Medieval Households,* 22.

22. Elliott, *Spiritual Marriage*, 38; Cf. Williams, *Ideas of the Fall and of Original Sin: A Historical and Critical Study*, 226–31.

23. Elliott, *Spiritual Marriage*, 44–45; cf. Jerome, *Adversus Jovinianum* I, PL 23, cols. 221–96 and *Adversus Helvidium* c.9–17, PL 23, cols.201–12, as cited in Elliot, *Spiritual Marriage*, 44.

24. Cf. Elliott, *Spiritual Marriage*, 45, 45 n; Augustine, *De Genesi ad litteram* (9.36.6, 9.19.36) as cited in Schmitt, *Le mariage chrétien dans l'ouvre de saint Augustine: une théologie baptismale de la vie conjugale*, 91–94.

25. Elliott, *Spiritual Marriage*, 47.

26. Cf. Sheehan, "Sexuality, Marriage, Celibacy," 172–75; Lospinoso, "Marriage," 209; Lucas, *Women in the Middle Ages: Religion, Marriage and Letters*, 70–71; Elliott, *Spiritual Marriage*, 132–34.

27. Sheehan, "Family and Marriage, Western European," 608–9.

28. Cf. L'Hermite-Leclercq, "Le donne nell'ordine feudale (XI–XII secolo)," 268; Klapisch-Zuber, "Women and the Family," 287–89; Duby, *Mâle Moyen Âge. De l'amour et autres essais*, 21–23.

29. Atkinson, *The Oldest Vocation: Christian Motherhood in the Middle Ages*, 13–15, 65–69, 75, 94–96, 117; Sheehan, "Family and Marriage," 609.

30. Cf. Elliott, *Spiritual Marriage*, 16; Peterson, *Clare of Assisi*, 8.

31. Although *sponsi* can be and is translated as the English neuter "spouses" in most religious texts, it is most correctly translated as the gender-specific "bridegroom" or "fiancé." We need to distinguish the term *sponsi* from the term *maritus* (husband), just as *sponsa* (bride/fiancée) is distinct from *uxor* (wife).

32. Besides daughters, they even had sons, such as Jacques di Vitry, who claimed Mary of Oignes as his spiritual mother. Gregory IX (then Cardinal Hugolino) even claimed Clare as the mother of his salvation (*matri salutis suae*): Letter of Cardinal Hugolino I. Cardinal Rainaldo called the Poor Ladies at San Damiano his mothers, sisters, and daughters: Letter of Cardinal Rainaldo I. English translations of both these letters can be found in Armstrong, ed. and trans., *The Lady: Clare of Assisi: Early Documents*, 129–30; 1133–34.

33. Cf. Weinstein and Bell, *Saints and Society*, 220–38.

34. Vauchez, *La santità nel Medioevo*, 243; Peterson, *Clare of Assisi*, 2. According to David Herlihy, besides feminization, this era also saw an urbanization and internalization of sanctity; cf. Herlihy, *Medieval Households*, 113–14.

35. Bynum, "Religious Women," 131.

36. Bynum, *Holy Feast and Holy Fast: The Religious Significance of Food to Medieval Women*, 280.

37. Cf. Bynum, *Holy Feast*, 279–88; Rohr and Martos, *The Wild Man's Journey: Reflections on Male Spirituality*, 11–17.

38. Cf. Turner, *Dramas, Fields and Metaphors: Symbolic Action in Human Society*; Turner and Turner, *Image and Pilgrimage in Christian Culture: Anthropological Perspectives*; Davis, "Anthropology and History."

39. Cf. Bynum, *Holy Feast*, 288.

40. Leclercq, *La figura della donna nel medioevo*, 7. (This and subsequent translations of this work are mine.)

41. It seems that the soul in relationship to God needs to express itself in feminine ways that are integrated into a man's maleness. In Jungian terms, a man must come into relationship with his anima if he is to have a capacity for meaning and valuation in his life; cf. Robert Johnson, *He: Understanding Masculine Psychology*, 31–50; Rohr and Martos, *The Wild Man's Journey*, 1–17.

42. One of these writers, a Cistercian nun named Liutgard of Tongern (a contemporary of Mary of Oignes) speaks of there being three couches in the Song of Songs. On the first couch, the soul, wounded through penitence, recognizes its sinfulness and need for the Spouse who saves. The second couch is the couch where the soul, trying to purify itself, is wearied by making war on itself through fasting and abstinence. It does not do this in order to save itself through its own merits, but rather to beautify itself for the Spouse who sanctifies. Finally, on the third couch, the soul, which rests sweetly in the arms of the Spouse who visits when He wills, is made glad and perfected through contemplation; cf. Taylor, *The Medieval Mind: A History of the Development of Thought and Emotion in the Middle Ages*, 480; Peterson, *Clare of Assisi*, 291, 295.

43. Bynum, *Holy Feast*, 126–27.

44. Cf. Peterson, *Clare of Assisi*, 51; Bynum et al., *Gender and Religion: On the Complexity of Symbols*, 259.

45. Ashley and Sheingorn trace their studies back to Voragine's *The Golden Legend*. The Church, as such, did not officially recognize the devotion to St. Joseph and the Holy Family until the late medieval era. Despite this, one has to recognize that these have their roots in the twelfth and thirteenth centuries; cf. Ashley and Sheingorn, eds., *Interpreting Cultural Symbols: St. Anne in Late Medieval Society*, 111–30, 178.

46. "Up to the twelfth century, Christians were expected to have affectionate or sibling or parental devotion (depending on respective ages) to their spouses." Boswell, *Same-Sex Unions in Premodern Europe*, 171.

47. The Church taught that love should be a part of every marriage, even arranged marriages. Love in the Middle Ages was more than just an emotion called *amore*; it was a respectful sentiment called *caritas*. Love, in a society that did not demand "emotional love" for marriage, was more a form of respect than an actual emotion. Cf. Leclercq, *La figura della donna*, 17–18.

48. A number of secular and ecclesiastical legends abound about the strength of a couple's love, even if that love went unconsummated. A popular hagiographic work to this effect was the marriage of St. Cunegunda to the Emperor Henry II. Their marriage went unconsummated and yet their love became as strong as that of Cicero's definition of friendship, which was applicable only to males; they came to have the same will, and what one began the other would hasten to see to completion. Their love was tested by rumors of Cunegunda's alleged infidelity, but in the end, their spiritual love was triumphant. Preachers not only held up positive role models of love such as Cunegunda and Henry II, they also condemned couples who did not love each other. Their message to the faithful was clear: love is essential to married life and its lack is a great fault; cf. Leclercq, *La figura della donna*, 21–24.

49. The Carolingian bishop and theologian Hincmar of Reims (842–82) seems to

have been the first to insist on consent and consummation as defining a valid marriage, but it wasn't until the twelfth century that the Church developed a systematic canon law for marriage; cf. Boswell, *Same-Sex Unions*, 166; Lucas, *Women in the Middle Ages*, 70–71.

50. Cf. Herlihy, *Medieval Households*, 80–81.

51. Cf. Elliott, *Spiritual Marriage*, 136, 142–55.

52. Cf. Herlihy, *Medieval Households*, 81.

53. Elliott, *Spiritual Marriage*, 138.

54. Alexander III was formed, theologically, in an Abelardian school of thought. He clarified the Church's position that, especially during times of fasting and abstinence, the continence of married couples described in ancient canons was to be considered as mere suggestion, but not precept. This clarification did much to encourage married couples to become part of apostolic movements and search for a life of devotion; cf. Rivi, *Francesco d'Assisi e il laicato del suo tempo*, 50–51.

55. Cf. Elliott, *Spiritual Marriage*, 139; Herlihy, *Medieval Households*, 81.

56. In a carnal world in which fornication is a constant danger, marriage was seen as the lesser of two evils. It was seen as a way to help discipline sexuality, as well as a way to avoid fornication. In this way, married couples were helpful to each other's spiritual well-being.

57. In traditional Catholicism, the faithful are divided into two states in life, the secular and the religious. Religious were primarily monastic and, at the time of Francis, expanded to include the mendicant communities as well. Unlike the seculars, who could marry and own property, religious lived in community and took vows of poverty, chastity, and obedience. For the first Christian millennium, the priests were primarily secular men who were ordained and placed in charge of a local community; they promised obedience to the local Bishop. Although some fourth-century councils in Spain recommended celibacy, the move to enforce clerical celibacy only began to take force in the late sixth century. Eventually, the Gregorian reform of the eleventh century tried to force celibacy on all priests. In 1123, the First Lateran Council called all priestly marriages invalid.

58. The anti-matrimonial polemic of the twelfth century slowly became pro-marriage by the start of the thirteenth century. The praise of marriage became an important pastoral theme. Marriage was proclaimed as being instituted directly by God in Eden, preserved from the destruction of the flood, and confirmed as something holy by the presence of Christ, Mary, and the apostles at the wedding of Cana. It was at this wedding celebration that Christ performed his first miracle. Marriage was the lifestyle that God had preordained for the mother of Christ. Finally, marriage accomplished the threefold task of generating offspring, keeping couples from fornication, and conferring a sacramental grace; cf. Vecchio, "La buona moglie," 130.

59. Ibid., 19–23.

60. The thirteenth-century Church dedicated itself to upholding the importance and the sanctity of marriage against heretical reactions—like those of the Cathars, who condemned matrimony as something worldly; cf. Leclercq, *La figura della donna*, 29–36; L'Hermite-Leclercq, "Le donne," 266–67.

61. Cf. Fenster, "Why Men?" (preface), ix–x; Pleck, *The Myth of Masculinity*; Brod, "The Case for Men's Studies," 264ff.

62. Bullough, "On Being a Male in the Middle Ages," 34. These roles are reminiscent of the tri-functional role attributed to the father in the second millennium BCE in Egypt.

63. I purposely use *genitor* here to distinguish from father. *Genitor, -oris* and *genetrix, -tricis* come from the root *gigno* (to beget, to bear, to bring forth) and thus are both intimately related to the conception and bearing of offspring. On the other hand, *pater, -ris* comes from the root *pa* (to nourish and/or to protect). Thus, the father was the one who protected and provided nourishment. The word *pater* carried with it no explicit reference to the generation of offspring (cf. Lat. Dict., 1313–14). The word *mater*, on the other hand, came from the root *ma* (to make and/or to measure). *Mater* was explicitly associated with the generation of offspring (cf. Lat. Dict., 1118).

64. Atkinson, *The Oldest Vocation*, 24, 46–51, 58–59, 113.

65. Elliott, *Spiritual Marriage*, 49.

66. C. Casagrande, "La donna custodita," 110–12.

67. The complete prayer reads, "You are blessed, O God of our fathers; blessed too is your name for ever and ever. Let the heavens bless you and all things you have made forevermore. You it was who created Adam, you who created Eve his wife to be his help and support; and from these two the human race was born. You it was who said, 'It is not right that the man should be alone; let us make him a helper like him.' And so I take my sister not for any lustful motive, but I do it in singleness of heart. Be kind enough to have pity on her and on me and bring us to old age together"; *New Jerusalem Bible*.

68. One notes that, taken out of context, these Pauline verses seem to place women in an inferior position to their husbands. But when they are placed in Paul's original context, which speaks of mutual submission (Eph 5:21), the husband is to govern his wife as Christ did the Church through sacrifice and service (Eph 5:25–30). This is a far cry from the male dominance promoted in medieval families.

69. Cf. C. Casagrande, "La donna custodita," 110; Elliott, *Spiritual Marriage*, 156–57; Vecchio, "La buona moglie," 144.

70. Canonists had fixed the age where a child could be engaged at seven years old, while marrying age was twelve for girls and fourteen for boys. While most girls would marry around the age of twelve, boys would usually not marry until their early twenties; cf. L'Hermite-Leclercq "Le donne," 268.

71. Vecchio, "La buona moglie," 144.

72. Cf. ibid., 135.

73. Ibid.

74. There are several legends of female saints who lived their lives as monks, even as abbots, only to be discovered as women when their bodies were being prepared for burial.

75. Bullough, "On Being a Male," 38; Vecchio, "La buona moglie," 135–36, 148–49.

76. In the Middle Ages, most of the anatomical and physiological theories of the Classical Period were incorporated into Christian thought. Not all of these theories were compatible with Christian doctrine; for example, Ovid's *Art of Love* and Constantine's *Viaticum* both taught that the only way to cure love-sickness in a male was through sexual intercourse. A man had to make sure that he used his wife "properly" due to the inconstant nature of her body and her incomplete reason. Thus, a wife required that a man never com-

promise his authority over her by becoming too emotionally involved with her. Cf. Bullough, "On Being Male," 39–40; Klapisch-Zuber, "Women and the Family," 305.

77. Thomasset, "La natura della donna," 39, 59ff.

78. Herophius discovered the ovum in 300 BCE, which was known as the female sperm in the Middle Ages. Galen (second century CE), who was extremely influential in the early Middle Ages, refuted Aristotle's theory that only the male seed was influential in the conception of a child. He claimed that the child was a product of both the male and female seed, without questioning the superiority of the male seed; cf. Atkinson, *The Oldest Vocation*, 49.

79. Bullough, "On Being Male," 40, 43; Atkinson, *The Oldest Vocation*, 47.

80. Vecchio, "La buona moglie," 131–32.

81. Cf. L'Hermite-Leclercq, "Le donne," 280–82

82. Vecchio, "La buona moglie," 136.

83. Cf. L'Hermite-Leclercq, "Le donne," 277.

84. Cf. Vecchio, "La buona moglie," 140.

85. Peterson, *Clare of Assisi*, 46.

86. St. Michael, defender of heaven and earth, was seen as the patron saint of pregnant women, because their death could mean the loss not only of this life, but also everlasting life; cf. Peterson, *Clare of Assisi*, 30–33.

87. Cf. Vecchio, "La buona moglie," 138–39.

88. Cf. Triviño, *Clara de Asís*, 38.

89. Cf. Aries, *Centuries of Childhood: A Social History of Family Life*.

90. Cf. Harris, *Our Kind*, 225.

91. Cf. Shahar, *Childhood in the Middle Ages*.

92. Peterson, *Clare of Assisi*, 63.

93. Cf. Herlihy, Destro, Adriana, and Mauro Pesce, 215–16.

94. Cf. L'Hermite-Leclercq, "Le donne," 261.

95. Cf. ibid., 262.

96. Girls were educated to be modest, sweet, reserved, and hard-working in order to attract a good husband and to be above reproach. If they learned to read, they did so with the Psalms. They were taught to cherish and treasure their virginity above all things in sight of a good marriage; cf. L'Hermite-Leclercq, "Le donne," 257, 263.

97. Cf. Lett, "Mais Si! Les parents aimaient leurs enfants," 17–18.

98. Shahar, *Childhood in the Middle Ages*, 112–15.

99. Cf. Lett, "Mais Si!" 18–19.

100. Vecchio, "La buona moglie," 148.

101. From Giacomo de Varagine's third sermon in *Sermones de sanctis per anni circulum, sermones quadragesimales, sermones de tempore*, as quoted in Bestor, "Ideas about Procreation and Their Influence on Ancient and Medieval Views of Kinship," 164.

102. Bestor, "Ideas about Procreation," 165.

103. According to medieval medical thought, a mother fed the child in her womb with her own menstrual blood. Once the child was born, the mother's menstrual blood was thought to become breast milk. In this way a mother continued to feed the child from her

own blood. It was commonly held that just as a man passed on his characteristics in the male seed at the moment of conception, so a mother passed on her characteristics in her milk while breastfeeding. For this reason, wet nurses were to be a last resort in supplying nourishment to a newborn child.; cf. Bestor, "Ideas about Procreation," 158, 161; Bartolomeus Anglicus and John Trevisa, *On the Properties of Things*, vol. I, 302–3; Atkinson, *The Oldest Vocation*, 57–60.

104. Cf. Vecchio, "La buona moglie," 149.

105. Peterson, *Clare of Assisi*, 18. There were many ways in which this new emphasis on the individual was being expressed in Christian spirituality. Moreover, it was not just in "traditional" religious settings that this was taking place. Marriage, that institution of questionable validity for the spiritual life, was also being affected to the point that it joined the ranks of the sacraments in this era. The growing emphasis on consent for the validity of marriage vows was another sign of how individuals were seeking autonomy from family structures that treated offspring as simply part of a social group.

106. Virtuous girls in Italy were expected to limit their contact with the world outside the home when they reached puberty; cf. Herlihy, *Women, Family*, 16.

107. Cf. Charron, *Da Narciso a Gesù*, 40–45, 49–64; Bynum, *Holy Feast*, 225.

108. Cf. Herlihy, *Medieval Households*, 83; Le Goff, "Introduction: Medieval Man," 23.

109. Cf. Stuard, "Burdens of Matrimony. Husbanding and Gender in Medieval Italy," 63–64; Gies and Gies, *Marriage and the Family*, 209–10.

110. Klapisch-Zuber, "Women and the Family," 297.

11. Cf. A. Fortini, *Nova vita* I, 46.

CHAPTER II: FRANCIS, SON OF A MERCHANT FAMILY

1. ICel 1.1; 2Cel 7.3; LegMai 1:1.1; 3Soc 2.1; JulSpi 1.1; HenAv 1:26–29; AnPer 3.2.

2. Cf. Cardini, "Francesco d'Assisi e l'Europa del suo tempo. Ricerca d'una risposta 'globale' al tema delle origini di una vocazione," 39; A. Fortini, *Francis of Assisi*, 40.

3. Cf. A. Fortini, *Francis of Assisi*, 1–165; Uribe, *Por los caminos de Francisco*, 19–28; Della Porta, *Guide to Assisi: History and Art*; Cardini, "Francesco e l'Europa," 38–46; Englebert, *Francis of Assisi*, 5–21.

4. Thomas was born in the town of Celano in central Italy. The date of his birth is uncertain, but some place it between 1185 and 1190, making him a contemporary of both Francis and Clare; cf. Hermann, "Celano: Introduction"; Da Campagnola, "Thomae de Celano: Introduzione."

5. Hermann, "Celano: Introduction."

6. Tunc profecto omni dissolutionis genere fluitantes, eo quod liceat eis explere omne quod libet, omni studio se tradunt flagitiis deservire.

7. miseri plerumque se nequiora fecisse quam fecerint, ne videantur abiectiores, quo innocentiores exsistunt.

8. Lanzoni, "Il sogno presagio della madre incinta nella letteratura medievale e antica," 226–28.

9. Of the modern collections of the Franciscan sources, only Habig, ed., *Omnibus* contains the story. The Latin manuscript of this particular version of the *Legend of the Three Companions* is found only in the sixteenth century Ms Vaticanus 7739. The story of the prophetic beggar however can also be found in De conformitate, 109, in De cognatione sancti Francisci by Arnaldo de Sarrant [MP 42 (1492), 125] in a manuscript from the end of the thirteenth century, [De conformitate, 108 n; Oliger, "Liber exemplorum Fratrum minorum saeculi XIII," in Antonianum 2 (1927), 262–63.

10. Domus, inquit, patris mei coniuncta est domui beati Francisci Referebat autem sic mater mea: Cum quiesceret in lecto post partum mater beati Francisci, ut solent mulieres in puerperio, et vicine mulieres alique circa eum, ecce peregrinus ad hostium quasi elemosinam petens cum accepisset partem pulli a matre beati Francisci mittente, instare cepit et dicere velle se videre puerulum natum. Et cum repelletur a mulieribus que ibi erant, cepit asserere quod nullo modo recederet nisi puerum prius videret. Tunc domina Pica mater: Afferte, inquit, puerum ut videat. Quem conplexum etc. dixit hoc modo: "Nati sunt duo pueri una die in vico isto, iste et alius. Unus, hic scilicet, erit de melioribus hominibus mundi, alter pessimus erit. Quod revera processu temporis verum esse rerum exitus docuit." This text is found in the *Liber exemplorum Fratrum Minorum saeculi XIII* in the Vatican Library Codex Ottoboniano Lateranensius no. 522. I have used the text as found in Oliger, "Liber exemplorum," 262–63.

11. "De conformitate vitae Beati Francisci ad vitam Domini Iesu, auctore Fr. Bartholomeo de Pisa Liber I Fructus I–XIII" in *Analecta Franciscana* 4 (1906): 108–9.

12. Qui habuit uxorem nomine iohanam / devotissimam supra modum: Hec enim sepulcrum domini / et locum beati michaelis archangeli ac limina apostolorum devotissime visitavit. et alia sanctuaria visitare cotidie affectabat. Cumque devotissime in suis oracionibus filium domino postularet: semper ipsum juxta dei beneplacita postulabat: Cum autem mater filium concepisset et / ipsa more solito ad partum devenisset, et languere cepisset. propter angustias sui partus : Et cum ipsa puerem parere non posset : ocurrit sibi memoriam partum virginis gloriose et locum humilitatis. in quo dominum parturivit. Unde affectans: statim stabulum ipsa peciit; et descendens cum ibi bovem et asinum adduxissent: juxta suum beneplacitum voluntatis. in medio eorum suum filium cum paucis doloribus parturivit. As found in Fierens, "La Question Franciscaine," 290–91.

13. The story of the stalleta seems to be a later invention which made its way into *Vita S. Francisci Anonyma Bruxellensis* (*Anonymous of Brussels*) in the later fourteenth or early fifteenth century: cf. Fierens, "La Question Franciscaine," 290–91; Abate, *La casa dove nacque San Francesco di Assisi nella sua documentazione storica*, 169ff; Bracaloni, *La Chiesa Nuova di San Francesco converso, casa paterna del Santo di Assisi*, 147ff; and A. Fortini, *Nova vita* II, 21ff.

14. A good merchant kept a strict record of his business. Thus, a solid education in reading, writing, and arithmetic was expected of him; cf. Herlihy, *Women, Family*, 14; Frugoni, *A Day in a Medieval City*, 137–46.

15. A. Fortini presents an interesting description of the child Francis's education; cf. A. Fortini, *Francis of Assisi*, 93–97.

16. 1Cel 16.1; 2Cel 13.5–7; 127.3; 3Soc 10.6; 23.8; 24.4–5; 33.2; AnPer 15.3.

17. Historians in the sixteenth and seventeenth centuries sought to align most saints with noble families. Francis was assigned to the Moriconi family of Lucca and his mother was said to have come from the noble house of Bourlemont in Provence. None of this can be proven, and Francis himself testified against it affirming that he was a commoner; EpOrd 39; Test 19. Cf. Englebert, *Francis of Assisi*, 11; Baronti, *Il Lucchese, San Francesco d'Assisi*; A. Fortini, *Francis of Assisi*, 89 n.

18. Many scholars tend to believe and affirm that Francis learned French from his mother whom they claim was French; Charron, *Da Narciso a Gesù*, 93–95. I do not agree. The French origin of Francis's mother is of late and dubious origin. Francis probably learned French from his father for the purposes of business.

19. Ibid., 40–41, 51.

20. Cf. ibid., 44.

21. "in sin"

22. Celano might simply be alluding to the prejudices against merchants in the Middle Ages. Most merchants, especially cloth merchants, were also money lenders tied closely to usury. This fact led many to consider the merchant to be useful yet not worthy of nobility. He was one who took advantage of people's need in order to make himself rich; cf. A. Fortini, *Francis of Assisi*, 37–42.

23. This refined manner was probably an indication of Francis's desire to be chivalrous. Chivalry and courtly love were all the rage in Europe at that time and the son of the ambitious Pietro di Bernardone could not have remained untouched by this fashion. Chivalry did much to soften the ruggedness of the knight, by educating him in courtesy, good manners, and fashionable dress. Although some would say that this formation was part of the feminization of the age, it seems to have been a way of holding in check the military class which was always tempted to abuse its power. Despite the fact that knights were soldiers, the codes of chivalry expected them to be courteous and kind toward the defenseless—primarily, women and the poor; cf. Charron, *Da Narciso a Gesù*, 120–22; Barbero and Frugoni, *Dizionario del Medioevo*, 68–70; Cardini, "Francesco d'Assisi e l'Europa," 49–50; A. Fortini, *Francis of Assisi*, 9–10, 479, 640; Frugoni, *Francis of Assisi: A Life*, 3, 8–11; Englebert, *Francis of Assisi*, 12–15.

24. Incipit transformari in virum perfectum, et alter ex altero fieri Regressus igitur domum, sequuntur eum filii Babylonis, et alio tendentem trahunt ad alia vel invitum. Nam iuvenum turba civitatis Assisii, quae ipsum olim habuerat suae vanitatis praeambulum, addit adhuc eum ad socialia prandia invitare, in quibus lasciviae semper et scurrilitati servitur. Eligitur ab eis in ducem, experta saepius liberalitate ipsius, qua indubitanter sciebant ipsum expensas pro omnibus soluturum. Obedientes se faciunt ut impleant ventrem, et patiuntur subici ut valeant saturari, Non respuit oblatum decus, ne notetur avarus, et inter mediationes sacras curialitatis est memor. Sumptuosum praeparat prandium, cibaria sapida duplicat, quibus repleti ad vomitum, plateas civitatis ebriis cantilenis commaculant. Sequitur Franciscus, ut dominus manibus baculum gestans; sed paulatim ab eis se corpore subtrahit, qui mente iam tota totus ad illa surduerat, corde Domino canens (2Cel 7.1–8).

25. A. Fortini provides an interesting description of the drunken feasts of the time in which all restrictions were lifted; cf. A. Fortini, *Francis of Assisi*, 98–102.

26. Cf. Charron, *Da Narciso a Gesù*, 28; Vauchez, *Santità nel medioevo*, 31, 543ff; Uribe, *Introduzione alle agiografie*, 44–62.

27. Cf. Oliger "Liber exemplorum," 262–63; Pellegrini, "Cronache e testimonianze," 2157 n.

28. Cf. A. Fortini, *Francis of Assisi*, 89 n; Fierens, "La Question Franciscaine," 290.

29. Cf. A. Fortini, *Nova vita* II, 94.

30. Shanahan, "Henry of Avranches: Poem on the Life of Saint Francis (*Legenda Sancti Francisci Versificata*)," 151 n.

31. Cf. A. Fortini, *Nova vita* II, 94.

32. According to Assisi's archives, Pietro and Pica seem to have had only two sons, Francis and Angelo. Of these, Francis was the elder; cf. A. Fortini, *Nova vita* II, 93–101.

33. This naming of a child, like the education and career choice of a child, was the right and duty of the father, not the mother; cf. Herlihy, *Women, Family*, 17.

34. 1Cel 13.1; JulSpi 8.4; HenAv 4:86; 3Soc 9.1; 18.2; LegMai 2:3.1.

35. In the Middle Ages, virility was a virtue that could be ascribed to either a man or a woman. Granted, it was more easily ascribed to men, and it would take an especially strong, determined, and self-assured woman to be admired as virile.

36. Charron, *Da Narciso a Gesù*, 46; A. Fortini, *Nova vita* I, 2, 111.

37. Ioannis proinde nomen ad opus ministerii pertinet quod suscepit, Francisci vero ad dilectationem famae suae…

38. Charron, *Da Narciso a Gesù*, 46–47.

39. Gurevich, "The Merchant," 248–51.

40. As quoted ibid., 251.

41. Cf. 2Cel 13.5; 3Soc 10.6.

42. Cf. A. Fortini, *Francis of Assisi*, 221; A. Fortini, *Nova vita* I, 2, 288.

43. Cf. 1Cel 12.1–4; 18.1; JulSpi 7.9–8.1; HenAv 1:33; 2:203–14; 3:9–10, 67; 3Soc 17.7–9; 2Cel 12.1; LegMai 2:2.2–7; AnPer 8.1.

44. non ad liberandum eum sed potius ad perderandum

45. Cf. 1Cel 10.1–2; JulSpi 7.1–2; 3Soc 16.7–8; LegMai 2:2.1.

46. perturbatus animo, plurimum sollicitus, dolore cordis

47. circuit usquequaque, tamquam sedulus explorator

48. Englebert, *Francis of Assisi*, 14.

49. Cf. 1Cel 13.7; JulSpi 8.9; HenAv 3:25–39; 99–146; LegMai 2:3.4.

50. enormiter vivere inter cognatos et notos et supra caeteros suam stultitiam exaltare

51. Mercibus intentum desiderioque flagrantem / Lucra reportandi

52. rusticum, mercenarium, imperitum et inutilem

53. Benedicat tibi Dominus!, quia verissima loqueris; talia enim decet audire filium Petri de Bernardone!

54. dicam libere: Pater noster qui es in caelis, non pater Petrus Bernardonis

55. in ipsius manibus facultatibus renuntiaret paternis et omnia redderet quae habebat

56. Cf. A. Fortini, *Francis of Assisi*, 222–27; A. Fortini, *Nova vita* II, 229–32.

57. Cf. A. Fortini, *Nova vita* II, 229–30, 237.

58. Audite omnes et intelligite. Usque modo Petrum Bernardonis vocavi patrem meum,

. . . volens amodo, dicere: Pater noster qui es in caelis non pater Petre Bernardonis (3Soc 20.4).

59. nudus abit coram patre, coram praesule, coram omnibus Assisii concivibus;

60. Cf. 1Cel 15.5; LegMai 2:4.5; JulSpi 9.5.

61. Franco Cardini claims that in Pietro's curses of his son, he was expressing his love for his child. "There must have been more love in each one of them than there would have been in a thousand caresses"; cf. Cardini, *Francesco d'Assisi*, 95. The translation is my own.

62. Cf. Habig, ed., *Omnibus*, 898 n.

63. Cf. A. Fortini, *Francis of Assisi*, 247; Englebert, *Francis of Assisi*, 40; Cardini, *Francesco d'Assisi*, 97–98; Frugoni, *Francis*, 33.

64. The expression *ceteris filiis* must have been a generic expression that should not be taken literally. According to A. Fortini, it is hard to believe that, if there had been other siblings, their names would not be preserved anywhere in hagiography or the documents of that period; cf. A. Fortini, *Nova vita* II, 95.

65. Shahar, *Childhood in the Middle Ages*, 219; cf. Beitscher "'As the Twig is Bent . . .': Children and Their Parents in an Aristocratic Society," 190.

66. It was only after three generations that the descendants of Angelo took up the name of Pietro again in a great grandchild of Angelo's son, Giovanetto, named Pietruccio; cf. A. Fortini, *Nova vita* II, 100.

67. Cf. A. Fortini, *Francis of Assisi*,. 475; A. Fortini, *Nova vita* I, 2, 158; II, 95.

68. Cf. A. Fortini, *Nova vita* II, 96–101.

69. Shahar, *Childhood in the Middle Ages*, 203.

CHAPTER III: CLARE'S NOBLE FAMILY

1. *Scipii* is the genitive form in Latin of what in Italian would be *Scipione*; cf. A. Fortini, *Nova vita* II, 315–16; A. Fortini, "Nuove notizie," 4–5.

2. Sources for Clare's genealogy are Ridolfi, *Historiarum Seraphicae Religionis libri tres*, f. 132v; Wadding, *Annales Minorum* a. 1212, n. 15; Vitalis, *Paradisus Seraphicus*, 268; and Loccatelli, *Vita di S. Chiara*, 32ff. Cf. A. Fortini "Nuove notizie," 4 n.

3. G. Fortini, "Noble Family," 50n, 52.

4. This genealogy is based on the works of both Arnaldo and Gemma Fortini. Italics are mine and indicate those family members mentioned in the Franciscan sources. I have excluded all descendents of Clare's generation except for Balvina and Amata (witnesses for Clare's Process). Cf. A. Fortini, *Nova vita* II, 315–49; A. Fortini, "Nuove notizie," 3–43; G. Fortini, "Noble Family," 48–67.

5. pater eius miles et tota utroque parente progenies militaris (LegCl 1.2).

6. Cf. Bartoli, *Clare of Assisi*, 17–18; A. Fortini, *Francis of Assisi*, 333; Frugoni, *A Day in a Medieval City*, 137–46.

7. la corte de casa sua fusse de le magiure de la cità.

8. The archives of Assisi show that Offreduccio had five sons, Monaldo, Paolo, Ugolino, Scipione, and Favarone. The other two knights might have married into the family, or might have been cousins of Monaldo. We cannot be sure who they were.

9. Bartoli, *Clare of Assisi*, 14.

10. Ibid.; A. Fortini, *Francis of Assisi*, 63–73.

11. Triviño, *Clara de Asís*, 20.

12. A. Fortini, *Francis of Assisi*, 329, 333.

13. Proc I:4; 16:1; 18:4; 19:1; 20:2.

14. Rossiaud, "The City-Dweller and Life in Cities and Towns," 146.

15. According to A. Fortini, Offreduccio of Bernardino was one of the nobles who signed a pact with the Cathedral of San Rufino in 1148. The pact was meant to limit the number of members in the powerful consortium to which they belonged, and to assure the protection of the Cathedral; cf. A. Fortini, *Francis of Assisi*, 70–71.

16. We need to keep in mind that, besides their fascination with lineage, medieval men so mistrusted women that for the most part only a noble woman could achieve sainthood; cf. Bartoli, *Clare of Assisi*, 31. These two witnesses seem to want to assure the tribunal that Clare, despite having spent most of her life as a poor woman, had very noble blood in her veins.

17. A. Fortini, *Francis of Assisi*, 338 n; A. Fortini, "Nuove notizie," 11; Triviño, *Clara de Asís*, 23.

18. A. Fortini, "Nuove notizie," 10, 10 n.

19. A. Fortini points out that, in medieval Umbrian dialect, the expression *vidde* could well have been used to indicate an intimate and friendly relationship, like the one that Pacifica had with Ortulana, whom she claims to have seen (*vidde*). Fortini affirmed that in Pietro's testimony, *vidde* is in contraposition to *non cognobbe*. Yet, Pietro does not mention *non cognobbe*. Rather, he used *cognobbe* twice to state that he knew Clare and he knew Favarone. He uses the word *vidde* twice as well: once, to state that he knew of Clare's noble family because he had "seen," and a second time to say that he had "seen" how her parents and relatives wanted to marry her off in a magnificent manner. In both cases, the word *vidde* seems to indicate knowledge of the facts; A. Fortini, *Nova vita*, 331–32.

20. Peterson, *Clare of Assisi*, 70–71.

21. A. Fortini, *Nova vita*, 332 n.

22. Cf. ibid., 333; 333 n; Bartoli, *Clare of Assisi*, 47–48.

23. Peterson, *Clare of Assisi*, 50.

24. nam quamvis maritali iugo subdita, quamvis curis familiaribus alligata

25. Proc 3:28; 6:12; BuCl 70; LegVer 185–91; LegCl 2.3–5.

26. Tu parturirai uno lume che molto illuminarà el mondo

27. Peterson, *Clare of Assisi*, 29.

28. Mariano da Firenze, "Libro delle dignità et excellentie del ordine della seraphica madre delle povere donne sancta Chiara da Asisi," 83.

29. Non molti anni dapoi passando della presente vita el suo marito messere Favarone rimase la beata Ortulana con le tre sue sancte figlole perseverando nelle opere della pietà et misericordia facendo helemosine allj poveri per l'amore di Dio, frequentando le chiese et li divini officij, et le predicationi con le sua dua maggiore figlole, et maximo quelle di sancto Francesco. Ma essendo finalmente da decte dua sue figliole abandonata et rimasta colla sua piccola figlola Beatrice, pensò et deliberò sequitare le loro sancte vestigie. Per la qual cosa

dato in cura di messere Monaldo la sua figlola Beatrice et la parte della sua heredità la quale li fu anchora stremata da sancta Chiara et distribuita a poveri, epsa madonna Ortulana, distribuito o per amore di Dio la sua dota, fu da sancto Francesco vestita et velata et in Sancto Damiano colle figlole rinchiusa; ibid., 147.

30. It is interesting to note that in the Umbrian version of the Process the witnesses referred to Clare's miracles as liberations; cf. Cavazos-González, "Liberation Spirituality and the Process of Canonization for St. Clare of Assisi."

31. Proc 4:11; LegVer 988–1000; LegCl 33.4–8.

32. Francis's early biographers show that he had to struggle with sin and moral conversion, Clare's biographers and witnesses show no such struggle. In doing so, their biographers fit both Francis and Clare into the normal patterns of the hagiographic stereotypes of the period; cf. Peterson, *Clare of Assisi*, 2; Vauchez, *La santità nel Medioevo*, 168–74.

33. Proc 17:1; 18:1; 19:2; 20:5; LegVer 194–99; LegCl 3.2.

34. fusse stata santificata nel ventre de la madre sua.

35. viveva spiritualmente come se credeva.

36. le quale lo Signore Dio haveva posto in lei.

37. The word *spiritus* is used ten times in *Legend of St. Clare of Assisi* but is capitalized only three times—twice in speaking of the Holy Spirit (LegCl 4.3; 62.11), once in reference to spirits as part of the powers and principalities found in Heb 12:9 (LegCl 5.1). Of the seven uncapitalized references to *spiritus*, once it refers to the Holy Spirit with the adjective *divino* (LegCl 24.10), and three times it refers to an inner disposition or virtue, such as nobility or repentance (LegCl 12.8; 13.1; 59.15). The remaining three references are vague and could mean either the Spirit of God or the human person's own spirit or intuition (LegCl 3.2; 4.6; 59.9).

38. spiritu interius conflante pariter et formante

39. This "mother bird" imagery is reminiscent of the Eucharistic symbol of the pelican feeding her young from her very breast.

40. Mente vigil, docilis animo, prelucida sensu,

41. Given that the Latin word *domina* can be translated by any of the English words *matron, wife, mistress*, or *lady*, I have chosen to use the Latin word.

42. We know that Clare lived with Benvenuta da Peroscia during the period of her exile (cf. Proc 11:2) and it was there that she must have met Phillippa.

43. In this period of Clare's youth, the archives of Assisi contain documentation of both nobles and merchants who sold their properties *pro famis necessitate*. In 1202, Bona, the daughter of Mesere Ugolino who lived near Clare's house, had to sell some of her property due to economic woes; cf. A. Fortini, *Francis of Assisi*, 112.

44. Sane cum ipsa, dum adhuc puella esset in saeculo, . . . claritatis et pietatis operibus vigilanter intenderet.

45. epsa digiunava et stava in oratione et faceva le alter opera pietose.

46. le cibi che li erano dati ad mangiare come in casa grande. Omaechevarria translates this phrase as "los alimentos que le daban como in grande casa para comer"; Omaechevarria, ed. and trans., *Escritos de Santa Clara y documentos complementarios*, 114. Armstrong avoids the detail *come in casa grande*, and translates it as "the food they were given to eat"; Armstrong, ed. and trans., *The Lady*, 195.

47. le cibi quali diceva mangiare

48. Et ut suum sacrificium gratius esset Deo, proprio corpusculo delicata subtrahebat cibaria, clamque per internuntios mittens, reficiebat viscera pupillorum.

49. Cf. A. Fortini, "Nuove notizie," 5–7.

50. It is believed that Ortulana took part in the widespread movement of female penitents in the Middle Ages. If this is true, Clare would have followed her mother's example and been influenced by this movement. This new expression of popular religiosity was especially successful among noblewomen, who had a certain anxiety and were uncomfortable with their wealth and status. Theirs was more than mere generosity and penance; it was a strong social critique that condemned wealth and comfort at the expense of the poor; cf. Lachance, *Angela of Foligno: Complete Works*, 34–36; Bynum, "Religious Women," 124.

51. *Pietà* can be translated as either devotion or charity and alms. In the manner that it is used by Sr. Pacifica, it is probable that "devotion" is the best translation, but without forgetting the allusion to charity and alms.

52. tanta fu la sanctità de la vita et la honestà delli costumi.

53. le quale Dio li haveva donate.

54. era a giovane prudente de etade de circha diciocto anni, et stava sempre in casa; et stava celata, non volendo essere veduta et così stava per modo che non poteva essere veduta da quelli che passavano innanti alla casa sua. Era ancho molto benigna et actendeva ad le altre opere bone.

55. in casa del padre fo de honestissima conversatione et ad tucti benigna et graziosa.

56. degiunava, orava, faceva de le elemosine quante poteva et voluntieri. Et quando stava ad sedere con quelli de casa, sempre voleva parlare de le cose de Dio.

57. allora epsa mammola era de tanta honestà in vita et in abito, come se fusse stata molto tempo nel monastario . . . portava a stamigna stamm[e]gna bianca socto gli altri vestimenti.

58. Proc 1:2; 2:2; 3:2; 7:2; 12:1, 16:2; 17:2; 18:1; 20:1.

59. The Church in the Middle Ages began to challenge the ancient practice of arranged marriages. Yet this established practice could not be overturned in a short period and had to be done in stages. In Clare's day, consent did not mean the right to choose a spouse. Rather it was the right to refuse or accept the spouse chosen by one's parents—a right that usually involved much family pressure for the desired consent.

60. Of all the witnesses, Ranieri is the only one who mentions Clare's physical beauty and he states that he asked her several times to consider getting married. Since he was not a member of her family, one can only surmise that he was asking her to marry him. He ended up marrying another woman in Clare's family, probably to ensure whatever political alliance he would have established through marriage with Clare.

61. audi che sancto Francesco haveva electa la via de la povertà.

62. Clare must have been aware that many Assisians ridiculed Francis and claimed that he had gone mad; cf. 3Soc 21.

63. propuse nel suo core di fare ancho lei quello medesimo

64. 2Cel 155 and SpecPer 51 recount that a young nobleman on the island of Cyprus was inspired to join the friars by the example of their fraternal love. The sources do not

mention the young man's name, but A. Fortini deduced that it must have been Rufino, the son of Scipione. Scipione owned an *isola* surrounded by three rivers near Assisi, it was called Insula Cipii. Fortini proposed that the event of 2Cel 155 and SpecPer 51 took place on the island of Cipii and not Cyprus, which would explain Rufino's being the young noble who became a Friar Minor; cf. A. Fortini, *Francis of Assisi*, 334–36, 335 n; *Fonti Francescane*, 739 n. 177.

65. permanere in verginità et vivere in povertà.

66. Like most noblewomen of her day, Clare had been taught to read the Psalms and the Lives of the Saints. Hagiography had given her the model of St. Agnes and other virgins who went against their families' wishes. When she heard of the radical change of Francis and her own cousin Rufino, she would have recognized the saintly struggle against the family. That a person of her noble status would have done the same as Francis and Rufino is no surprise since hagiographic literature was full of noble ladies who had gone against the family in order to follow Christ. Cf. Bynum, *Holy Feast* , 280.

67. quelli che lavoravano in Sancta Maria de la Porziuncola.

68. The *Legendae* make no explicit reference to Rufino's joining the Friars Minor. We can deduce, however, that since he is numbered with Leo and Angelo as one of the "three companions" and is named by Francis in his list of the friars who make up the perfect friar, that he came to the Order during the early years; cf. Greccio Letter (3Soc I.1); SpecPer 85; Englebert, *Francis of Assisi*, 89; Giandomenico, "Rivotorto," 1750.

69. Cf. 1Cel 32; 3Soc 49; LegMai 3:10.

70. According to St. Bonaventure, Francis already preached in San Rufino while he was still living in an abandoned place near Assisi (probably Rivo Torto) prior to moving to the Portiuncola. The response to his preaching was impressive, in that many, including Clare, desired to live his way of life; LegMai 4:4–6.

71. Proc 3:1; 4:2; 6:1; 16:3.

72. Proc 1:2; 3:1; 4:2; 6:1; 12:2; 16:3,6; 17:3; 20:6.

73. Cf. A. Fortini, *Francis of Assisi*, 70.

74. Peterson, *Clare of Assisi*, 48.

75. andava secretamente (ad parlare ad sancto Francesco) per non essere veduta da le parenti.

76. Clare lived in a period that considered only those who entered ecclesial service to be perfect. These priests, religious, or penitents were persons who, having entered religious life, lived under the protection of the Church and were not subject to civil law.

77. Cf. 1Cel 16; LegMai 2:5.

78. Proc 1:2; 3:1; 4:2; 6:1; 12:2; 16:3,6; 17:3; 20:6.

79. Proc 12:2; 13:1; 17:5; 18:3; 20:6; BuCl 21; LegVer 279–81; LegCl 7.6–8.2.

80. In popular Umbrian culture, the *uscio* was often called "the door of the dead." A. Fortini explains that this has no historical foundation. The *uscio* in fact was used mainly to escape during war times. H. Moak, translator of A. Fortini's book, adds that according to Umbrian tradition the *uscio* was used not only in times of war but also for a bride to pass through on her wedding day; cf. A. Fortini, *Francis of Assisi*, 329; 329 n.

81. Proc 12:4; 18:3; 20:6; BuCl 21;LegVer 300–311; LegCl 9.1–6.

82. Proc 12:4; 18:3; 20:6; LegVer 297; LegCl 8.5. Although these references do not mention that Clare was in San Paolo as a servant, I agree with M. Bartoli that she most certainly was not there as a choir nun; cf. M. Bartoli, *Clare of Assisi*, 46–50.

83. It is interesting to note that Messere Ugolino and Ioanni de Ventura, the older of the male witnesses, spoke of the importance of Clare's family, highlighting the Offreduccio lineage and the number of knights in the family, yet they also made no mention of the family's violent response to Clare's flight. This might be because such a reaction would have placed her family in a bad light—since Clare was, by then, thought to be a saint rather than a rebellious daughter.

84. It seems that Clare sold her inheritance before her flight from home, according to the author of *Clare's Legend*. Yet Beatrice's testimony puts this affirmation in doubt.

85. Cf. Triviño, *Clara de Asís*, 71–73.

86. The sale of Clare's inheritance raises some important questions as to what possibility a young woman would have of ownership and the ability to make legal transactions, such as the sale of property. Besides her clothing and jewels, a young woman in Umbria would have had the right to an inheritance from her father. As a person of legal age, Clare had certain rights according to the juridical norms of her day and of her region. Being a single adult, she was legally able to sell without her family's consent; cf. Triviño, *Clara de Asís*, 69–70; A. Fortini, *Francis of Assisi*, 338 n.

87. Only her sister Beatrice explicitly stated that Clare "tucto quello cue recevve of the vendita of epsa heredità, lo distribuì alli poveri." The other witnesses simply say, "sua eredità vendecte et distribui alli poveri."

88. Cf. Triviño, *Clara de Asís*, 70.

89. We know that in 1238, the Damianites, which already numbered sixty sisters, sold a property. This might have been part of either Clare's or Beatrice's inheritance. Cf. Armstrong, ed. and trans., *The Lady*, 146 n; Wadding, *Annales Minorum* III, 14–15.

90. While the year that Beatrice joined the Damianites can be traced to 1229, the year of Ortulana's entrance cannot be traced. Cecilia di Gualtieri Cacciaguerra claims to have spoken with Ortulana about Clare's birth around the time of Francis's death (Proc 6:12). This testimony seems to indicate that Ortulana was already at San Damiano by 1226, but it is not necessarily so, because Ortulana simply might have spoken with Cecilia in the place where one speaks to the sisters; cf. G. Casagrande, "Le compagnie di Chiara," 387 n; Armstrong, ed. and trans., *The Lady*, 170n 183 n.

91. Pacifica was the blood sister of Madonna Bona and was counted among Clare's relatives by Friars Mariano da Firenze and Luke Wadding. Cf. Mariano da Firenze, "Libro delle degnità," 151–53; Wadding, *Annales Minorum* III, 14–15.

92. Amata and Balvina de Mesere Martino da Cocorano were the daughters of one of Clare's cousins, and, according to the kinship ties of that period and culture, they were considered Clare's carnal nieces. Amata entered religious life thanks to the prayers of Clare. Apparently, according to Friar Mariano, she "lived in the world following its vanity and did not take care to live religiously." Clare not only prayed for her, but also preached to her until 1228, when she, "according to the desire of St. Clare, renounced the world and her relatives" in order to live in San Damiano. Cf. Mariano da Firenze, "Libro delle degnità," 149–51;

A. Fortini, *Francis of Assisi*, 352, 352n, 354, 366 n; A. Fortini, *Nova vita*, 334–39; Lazzeri, "Il processo di canonizzazione," 403–507; Armstrong, ed. and trans., *The Lady*, 162, 171.

93. Mariano da Firenze, "Libro delle degnità," 135.

94. Beatrice joined the Damianites in 1229 at the age of 18, when her uncle Monaldo had tried to marry her off. Given her age at that time, she would have been two years old when Clare abandoned her father's house. This explains why her testimony about Clare's conversion (Proc 12:2–5) sounds like a repetition of what she heard rather than what she saw; cf. Mariano da Firenze, "Libro delle degnità," 148–49; G. Casagrande, "Le compagnie," 386.

95. It is thanks to the late fifteenth-century humanist, Ugolino Verino that we know Agnes's baptismal name. In his *Vita di S. Chiara vergine, riformatrice del sexo femineo*, he makes reference to her uncle Monaldo having called her Catherine during his attempt to take her back from the Church of San Paolo (*Archivum Franciscanum Historicum* 13 [1920], 275). Given Ortulana's pilgrimage to the Holy Land, it was probably out of devotion to Saint Catherine of Alexandria, virgin and martyr, that she named her second daughter Catherine. Saint Catherine, who had given up her riches in order to serve Christ, was the patroness of pilgrims to the Holy Land; cf. Omaechevarria, ed. and trans., *Escritos de Santa Clara* 367–68 n; A. Fortini, *Francis of Assisi*, 330–31; Lainati, *Santa Chiara d'Assisi. Cenni Biografici di S. Agnese d'Assisi*, 132–33.

96. Mirandus enim utrique mutuus insederat amor, qui novam divulsionem, licet affectu dissimili, utrique fecerat dolorasam.

97. LegCl 24.1–28.8; "Vita Sororis Agnetis, Germanae Sanctae Clarae," 173–82; Mariano da Firenze, "Libro delle degnità," 148–49.

98. Agnes's conversion and ordeal are mentioned in *Clare's Legend* as being the first signs of Clare's powerful prayer, but although Agnes is mentioned in the Process, her conversion and ordeal are completely ignored. This may have been because the focus of attention was on Clare's life. It may also be that, given the proximity to Clare's family, such testimony would have offended and embarrassed members of the family who might have participated in the physical violence against Agnes; cf. Cadderi, "Santa Agnese d'Assisi," 12.

99. "Vita sororis Agnetis," 173–82.

100. Only the "Vita sororis Agnetis" gives any indication that her original name had been changed to Agnes, but never refers to what that original name might have been, calling her Agnes, instead.

101. Agnes was sent as abbess to Santa Maria del Sepolcro in Monticello to reform that monastery which had been founded in 1219 by Madonna Avegnente, an Admirer of Francis. From the outset, that monastery was linked to the community of sisters at San Damiano. If we are to believe the XXIV Generali, Agnes was made the abbess as a result of Francis's desire that Agnes be sent there. More than likely, Agnes did not go to Monticello until after the year 1228, having been sent there by Pope Gregory IX. Her letter makes a veiled mention of the *Privilegium paupertatis*, which was granted to the monastery in Monticello by Gregory IX in 1230 or 1232, a few years after he had granted it to the monastery in San Damiano. The mention of Brother Elias in Agnes's letter indicates that she was writing during his administration as general minister (1232–39). The tenor of her letter leads

us to believe that she wrote it shortly after her arrival in Monticello, thus placing her arrival there around the year 1232; cf. Omaechevarria, ed. and trans. *Escritos de Santa Clara*, 367–68; Cadderi, "Santa Agnese d'Assisi," 14–18; Lainati, *Santa Chiara d'Assisi*, 117–20.

102. maxima tribulatio et immensa tristia

103. *The Martyrologium Franciscanum* of 1653 records 1253 as the year of Ortulana's death—although she probably died around the year 1238. In either case, she was alive when Agnes wrote her letter; cf. Arturo du Monstier di Rouen, *Martirologio francescano*, 4–5.

104. Cadderi, "Santa Agnese d'Assisi," 16.

CHAPTER IV: KINSHIP IN THE OPUSCULA OF FRANCIS

1. Nguyên-Van-Khanh, *Teacher of His Heart*, 23; cf. Paolazzi, *Lettura degli "Scritti,"* 6.

2. A good explanation of how Francis's opuscula came to be can be found in Esser, ed., *Gli scritti*, 74–78.

3. This exhortation is not found in Esser's work; it has been added to the list of Francis's opuscula by Friar Giovanni Boccali; cf. Boccali, "Parole di esortazione alle 'poverelle' di San Damiano"; Boccali, "Canto di esortazione alle 'poverelle' di San Damiano."

4. Despite Francis's request that copyists remain faithful to his text (Test 35), the many copyists throughout the centuries who tried to correct grammatical errors in his writings have led to textual variations. The critical edition of Francis's opuscula done by Esser presents a great number of variations in the manuscripts and incunabula; cf. Esser, ed., *Gli scritti*, 21–58.

5. Armstrong and Brady, Francis and Clare: The Complete Works, 6; cf. Paolazzi, *Lettura degli "Scritti,"* 8; Armstrong et al., *The Saint: Francis of Assisi: Early Documents* I, 13.

6. RnB 24.1–2; EpRect 9; EpMin 21; 1EpFid 2.20; 2EpFid 88; 1EpCus 9; EpCler 15; EpOrd 47; Test 36.

7. Cf. 3Soc 29.

8. Vandenbroucke, "New Milieux, New Problems from the Twelfth to the Sixteenth Century," 243.

9. I found various discrepancies in the numbering of the Sacred Scripture texts used by Francis (cf. Ruyter, "Bible Interpretation," 79; Matura, *François d'Assise, "auteur spirituel,"* 35). Therefore, I chose to do my own numbering based on Menestò and Brufani, eds., *Fontes Franciscani*; Armstrong and Brady, *Francis and Clare*; and Armstrong et al., *The Saint*.

10. Matura, *François d'Assise, "auteur spirituel,"* 35; this and all translations of this work are my own.

11. Matura claimed that in his opuscula Francis used the Scriptures in five different ways: (1) inspiration for his own words, (2) explicit citations as either points of departure or confirmations, (3) meditated and explained texts, (4) ensembles of Gospel texts, and (5) bouquets of texts from various books around a certain theme; Matura, *François d'Assise, "auteur spirituel,"* 37–43.

12. Cf. OffPass 1.5, 9; 2.11; 4.9; 5.9; 6.11–12; 7.3; 14.1; 15.3, 7. Other examples of this are found in LDei 2 and RnB 23.1.

13. Adm 5.1; 6.1; 2EpFid 34; IEpCus 6.

14. 2EpFid 48–56; RnB 22.27; 23.4–7; Adm 15.1; ExhLD 7.

15. ExPat 2; RnB 23.6, 9; OffPass Ant. 2–3; 9.12; Test 40.

16. Cf. CSol; In the Canticle of Brother Sun, he never once refers to any creature as father; he does refer to the earth as both mother and sister. This is very much in keeping with the maternal-fraternal vocation and tension of the Friars Minor which we will consider later in this chapter.

17. Shahar, *Childhood in the Middle Ages*, 187–208. Breaking away from one's family of origin seems to have been part of a general tendency to break away from social patterns that seem to have influenced most religious and social movements and groups in the latter twelfth and early thirteenth century; cf. Vandenbroucke, "New Milieux," 261.

18. Salimbene de Adam da Parma, *Cronaca*, nos. 219–27; 307–8. For an analysis of Salimbene's break with his family of origin, see Paul and D'Alatari, *Salimbene da Parma*, 83–89.

19. Shahar, *Childhood in the Middle Ages*, 203–5.

20. Omnis, qui reliquerit patrem aut matrem, fratres aut sorores, uxorem aut filios, domos aut agros propter me, centuplum accipiet et vitam aeternam possidebit.

21. Admonition 7 and both redactions of Letter to the Faithful describe the process of inheritance and the hypocrisy that it revealed in kinfolk. In Admonition 7, Francis warns against using the word (of God) to acquire riches for one's relatives and friends. He seeks to enlighten people regarding the futility, danger, and uselessness of amassing wealth in order to leave it to ungrateful and hypocritical wives, children, relatives, and friends. They will criticize the deceased for not having left more and he will have died without having done penance. Francis's description of the dying man seems to indicate personal experience. It may be that he is referring to the death of his father's father. Or he might even be referring to his own father's death. In either case, the description of the man who died without having made retribution to the people he had cheated and stolen from seems to indicate that he was a merchant and/or usurer, like the men of the di Bernardone household: cf. IEpFid 2.16–18; 2EpFid 71–85.

22. Salimbene de Adam da Parma, *Cronaca*, nos. 222–24.

23. RnB 22.18.

24. Cf. Mt 13:1–23; Mk 4:1–20; Lk 8:5–15

25. 3Soc 60.

26. ICel 24; 2Cel 15; 3Soc 29.

27. The person in question probably did so as a security measure so that his kinfolk would take him back in case he found the life of a Friar Minor too hard to handle; cf. Leg-Mai 7:3; LegPer 20. Only in the case of Friar John the Simple did Francis allow a friar to give his only possession (an ox) to his impoverished family, but even then he did so pointing out that he would let the family keep the ox, but he would take their son from them; cf. 2Cel 190; LegPer 19.

28. 3Soc 45; cf. AnPer 29.

29. AnPer 41.4–7.

30. Accrocca and Ciceri, *Francesco e i suoi frati*, 162. Thanks to Francis, Clare, and their followers, the radical break with the family, especially with the father, became a prominent feature in the topos of sanctity and hagiography; Vauchez, *Santità nel medioevo*, 144–45.

31. Celano explains that Francis used to call the mother of a friar the mother of every friar. Still, there is only one reference to continued contact with a parent in the sources. It is the case of a poor woman who had two sons in the Order. Francis gave her a copy of the Gospels so that she might sell it to meet her needs. It should be noted, however, that nowhere in the story is there any reference to the mother having seen her sons during the interaction; 2Cel 91; LegPer 56.

32. 2EpFid I, 86, 88; EpOrd I, 38; RnB Pro. I; 16.7; 17.16; 21.2; 22.27; 23.11; LHor 4.

33. RnB 3.10 (Francis uses it three times in this verse); 24.5; LHor 9; OffPass I.10; Ant. 2; 9.12; ExPat 10.

34. As an adolescent, Francis was molded by a fascination with chivalry and the troubadours. Part of Francis's interest in and experience of the Trinity and the role of the Holy Spirit, whom troubadours called "sweet guest of the soul" (*dulcis hospes animae*), may have come from the religious piety of chivalry and courtly love. The Provençal literature of the troubadours had various expressions which manifested marked devotion to the Trinity—with a preference for devotion to the Holy Spirit. Cf. Zorgi, *Valori religiosi nella letteratura provenzale. La spiritualità trinitaria*; Vandenbroucke, "New Milieux," 282.

35. McGinn, *The Flowering of Mysticism: Men and Women in the New Mysticism—1200–1350*, 51.

36. Ibid., 52.

37. Cf. Vandenbroucke, "New Milieux," 273–74, 279–80.

38. Here I use McGinn's understanding of democratization and secularization as opening the experience of God to everyone, even those "in the world"; cf. McGinn, *The Flowering of Mysticism*, 13.

39. Paolazzi, *Lettura degli "Scritti,"* 157; this and other translations of this work are my own.

40. The Latin text is found in Appendix E.

41. This is not the only place where Francis pairs men and women, rather than use the term *homines* that presumably includes both men and women; cf. RnB 23.7 (*religiosos et religiosas; vergines et continentes; masculos et feminas*); 2EpFid I (*masculis et feminis*); 88 (*illi et illae*). Everywhere else, when he wants to refer to people in general, he uses *homines* (cf. Adm; EpOrd; RnB; SalVir; etc.), which he also uses in the singular to indicate a male; cf. Test 32.

42. Anthropologists suggest that the reversal of symbols or the use of dichotomies provides "liminality" which allows one to escape from role or status and cross boundaries and limits to take on a contradictory role. This process of liminality is momentary and serves to strengthen the normal role or status; cf. Bynum, *Holy Feast*, 279–80.

43. This type of thinking was so ingrained in medieval culture that even Friars Minor

like Anthony of Padua (Lisbon) pronounced man a symbol of clarity and woman a symbol of sensuality; cf. Merino, "Il linguaggio antropocentrico in rapporto all'universo di significazione del femminile in alcuni temi della teologia," 13.

44. Male symbolized divinity, clergy, office, spirit, and authority—all of which were cut off from nature—while female symbolized the natural realm, body, laity, humanity, and inner aspirations. While women were encouraged to develop their strength, men were encouraged to develop their weakness in order to come to God; cf. Bynum, *Jesus as Mother: Studies in the Spirituality of the High Middle Ages*; Bynum, *Holy Feast*, 282–96.

45. Gniecki, *Visione dell'uomo negli scritti di Francesco d'Assisi*, 23–24; Hubaut, "Le Mystère de la vivante Trinité dans la vie et la prière de Saint François d'Assise," 44.

46. The soul can be likened to a wife who receives the seed of her husband (God) and generates a son. While reception may seem to be a passive act, generation and birthing are most certainly active realities, as is also raising the son to recognize and serve his father.

47. The soul can be likened to a knight who battles against the enemies of his Lord, most of whom are found within the knight himself. Thus, his struggle becomes an active inner pilgrimage to his homeland where he will passively receive his Lord's welcome.

48. Cf. Bynum, Jesus as Mother, 113–26; Bynum, Holy Feast, 283; Ago, La "Salutatio Beatae Mariae Virginis" di San Francesco di Assisi, 123–27.

49. Omnes qui Dominum diligunt . . . et diligunt proximos suos . . . et odio habent corpora eorum cum vitiis et peccatis, et recipiunt corpus et sanguinem Domini nostri Jesu Christi, et faciunt fructus dignos poenitentiae. Although Francis spells out more fully these conditions in the first part of 2EpFid, they are basically the same conditions.

50. Nguyên-Van-Khanh, *Teacher of His Heart*, 100–101

51. For the most part, it is difficult in Francis's opuscula to distinguish whether or not one should translate *frater* with *friar* or with *brother*. We find the term *frater, -ris* 263 times in the opuscula. More than likely, with the exception of the title *Fratrum/es Minorum/es* (8 times), Francis understood the term *frater* as *brother*, even when used as a title for himself, Leo, Anthony, or others.

52. *Father* is found 99 times in the opuscula (*son* is found only 55 times) and usually refers to God the Father. Twice it is used to refer to the human father and once to state "call no one your father"; cf. RnB 1.4–5; 22.34. Twenty-one times it is used as part of the "Gloria" or the "Our Father."

53. Cf. 1EpFid 1.19; 2EpFid 8, 10, 56, 57, 60; RnB 2.41, 42.45, 55.

54. Cf. LDei 2; LHor 4; OffPass 1.5, 9; 2.11; 3.3; 4.9; 5.9, 15; 6.11–12; 7.3; 14.1; 15.3–4; RnB 23.1.

55. Cf. 2EpFid 3, 4, 10, 52, 56, 67; Adm 1.1, 2, 3, 5, 7, 18; EpOrd 33, 46; OffPass 7.10; RnB 16.8, 9; 22.42; 23.4.

56. Cf. 1EpFid 1.9, 11; 2.8; 2EpFid 4, 8, 11, 19, 49, 52, 54; FormViv 1; OffPas Ant. 2; RnB 17.16; 21.2; 22.27; 22.30, 34; 22.42; 23.10; SalBVM 1.

57. Cf. Esser, ed., *Gli scritti*, 341–42; Armstrong et al., *The Saint*, 158–60.

58. O sanctissime Pater noster: creator, redemptor, consolator et salvator noster.

59. Cf. Nguyên-Van-Khanh, *Teacher of His Heart*, 116–21.

60. LDei 2; 1EpFid 1.14; 2EpFid 56; OffPass 1.5, 9; 4.9; 5.9; 6.12; RnB 22.45; 23.1.

61. ExPat I; OffPass 2.11; 3.3; 6.11; 7.3, 10; 14.1; 15.3; SalBVM 2; EpOrd 46; RnB 23.63.

62. IEpFid I.11; 2EpFid 21, 54; OffPass Ant. 2; 7.3, 10; FormViv I.

63. 2EpFid 4; OffPass Ant. 2; 3.3; FormViv I; RnB 23.1; Test 40.

64. summum bonum es, aeternum, a quo omne bonum, sine quo nullum bonum.

65. RnB 16.8; 23.4; Adm I.2, 4. In the "Office of the Lord's Passion," the affirmation "my Father" occurs only where it would seem to come from the mouth of Jesus; OffPass 1.5; 2.11; 3.3; 5.15; 6.15; 15.4; cf. Lehmann, *Francesco, maestro di preghiera*, 132–33.

66. In knowing God, the faithful discover His greatness and generosity; in serving Him, they discover that God recompenses them with joy; and in loving Him, they seek to respond to God in a wholehearted and totally self-giving way in the service of His love.

67. A person's childhood experiences of interpersonal relationships shape how she will ultimately relate to the world. This is also true of the relationship with God, which is especially tied to childhood experiences of significant others such as parents. As the child grows and receives catechetical instruction, his image of God will either be an extension of or the complete opposite of his image of his parents; cf. Michael St. Clair, *Human Relationships and the Experience of God: Object Relations and Religion*, 7–10, 11–13.

68. RnB 23.1; FormViv I; OffPass Ant. 2; 1.5, 11; 7.3; 14.1; LDei 2; EpOrd 33.

69. A synoptic table in Latin of 2EpFid 57–60 and RnB 22.41–55 can be found in Appendix F.

70. filias et ancillas altissimi summi Regis Patris caelestis.

71. Mary is found only fourteen times in Francis's writings, not counting the various times the Antiphon of the Office of the Lord's Passion is used; cf. RnB 9.5; 23.3, 6.64; Adm I.16; 2EpFid 4, 5; EpOrd 21, 38; SalBVM; ExLD 4; OffPass Ant. 2-3; 15.3; ExPat 7.

72. filia et ancilla altissimi summi Regis Patris caelestis.

73. RnB Pro. 2.10; 24.4; RB I.3; 2.13; 12.4; Test 15.

74. Cf. Blaise, Lexicon Latinitatis Medii Aevi, 661; Niermeyer, Mediae Latinitatis Lexicon Minus, 1313–14.

75. Cf. CompAs 100.3.

76. Cf. CompAs 58.8–10; Other applications of father as role can be found in reference to the General Minister as familiae pater (2Cel 184.4); to the Cardinal of Ostia as papa of the Order (3Soc 65.3); and, in a late source, Francis refers to the friars filii pauperis patris (SpecPer 15.8); and in the *Little Flowers of St. Francis* (Fioretti) where Francis, in a post-mortem vision, calls himself a particular friar's father (Fioretti 5th Consideration on the Stigmata). Applications of the title *father* can be found in Angelo Clareno's Seven Tribulations, where Francis refers to the Cardinal protector by the title *reverend father* (*Sette Tribolazioni* II.4), and in a story where Francis called a priest father (Fioretti 19) which probably reflects the fact that, by the time the story was written, the title *father* was moving from an exclusively select group of spiritual leaders to refer to any priest and/or religious.

77. 2Cel 16–17; 137; LegMai 3:10.2-4; 8:1.3; 3Soc 50. 2Cel 120; 180; 191 are also worth noting in that it is difficult to ascertain if the maternal reference is to Francis or the whole Brotherhood.

78. CompAs 100.3–4.

79. Friar Thomas of Tuscany (or Pavia) testified that Pacifico was of such holiness that Francis would call him mother (*Fonti Francescane*, 2677).

80. Paolazzi, *Lettura degli "Scritti,"* 156.

81. It is the only book in the Scriptures to deal with human passion and thus was ripe with symbolism that could be allegorized to explain a soul's passion for God; cf. Boswell, *Same-Sex Unions*, 128.

82. This lack of explicit reference to the Song of Songs has caused Dominique Gagnant to hypothesize that Francis was probably not directly familiar with the sermons of Bernard of Clairvaux, although he does claim that the Cistercian's spirituality had permeated Christianity by the time of Francis. Thus, spousal language taken from his writings might have been known to Francis; cf. Gagnant, "Le symbole de la femme chez Saint François d'Assise," 267.

83. Leclercq, *La figura della donna nel medioevo*, 7. This and subsequent translations of this work are mine.

84. We have seen that love-sickness was considered "womanly," but, regarding the soul's relationship with God, spiritual writers and mystics of the period encouraged it. It seems that the soul, in relationship to God, needs to express itself in feminine ways which are integrated into a man's maleness. In Jungian terms, a man must come into relationship with his anima if he is to have a capacity for meaning and valuation; cf. Robert A. Johnson, *He: Understanding Masculine Psychology*, 4, 31–50; Rohr and Martos, *The Wild Man's Journey*, 1–17.

85. As noted in McGinn, *The Flowering of Mysticism*, 104.

86. coniungitur fidelis anima Jesu Christo

87. Armstrong and Brady, *Francis and Clare*; Paolazzi, *Lettura degli "Scritti"*; Ago, *La "Salutatio Beatae Mariae Virginis"*; Habig, ed., *Omnibus*; the *Fonti Francescane*; and others offer no explanation for this title. Optatus Van Asseldonk, however, did not shy away from grappling with it. He first did so for his intervention in the 1975 *Congressus mariologici-mariani internationalis*, held in Rome. He sought to explain that, even though Francis was probably the first to concretize the title *Sponsa Spiritus Sanctus*, he was not the first to make reference to Mary's spousal relationship to the Holy Spirit. Van Asseldonk traces this spousal relationship of Mary as far back as the fourth century and then presents an excursus in which he shows how various Eastern and Western writers had made use of a spousal union between Mary and the Holy Spirit, whom some authors call Mary's *maritus*; Van Asseldonk, *La lettera e lo Spirito. La tensione vitale nel Francescanesimo ieri e oggi*, 106–8, 131–32; Van Asseldonk, *Maria, Francesco e Chiara*, 32–40, 97. Another scholar who has not been afraid to tackle this Marian title is Leonhard Lehmann. According to Lehmann, although Francis was the first to apply this title directly to Mary, another writer, Cosmas the Vestititore (of the early ninth century) had already used the title in speaking of St. Joachim as "the father of the Spouse of the Holy Spirit"; cf. Lehmann, *Francesco, maestro di preghiera*, 162, 165–66.

88. Cf. Matura, *François d'Assise, "auteur spirituel,"* 137.

89. Despite the Church's stress on the importance of the mutual consent of both part-

ners in marriage, it was still a common practice at the time of Francis for fathers to choose brides for their sons. Francis was a product of his age and would not have considered it strange for the Father to choose brides for the rest of the Trinity. These brides, after all, would be expected to enrich His household with children.

90. Clare, in her letters, did not hold on to this honor. Her spousal language always indicates Christ as spouse; 1EpAgn 7, 12, 24; 2EpAgn 1, 20; 4EpAgn 1, 15.

91. Cf. RnB 2.14; 5.10, 17; 8.1; 16.8; 22.6, 11; RB 1.1; 12.4; 1EpFid 2.12; 2EpFid 18, 37, 69; Adm 3.1.

92. eligendo vivere secundum perfectionem sancti Evangelii.

93. curam diligentem et sollicitudinem specialem

94. curas et sollicitudines huius saeculi

95. curis et sollicitudinibus huius saeculi et curis huius vitae.

96. habere Spiritum Domini et sanctam eius operationem;

97. carnaliter et non spiritualiter ambulare.

98. Cf. RnB 22.15; RB 7.3.

99. glorious, holy and magnificent (gloriosum, sanctum et magnum).

100. holy, consoling, beautiful, and Admirable (sanctum, praeclarum, pulchrum, et admirabilem).

101. sanctum, dilectum, beneplacitum, humilem, pacificum, dulcem et amabilem et super omnia desiderabilem.

102. 2Cel 198; LegMai 2:81-4; 9:3.1—4.

103. verum Deum et verum hominem ex gloriosa semper Virgine beatissima sancta Maria; cf. OffPass 15.3; SalBVM.

104. imaginem dilecti Filii sui secundum corpus et similitudinem secundum spiritum.

105. Even though Francis asserts the fragile, weak, and sinful nature of the flesh (cf. RnB 22.5; Adm 1.6; 12.2; 1EpFid 2.3, 11; 2EpFid 45; 65; 69; SalVir 10), he did not refrain from insisting that the Son took on real human flesh and keeps taking on flesh in the Eucharist (cf. RnB 20.5; Adm 1.11, 19, 20; 2EpFid 4; 23).

106. Et postquam Dominus dedit mihi de fratribus, nemo ostendebat mihi, quid deberem facere, sed ipse Altissimus revelavit mihi quod deberem vivere secundum formam sancti Evangelii. Et ego paucis verbis et simpliciter feci scribi et dominus Papa confirmavit mihi. Et illi qui veniebant ad recipiendam vitam, omnia quae habere poterant, dabant pauperibus; et erant contenti tunica una, intus et foris repeciata, cum cingulo et braccis. Et nolebamus plus habere.

107. Francis uses the term *Lord* in his opuscula 380 times. Of these, 85 are found in the Office of the Lord's Passion, where *Lord* refers to God (Father), and in OffPass 11:6 he specifies that the Lord sent Jesus Christ. Francis specifies the Lord as being Jesus Christ 62 times, and another 71 times he uses the word *Lord* to implicitly mean Jesus ("the Lord says in the Gospel"; "the body and blood of the Lord"). He refers to *Lord* as being the whole of the Trinity only five times. The other times he uses *Lord*, he seems to refer to the whole of the Godhead, especially in his prayers, but at times it could easily refer to Jesus Christ. He uses the word *lord* to refer to the Cardinal Protector, the Pope, or the General Minister 14 times.

108. 1Cel 24–27, 32–33; 2Cel 15–17; LegMai 3:3.2–10; 3Soc 27–35; AnPer 10–17, 31–36.

109. RB 1.2.

110. This being so, the Salutation of the Virtues has been referred to as the Greeting to the virtues found in Mary; cf. Armstrong and Brady, *Francis and Clare*, 151 n. 1; Armstrong et al., *The Saint*, 164.

111. Nowhere in his opuscula does Francis ever use the word *superior* to refer to a leader in his brotherhood. Rather, he calls them ministers, custodians, and guardians/custodians (cf. RnB; RB; RegEr; Test; EpOrd; EpMin). Seven times, however, Francis does use the word *praelatus* in his opuscula. Two of these times he is definitely referring to prelates outside the order, that is to say, to bishops and others. The other five times are found in the Admonition 3 and can easily refer to bishops, abbots, priors, and even ministers and guardians. It seems that even though the Admonitions were given to the Friars, Francis in using a more universal language in hopes that his Admonitions will serve as exhortations for all religious and all the faithful.

112. Adm 3.7; 2EpFid 41.

113. Misogyny discriminates against women because of their gender. In extreme cases in the Middle Ages, this prejudice considered woman to be the door of sin and an instrument of the devil. Marian devotion and courtly love seem to have been part of the challenge to misogyny; cf. Sanz Montes, "Lo femenino en la vida y espiritualidad de Francisco de Asís" 39–41.

114. Francis's legendae reveal Francis as a friend of various women; Lady Clare and Lady Jacopa being the best known; cf. Sanz Montes, "Lo femenino," 47.

115. Although Francis had a disordered adolescence and did his share of carousing, it would not be far-fetched to believe that he was still able to retain his virginity. As a youth, Francis was deeply affected by chivalry and knightly codes of conduct that would have kept him from prostitutes and other women who could lead him to carnal sin; cf. Sanz Montes, "Lo femenino," 36–37; Johnson, *He*, 29, 33–38, 43.

116. Where Non-Bulled Rule 12 was more of a word of counsel, an admonition, or exhortation, the same passage in Bulled Rule 11 becomes nothing more than regulation.

117. I agree with J. M. Charron that *Jesus* and *mother* are more important identification factors for Francis; cf. Charron, *Da Narciso a Gesù*, 74–75. But Charron neglects to list *brother* as a way of identifying Francis and his brothers. As we will see later in this chapter, *brother* is an important way of being identified to Francis, one that he ties closely to that of *mother* and *Jesus*.

118. RnB 1.1; RB 1.2. Clare, in her own Form of Life, takes up this vow (RCl 1.2), but she refers to poverty 37 times in her eight writings while Francis only uses the word *poverty* 16 times in his 38 writings.

119. Cf. Adm 11.3; SalVir 14; RB 10.3

120. All the accounts of this parable claim that it was the Lord himself who suggested it to Francis. According to the legendae, it would have been the Lord who suggested the spousal/maternal role as his relationship to Jesus and the friars. 2Cel 16.4 even goes so far as to state that *familiaris allocutio Christi* to Francis, which is to say, He spoke to Francis

in the manner of family or as one belonging to the same household; 2Cel 16.4–17.2; 3Soc 50.1–51.4; AnPer 35.3–8.

121. When it comes to all the faithful mothering Christ, Francis breaks open a medieval convention that saw Christ, the Church, and even Bishops and Abbots as nursing mothers of the faithful (body of Christ). Cf. Clement of Alexandria, *Paedagogus*, Book I, chap. 6; Ireneus, *Against Heresies*, Book III, chap. 24, par. 1; Bynum, *Jesus as Mother*, 125–28.

122. Cf. McGinn, *The Flowering of Mysticism*, 65; Bynum, *Jesus as Mother*, 115–25, 146–59.

123. 1Cel 84–87; 2Cel 199–200; 3Cel 19; LegMai 10:7; LegPer 110; EpCl 2, 4.

124. Francis's mercantile and middle-class formation manifests itself continually in his writings. He uses concrete examples taken from the *cotidiano* or "culture of life," rather than resorting to literary or abstract symbolism. Cf. Paolazzi, *Lettura degli "Scritti,"* 18.

125. It is important to note that medieval art rarely separated Mary from her Son as does later art. Mary could only be understood in relationship to her Son, either as Mother or as Queen Mother; she is always shown with Jesus; cf. Vandenbroucke, "New Milieux," 251.

126. Recent attempts include these: De Ventosa, "La devoción a María en la espiritualidad de San Francisco I"; López, "El tema mariano en los escritos de Francisco de Asís,"; Van Asseldonk, *La lettera e lo Spirito*; Van Asseldonk, *Maria, Francesco e Chiara*; Motte, "La 'Poverella…', la 'Cara Poverella.'" 241–44; Menard, "Maria vista da Francesco," 245–52; Lehmann, *Francesco, maestro di preghiera*, 157–88; Ago, La *"Salutatio Beatae Mariae Virginis."*

127. eo quod Dominum majestatis fratrem nobis effecerit; this was an explanation that Bonaventure saw fit to repeat in his *Major Life of St. Francis*; cf. LegMai 9;3.1.

128. Francis was a man of the High Middle Ages. The Christian art that nurtured his initial image of Christ was closely aligned with Byzantine art and portrayed Christ as the Divine teacher, king, and judge. It was only after Francis's death that the growing depiction of Christ's humanity exploded in Western art.

129. In this respect, Francis's devotion to Mary is closely tied to his high regard for the clergy.

130. It is interesting to note that even though the Ave Maria was a prayer already known by the end of the ninth century, Francis never once made reference to it (cf. Vandenbroucke, "New Milieux," 252–53). While he continually recommended the *Pater noster* as a daily practice, he never once recommended daily prayer to Mary—aside from her Antiphon in the Office of the Lord's Passion. Francis's devotion to Mary never lapsed into the exaggerated Marianism that proposes she be honored but not imitated. He kept Mary forever connected to the mystery of the Incarnation and never lost sight of the roles of the Father and the Holy Spirit in her life. I agree with Jean-Marc Charron that Francis's devotion to Mary was in reality a devotion to Mary's maternity; cf. Charron, *Da Narciso a Gesù*, 89–90, 105.

131. Istud Verbum Patris tam dignum, tam sanctum et gloriosum nuntiavit altissimus Pater de caelo per sanctum Gabrielem angelum suum in uterum sanctae ac gloriosae virginis

Mariae, ex cuius utero veram recepit carnem humanitatis et fragilitatis nostrae. N.B. Francis like his contemporaries refers to the Word of God as *verbum* in keeping with the concept of the Logos being the active and creative Word of God.

132. Et gratias agimus tibi, quia sicut per Filium tuum nos creasti, sic per sanctam dilectionem tuam, qua dilexisti nos (cf. Joa 17,26) ipsum verum Deum et verum hominem ex gloriosa semper Virgine beatissima sancta Maria nasci fecisti et per crucem et sanguinem et mortem ipsius nos captivos redimi voluisti.

133. Audite, fratres mei: Si beata Virgo sic honoratur, ut dignum est, quia ipsum portavit in sanctissimo utero.

134. Cf. De Ventosa, "La devoción a María," 249–74, 256–57; Gniecki, *Visione dell'uomo*, 24, 45; Vandenbroucke, "New Milieux," 271–73.

135. Francis's description of himself as a poor mother might also reflect his understanding of Mary's impoverished life in Nazareth. She, like Francis in the parable, bears a child for a great King, yet absent Father. She, like Francis, gives the Son back to the Father, whose will she has educated Jesus to do. Francis's children, although invited to carry their cross (RnB I.3), are not sent to die on that cross; rather, thanks to Mary's Son, who died on the Cross, they are brought into the Kingdom of the Father.

136. For a good explanation of the various types of maternity discussed by patristic writers, see Simbula, *La maternità spirituale di Maria in alcuni autori Francescani del seculo XIII – XV*, 16.

137. Cf. Paolazzi, *Lettura degli "Scritti,"* 51; Esser, ed., *Gli scritti*, 552.

138. portamus eum in corde et corpore nostro; parturimus eum

139. He will not even allow the friars to be godparents, because of the responsibilities involved in that juridical form of kinship; RB 11.3.

140. As I have previously noted, the Middle Ages did not shy away from the maternity of Jesus. Although Francis himself does not refer to Jesus' birthing the Church or the faithful soul, he does insist on the faithful person being nourished by Christ.

141. Simbula, Maternità spirituale, 84.

142. For a study of these titles in Francis's opuscula, see Nguyên-Van-Khanh, *Teacher of His Heart*, chaps 1–5.

143. Francis refers to priests some 32 times and to clerics some 29 times in his opuscula.

144. sanctificatur per verba Domini super altare per manum sacerdotis.

145. Because of their office, which deals with the Body and Blood of the Lord, all priests, even those in sin, should be respected (2EpFid 33).

146. se nobis ostendit in sacro pane.

147. sicut quando a regalibus sedibus venit in uterum Virginis; . . . quotidie descendit de sinu Patris super altare in manibus sacerdotis.

148. SalBVM 4; in the thirteenth century and the Late Middle Ages, there was an increased production of statues of Mary that opened up to reveal the Trinity or that served as tabernacles and monstrances for the Blessed Sacrament; cf. Bynum, *Holy Feast*, 268, plate 13 (following page 302).

149. Bynum, *Holy Feast*, 57, 268. In the same vein, Bernard of Clairvaux suggested,

in the twelfth century, that Mary was both mother and celebrant, who provides the faithful with the body of Christ: "Offer your son, sacred Virgin, and present the blessed fruit of your womb to God. Offer the blessed host, pleasing to God, for the reconciliation of all." (From Bernard of Clairvaux's Sermon 3 on the Purification of Mary par 2, PL 183, col. 370 as quoted in Bynum, *Holy Feast*, 268.)

150. The image of Mary the Virgin who incarnated the Son became a prominent factor in the Church's insistence that only celibate men could be ordained, for only virgins should handle the body of Christ upon the altar; cf. Petri Damiani, "Opusculum 18.1 De coelibatu sacerdotum, c. 3" PL 145, 384, as cited in Atkinson, *The Oldest Vocation*, 116–17.

151. Bynum, *Holy Feast*, 268–69, 285, 409 n.

152. The other man was Henry Suso in the fourteenth century. Bynum claims this is only true if we define feminine spirituality to mean "affective, exuberant, lyrical and filled with images." Other aspects of female spirituality and piety are devotion to Christ's humanity and emotional identification with the events of Christ's earthly life; Bynum, *Holy Feast*, 105. Although Church men were leery of anything in a man that might cause him to appear womanish, feminization was important in the culture of chivalry and courtly love. Feminization also became an important factor in the definition of sanctity in the High Middle Ages; cf. Charron, *Da Narciso a Gesù*, 107–29; Vauchez, *Santità nel medioevo*, 169–74; Bynum, *Jesus as Mother*; Atkinson, *The Oldest Vocation*, 101–43.

153. Bynum, *Holy Feast*, 95.

154. Ibid., 289.

155. The symbols, visions, and experiences of consecrating priests as pregnant women in the Middle Ages do not express any gender confusion. Rather, they express that all symbolic reality has fertile paradoxical qualities that allow priests and even Christ to be seen as women who prepare the meal and feed the family, or as pregnant and lactating women; cf. Bynum, *Holy Feast*, 278.

156. Cf. Bynum, *Jesus as Mother*, 110–69; Cabassut, "Une dévotion médiéval peu connu: la Dévotion à 'Jésus Notre Mère'"; Vandenbroucke, "New Milieux," 244.

157. Bynum, *Holy Feast*, 94.

158. Cf. Anselm's Prayer to St. Paul in Opera Omnia 3.33, 39–41 as cited in Bynum, *Jesus as Mother*, 113–14.

159. RB 6.9; RegEr.

160. Of the 38 times that Francis refers to the Blood of Christ, 28 times it is in conjunction with his Body, 3 times with his Flesh, and 7 times it is by itself.

161. In the High and Late Middle Ages, several mystics received the Virgin's milk (cf. Atkinson, *The Oldest Vocation*, 142). Francis never once refers to this phenomenon, however. It seems that he preferred to receive the blood of the nursing Christ.

162. In LegMai 3:7.3–4, Bonaventure describes Francis as a mother who births the Friars and the faithful for Christ. This maternal imagery in Francis's hagiography is touched upon in various works; cf. Zavalloni, *La personalità di Francesco d'Assisi*, 65–67; Charron, *Da Narciso a Gesù*, 79–105; Van Asseldonk, "Madre."

163. diligat et nutriat fratrem suum, sicut mater diligit et nutrit filium suum.

164. si mater nutrit et diligit filium suum carnalem, quanto diligentius debet quis diligere et nutrire fratrem suum spiritualem.

165. Matura, *François d'Assise, "auteur spirituel,"* 127.

166. Ita dico tibi, fili mei, sicut mater.

167. This does not mean that ministers and guardians have no say in how or where a brother lives and ministers. Rather, it means that ministers need to enter into a dialogue with a particular friar taking into account both the community's and the individual's needs and then find a way to meet both. The provincial minister in a particular way is called to give a brother the freedom and responsibility to decide whether what a minister desires for him is compatible with his conscience and with his understanding of the Gospel life.

168. Flew, *The Idea of Perfection in Christian Theology: An Historical Study of the Christian Ideal for the Present Life,* 196.

CHAPTER V: KINSHIP IN CLARE'S OPUSCULA

1. Many people are familiar with Francis's writings found in Habig, ed., *Omnibus,* but few know of Clare's earliest (1953) English translation: *The Legend and Writings of Saint Clare of Assisi: Introduction, Translation, Studies.*

2. After the seventh centenary of her death in 1953, articles and books concerning Clare have multiplied. Although these are many, a few are particularly noteworthy: Pyfferoen and Van Asseldonk, "Maria Santissima"; Lainati, "The Enclosure of St. Clare and the First Poor Clares in Canonical Legislation and in Practice"; Bartoli, "Analisi storica e interpretazione psicanalitica di una visione di S. Chiara d'Assisi"; Triviño, *Clara de Asís*; Bartoli, *Clare of Assisi*; Peterson, *Clare of Assisi*; Purfield, *Reflets dans le miroir. Images du Christ dans la vie spirituelle de Sainte Claire d'Assise*; Savey, "Les Autorités de Claire" ; Pozzi and Rima, eds. and trans., *Chiara d'Assisi, Lettere Ad Agnese. La Visione Dello Specchio.*

3. *Fonti Francescane. Scritti e biografie di san Francesco d'Assisi; cronache e altre testimonianze del primo secolo francescano; scritti e biografie di santa Chiara d'Assisi.*

4. Placing Francis's and Clare's opuscula in the same book is an outward manifestation of the Franciscan family's desire to see Clare as the mother of the family and the most faithful among Francis's early companions. Examples of such works are these: *Textus opusculorum S. Francisci et Clarae Assisiensum, variis adnotationibus ornatus, cura et studio Ioannis M. Boccali in lucem editus*; Canonici, L., ed. and trans. *Textus opusculorum S. Francisci et Clarae Assisiensum*; Vorreux, ed. and trans. *Les écrits de saint François et de sainte Claire d'Assise*; Julio Herranz et al., eds. and trans., *Los escritos de Francisco y Clara de Asís*; Iriarte, ed. *Los escritos de Francisco y Clara de Asís.*

5. Armstrong and Brady, eds. and trans., *Francis and Clare.*

6. Like Heloïse, Hildegard of Bingen, and a handful of others, Clare is one of the extremely few women who left writings from early and medieval Christianity. Being able to read and write was a privilege only afforded noble and religious women; cf. Becker et al., trans., *Claire d'Assise: Écrits,* 35–37, 39–41.

7. Uribe, "Il Cristo di Santa Chiara. Gesù Cristo nella esperienza e nel pensiero di Chiara d'Assisi," 39.

8. I found no previous count of Clare's scriptural references and based my count on the *Fonti Francescane* and Armstrong and Brady, eds. and trans., *Francis and Clare.*

9. She quoted or alluded to some 168 passages from Scripture in 197 verses of her writings.

10. These are divided as follows: BenCl (3), 2EpAgn (4), EpErm (4), 4EpAgn (5), 3EpAgn (8), TestCl (9), 1EpAgn (11), and RCl (12).

11. The rest are divided as follows: BnLeo; CSol; EpAnt; EpLeo; EpMin; LDei; LHor (1 each); EpOrd; EpRect Test (2 each); ExPat (4); Adm (5); OffPass (6). Although one can imagine that she had copies of Francis' Rules and some of his other opuscula, it would be hard to believe that she had access to all of his opuscula.

12. Clare made use of Paul's Second Letter to the Corinthians some 21 times in her opuscula. It seems that, from that Epistle, Clare developed a notion of the Father of mercies sending the Spouse who became poor for our sake in order to help transform the sisters and thus diffuse the perfume of their way of life. If the sisters are called to persevere in this way of life, it is because of the Spouse who joins them to the household of the Father of mercies (2 Cor 1:3; 2:15; 3:3, 18; 5:18; 8:2, 6, 9; 11:2; 13:11).

13. Peterson, *Clare of Assisi*, 322.

14. Hugolino was an Admirer of the Cistercians and sought to bring Clare and her sisters under their tutelage. Clare herself seems to have been influenced by Cistercian spirituality in her spousal imagery and even in the vision of Francis's breast; cf. Bartoli, *Clare of Assisi*, 130, 151, 154.

15. Cf. Hames, "Bridal Mysticism"; Malatesta, "Marriage, Mystical."

16. Bynum, *Holy Feast*, 126–27.

17. These carry degrees of servanthood and relationship to the household they serve. They include the slave girl, *serva*, the handmaids, *famula* and *ancilla* (which is best understood as "beloved servant girl"). *Servus* was the general term used for servant or slave, while *famulus* denoted a servant or a noble who wasn't a knight and who was part of the household under a paterfamilias. *Ancilla* on the other hand was a term of endearment for a servant girl and was usually tied to the service of God. In some cases, it was used to denote a nun coming from the lower classes; cf. Godet, "Chiara e la vita al femminile. Simboli di donna nei suoi scritti," 162; Uribe, "Cristo en la experiencia y en las enseñanzas de Santa Clara. Aproximaciones al pensamiento cristologico de Clara de Asís," 439 n; Uribe, "Il Cristo di Santa Chiara," 22–23; Niermeyer, *Mediae Latinitatis Lexicon Minus*, 42, 409, 967; Blaise, *Dictionnaire Latin-Français*, 80, 345, 756–57; Blaise, *Lexicon Latinitatis Medii Aevi*, 45, 373, 843.

18. 3EpAgn 2 (*serva*); 1EpAgn 2, 33; 4EpAgn 2; RCl 8.2 (*famula*); 1EpAgn 2; 2EpAgn 1, 2; 3EpAgn 2; 4EpAgn 2; EpErm 1; RCl 1.3; 6.3; 10.4, 5; TestCl 37, 79; BenCl 6, 9 (*ancilla*).

19. "Sacred Exchange" is actually the title of a famous thirteenth-century treatise on Francis's marriage to Lady Poverty. Although, Clare herself never used the phrase *sacrum commercium*, her opuscula reflect this Franciscan tradition. For her, poverty is incarnated in the divine Spouse who, out of love, became the poor and naked Christ. Celano, in his Vita Secunda, had already alluded to a spousal relationship with poverty as the *sacrum commercium* by which one trades all one has, including the family, for a treasure that is eternal; 2Cel 55.

20. Armstrong and Brady, eds. and trans., *Francis and Clare*, 190; Cremaschi and Acquadro, *Scritti di Santa Chiara*, 111; Omaechevarria, ed. and trans. *Escritos de Santa Clara*, 376–77.

21. It was with the aid of her mother and her brother, King Wenceslaus I, that in 1233 she founded a monastery based on the Poor Sisters at San Damiano for five sisters from Trent. She herself entered that monastery in 1234.

22. Mueller, *Clare of Assisi: The Letters to Agnes*, 35.

23. 1EpAgn 24; 2EpAgn 1; 3EpAgn 1; 4EpAgn 4, 17.

24. Cf. 3EpAgn 24–28.

25. Proportionately, Clare emphasized the following of Christ in her opuscula much more than Francis did in his; cf. Uribe, "Cristo en la experiencia," 460 ns. 109 and 111.

26. Cui si compateris conregnabis, condolens congaudebis, in cruce tribulationis commoriens cum ipso in sanctorum splendoribus mansiones aethereas possidebis, et nomen tuum in libro (vitae) notabitur futurum inter homines gloriosum. Propter quod in aeternum et in saeculum saeculi regni caelestis gloriam pro terrenis et transitoriis, aeterna bona pro perituris participes et vives in saecula saeculorum.

27. Uribe, "Cristo en la experiencia," 462.

28. She mentions poverty directly some 41 times in her opuscula, 14 times in her 1–4EpAgn, 14 times in her RCl, 13 times in her TestCl. Francis on the other hand mentioned poverty only 16 times in all of his opuscula.

29. cura diligens et solicitudo specialis; cf. RCl 6.4.

30. trangressio primi parentis.

31. Clare's contagious enthusiasm for the Franciscan lifestyle is part and parcel of Clare's pedagogy for life. She is still very much an important model for the Franciscan family today. Triviño, *La vía de la belleza: Temas espirituales de Clara de Asís*, 21–43.

32. Clare especially turns to the Sacred Scripture to insist on persevering until the end; cf. 2EpAgn 7, 10, 11, 14; EpErm 6, 9, 14; RCl 6.7; 10.13; 12.13; TestCl 4, 18, 71, 73.

33. BenCl 2–5.

34. Ego Clara, ancilla Christi, plantula beatissimi patris nostri sancti Francisci, soror et mater vestra et aliarum sororum pauperum, licet indigna, rogo Dominum nostrum Jesum Christum per misericordiam suam et intercessionem sanctissimae suae genitricis sanctae Marie et beati Michaelis archangeli et omnium sanctorum angelorum Dei, beati Francisci patris nostri et omnium sanctorum et sanctarum, ut ipse Pater caelestis det vobis et confirmet istam sanctissimam suam benedictionem in caelo et in terra: in terra, multiplicando vos in gratia et in virtutibus suis inter servos et ancillas suas in Ecclesia sua militanti; et in caelo, exaltando vos et glorificando in Ecclesia triumphanti inter sanctos et sanctas suas. BenCl 6–10.

35. The mirror is something important in Clare's spirituality. She mentions it twelve times in her writings, inviting her sisters to see themselves in the mirror that is Jesus Christ; cf. Dozzi, "Chiara e lo specchio"; Uribe, "Cristo en la experiencia," 449 n. 67; Peterson, *Clare of Assisi*, 281–84.

36. Handmaid of Christ

37. She refers to him as the Lord Jesus Christ 11 times (1EpAgn 7, 12, 17; RCl 1.1;

6.7; 8.6; 10.6; 12.13; TestCl 56, 77; BenCl 7) as Jesus Christ 7 times(1EpAgn 2, 4, 34; 2EpAgn 1, 3; EpAgn 4; 4EpAgn 15); as Christ 15 times (1EpAgn 18, 28, 31; 2EpAgn 18; 3EpAgn 1, 2, 11; 4EpAgn 2, 37; RCl 1.3; TestCl 37, 48, 57, 59; BenCl 6.7. She also refers to him as the Son of God 13 times (TestCl 5, 35, 46), as the Son of Man (1EpAgn 18), the Son of the Most High (1EpAgn 24; 3EpAgn 17), Son of the Virgin (1EpAgn 24; 3EpAgn 17–18; TestCl 46), or simply the Son (3EpAgn 18; BenCl 1). She also calls him Mirror (3EpAgn 12; 4EpAgn 14, 15, 18, 19, 22, 23, 24), Spouse (1EpAgn 7; 2EpAgn 20, 24; 4EpAgn 30), and King (4EpAgn 1, 21).

38. As with many Christian authors, it can be confusing as to which member of the Godhead the title *Lord* refers to. Clare uses the title *Lord* some 79 times in her opuscula: six times in reference to the Pope or a cardinal. The other 73 times, Clare uses *Lord* to speak of God (RCl 6.10); the Father (TestCl 46); the Spirit (2EpAgn 14; RCl 10.9); the Spouse (1EpAgn 7; 2EpAgn 24). In 17 cases, *Lord* explicitly or implicitly refers to Jesus (1EpAgn 7, 12, 17, 19; 4EpAgn 21; RCl 1.1; 3.9, 14; 6.7; 8.3, 6; 9.9; 10.6; TestCl 56, 75, 77; BenCl 7). Judging by her preference to connect the title *Lord* to Jesus, the other 50 uses of the title probably refer to Jesus Christ.

39. As with *Lord*, the title *King* in Clare is applied indiscriminately to both the Father (RCl 6.3) and the Son (4EpAgn 1, 21). In other cases, the reference is not clearly tied to the Son (2EpAgn 1, 5; 3EpAgn 1; 4EpAgn 4, 17, 27), but given the spousal language and imagery in which the title is used, it can only indicate Jesus.

40. Clare calls herself Christ's *famula* (1EpAgn 2; 4EpAgn 2) and *ancilla* (RCl 1.3; BenCl 6; 3EpAgn 2; EpErm 1). She also call herself the *serva* (3EpAgn 2) and *ancilla* of the sisters or rather the *ancillarum* of Christ (RCl 10.5; TestCl 37; 1EpAgn 2; 4EpAgn 2). *Ancilla*, as opposed to *famula* and *serva*, denotes a sense of endearment, and in the Middle Ages, it was the preferred title given to women religious.

41. In one case, she specifically refers to God the Father (1EpAgn 14), while in three other cases, she alludes to God's paternity by referring to Jesus as the Son of God (TestCl 5, 35, 46).

42. Clare used the Trinitarian formula only once in her opuscula (BenCl 1).

43. 2EpAgn 14; RCl 6.3; 10.9; TestCl 11; BenCl 1. It seems that Jesus Christ is "the Absolute" for Clare, which is to say the foundation, the center of her vocation and life; Uribe, "Cristo en la experiencia," 440–45.

44. Cf. Proc 18:3; 20:5.

45. 1EpAgn 24; TestCl 77.

46. Although it was only in the High Middle Ages that the Church began to seriously develop a Christian concept of marriage and family life, it would seem that from the beginning Christianity began to insist on marriage as a covenant of love between the two spouses rather than a social alliance between two families with the offspring as chattel for barter; cf. Sheehan, "Family and Marriage, Western European," 608–9. Marriage was primarily seen as a social endeavor, to which the Church insisted belonged the presence of *affectio maritalis* which designated the "proper attitude" that the spouses should have for each other; cf. Elliott, *Spiritual Marriage*, 47, 139, 165 n. 106.

47. Clare never once referred to Christ as her husband in the opuscula, yet her de-

scription of the husband in the letters to Agnes led one to understand that in her life she truly saw him as her *sponsum*, thus I will refer to him as her husband, groom, or spouse periodically in this book.

48. RCl 6.3; TestCl 24, 1EpAgn 24; 2EpAgn 14; 3EpAgn 17.

49. RCl 6.3; TestCl 14, 24; BenCl 8.

50. In calling the Father *King*, Clare is simply quoting Francis's use of this title for the Father. She, on the other hand, usually refers to the Son as King.

51. *Misericordia* in the Middle Ages was connected with the concept of mercy, pity, compassion, clemency, forgiveness, grace, and condescension. It was usually a virtue ascribed to God and rulers. Legally, it referred to advantages of an heir, to the forgiveness of debt, to amnesty, and to special privileges and gifts given to monks, like a dispensation from a prescription of a monastic Rule; cf. Blaise, *Dictionnaire Latin-Français*, 534; Niermeyer, *Mediae Latinitatis Lexicon Minus*, 692–93.

52. "benedictus Deus et Pater Domini nostri Iesu Christi Pater misericordiarum et Deus totius consolationis qui consolatur nos in omni tribulatione nostra ut possimus et ipsi consolari eos qui in omni pressura sunt per exhortationem qua exhortamur et ipsi a Deo quoniam sicut abundant passiones Christi in nobis ita et per Christum abundat con- solatio nostra sive autem tribulamur pro vestra exhortatione et salute sive exhortamur pro vestra exhortatione quae operatur in tolerantia earundem passionum quas et nos patimur ut spes nostra firma pro vobis scientes quoniam sicut socii passionum estis sic eritis et con- solationis" (2Cor 1:3–7, Douay-Rheims Latin Bible). http://www.drbo.org/lvb/chap- ter/54001.htm (accessed 14 June, 2009).

53. Francis is her second; TestCl 38.

54. 3EpAgn 30, 36; RCl 6.1; TestCl 5, 24, 36, 46.

55. 3EpAgn 24; RCl 6.7; 8.6; 12.13.

56. She was Jacob's chosen bride, who could only become his wife after he had been tricked into marrying Leah and had worked for years for her father. Once married, however, it seemed that she was sterile and only after several years was she able to birth two sons. Rachael was a model of perseverance and patience and was rewarded by God for her stead- fastness, despite all odds (Gen 29–35); Cremaschi and Acquadro, *Scritti di Santa Chiara*, 211 n; Godet, "Chiara e la vita al femminile," 163.

57. Clare of Assisi recommends the martyr Agnes to Agnes of Prague in her 4EpAgn as an example of holding on to the Lamb/Spouse who takes away the sins of the world (4EpAgn 8). Clare had already referred to the Office of St. Agnes in 1EpAgn 10–11 and again in 3EpAgn 16; cf. Armstrong, ed. and trans., *The Lady*, 44 ns; 54.

58. As previously mentioned, the Anglophonic world uses the word *spouse* to speak of bride, wife, bridegroom, and husband. This has led to a lumping together of bridal and marital symbolism into one spousal spirituality as if a fiancée (bride) and wife or a groom and a husband were the same thing. However, the Latin origin of that word (*sponsa, -ae* and *sponsum, -i*) specifically denoted the roles of fiancée and fiancé. As such, what is com- monly denoted as spousal spirituality is meant to indicate the transforming union of the soul to God as a process of courtship. This process moves into betrothal leading up to final consumption on what could be seen as (to borrow from contemporary nuptial practices) a

heavenly honeymoon. Cf. Hames, "Bridal Mysticism," 106; Malatesta, "Marriage, Mystical"; Brunet, "Figures de l'Eglise"; Adnès, "Mariage, spirituel." Caroli, ed., *Dizionario Francescano. Spiritualità* includes articles on the spiritual themes of affectivity, brotherhood, and mother. It lacks an article on spousal spirituality. (There is nothing on father, either). The editor limits any discussion of spousal spirituality within Franciscanism to the theme of virginity; cf. Izzo, "Verginità."

59. "to promise," "to pledge"; RCl 6.3; 4EpAgn 8.

60. "fiancée," "girlfriend"; 1EpAgn 24; 2EpAgn 1; 3EpAgn 1; 4EpAgn 1, 4, 15, 17.

61. "fiancé," "boyfriend"; 2EpAgn 20, 24; 4EpAgn 30.

62. Francis, in his opuscula, uses the term *uxor, -oris* a total of six times and always in reference to the carnal wife. This he does in two different situations: in reference to entering the Order (RnB 1.4, 5; RB 2.4), and in speaking of the hypocrisy of the carnal family (2EpFid 73).

63. 2EpAgn 1; 4EpAgn 15.

64. Agnes is mother, sister, and daughter of Christ; 1EpAgn 12, 24; 3EpAgn 1; 4EpAgn 4, 17. She is also mother, sister, and daughter of Clare; 1EpAgn 12; 2EpAgn 1; 3EpAgn 1; 4EpAgn 1, 5, 33, 36, 37, 38, 39. For an enlightening description of Clare's use of the kinship roles of mother, sister, and bride, cf. Schlosser, "Mother, Sister, Bride: The Spirituality of St. Clare."

65. For a clearer understanding of Clare's use of mirror in the context of mirror writings of her day, cf. Dozzi, "Chiara e lo Specchio"; Purfield, *Reflets dans le Mirior*; Rodriguez Herrera, "Aspecto literario de los escritos de Santa Clara"; Pozzi and Rima, eds. and trans., *Chiara d'Assisi, Lettere ad Agnese*, 90–96.

66. sponsum tuum prae filiis hominum speciosum.

67. Van Asseldonk, *Maria, Francesco e Chiara*, 127.

68. Cf. Elliott, *Spiritual Marriage*, 153.

69. Rodriguez Herrera, "Aspecto literario," 160.

70. Here, we will only consider those mirror references in which Christ/God is the mirror. We need to acknowledge, however, that in Clare's Testament the mirror is no longer Christ, but the sisters themselves are called to be mirrors for others; cf. TestCl 19–21.

71. Hoc speculum quotidie intuere, o Regina, sponsa Jesu Christi, et in eo faciem tuam iugiter speculare, ut sic totam interius et exterius te adornes amictam circumdatamque varietatibus, omnium virtutum floribus et vestimentis pariter adornata, sicut decet, filia et sponsa carissima summi Regis. In hoc autem speculo refulget beata paupertas, sancta humilitas et ineffabilis caritas, sicut per totum speculum poteris cum Dei gratia contemplari. Attende, inquam, principium huius speculi paupertatem positi siquidem in praesepio et in panniculis involuti. O miranda humilitas, o stupenda paupertas! Rex angelorum, Dominus caeli et terrae in praesepio reclinatur. In medio autem speculi considera humilitatem, saltem beatam paupertatem, labores innumeros ac poenalitates quas sustinuit pro redemptione humani generis. In fine vero eiusdem speculi contemplare ineffabilem caritatem, qua pati voluit in crucis stipite et in eodem mori omni mortis genere turpiori.

72. There are several references in Tobit where wives are referred to as sisters.

73. It is worth noting here that the modern translations have this word as "co-worker,"

"cooperadora," and "collaboratrice," while Clare's original word, *adiutricem*, is more reminiscent of Tobit's reference to Eve as Adam's helpmate.

74. Luke creates an intimate connection between Mary and the Holy Spirit in his writings. Besides having the Spirit come upon her, she is present when the Spirit inspires Elizabeth, Zechariah, and Simeon, as well as when the Spirit descends on the disciples of her Son: cf. Lk 1:35, 41, 67; 2:27; Acts 1:14–2:4.

75. Iriarte—referring to Gregory IX's having called her the "reliquary" of the Holy Spirit as proof—insists that Clare felt betrothed to the Holy Spirit; Iriarte, *Vocación Franciscana. La Opción de Francisco y Clara de Asís*, 135. Although it is true that people who knew her attested to Clare's close connection with the Holy Spirit, her opuscula do not reflect a nuptial understanding of her relationship to the Spirit of the Lord.

76. *Et sicut Dominus dedit nobis beatissimum patrem nostrum Franciscum in fundatorem, plantatorem et adiutorem nostrum in servitio Christi et in his quae Domino et beato patri nostro promisimus, qui etiam dum vixit sollicitus fuit verbo et opere semper excolere et fovere nos, plantulam suam, sic recommendo et relinquo sorores meas, quae sunt et quae venturae sunt, successoris beatissimi patris nostri Francisci et toti religioni, ut sint nobis in adiutorium proficiendi semper in melius ad serviendum Deo et observandam praecipue melius sanctissimam paupertatem.*

77. She refers to father Francis 17 times in TestCl (5, 7, 17, 24, 30, 36, 38, 40, 46, 47, 48, 50, 52, 57, 75, 77, 79), 3 times in BenCl (6, 7, 8).

78. Dalarun, *Francesco: un passaggio. Donna e donne negli scritti e nelle leggende di Francesco d' Assisi*, 15.

79. Cf. Godet, "Chiara e la vita al femminile," 165–67.

80. The Latin word, *fovere* (a process of warming, fostering, nurturing, pampering, fondling, loving, and encouraging), is reminiscent of both gardening and raising a child; Blaise, *Dictionnaire Latin-Français*, 362.

81. *Genuit* comes from *gignere* (to beget, cause, bear, or produce); Blaise, *Dictionnaire Latin-Français*, 376, 814–15. The word *gigno, -ere* is not found in Niermeyer, *Mediae Latinitatis Lexicon Minus*. But in the Vulgate, *genuit* is used to mean "beget" (cf. Mt 1). In the process of procreation, medieval scholars and physicians saw the male parent as actively implanting the human form and soul of the child in the embryo; this was condensed and fermented in the female's womb. Thus, the male action was considered to be that of begetting (*gignere*) as opposed to that of the female which was to generate (*generare*); cf. Atkinson, *The Oldest Vocation*, 24, 49, 50.

82. RCl 1.3; BenCl 6. She also called herself *plantula* (TestCl 49).

83. Peterson, *Clare of Assisi*, 45–46. According to psychological studies, early interpersonal relationships cause "rich images which function as psychological structures in the mind and shape how the person's resultant personality relates to the world"; Michael St. Clair, *Human Relationships*, 7.

84. Riferiva anco epsa madonna Chiara che una volta in visione, li pareva che epsa portava ad sancto Francesco uno vaso de acqua calda, con uno sciucchatoio da sciucchare le mane, et salliva per una scala alta, ma andava cusì legieramente, quasi come andasse per piana terra. Et essendo pervenuta ad sancto Francesco, epso sancto trasse dal suo seno una

mammilla et disse ad essa vergine Chiara: "Viene, receve et sugge". Et avendo lei succhato, epso sancto la admonìva che suggesse un'altra volta; et epsa suggendo, quello che de lì suggeva, era tanto dolce et delectevole che per nesuno modo lo poteria explicare. Et havendo succhato, quella rotondità overo boccha de la poppa, donde escie lo lacte, remase intra li labri de epsa beata Chiara; et pigliando epsa con le mane quello che li era remaso nella boccha, li pareva che fusse oro così chiaro et lucido, che ce se vedeva tucta, come quasi in uno specchio. Proc 3:29.

85. Sisters Philippa, Cecilia, Balvina, and Amata gave testimony about this dream/vision: "Cecilia . . . disse de la visione de la mammella de sancto Francesco, quello che sora Phylippa, excepto che non se recordava of quello che epsa haveva dicto de la boccha de la mammella, che sancta Chiara retenne ne la boccha sua" (Proc 6:13); cf. Proc 4:16; 7:10.

86. Cf. Uribe, "Una curiosa 'visión' de Santa Clara interpretada desde diversos puntos de vista," 237.

87. Verbal and visual images of Jesus, Mary, abbots, bishops, and Charity breastfeeding Christians and the needy were not uncommon in Christian literature and art; cf. Bynum, *Jesus as Mother*, 115–19, 122, 124; Bynum, *Holy Feast*, 270–71; Bartoli, *Clare of Assisi*, 154.

88. Cf. Bartoli, "Analisi storica"; Bartoli, *Clare of Assisi*, 141–57.

89. Bartoli divides the vision as follows: (1) The hot water is a reminder of the service that Clare gave Francis when he was infirm and in need of care; (2) the stairs demonstrate that Clare saw herself was lesser than Francis; (3) Francis's nursing of Clare affirms her filial dependence on Francis: (4) the sweet milk was an unconscious memory of the physical and psychological satisfaction that she felt when, as a babe, she nursed at the breast; (5) Francis's nipple remaining in her mouth is Clare's desire to become one with Francis; and (6) the breast transformed into a mirror of gold in Clare's hands reflects that her renunciation of her wealth won her something immeasurably more valuable—the primitive ideal of the Franciscan way of life; Bartoli, *Clare of Assisi*, 145–48.

90. Cf. Peter Van Leeuwen, "Clare's Dream of Francis."

91. Carstens, "Spiritual Mothering."

92. Cf. Bynum, *Holy Feast*, 101–2.

93. According to the medieval mentality, Christ, the Virgin, or a saint might appear to announce an imminent death; cf. Rotzetter, "Il servizio negli scritti di Chiara: subordinazione o maturità?" 339.

94. She also affirmed that none of the saints cancel each other out in the vision; Clare does not absorb Francis, nor vice versa. Rather, the two find themselves united in the love of the Spirit; cf. Triviño, *Clara de Asís*, 250–60.

95. Peterson, *Clare of Assisi*, 185–90.

96. Clare's response to this affirmation of the pope seems to have been this vision where it is affirmed that the form of life is a rich and sweet milk that comes from Francis himself. Having imbibed, Clare came to see herself reflected in the breast from which the milk had come, which is to say she had become another Francis; cf. Accrocca, "Chiara 'alter Franciscus,'" 74–77; Marini, "Ancilla Christi, plantula sancti Francisci. Gli scritti di Santa Chiara e la regola," 125–26.

97. Uribe affirms that the love for God/Christ does not exclude human love and that human love can be purifying, mediating, and fecund in assisting the ascending journey of identification with God. Uribe ends by saying that, besides the deep affective communion between the two saints of Assisi, "one perceives the great sense of security and the firm will of Clare in the tenacious reaffirmation of her fidelity to the intuition of Francis"; cf. Uribe, "Una curiosa 'visión,'" 246–48.

98. Pozzi and Rima, eds. and trans., *Chiara d'Assisi, Lettere ad Agnese*, 58–96.

99. Christian society understood that, at times, a mother (or a father, if the mother had died in childbirth) had no choice but to turn to a wet nurse to assist with the feeding of an infant; for this purpose, moral and physical qualifications for choosing a wet nurse were provided; cf. Gies and Gies, *Marriage and the Family*, 200–201; Peterson, *Clare of Assisi*, 46–49; Shahar, *Childhood in the Middle Ages*, 55–59, 77–83.

100. Cf. Bartoli, *Chiara d'Assisi*, 154–55.

101. This does not mean that Clare received this vision in 1238 as Marini and Accrocca affirm. Rather, it probably happened in the period just before her death. During this time, she surely must have reflected on her life and on the variety of occasions on which she had to defend her community against changes and compromises that had already affected the Order of Friars Minor at the hands of Gregory IX; cf. Accrocca, "Chiara 'alter Franciscus,'" 74–77; Marini, "Ancilla Christi," 125–26.

102. The authors of Francis's vitae recall the maternal imagery that Francis used for himself regarding his role in the brotherhood. Cf. Sabatier, *Études Inédites sur S. François d'Assise*, 17.

103. If she used the word in her Form of Life for the Poor Sisters, it was probably due to the insistence of those who helped her in its redaction.

104. illa quae est in officio sororum.

105. Although Clare refers often to the mother of Jesus Christ, she mentions her by name only four times; 3EpAgn 36, TestCl 46, 77; BenCl 7. She refers to Mary as mother eight times; 3EpAgn 18; RCl 2.24; 6.7; 8.6; 12.13; TestCl 75, 77; BenCl 7; and as Virgin another eight times 1EpAgn 19, 24; 3EpAgn 17, 24; RCl 3.14; TestCl 46, 75, 77. Most of the uses of the title *Virgin* are tied to maternity in either an explicit or implicit fashion; 1EpAgn 19, 24; 3EpAgn 17, 24; TestCl 46, 75, 77.

106. Ilia Delio indicates that Clare's (and I would add Francis's) image of Mary is not devotional but imitational. In her maternity, Mary becomes a model of the "mysticism of motherhood"; Delio, *Franciscan Prayer*, 150.

107. In 3EpAgn 17, Clare speaks of having to respect those in authority even without having to adhere to their counsel if it goes against the way of poverty. This concept of owing respect seems to be something that was ingrained into noble children as a form of the love that was owed to parents and eventually to the spouse and in-laws. Even in marriage, *Christianitas* did not demand "emotional love" but rather a love that was expressed as mutual respect.

108. Ipsius dulcissimae Matri adhaereas, quae talem genuit Filium, quem caeli capere non poterant, et tamen ipsa parvulo claustro sacri uteri contulit et gremio puellari gestavit.

109. Cf. 1EpFid 1.10; 2EpFid 53.

110. Delio ties the divine maternity of believers to Clare's invitation to gaze upon, consider, contemplate, and imitate the mirror that is Christ; Delio, *Franciscan Prayer*, 151–52.

111. Schlosser, "Madre-sorella-sposa nella spiritualità di Santa Chiara," 179; Bartoli, *Clare of Assisi*, 125–28; Marchitielli, "L'alleanza sponsale con Cristo nelle lettere di S. Chiara a S. Agnese di Praga," 310.

112. et si mater diligit et nutrit filiam suam carnalem, quanto diligentius debet soror diligere et nutrire sororem suam spiritualem? Cf. RnB 9.11; RB 6.8.

113. It is interesting to note that nowhere in the Franciscan sources does Francis refer to God the Father as Mother. Clare, on the other hand, does. This may be because Clare, unlike Francis, likely never had much of a relationship with her father, either because he died while she was still young or because he was so frequently off at war. The prominent father figure in her life was her Uncle Monaldo, who was not a genitor but rather a paterfamilias. He certainly was far from being the symbol of care and nurture that Clare's mother, Ortulana, must have been, and that Clare needed at the moment of death.

114. Clare uses the term *sister/s* 110 times in her writings while she uses *mother* in reference to herself and the other sisters only 15 times. Rather than refer to herself as the mother of the sisters, she refers to herself as their servant.

115. In her Form of Life for the Poor Sisters (RCl), she refers to herself and the future abbesses implicitly by the title *sister* rather than *mother*. She also acknowledges that she is mother and sister to the poor sisters; BenCl 6.

116. This was probably because while *serva* is a female *servo*, a mother is not a female father. Rather, a mother was part of the family governed by the father. Thus, it seems that Clare did not want the Abbess to forget that she was a member of the community. Cf. Schlosser, "Madre-sorella-sposa," 171.

117. Ibid., 177.

118. 2EpAgn 9, 17, 19; RCl 2.17; 3.10; 4.24; 9.3; TestCl 66.

119. RnB 23.6; EpOrd 38; OffPass Ant. 2.

120. However, we have seen that, at least as regards "father" Francis, Clare ascribes to him an implicit gender reversal by calling herself his *plantula*.

CONCLUSION

1. Lehmann, *Francesco, maestro di preghiera*, 162.

2. Although Fernando Uribe attributed the adjective *regal* to Clare's spirituality (cf. Uribe, "Il Cristo di Santa Chiara," 39), I believe that Francis shared in this same spirituality unconsciously.

3. Russell, "Sociology and the Study of Spirituality," 34.

4. Most of the Scriptural references to God's paternity can be found in the Christian Scriptures. This should not come as a surprise, given Jesus' intimate relationship with God as Father (cf. Mt 11:27; Mk 14:36; Lk 10:22; Jn 3:35; 8:16ff). The Hebrew Scriptures, however, do not ignore this attribute of God, but describe God as Father in Is 63:16; Job 31:18; Ps 2:7; 68:6; Mal 1:6; 2:10, among many other places.

5. Cf. Ps 27:10; Is 49:15; 66:9–13.

6. God, as Spouse of Israel, can be found not only in Is 62:4–5 and Jer 2:2, but also in much of the prophet Hosea and in the allegorical reading of the Song of Songs.

7. Thadée Matura asserts this as well. He points out that many erroneously tend to center Francis's spirituality on Christ. Matura affirms what our reading of Francis's opuscula reveals—that the Father has primacy of place in Francis's spirituality. Matura goes on to call this primacy of the Father a "monarchy," alluding to a sense of nobility without explaining why; cf. Matura, *François d'Assise, "auteur spirituel,"* 139–42.

8. One will not find any maternal imagery applied to the first person of God in the Christian Scriptures. Rather, one finds maternity applied to Mary, the mother of Jesus, who is given as mother to the beloved disciple (Jn 19:27), the heavenly Jerusalem is called mother of the faithful (Gal 4:26), and Paul compares himself to both a nursing and affectionate mother and an educating father in his relationship to the Thessalonians (1 Thes 2:7–12). If there is only one Father, as both Jesus and Francis attest (RnB 22:34; Mt 23:9), then the only other generative role left for everyone else is that of mother.

9. In his Office of the Lord's Passion, Antiphon 2.2 (OffPass Ant. 2.2), Francis refers to Mary as the "spouse of the Holy Spirit," a title that he attributes also to Clare and her sisters. It would seem that, in the mind of Francis and eventually in the mind of Clare, Mary became a model for the kinship of the faithful with God. As Van Asseldonk has written, Mary has become, "in the community of the faithful, the mother-sister, model of the faith of the Church"; Van Asseldonk, *Maria, Francesco e Chiara,* 379.

10. Bernardus Claraeuallensis, "Sermones De diversis," sermo 3.1.21, p. 86; sermo 22.2.7, p. 171; sermo 30.I.11, p. 214; sermo 40.I.12, p. 234; sermo 121.3 , p. 398. "Every school of spirituality manifests some special aspect of the inexhaustible plenitude of Christ's sanctity. It is this that gives it a special 'cachet,' a center of spiritual unity, a way of holiness. As a matter of fact, the end of every school is charity and the ultimate means is humility through which charity flourishes, because charity is a theological virtue and a gratuitous gift which is neither acquired nor merited." Cf. Breton, "Franciscan Spirituality."

11. Cf. McGinn, *The Foundations of Christian Mysticism: Origins to the Fifth Century,* 125.

12. Cf. 2 EpFid 48–56; 2EpAgn 1; 3EpAgn 1; 4EpAgn 4, 17.

13. Cf. 2EpFid 33; EpOrd 21–22. Citing Petri Damiani ("Sermones 45 in Nativitate Beatae Mariae Virginis 2" PL 144, 734a,b), Oktavian Schmucki claims that Francis connected the work of the priest in the celebration of the Eucharist with a popular Marian teaching of his time. Schmucki, "Francis' Devotion toward the Blessed Virgin Mary," 209–10, 209 n.

14. Western societies' contemporary emphasis on a child being nurtured, cared for, and educated by both father and mother during and even past the weaning period is not congruent with the child-rearing practices of the Middle Ages. Yet today's child-rearing practices can give new insight into how God the Father works together with the faithful mother and vice versa. This would make an interesting study that is beyond the scope of our present work.

15. Van Asseldonk, *Maria, Francesco e Chiara,* 521.

16. Cf. Specifically, we are told that Francis chose Friar Elias to be his mother: 2Cel 98.

17. Frohlich, "Spiritual Discipline, Discipline of Spirituality: Revisiting Questions of Definition and Method."

18. Franciscans have a long tradition of not shying away from using the sciences in the study of theology. In section 26 of his *De reductione artium ad theolgiam*, Saint Bonaventure claims, "And so it is evident how the manifold Wisdom of God, which is clearly revealed in Sacred Scripture, lies hidden in all knowledge and in all nature. It is evident, too, how all divisions of knowledge are handmaids of theology, and it is for this reason that theology makes use of illustrations and terms pertaining to every branch of knowledge. . . . And this is the fruit of all sciences, that in all, faith may be strengthened, God may be honored, character may be formed and consolation may be derived from union of the Spouse and His beloved, a union which takes place through charity." (Et sic patet, quomodo "multiformes sapientia Dei", quae lucide traditur in sacra Scriptura occultur in omni cognitione et in omni natura. Patet etiam, quomodo omnes cognitiones famulantur theologiae; et ideo ipsa assumit exampla et utitur vocabulis pertinentibus ad omne genus cognitionis. . . . Et hic est fructus omnium scientiarum, ut in omnibus aedificetur fides, "honorificetur Deus", componantur mores, hauriantur consolationes, quae sunt in unione sponsi et sponsae, quae quidem fit per caritatem.) Healy, *St. Bonaventure's De reductione artium ad theolgiam: A Commentary with an Introduction and Translation*, 40–41.

19. Cf. Lehmann, "The Man Francis as Seen in His Letters," 181.

APPENDICES

1. This number includes eight *opuscula dictata* which have been transmitted in other sources (cf. Esser, ed., *Gli scritti*, 31–35).

2. Lemmens, ed., *S. Franciscus Assisiensis, Opuscula*. Cf. Nguyên-Van-Khanh, *Teacher of His Heart*, 31; Matura, *François d'Assise, "auteur spirituel,"* 27–28; Paolazzi, *Lettura degli "Scritti,"* 15–17.

3. Armstrong and Brady, eds. and trans., *Francis and Clare*, 8.

4. Regarding the English translations of the titles, I stay as faithful to the Latin titles as possible. For the benefit of a more international audience, the abbreviations are based on the Latin titles.

5. Francis wrote to various types of people. Some of the opuscula were meant for a particular person (Leo, for example) or for a particular group (rulers, the Friars, or the Damianites) while others were meant for all Christians.

6. For more critical information on Clare's opuscula, see Omaechevarria, ed. and trans., *Escritos de Santa Clara*; Becker, et al., eds., *Claire d'Assise: Écrits*, 169–234; Armstrong et al., ed. and trans., *The Lady*; Bartoli and Zoppetti, trans., *S. Chiara d'Assisi: Scritti e documenti*; E. Paoli, "Clarae Assisiensi opuscula. Introduzione."

7. When citing the vitae, I employ a slightly modified version of the numbering system used in the Edizioni Porziuncola version of Menestò and Brufani, eds., *Fontes Franciscani*.

I use a period instead of a comma when citing the sources. The number before the period is the number of the section (not the chapter). The verse or verses follow the period. When citing the *Process of Canonization for St. Clare of Assisi*, Bonaventure's *Major Life of St. Francis*, or Henry of Avranches' *Legend of St. Francis*, however, I cite the chapter and then the section and verse(s), so that LegMai 2:1.3–7 is chapter 2, section 1, verses 3 through 7 of the *Major Life of St. Francis*.

8. Scholars of the Franciscan Question continue to debate the dating and interdependence of these sources.

9. Most scholars agree that the Assisi Compilation (CompAs) and the Legend of Perugia (LegPer) were originally the same document. The manuscript tradition and the work of various scholars have produced two separate but very similar documents. Of these two, the Assisi Compilation is probably the older. Cf. Armstrong, Hellman, and Short, eds. and trans., *The Founder: Francis of Assisi: Early Documents*, 2, 113–17.

BIBLIOGRAPHIES

COMBINED LIST

This combined list of references contains all the primary sources and pertinent studies. The primary sources are listed again in subsequent bibliographies of opuscula, vitae, other sources, and translations and commentaries.

Abate, Giuseppe. *La casa dove nacque San Francesco di Assisi nella sua documentazione storica.* Roma: Presso "Miscellanea francescana," 1966.

Accrocca, Felice. "Chiara 'alter Franciscus.'" In Accrocca et al., eds., *Chiara d'Assisi con Francesco sulla via di Cristo*, 69–87.

———, and Antonio Ciceri. *Francesco e i suoi frati.* Milano, Italy: Biblioteca francescana, 1998.

———, et al., eds. *Chiara d'Assisi. Con Francesco sulla via di Cristo.* Assisi: Porziuncola, 1993.

Adnès, Pierre. "Mariage, spirituel." In *Dictionnaire de Spiritualité* X. Paris: G. Beauchesne, 1980, 388–408.

Ago, Lorenzo Maria. *La "Salutatio Beatae Mariae Virginis" di San Francesco di Assisi. Monumenta Italica Mariana. Studi e testi*, 3. Roma: Edizioni Monfortane, 1998.

Anonymus Perusinus. "De inceptione vel fundamento Ordinis et actibus illorum fratrum Minorum qui fuerunt primi in religione et socii B. Francisci." In Menestò and Brufani, eds., *Fontes Franciscani*, 1311–51.

Archivum Franciscanum Historicum: Periodica publicatio trimestris. cura pp. Collegii D. Bonaventurae. Quaracchi, Italy: Ad Claras Aquas, 1908.

Aries, Philippe. *Centuries of Childhood: A Social History of Family Life.* Translated by Robert Baldick. New York: Knopf, 1962.

Armstrong, Regis J., ed. and trans. *The Lady: Clare of Assisi: Early Documents.* New York: New City Press, 1993.

———, and Ignatius Brady, eds. and trans. *Francis and Clare: The Complete Works.* New York: Paulist Press, 1982.

———, J. A. W. Hellman, and W. J. Short, eds. and trans. *The Saint: Francis of Assisi: Early Documents*, vol. 1. New York: New City Press, 1999.

———, J. A. W. Hellman, and W. J. Short, eds. and trans. *The Founder: Francis of Assisi: Early Documents*, vol. 2. New York: New City Press, 2000.

Arturo du Monstier di Rouen. *Martirologio francescano.* Ignazio Beschin e Giuliano eds. Palazzolo. Vicenza: Ex Typographia Commerciali, 1939.

Ashley, Kathleen, and Pamela Sheingorn, eds. *Interpreting Cultural Symbols: St. Anne in Late Medieval Society.* Athens: University of Georgia Press, 1990.

Atkinson, Clarissa W. *The Oldest Vocation: Christian Motherhood in the Middle Ages.* Ithaca, NY: Cornell University Press, 1991.

Baldelli, Ignacio, and Angiola Maria Romanini, eds. *Francesco, il francescanesimo e la cultura della nuova Europa.* Roma: Istituto della enciclopedia italiana, 1986.

Barbero, Alessandro, and Chiara Frugoni. *Dizionario del Medioevo.* Roma: Laterza, 1994.

Baronti, Remo. *Il Lucchese, San Francesco d'Assisi.* Vigodarzere, Italy: Progetto Editoriale Mariano, 1993.

Bartoli, Marco. "Analisi storica e interpretazione psicanalitica di una visione di S. Chiara d'Assisi." *Archivum Franciscanum Historicum* 73 (1980): 449–72.

———. *Clare of Assisi.* Quincy, IL: Franciscan Press, 1993.

———. *Chiara d'Assisi.* Roma: Istituto storico dei cappuccini, 1989.

———, and G. Ginepro Zoppetti, trans. *S. Chiara d'Assisi: Scritti e documenti.* Assisi: Editrici Francescane, 1994.

Bartolini, Rino. *Lo Spirito del Signore. Francesco di Assisi guida all'esperienza dello Spirito Santo*. Assisi: Studio teologico "Porziuncola," 1993.

Bartholomeo de Pisa. *De conformitate vitae Beati Francisci ad vitam Domini Iesu*, Liber I Fructus I–XIII. (*Analecta Franciscana*, vol. 4). Quaracchi, Italy: Ad Claras Aquas, 1906.

Becker, Marie-France, Jean-Francois Godet, and Thaddee Matura, trans. *Claire d Assise: Écrits*. Paris: Editions du Cerf, 1986.

Beitscher, Jane K. "'As the Twig is Bent . . .': Children and Their Parents in an Aristocratic Society." *Journal of Medieval History* 2 (1976): 181–91.

Bernardus Claraeuallensis. "Sermones De Diversis." In *Cetedoc Library of Christian Latin Texts* [version 3.0] vol. 6.1. Turnhout, Belgium: Brepols, 1996.

Bestor, Jane Fair. "Ideas about Procreation and Their Influence on Ancient and Medieval Views of Kinship." In Kertzer and Saller, eds., *The Family in Italy*, 150–67.

Blaise, Albert. *Dictionnaire Latin-Français des auteurs Chrétiens*. Turnhout, Belgium: Brepols, 1954.

Blaise, Albert. *Lexicon Latinitatis Medii Aevi: praesertim ad res ecclesiasticas investigandas pertinens = Dictionnaire latin-français des auteurs du Moyen-Age*. Turnhout, Belgium: Brepols, 1975.

Bly, Robert. *Iron John: A Book about Men*. Reading, MA: Addison-Wesley, 1990.

Boccali, Giovanni. "Canto di esortazione alle 'poverelle' di San Damiano." *Collectanea Franciscana* 48 (1978): 5–29.

―――. "Parole di esortazione alle 'poverelle' di San Damiano." *Forma Sororum* 14 (1977): 54–70.

―――. "Testamento e benedizione di S. Chiara. Nuovo codice latino." *Archivum Franciscanum Historicum* 82 (1989): 283–94.

Bonaventurae de Balneoregio, "Legenda Maior S. Francisci." In Menestò and Brufani, eds., *Fontes Franciscani*, 777–961.

Bonaventurae de Balneoregio. "Commentaria in quatuor libros Sententiarum." In PP. Collegium S. Bonaventurae, ed., *Opera omnia*, ii. Quaracchi, Italy: Ex Typographia Collegii S. Bonaventurae, 1882.

Boswell, John. *Same-Sex Unions in Premodern Europe*. New York: Villard, 1994.

Bracaloni, Leone. *La Chiesa Nuova di San Francesco converso, casa paterna del Santo di Assisi*. Todi: Tipografia Tuderte, 1943.

Breton, Valentin. "Franciscan Spirituality." In Jean Gautier, *Some Schools of Catholic Spirituality*. Paris: Desclee, 1959. http://www.ewtn.com/library /SPIRIT /FRANSPIR.TXT (accessed 15 June, 2009).

Brod, Harry. "The Case for Men's Studies." In *The Making of Masculinities*, edited by Harry Brod, 261–73. Boston: Allen & Unwin, 1987.

Brooke, Christopher Nugent Lawrence. *The Medieval Idea of Marriage*. Oxford: Oxford University Press, 1989.

Brown, Peter. *The Cult of the Saints*. Chicago: University of Chicago Press, 1981.

Brunet, Robert. "Figures de l'Eglise." In *Dictionnaire de Spiritualité* IV.1, 392–96. Paris, 1960.

Bughetti, B. "Legenda versificata S. Clarae Assisiensis." *Archivum Franciscanum Historicum* 5 (1912): 241–60; 459–81.

Bullough, Vern L. "On Being a Male in the Middle Ages." In Lees et al., eds., *Medieval Masculinities*, 31–46.

Bynum, Carolyn Walker. "Religious Women in the Later Middle Ages." In Rait, ed., *Christian Spirituality: High Middle Ages and Reformation*, 121–39.

———. *Holy Feast and Holy Fast: The Religious Significance of Food to Medieval Women*. Berkeley: University of California Press, 1987.

———. *Jesus as Mother: Studies in the Spirituality of the High Middle Ages*. Berkley: University of California Press, 1982.

————, Steven Harrell, and Paula Richman. *Gender and Religion: On the Complexity of Symbols.* Boston: Beacon, 1986.

Cabassut, André. "Une dévotion médiéval peu connu: la dévotion à 'Jésus Notre Mère,'" *Revue d'ascétique et de mystique* 25 (1949): 234–45.

Cadderi, Carlo. "Santa Agnese d'Assisi." *Frate Francesco* 65, no. 2 (aprile–giugno 1998): 5–20.

Canonici, Luciano, ed. and trans. *Textus opusculorum S. Francisci et Clarae Assisiensum. Variis adnotationibus ornatus, cura et studio Ioannis M. Boccali in lucem editus.* Assisi: Edizioni Porziuncola, 1978.

Cardini, Franco. "Francesco d'Assisi e l'Europa del suo tempo. Ricerca d'una risposta 'globale' al tema delle origini di una vocazione." *Studi Franciscani* 79 (1982): 15–53.

————. *Francesco d'Assisi,* 3 ed. Milano, Italy: A. Mondadori, 1994.

Caroli, Ernesto, ed. *Dizionario Francescano. Spiritualità,* 2 ed. Padova, Italy: Edizioni Messaggero, 1995.

Carstens, Carol. "Spiritual Mothering." *The Cord* 36 (1986): 216–23.

Casagrande, Carla. "La donna custodita." In Klapisch-Zuber, ed., *Storia delle donne in occidente,* 88–128

Casagrande, Giovanna. "Le compagnie di Chiara." In *Chiara di Assisi. Atti del XX Convegno Internazionale. Assisi, 15–17 ottobre 1992.* 383–425. Spoleto: Centro italiano di studi sull'Alto Medievo, 1993.

Cavazos-González, Gilberto. "Spirituality." Miguel A. De La Torre, ed. *Hispanic American Religious Cultures,* vol. 2. Santa Barbara, CA: ABC-CLIO 2009, 749-760.

————. "*La Cotidianidad Divina*: A Latin@ Method of Spirituality." *Journal of Hispanic/Latino Theology* (2008). http://www.latinotheology.org/2008/ latinoa_ method_spirituality (accessed 12 September 2008).

————. "Liberation Spirituality and the Process of Canonization for St. Clare of Assisi." *The Cord* 52 (2002): 142–52.

————. *Greater than a Mother's Love: Kinship in the Spirituality of Francis and Clare of Assisi*. Pars Dissertationis. Facultas Theologiae – Sectio Spiritualitas Thesis ad Lauream 383. Romae: Pontificium Athenaeum Antonianum, 2001.

Charron, Jean-Marc. *Da Narciso a Gesù. La ricerca dell'identità in Francesco d'Assisi*. Padova, Italy: Edizioni Messaggero, 1995.

Chiara d'Assisi. *Atti del XX Convegno Internazionale*. Assisi 15–17 ottobre 1992. Spoleto: Centro italiano di studi sull'alto medioevo, 1993.

Clarae Assisiensis. "Opuscula." In Menestò and Brufani, eds., *Fontes Franciscani*, 2262–2324.

Clareno, Angelo. "Cronaca o Storia delle Sette Tribolazioni dell'Ordine dei Minori." In Menestò and Brufani, eds., *Fontes Franciscani*, 1738–96.

Clement of Alexandria. *Paedagogus* Book 1. Calvin College: Christian Classics Ethereal Library. http://www.ccel.org/ccel/schaff/anf02.vi.iii.i.vi.html (accessed 22 February, 2010).

Covi, Davide, and Dino Dozzi, eds. *Chiara, Francescanesimo al Femminile*, 2 ed. Roma: Edizioni Dehoniane, 1992.

Cremaschi, Chiara Giovanna, and Chiara Agnese Acquadro. *Scritti di Santa Chiara d'Assisi*. Assisi: Edizioni Porziuncola, 1994.

Da Campagnola, Stefano. "Francisci Assisiensis Opuscula: Introduzione." In Menestò and Brufani, eds., *Fontes Franciscani*, 3–22.

————. "Thomae de Celano 'Introduzione.'" In Menestò and Brufani, eds., *Fontes Franciscani*, 259–71.

Dalarun, Jacques. *Francesco: un passaggio. Donna e donne negli scritti e nelle leggende di Francesco d' Assisi*. Roma: Viella, 1994.

————. *Francis of Assisi and the Feminine*. St. Bonaventure, NY: Franciscan Institute Publications, 2006.

Danieli, Rodolfo. "La famiglia nel diritto romano e intermedio." In *Enciclopedia Cattolica* 5, 989–94. Città del Vaticano: Ente per l'Enciclopedia cattolica e per il Libro cattolico, 1949.

Davis, Natalie Zemon. "Anthropology and History." In *Society and Culture in Early Modern France*, 97–151. Stanford: Stanford University Press, 1975.

Delio, Ilia. *Franciscan Prayer.* Cleveland, OH: St. Anthony Messenger Press, 2004.

Della Porta, Pier Maurizio. *Guide to Assisi: History and Art.* Assisi: Coop. Editrice Minerva, 1992.

Destro, Adriana, and Mauro Pesce. *Antropologia delle origini cristiane.* Roma: Laterza, 1995.

De Ventosa, Feliciano. "La devoción a María en la espiritualidad de San Francisco." *Estudios Franciscanos* 62 (1961): 249–74.

Dhont, Rene-Charles. *Chiara madre e sorella.* Milano, Italy: Edizione Biblioteca Francescani, 1980.

Di Fonzo, Lorenzo. "Questione Francescana." In *Dizionario degli Istituti di Perfezione* VII, edited by Guerrino Pelliccia and Giancarlo Rocca, 1133–54. Roma: San Paolo Edizioni, 1983.

Downey, Michael, ed. *The New Dictionary of Catholic Spirituality.* Collegeville, MN: Liturgical Press, 1993.

Dozzi, Davide. "Chiara e lo specchio." In Covi and Dozzi, eds., *Chiara, Francescanesimo al Femminile*, 290–318.

Duby, Georges. *Mâle Moyen Âge. De l'amour et autres essais.* Paris: Flammarion, 1988.

———. *The Three Orders: Feudal Society Imagined.* Translated by Arthur Goldhammer. Chicago: University of Chicago Press, 1980.

Elliott, Dyan. *Spiritual Marriage: Sexual Abstinence in Medieval Wedlock.* Princeton, NJ: Princeton University Press, 1993.

Englebert, Omer. *St. Francis of Assisi: A Biography*. Ann Arbor, MI: Servant Books, 1979.

Esser, Kajetan, ed. *Gli scritti di S. Francesco d'Assisi. Nuova edizione critica e versione italiana*. Translated by Alfredo Bizzotto, Sergio Cattazzo, and Vergilio Gamboso. Padova, Italy: Edizioni Messaggero, 1982.

Espín, Orlando. *Futuring Our Past: Explorations in the Theology of Tradition*. Maryknoll, NY: Orbis, 2006.

Fenster, Thelma S. "Why Men?" In Lees et al., eds., *Medieval Masculinities*, ix–xiii.

Fierens, A. "La question Franciscaine. Vita Sancti Francisci anonyma Bruxellensis d'après le manuscrit II.2326 de la Bibliothèque Royale de Belgique." *Revue d'Histoire Ecclésiastique* 8 (1907): 286–304, 498–513; 9 (1908): 38–47, 703–27; 10 (1909): 42–65, 303–7.

Flanagan, Kieran. *A Sociology of Spirituality*. Burlington, CT: Ashgate, 2007.

Flew, Robert Newton. *The Idea of Perfection in Christian Theology: An Historical Study of the Christian Ideal for the Present Life*, 2 ed. Oxford: Clarendon, 1968.

Fonti Francescane. Scritti e biografie di San Francesco d'Assisi; Cronache e altre testimonianze del primo secolo francescano; scritti e biografie di Santa Chiara d'Assisi, 4 ed. Padova, Italy: Edizioni Messaggero, 1990.

Fortini, Arnaldo. "Nuove notizie intorno a S. Chiara d'Assisi." *Archivum Franciscanum Historicum* 46 (1953): 3–43.

———. *Francis of Assisi*. Translated by Helen Moak, New York: Seabury, 1981.

———. *Nova vita di San Francesco*, vols. I–V. Assisi: Edizioni Porziuncola, 1959.

Fortini, Gemma. "The Noble Family of St. Clare of Assisi." *Franciscan Studies* 42 (1982): 48–67.

Franceschini, Ezio. *Nel segno di Francesco*. Edited by Fausta Casolini and G. Giamba. Assisi: Edizioni Porziuncola, 1988.

Francesco d'Assisi. *Scritti: Testo latino e traduzione italiana*. Padova, Italy: Editrici Francescane, 2002.

Francisci Assisiensis. "Opuscula." In Menestò and Brufani, eds., *Fontes Franciscani*, 23–245.

"Frate Nicola d'Assisi." In *Fonti Francescane*, no. 2686.

Frohlich, Mary. "Spiritual Discipline, Discipline of Spirituality: Revisiting Questions of Definition and Method." *Spiritus: A Journal of Christian Spirituality* I (Spring 2001): 65–78.

Frugoni, Chiara. *Francis of Assisi: A Life*. New York: Continuum, 1998.

———. *A Day in a Medieval City*, Chicago, IL: University of Chicago Press, 2006.

Fumagalli, Mariateresa, and Beonio Brocchieri. "The Intellectual." In Le Goff, ed., and Cochrane, trans., *Medieval Callings*, 181–209.

Gagnant, Dominique. "Le symbole de la femme chez saint François d'Assise." *Laurentianum* 18 (1977): 256–91.

García, Sixto. "Hispanic Theologians as Actors, Prophets and Poets of Their Communities." *Journal of Hispanic Latino Theology* (1999). http://www.latinotheology.org /fileshare/files/27/6-4/Hispanic_Theologians_Actors_Poets_Prophets.pdf (accessed 5 November, 2008).

Giacometti, Luigi, ed. *Dialoghi con Chiara d'Assisi: Atti delle giornate di studio e riflessione per l'VIII centenario di Santa Chiara*, (ottobre 1993–luglio 1994). Assisi: Edizioni Porziuncola 1995.

Giandomenico, Nicola. "Rivotorto." In Caroli, ed., *Dizionario Francescano. Spiritualità*, 2 ed., 1747–58.

Gies, Frances, and Joseph Gies. *Marriage and the Family in the Middle Ages*. New York: Harper and Row, 1978.

Gniecki, Czeslaw. *Visione dell'uomo negli scritti di Francesco d'Assisi*. Roma: Antonianum, 1987.

Godet, Jean François. "Chiara e la vita al femminile. Simboli di donna nei suoi scritti." In Covi and Dozzi, eds., *Chiara, Francescanesimo al Femminile*, 2 ed., 143–68.

Goody, Jack. *The Development of the Family and Marriage in Europe*. Cambridge: Cambridge University Press, 1983.

Guerra, José Antonio, ed. *San Francisco de Asís. Escritos, biografías, documentos de la época*, 6 ed. Madrid: Biblioteca de Autores Cristianos, 1995.

Gurevich, Aron J. "The Merchant." In Le Goff, ed., and Cochrane, trans., *Medieval Callings*, 243–84.

Guttmacher, Adolf. "Family and Family Life." In *The Jewish Encyclopedia* V, 336–38. New York: Katy, 1965.

Habig, Marion A., ed. *St. Francis of Assisi Writings and Early Biographies: English Omnibus of the Sources for the Life of St. Francis*, 3 ed. Chicago: Franciscan Herald Press, 1973.

Hames, Susan E. "Bridal Mysticism." In Downey, ed., *The New Dictionary of Catholic Spirituality*, 106.

Harris, Marvin. *Our Kind: Who We Are, Where We Came From, Where We Are Going*. New York: Harper Perenniel, 1990.

Healy, Emma Thérèse. *St. Bonaventure's De reductione artium ad theologiam: A Commentary with an Introduction and Translation*. St. Bonaventure, NY: The Franciscan Institute, 1955.

Hellman, J. A. Wayne. "Spiritual Writing, Genres of." In Downey, ed., *The New Dictionary of Catholic Spirituality*, 922–30.

Herlihy, David. "The Family and Religious Ideologies in Medieval Europe." *Journal of Family History* 12 (1987): 3–17.

———. *Medieval Households*. Cambridge, MA: Harvard University Press, 1985.

———. *Women, Family and Society in Medieval Europe: Historical Essays, 1978–1991*. Providence RI: Berghahn, 1995.

Hermann, Placid. "Celano: Introduction." In Habig, ed., *Omnibus*, 179–212.

Herranz, Julio, Javier Garrido, and José Antonio Guerra, eds. and trans. *Los escritos de Francisco y Clara de Asís*, 2 ed. Aranzazu, Colombia: Ediciones Franciscanas, 1980.

House, Adrian. *Francis of Assisi: A Revolutionary Life*. Mahwah, NJ: Hidden Spring, 2001.

Hubaut, Michel. "Le Mystère de la vivante Trinité dans la vie et la prière de Saint François d'Assise." *Evangile Aujourd'Hui* 95 (1977): 43–50.

Ireneus, *Against Heresies* Book III. Calvin College: Christian Classics Ethereal Library. http://www.ccel.org/ccel/schaff/anf01.ix.iv.xxv.html (accessed 22 February, 2010).

Iriarte, Lázaro. *Vocación Franciscana. La opción de Francisco y Clara de Asís*, 3 ed. Valencia, Spain: Editorial Asís, 1989.

Iriarte, Lázaro, ed. *Los escritos de Francisco y Clara de Asís*. Valencia, Spain: Editorial Asís, 1981.

Izzo, Leonardo. "Verginità." In Caroli, ed., *Dizionario Francescano. Spiritualità*, 2 ed., 2159–78.

Johnson, Robert A. *He: Understanding Masculine Psychology*, 4 ed. King of Prussia, PA: Religious Publishing, 1976.

Kertzer, David I., and Richard P. Saller, eds. *The Family in Italy from Antiquity to the Present*. New Haven, CT: Yale University Press, 1991.

Klapisch-Zuber, Christiane. "Women and the Family." In Le Goff, ed., and Cochrane, trans., *Medieval Callings*, 285–311.

———, ed. *Storia delle donne in occidente. Il Medioevo*. Roma: Laterza 1990.

Kazantzakis, Nikos. *Saint Francis*. Translated by Peter A. Bien. Chicago: Loyola Press, 2005.

Lachance, Paul. *Angela of Foligno: Complete Works*. New York: Paulist Press, 1993.

Lainati, Chiara Augusta. "The Enclosure of St. Clare and the First Poor Clares in Canonical Legislation and in Practice." *The Cord* 28 (1978): 4–15, 47–60.

————. Santa Chiara d'Assisi. *Cenni biografici di S. Agnese d'Assisi*. Assisi: Edizioni Porziuncola, 1983.

Lanzoni, Francisco. "Il sogno presagio della madre incinta nella letteratura medievale e antica." *Analecta Bollandiana* 45 (1926): 225–68.

Larrañaga, Ignacio. *El hermano de Asís. Vida profunda de San Francisco*, 5 ed. Buenos Aires, Argentina: Grupo Ilhsa, 1996.

Lazzeri, Zeffirino. "Il processo di canonizzazione di S. Chiara d'Assisi." *Archivum Franciscanum Historicum* 13 (1920): 403–507.

The Legend and Writings of Saint Clare of Assisi: Introduction, Translation, and Studies. St. Bonaventure, NY: Franciscan Institute, 1953.

"Legenda Sanctae Clarae Virginis." Found in Ms 338 of the *Biblioteca Comunale di Assisi*. Edited by Francesco Pennachi. Assisi, 1910.

Leclercq, Jean. *La figura della donna nel medioevo*. Translated by Antonio Tombolini. Milano, Italy: Editoriale Jaca Book, 1994.

————, François Vandenbroucke, and Louis Bouyer. *The Spirituality of the Middle Ages (History of Christian Spirituality II)*. Translated by the Benedictines of Holme Eden Abbey. London: Burns & Oats, 1968.

Lees, Clare A., Thelma S. Fenster, and Jo Ann McNamara, eds. *Medieval Masculinities. Regarding Men in the Middle Ages*. Minneapolis: University of Minnesota Press, 1994.

Le Goff, Jacques. "Introduction: Medieval Man." In Le Goff, ed., and Cochrane, trans., *Medieval Callings*, 1–35.

————. *Saint Francis of Assisi*. London: Routledge, 2004.

————, ed., and Lydia G. Cochrane, trans. *Medieval Callings*, 4 ed. Chicago: University of Chicago Press, 1996.

Lehmann, Leonhard. *Francesco, maestro di preghiera*. Roma: Istituto Storico dei Cappuccini, 1993.

————. "The Man Francis as Seen in His Letters." *Greyfriars Review* 5 (1991): 159–90.

Lemmens, Leonard, ed. *S. Franciscus Assisiensis. Opuscula*, 2 ed. Quaracchi, Italy: Ad Claras Aquas, 1941 (1 ed., 1904).

Lenzen, Dieter. *Alla riceca del padre, Dal patriarcato agli alimenti*. Roma: Laterza, 1994.

Leo and companions. *Compilatio Assisiensis: dagli scritti di Fra Leone e compagni su S. Francesco d'Assisi*, 2 ed. Translated by Marino Bigaroni. Assisi: Porziuncola, 1992.

Lett, Didier. "Mais Si! Les parents aimaient leurs enfants." *Historia Spécial* 42 (1996): 17–18.

Lewis, Charlton T., and Charles Short. *A Latin Dictionary*, 2 ed. Oxford: Clarendon, 1955.

L'Hermite-Leclercq, Paulette. "Le donne nell'ordine feudale (XI–XII secolo)." In Klapisch-Zuber, ed., *Storia delle donne in occidente*, 2 ed., 251–309.

Loccatelli, Vincenzo. *Vita di S. Chiara*. Napoli: Andrea Festa, 1855.López, Sebastián. "El tema mariano en los escritos de Francisco de Asís." *Selecciones de franciscanismo* 16 (1987): 171–86.

Lospinoso, Mariannita. "Matrimonio." In *Grande dizionario enciclopedico UTET* XIII, 208. Torino, Italy: UTET, 1992.

Lucas, Angela M. *Women in the Middle Ages: Religion, Marriage, and Letters*. Brighton, Sussex, UK: Harvester Press, 1988.

Malatesta, Edward J. "Marriage, Mystical." In Downey, ed., *The New Dictionary of Catholic Spirituality*, 631.

Manselli, Raoul. *St. Francis of Assisi.* Translated by Paul Duggan. Chicago: Franciscan Herald Press, 1988.

Marchitielli, Elena. "L'Alleanza sponsale con Cristo nelle lettere di S. Chiara a S. Agnese di Praga." In Giacometti, Luigi, ed., *Dialoghi con Chiara d'Assisi*, 309–22.

Mariano da Firenze. *Libro delle dignità et excellentie del ordine della seraphica madre delle povere donne sancta Chiara da Asisi. Introduzione, note e indici Giovanni Boccali.* Firenze: Studi Franciscani, 1986.

Marini, Alfonso. "Ancilla Christi, plantula sancti Francisci. Gli scritti di Santa Chiara e la regola." In *Chiara d'Assisi. Atti del XX Convegno Internazionale. Assisi 15–17 ottobre 1992*, 107–56. Spoleto: Centro italiano di studi sull'alto Medioevo, 1993.

Martin, David. *Reflections on Sociology and Theology.* Oxford: Oxford University Press, 1997.

Matura, Thadée. *François d'Assise, "auteur spirituel." Le message de ses écrits.* Paris: Editions du Cerf, 1996.

———. *Francis of Assisi: Writer and Spiritual Master.* Cincinnati, OH: St. Anthony Messenger, 2005.

McGinn, Bernard. *The Flowering of Mysticism: Men and Women in the New Mysticism—1200–1350 (The Presence of God: A History of Western Christian Mysticism, vol. 3).* New York: Crossroad, 1998.

———. *The Foundations of Christian Mysticism: Origins to the Fifth Century (The Presence of God: A History of Western Christian Mysticism, vol. 1).* New York: Crossroad, 1997.

———, John Meyendorf, and Jean Leclercq, eds. *Christian Spirituality: Origins to the Twelfth Century (World Spirituality: An Encyclopedic History of the Religious Quest, vol. 16).* New York: Crossroad, 1985.

McNally, R. E., "Middle Ages." In *New Catholic Encyclopedia* IX, 812–13. Washington, DC: Catholic University of America, 1967.

Menard, André, "Maria vista da Francesco." In Redactors of Evangile Aujourd'Hui, eds. *La Spiritualità di Francesco d'Assisi* (Milano 1993), 245–52.

Menestò, Enrico, and Stefano Brufani, eds. *Fontes Franciscani.* Assisi: Edizioni Porziuncola, 1995.

Merino, Antonio. "Il linguaggio antropocentrico in rapporto all universo di significazione del femminile in alcuni temi della teologia." In *Il carisma materno di Francesco d'Assisi*, edited by OFS-Centro Nazionale, 13–17. Assisi: Porziuncola, 1996.

Migne, Jacques-Paul, ed. *Patrologiae cursus completus: series latina*, 221 vols. Paris, 1841–1864.

Miskuly, Jason M. "Julian of Speyer: Life of St. Francis. Introduction." *Franciscan Studies* 49 (1989): 93–115.

Moore, Robert, and Douglas Gillette. *King, Warrior, Magician, Lover: Rediscovering the Archetypes of the Mature Masculine.* San Francisco: Harper San Francisco, 1990.

Motte, Ignace-Étienne. "La 'poverella' . . . la 'chère petite pauvre.'" *Evangile Aujourd'Hui* 137 (1988): 2–4.

Mueller, Joan. *Clare of Assisi: The Letters to Agnes.* Collegeville, MN: Liturgical Press, 2003.

Nanko-Fernández, Carmen. "Lo Cotidiano." Miguel A. De La Torre, ed. *Hispanic American Religious Cultures*, vol. 1. Santa Barbara, CA: ABC-CLIO 2009, 158–60.

———. "Traditioning *Latinamente*: A Theological Discussion on *la Lengua Cotidiana*." *Learn@CTU.* http://learn.ctu.edu/Lectures_and_Conferences/Nanko_Traditioning.pdf (accessed 25 April 2007).

———. "From *Pájaro* to Paraclete: Retrieving the Spirit of God in the Company of Mary." *The Journal of Hispanic/Latino Theology* (2007). http://www.latinotheology.org/2007/company_of_mary (accessed 15 April, 2008).

The New Jerusalem Bible: Reader's Edition. Edited by Bonifatio Fischer et al. Stuttgart: Deutsche Bibelgesellschaft, 1969.

Nguyên-Van-Khanh, Norbert. *Teacher of His Heart: Jesus Christ in the Thought and Writings of St. Francis.* Translated by Edward Hagman. St. Bonaventure, NY: Franciscan Institute, 1994.

Niermeyer, J. F. *Mediae Latinitatis Lexicon Minus.* Leiden: Brill, 1984.

Oliger, Livarius. "Liber exemplorum Fratrum minorum saeculi XIII (excerpta e cod. Ottob. Lat. 522)." *Antonianum* 2 (1927): 213–76.

Omaechevarria, Ignacio, ed. and trans. *Escritos de Santa Clara y documentos complementarios,* 3 ed. Madrid: Editorial Católica, 1993.

Osiek, Carolyn. "Family Matters." In *A People's History of Christianity: Vol I: Christian Origins,* edited by Richard A. Horsley. Minneapolis: Fortress, 2005.

Ortolani da Pesaro, Ciro. *La madre del Santo d'Assisi.* Tolentino: Stab. Tipografico "F. Filelfo," 1926.

Paolazzi, Carlo. *Lettura degli "Scritti" di Francesco d'Assisi,* 2 ed. Milano, Italy: Biblioteca Francescana, 1992.

Paoli, E. "Clarae Assisiensi opuscula. Introduzione." In *Fonti Francescane,* 2223–60.

Parmisano, Fabian. "Love and Marriage in the Middle Ages." *New Blackfriars* 50 (1969): 599–608, 649–60.

Paul, Jacques, and Mariano D'Alatari. "Salimbene da Parma testimone e cronista." In *Bibliotheca Seraphico-Capuccina* 41. Roma: Istituto dei Cappucini, 1992.

Pellegrini, Luigi. "Cronache e Tesimonianze." In *Fonti Francescane,* 1797–2205.

Peters, Edward. "Middle Ages." In *New Catholic Encyclopedia,* 2 ed., IX, 609–16. Washington, DC: Catholic University of America, 2003.

Peterson, Ingrid. *Clare of Assisi: A Biographical Study.* Quincy, IL: Franciscan Press, 1993.

Petri Damiani, "Opusculum 18.1 De coelibatu sacerdotum, c. 3." In Migne, Jacques-Paul, ed., *Patrologiae cursus completus: series latina*, vol. 145 (Paris, 1853), col 379–88.

———. "Sermones 45 In Nativitate Beatae Mariae Virginis 2." In Migne, Jacques-Paul, ed., *Patrologiae cursus completus: series latina*, vol. 144 (Paris, 1853), col 740–48.

Petri Lombardi. *Sententiae in IV Libris Disctintae*. Grottaferrata: Editiones Collegii S. Bonaventurae ad Claras Aquas, 1971–81.

Pleck, Joseph H. *The Myth of Masculinity*. Cambridge: MIT Press, 1981.

Pozzi, Giovanni, and Beatrice Rima, ed. and trans. *Chiara d'Assisi, Lettere ad Agnese. La visione dello specchio*. Milano, Italy: Adelphi, 1999.

Purfield, Brian E. Reflets dans le mirior. *Images du Christ dans la vie spirituelle de sainte Claire d'Assise*. Paris: Editions franciscains,1993.

Pyfferoen, Ilario, and Optatus Van Asseldonk. "Maria Santissima e lo Spirito Santo in San Francesco d'Assisi." *Laurentianum* 16 (1975): 446–74.

Rait, Jill, ed. *Christian Spirituality: High Middle Ages and Reformation (World Spirituality: An Encyclopedic History of the Religious Quest 17)*. New York: Crossroad, 1988.

Ridolfi, Pietro. *Historiarum seraphicae religionis libri tres seriem temporum continentes quibus breui explicantur fundamenta, universique ordinis amplificatio, gradus, et instituta; nec non uiri scientia, uirtutibus, et fama praeclari*. Venetiis: Franciscun de Franciscis; 1586.

Rivi, Prospero. *Francesco d'Assisi e il laicato del suo tempo. Le origini dell'Ordine Francescano Secolare*. Padova, Italy: Edizioni Messaggero, 1989.

Rodriguez Herrera, Isidoro. "Aspecto literario de los escritos de Santa Clara." *Verdad y Vida* 52 (1994): 147–65.

Rohr, Richard, and Joseph Martos. *The Wild Man's Journey: Reflections on Male Spirituality*. Cincinnatti: St. Anthony Messenger Press, 1992.

Rossiaud, Jacques. "The City-Dweller and Life in Cities and Towns." In Le Goff, ed., and Cochrane, trans., *Medieval Callings*, 139–79.

Rotzetter, Anton. "Il servizio negli scritti di Chiara. Subordinazione o maturità?" In Covi and Dozzi, eds., *Chiara, Francescanesimo al Femminile*, 2 ed., 319–57.

———. *Chiara d'Assisi. La prima francescana.* Translated by Cristina Riva. Milano, Italy: Biblioteca Francescana, 1993.

Russell, Anthony. "Sociology and the Study of Spirituality." In *The Study of Spirituality*, edited by Cheslyn Jones, Geoffrey Wainwright, and Edward Yarnold, 33–38. Oxford: Oxford University Press, 1986.

Sabatier, Paul. *Études inédite sur S. François d'Assise.* Paris: Librairie Fischbacher, 1932.

———. *The Road to Assisi: The Essential Biography of St. Francis.* Edited with introduction by Jon Sweeney. Brewster, MA: Paraclete Press, 2003.

———. *Vita di San Francesco d'Assisi.* Translated by Giuseppe Zanichelli. Milano, Italy: A. Mondadori, 1978.

Salimbene de Adam da Parma. *Cronaca.* Translated by Berardo Rossi. Bologna, Italy: Radio TAU, 1987.

Sanz Montes, Jesús. "Lo femenino en la vida y espiritualidad de Francisco de Asís." *Verdad y Vida* 50 (1992): 27–51.

Savey, Catherine. "Les autorités de Claire." In *Sainte Claire d'Assise et sa postérité. Actes du colloque international organisé a l'occasion du VIIIe centenaire de la naissance de sainte Claire.* Nantes, France: Association Claire Aujourd'hui, 1995.

Schlosser, Marrianne, "Madre-sorella-sposa nella spiritualità di Santa Chiara." In Covi and Dozzi, eds., *Chiara, Francescanesimo al Femminile*, 2 ed., 169–87.

———. "Mother, Sister, Bride: The Spirituality of St. Clare." *Greyfriars Review* 5 (1991): 233–50.

Schmitt, Emile. *Le mariage chrétien dan l'ouvre de saint Augustin: une théologie baptismale de la vie conjugale.* Paris: Etudes augustiniennes, 1983.

Schmucki, Oktavian. "St. Francis' Devotion toward the Blessed Virgin Mary." *Greyfriars Review* 5 (1991): 201–32.

Scroggs, Robin. "The Sociological Interpretation of the New Testament: The Present Stage of Research." *New Testament Studies* 26 (1980): 164–79.

Secondin, Bruno. *Spiritualità in dialogo. Nuovi scenari dell'esperienza spirituale.* Milano, Italy: Paoline, 1997.

Seton, Walter W. "The Italian Version of the Legend of Saint Clare by the Florentine Ugolino Verino." *Archivum Franciscanum Historicum* 12 (1919), 595–659.

Seymour, M. C., gen. ed. *On the Properties of Things: John Trevisa's Translation of Bartholomaeus Anglicus* De proprietatibus rerum, vol. I. Oxford: Clarendon, 1975.

Shahar, Shulamith. *Childhood in the Middle Ages.* New York: Routledge, 1992.

Shanahan, G. "Henry of Avranches: Poem on the Life of Saint Francis (*Legenda Sancti Francisci Versificata*)." *Franciscan Studies* 48 (1988): 125–227.

Sheehan, Michael. "Family and Marriage, Western European." In *Dictionary of the Middle Ages,* edited by Joseph Reese Strayer, 608–12. New York: Scribner, 1989.

———. "Sexuality, Marriage, Celibacy, and the Family in Central and Northern Italy: Christian Legal and Moral Guides in the Early Middle Ages." In Kertzer, *The Family in Italy,* 168–83.

Simbula, Giuseppe. *La maternità spirituale di Maria in alcuni autori francescani del secolo XIII–XV.* Roma: Miscellanea francescana, 1967.

St. Clair, Michael. *Human Relationships and the Experience of God: Object Relations and Religion.* New York: Paulist Press, 1994.

Stuard, Susan Mosher. "Burdens of Matrimony. Husbanding and Gender in Medieval Italy." In Lees et al., eds., *Medieval Masculinities*, 61–72.

Taylor, Henry Osborn. *The Medieval Mind: A History of the Development of Thought and Emotion in the Middle Ages*. London: Macmillan, 1938.

Textus opusculorum S. Francisci et Clarae Assisiensum, variis adnotationibus ornatus. cura et studio Ioannis M. Boccali in lucem editus. Assisi: Edizioni Porziuncola, 1976.

Thomasset, Claude. "La natura della donna." In Klapisch-Zuber, ed., *Storia delle donne in occidente*, 56–87.

Trettel, Efrem. *Francis*. Chicago: Franciscan Herald Press, 1975.

Triviño, María Victoria. *Clara de Asís ante el espejo: historia y espiritualidad*. Madrid: Ediciones Paulinas, 1991.

———. *La vía de la belleza: Temas espirituales de Clara de Asís*. Madrid: Biblioteca de Autores Cristianos, 2003.

Turner, Victor Witter. *Dramas, Fields and Metaphors: Symbolic Action in Human Society*. Ithaca, NY: Cornell University Press, 1974.

———, and Edith L. B. Turner. *Image and Pilgrimage in Christian Culture: Anthropological Perspectives*. Oxford: Colombia University Press, 1978.

Ugolini d'Ostia. "Lettera del Cardinale Ugolini a S. Chiara." *Vita Minore* 62 (1991): 65–66.

Ulivi, Ferruccio. *Le mura del cielo*. Milano, Italy: A. Mondadori, 1991.

Uribe, Fernando. "Cristo en la experiencia y en las enseñanzas de Santa Clara. Aproximaciones al pensamiento Cristologico de Clara de Asís." *Selecciones de Franciscanismo* 22 (1993): 437–64.

———. "Il Cristo di Santa Chiara. Gesù Cristo nella esperienza e nel pensiero di Chiara d'Assisi." In Giacometti, ed., *Dialoghi con Chiara d'Assisi*, 21–51.

————. "Una curiosa 'visión' de Santa Clara interpretada desde diversos puntos de vista." *Selecciones de Franciscanismo* 24 (1995): 236–48.

————. *Introduzione alle agiografie di S. Francesco e S. Chiara d'Assisi* (sec XIII–XIV). Roma: P.A.A., 1996.

————. *Por los caminos de Francisco.* Roma: P.A.A., 1989.

Van Asseldonk, Optatus. *Maria, Francesco e Chiara: Una spiritualità per domani.* Roma: Collegio S. Lorenzo da Brindisi, 1989.

————. *La lettera e lo Spirito. La tensione vitale nel Francescanesimo ieri e oggi.* Roma: Editrice Laurentianum, 1985.

————. *Lo Spirito dà la vita. Chiara, Francesco e i penitenti.* Roma: Editrice Laurentianum, 1994.

————. "Madre." In Caroli, ed., *Dizionario Francescano. Spiritualità,* 2 ed., 1037–48.

Vandenbroucke, François. "New Milieux, New Problems from the Twelfth to the Sixteenth Century." In Leclercq et al., *The Spirituality of the Middle Ages,* 240–85.

Van Leeuwen, Peter. "Clare's Dream of Francis." *Haversack* 9, no. 2 (1985): 13–18.

Vauchez, André. *La santità nel Medioevo.* Bologna, Italy: Societá editrice il Mulino, 1981.

Vecchio, Silvana. "La buona moglie." In Klapisch-Zuber, ed., *Storia delle donne in occidente,* 129–65.

"Vita sororis Agnetis, germanae sanctae Clarae." *Chronica XXIX Generalium ordinis Minorum cum pluribus appendicibus,* (*Analecta Franciscana* vol. 3). Quaracchi, Italy: Ad Claras Aquas, 1897, 173–82.

Vitalis, Salvator. *Paradisus Seraphicus: portiuncula sacra S. Mariae Angelorum , alma basilica Vallis Assisi.* Mediolani: Ex Typ. Io. Petri Cardi, 1645.

Vorreux, Damien, ed. and trans. *Les écrits de saint François et de sainte Claire d'Assise*. Paris: Éditions Franciscaines, 1979.

Wadding, Lucas. *Annales Minorum seu trium Ordinum a S. Francesco Institutorum*. Quaracchi, Italy: Ad Claras Aquas, 1931.

Weinstein, Donald, and Rudolf M. Bell. *Saints and Society: The Two Worlds of Western Christendom, 1000–1700*. Chicago: University of Chicago Press, 1982.

Williams, Norman Powell. *Ideas of the Fall and of Original Sin: A Historical and Critical Study*. London: Longmans, Green, 1927.

Zavalloni, Roberto. *La personalità di Chiara d'Assisi*. Assisi: Edizioni Porziuncola, 1993.

———. *La personalità di Francesco d'Assisi. Studio psicologico*. Padova, Italy: Edizioni Messaggero, 1991.

Zorgi, Diego. *Valori religiosi nella letteratura provenzale. La spiritualità trinitaria*. Milano, Italy: Vita e Pensiero, 1954.

PRIMARY SOURCES
OPUSCULA OF FRANCIS AND CLARE

Boccali, Giovanni. "Testamento e benedizione di S. Chiara. Nuovo codice latino." *Archivum Franciscanum Historicum* 82 (1989): 283–94.

Clarae Assisiensis. "Opuscula." In Menestò and Brufani, eds., *Fontes Franciscani*, 2262–2324.

Esser, Kajetan, ed. *Gli scritti di S. Francesco d'Assisi. Nuova edizione critica e versione italiana*. Translated by Alfredo Bizzotto, Sergio Cattazzo, and Vergilio Gamboso. Padova, Italy: Edizioni Messaggero, 1982.

Francesco d'Assisi. *Scritti: Testo latino e traduzione italiana*. Padova, Italy: Editrici Francescane, 2002.

Francisci Assisiensis. "Opuscula." In Menestò and Brufani, eds., *Fontes Franciscani*, 23–245.

Lemmens, Leonard, ed. *S. Franciscus Assisiensis*. Opuscula, 2 ed. Quaracchi, Italy: Ad Claras Aquas, 1941; I ed., 1904.

Textus opusculorum S. Francisci et Clarae Assisiensum, variis adnotationibus ornatus. cura et studio Ioannis M. Boccali in lucem editus. Assisi: Edizioni Porziuncola, 1976.

VITAE OF FRANCIS AND CLARE

Anonymus Perusinus. "De inceptione vel fundamento Ordinis et actibus illorum fratrum Minorum qui fuerunt primi in religione et socii B. Francisci." In Menestò and Brufani, eds., *Fontes Franciscani*, 1311–51.

Bonaventurae de Balneoregio, "Legenda Maior S. Francisci." In Menestò and Brufani, eds., *Fontes Franciscani*, 777–961.

Bughetti, B. "Legenda versificata S. Clarae Assisiensis." *Archivum Franciscanum Historicum* 5 (1912): 241–60; 459–81.

Fierens, A. "La question Franciscaine. Vita Sancti Francisci anonyma Bruxellensis d'après le manuscrit II.2326 de la Bibliothèque Royale de Belgique." *Revue d'Histoire Ecclésiastique* 8 (1907): 286–304, 498–513; 9 (1908): 38–47, 703–27; 10 (1909): 42–65, 303–7.

Lazzeri, Zeffirino. "Il processo di canonizzazione di S. Chiara d'Assisi." *Archivum Franciscanum Historicum* 13 (1920): 403–507.

"Legenda Sanctae Clarae Virginis." Found in Ms 338 of the *Biblioteca Comunale di Assisi*. Edited by Francesco Pennachi. Assisi, 1910.

Leo and companions. *Compilatio Assisiensis: dagli scritti di Fra Leone e compagni su S. Francesco d'Assisi*, 2 ed. Translated by Marino Bigaroni. Assisi: Porziuncola, 1992.

Menestò, Enrico, and Stefano Brufani, eds. *Fontes Franciscani*. Assisi: Edizioni Porziuncola, 1995.

Other Sources

Arturo du Monstier di Rouen. *Martirologio francescano.* Ignazio Beschin e Giuliano eds. Palazzolo. Vicenza: Ex Typographia Commerciali, 1939.

Bartholomeo de Pisa. *De conformitate vitae Beati Francisci ad vitam Domini Iesu,* Liber I Fructus I–XIII. (*Analecta Franciscana,* vol. 4). Quaracchi, Italy: Ad Claras Aquas, 1906.

Bernardus Claraeuallensis. "Sermones De diversis." In *Cetedoc Library of Christian Latin Texts* [version 3.0] vol. 6.1. Turnhout, Belgium: Brepols, 1996.

Bonaventurae de Balneoregio, *Commentaria in quatuor libros Sententiarum,* ed. PP. Collegium S. Bonaventurae, *Opera omnia,* ii. Quaracchi, Italy: Ex Typographia Collegii S. Bonaventurae, 1882.

Clareno, Angelo. "Cronaca o Storia delle Sette Tribolazioni dell'Ordine dei Minori." In Menestò and Brufani, eds., *Fontes Franciscani,* 1738–96.

"Frate Nicola d'Assisi." In *Fonti Francescane,* no. 2686.

Healy, Emma Thérèse. *St. Bonaventure's De reductione artium ad theologiam: A Commentary with an Introduction and Translation.* St. Bonaventure, NY: The Franciscan Institute, 1955.

Mariano da Firenze. Libro delle dignità et excellentie del ordine della seraphica madre delle povere donne sancta Chiara da Asisi, introduzione note e indici Giovanni Boccali. Firenze: Studi Franciscani, 1986.

Oliger, Livarius. "Liber exemplorum Fratrum minorum saeculi XIII (excerpta e cod. Ottob. Lat. 522)." *Antonianum* 2 (1927): 213–76.

Petri Damiani, "Opusculum 18.1 De coelibatu sacerdotum, c. 3." In Migne, Jacques-Paul, ed., *Patrologiae cursus completus: series latina,* vol. 145 (Paris, 1853), col 379–88.

―――. "Sermones 45 In Nativitate Beatae Mariae Virginis 2." In Migne, Jacques-Paul, ed., *Patrologiae cursus completus: series latina,* vol. 144 (Paris, 1853), col 740–48

Petri Lombardi. *Sententiae in IV Libris Disctintae,* Grottaferrata : Editiones Collegii S. Bonaventurae ad Claras Aquas, 1971–81.Ridolfi, Pietro. *Historiarum
seraphicae religionis libri tres seriem temporum continentes quibus breui explicantur fundamenta, universique ordinis amplificatio, gradus, et instituta; nec
non uiri scientia, uirtutibus, et fama praeclari.* Venetiis: Franciscun de Franciscis,
1586.

Seton, Walter W. "The Italian Version of the Legend of Saint Clare by the Florentine Ugolino Verino." *Archivum Franciscanum Historicum* 12 (1919): 595–
659.

Ugolini d'Ostia. "Lettera del Cardinale Ugolini a S. Chiara." *Vita Minore* 62
(1991): 65–66.

"Vita sororis Agnetis, germanae sanctae Clarae." In *Chronica XXIX Generalium
ordinis Minorum cum pluribus appendicibus,* (*Analecta Franciscana* vol. 3).
Quaracchi, Italy: Ad Claras Aquas, 1897, 173–82.

Vitalis, Salvator. *Paradisus Seraphicus: portiuncula sacra S. Mariae Angelorum,
alma basilica Vallis Assisi.* Mediolani: Ex Typ. Io. Petri Cardi, 1645.

Wadding, Lucas. *Annales Minorum seu trium Ordinum a S. Francesco Institutorum.* Quaracchi, Italy: Ad Claras Aquas, 1931.

TRANSLATIONS AND COMMENTARIES

Armstrong, Regis J., ed. and trans. *The Lady: Clare of Assisi: Early Documents.* New York: New City Press, 1993.

————, and Ignatius Brady, eds. and trans. *Francis and Clare: The Complete Works.* New York: Paulist Press, 1982.

————, J. A. W. Hellman, and W. J. Short, eds. and trans. *The Saint: Francis of Assisi: Early Documents*, vol. 1. New York: New City Press, 1999.

————, J. A. W. Hellman, and W. J. Short, eds. and trans. *The Founder: Francis of Assisi: Early Documents*, vol. 2. New York: New City Press, 2000.

Bartoli, Marco, and G. Ginepro Zoppetti, trans. *S. Chiara d'Assisi: Scritti e documenti.* Assisi: Editrici Francescane, 1994.

Becker, Marie-France, Jean-Francois Godet, and Thaddee Matura, trans. *Claire d Assise: Écrits.* Paris: Editions du Cerf, 1986.

Canonici, Luciano, ed. and trans. *Textus opusculorum S. Francisci et Clarae Assisiensum. Variis adnotationibus ornatus, cura et studio Ioannis M. Boccali in lucem editus.* Assisi: Edizioni Porziuncola, 1978.

Cremaschi, Chiara Giovanna, and Chiara Agnese Acquadro, trans. *Scritti di Santa Chiara d'Assisi.* Assisi: Edizioni Porziuncola, 1994.

Fonti Francescane. Scritti e biografie di San Francesco d'Assisi; Cronache e altre testimonianze del primo secolo francescano; scritti e biografie di Santa Chiara d'Assisi, 4 ed. Padova, Italy: Edizioni Messaggero, 1990.

Guerra, José Antonio, ed. *San Francisco de Asís. Escritos, biografías, documentos de la época,* 6 ed. Madrid: Biblioteca de Autores Cristianos, 1995.

Habig, Marion A., ed. St. Francis of Assisi Writings and Early Biographies. *English Omnibus of the Sources for the Life of St. Francis,* 3 ed. Chicago: Franciscan Herald Press, 1973.

Herranz, Julio, Javier Garrido, and José Antonio Guerra, eds. and trans. *Los escritos de Francisco y Clara de Asís*, 2 ed. Aranzazu, Colombia: Ediciones Franciscanas, 1980.

Iriarte, Lázaro, ed. *Los escritos de Francisco y Clara de Asís*. Valencia, Spain: Editorial Asís, 1981.

The Legend and Writings of Saint Clare of Assisi: Introduction, Translation, and Studies. St. Bonaventure, NY: Franciscan Institute, 1953.

Omaechevarria, Ignacio, ed. and trans. *Escritos de Santa Clara y documentos complementarios*, 3 ed. Madrid: Editorial Católica, 1993.

Pozzi, Giovanni, and Beatrice Rima, eds. and trans. *Chiara d'Assisi, Lettere ad Agnese. La visione dello specchio*. Milano, Italy: Adelphi, 1999.

Salimbene de Adam da Parma. *Cronaca*. Translated by Berardo Rossi. Bologna, Italy: Radio TAU, 1987.

Seymour, M. C., gen. ed. *On the Properties of Things: John Trevisa's Translation of Bartholomaeus Anglicus De proprietatibus rerum*, vol. I. Oxford: Clarendon, 1975.

Shanahan, G. "Henry of Avranches: Poem on the Life of Saint Francis (Legenda Sancti Francisci Versificata)." *Franciscan Studies* 48 (1988): 125–227.

Vorreux, Damien, ed. and trans. *Les écrits de saint François et de sainte Claire d'Assise*. Paris: Éditions Franciscaines, 1979.